A BASIC ENGLISH-SHONA DICTIONARY

DESMOND DALE S.J.

A BASIC ENGLISH — SHONA DICTIONARY

Illustrated

MAMBO PRESS
Published in association with
LITERATURE BUREAU

MAMBO PRESS
P.O. Box 779, Gweru, Zimbabwe
Tel: 263 - 054 - 24016/7 or 25807
Fax: 263 - 054 - 21991
E-mail: mambopress@telco.co.zw

BASIC ENGLISH - SHONA DICTIONARY

First Published 1975
Reprinted 1979, 1981, 1984, 1987, 1990, 1994, 1997, 1999, 2004

ISBN 0 86922 014 4

Printed and published in Zimbabwe
by Mambo Press, Senga Road, Gweru
2004

To my father, Tom Dale, as a small token of appreciation and to the youth of this country in the hope that Christian justice and charity will guide them to weld diverse racial elements into a happy and harmonious society.

INTRODUCTION

This dictionary aims to serve many needs: of Europeans and even primary school Africans. It restricts itself to common and useful words. Where it was possible to do so, purely dialect variations have been avoided. Words that are widely used and generally understood have been preferred.

An attempt has been made here to provide a vocabulary that is up-to-date and adapted to the modern world. This has led to the inclusion of many borrowed words. Very often Shona has no indigenous words to describe modern terms. It has done what every language does in similar circumstances: it has borrowed from other languages, whose cultural influence was strongest. In the present Rhodesian context, English undoubtedly has the main cultural influence, and it is from English that most borrowed words derive. These words have passed into current use and, in many cases, have found no Shona substitutes. This is partly because every child in our schools knows some English. It is partly because the adult, at his place of work, or even at leisure, widens his English contact and English vocabulary. Some of these words, naturally, get accepted into the Shona vocabulary — often in a form that is not easily recognizable to native English-speakers. The end result is that Shona is the richer for having borrowed; it is not necessarily debased by the process.

The basic vocabulary of this dictionary is that of Father E. Biehler S.J., who compiled his pioneer work at Chishawasha, outside Salisbury, in 1906. It was revised and reprinted four times by 1950, by which time it became clear that a more inclusive and up-to-date work was needed, which took account of the development of Bantu linguistic studies.

I have always been persuaded that there was a need for two dictionaries: one, a popular collection of everyday words to help the European beginner — which this volume aims to do; the other, more scholarly and comprehensive, to help the serious student — which Father Hannan's Shona Dictionary has done so admirably and will continue to do.

Father Biehler's dictionary contained approximately 5 000 English entries. This one contains an additional 2 000 entries. My criterion for selecting what was to be included here was ultimately my own judgement. But I have also been influenced by considerations of the type of person who would be likely to use this book: African children, of course, but all those whose routine brings them into daily contact with Africans and who would be most disposed to speak Shona. Therefore, I have considered such users as doctors, nurses, farmers, mechanics, housewives, civil servants, missionaries and field-workers of every description. All those, in short, who have frequent dealings with Shona people, have been considered. I hope the result will satisfy them, at least to the point of giving them the initial vocabulary they need. I have tried, in my judgement, not to be partisan, and to be open-minded in making my selection of words.

Abbreviations used have reference to the English grammatical terms, not the Shona. Many Shona verbs serve as adjective equivalents. In these cases the entry vb. & adj. has been made. Nouns are recognized by the addition of a number, indicating the noun class to which the noun belongs. For this reason, a basic acquaintance with the Shona language structure is required for this dictionary to serve its fullest use. Many Shona verbs are stative: they are past in form, but present in meaning, and this characteristic has been noted. Derivations from English, Afrikaans and other languages have also been noted. Derivative stems of verbs have the verb stem from which they are derived indicated in the dictionary by means of the convention: cf. To contrive an alternative convention did not prove possible.

If a dictionary is to be popular in these days of developed printing techniques, it must contain illustrations. With the cooperation of Mambo Press, the publishers, and other publishers and authors — in Rhodesia, South Africa and the United Kingdom — illustrations have been provided. To a generation that has become urbanized, illustrations of local fauna and flora will be of special interest. They will help to foster greater attention to the riches of Zimbabwe's wild-life. Nothing but good can be the result of this!

With the help and kindly interest of my colleague, Father Michael Hannan S.J., I have been able to indicate the dialect distribution of my various entries. Where the entry had a basically Central Shona distribution, KZ, I have not bothered to indicate this, but other combinations have been noted.

ACKNOWLEDGEMENTS

It is very difficult, in a work of this kind, to render adequate thanks where thanks are due. A very big debt of gratitude is due to Mr Tobias Chawatama, Language Informant at Prestage House, who over the years has assisted me closely at every stage of my work. To him are due the tone markings, the sheer drudgery and some of the research that has gone into this book. From him, naturally, I have learned a good deal of the Shona I know. Second, great imagination and generosity were shown by the Anglo American Companies for sponsoring the illustrations; to them and the publishers is due the modest selling price. To Mr. Walter Krog and Mr. Charles Singende of Zimbabwe Literature Bureau for their scrutiny of the manuscript, practical help and encouragement, I am indeed grateful.

For the illustrations my sincere thanks are due to a host of artists and publishers. Special thanks to Sister M. Georgina O.P., of Harare Dominican Convent, for her willing cooperation so generously given. To Mrs. Annette Maberly of the Eastern Transvaal is due permission ro reproduce the many excellent wild-life illustrations of C.T. Astley Maberly; likewise, his publishers: Thos. Nelson & Co., who have been particularly kind and helpful; so also have been Books of Africa (T.V. Bulpin) in Cape Town and artist, A.A. Telford, living in Knysna, C.P. To Mrs. T. Donnelly of the Bulawayo Museum I am especially indebted. The publishers of the Bundu Books and Mr. Russell Williams, illustrator of Book 1, have given me their permission to use illustrations of Zimbabwean trees. Oxford University Press have granted me permission to reproduce a vast number of their illustrations — the greatest number from any one source — from their Progressive English Dictionaries. Longmans, Green and Co. granted permission to reproduce drawings of artist E. Cardwell from 'Jock of the Bushveld', whose illustrations would not be complete unless they included the famous Jock, who appears here as a puppy.

I received great help from Mr. Power (A.P.) Jackson, retired District Commissioner and official Interpreter to the Council of Chiefs, who went to a lot of trouble to verify the accuracy of my wild-life entries. To the following authors, artists and publishers I wish also to express my thanks:-

G.G. Arnott, Peter Ginn, Russell Williams and Longman Rhodesia Ltd for illustrations from *Bundu Book I* and *Birds Afield*..

Dreyer Printers and Publishers, Bloemfontein, for the illustrations of

C.T. Astley Maberly, appearing in their book *The Call of the Bushveld* by A.C. White.

Mambo Press, Gwelo, and author D.M. Chavunduka for illustrations appearing in *Kuchengeta Imbwa*.

Thomas Nelson and Sons and author Mrs. Margaret Bevis of Durban for illustrations in their book *The Insects of Southern Africa*.

Mrs. Shirley Sinclair for illustrations appearing in her book *The Story of Melsetter*.

Dr. S.H. Skaife and Longman Southern Africa Ltd, Cape Town, for illustrations from *African Insect Life*.

Tafelberg-Uitgewers of Cape Town and author Anna Rothmann for illustrations of C.T. Astley Maberly appearing in *Elephant, Shrew and Company* and *The Crow and Company*.

Howard Timmins of Cape Town and author T.V. Bulpin for the illustrations of C.T. Astley Maberly appearing in *Storm over the Transvaal* and *Lost Trails of the Transvaal.*

John Voelcker Bird Book Fund for permission to reproduce the illustrations of N.C.K. Lighton, appearing in *Birds of South Africa* by Dr. Austin Roberts.

Wildlife Society of South Africa, Pinetown, Natal, and African Wildlife for permission to reproduce the illustrations of C.T. Astley Maberly from *Memories of a Game Ranger* by Harry Wolhuter. Also the trustees of A.M. Wolhuter for the same permission.

ABBREVIATIONS

Abs pron	Absolute pronoun
adj	adjective
adv	adverb
Afrik	Afrikaans
B Bk	Bundu Book
cc	concord
cf	confer (Commonly used to denote words derived from other languages)
Colloq	colloquial
Conj	conjunction
Cop	copulative verb (It is)
cp	compare
dem	demonstrative
Eng	English
esp	especially
f	female
fut	future
H	high tone
i	instransitive verb
ideo	ideophone
infin	infinitive
inter	interjection
interrog	interrogative
K	Karanga dialect
Ko	Korekore dialect
L	Low tone
Lat	Latin
lit	literally
loc	locative
M	Manyika dialect
m	male
n	noun
neg	negative
p	page
partic	participial or participle
PC	possessive concord
PG	Birds of the Highveld, Peter Ginn
plur	plural
PP	past participle
prep	preposition
pron	pronoun
prov	proverb
PT	past tense
R	Birds of South Africa Dr. Austin Roberts
rec past	recent past
reflex	reflexive form of the verb with object cc *-zvi-*
rel	relative mood
sing	singular
sp	species
subj	subjunctive mood
suff	suffix
t	transitive verb
usu	usually
var	variety
vb	verb
veg	vegetable
Z	Zezuru dialect

GENERAL CHARACTERISTICS

NOUN CLASSES

Class	Prefix	Example		Subject Ccs of the verb
1	MU-	mukomana (*boy*)	Humans and human agents	a-
2	VA-	vakomana (*boys*)		va-
1a	—	baba (*father*)	Honorific titles	a-
2a	VA-	vababa (*fathers*)	Used in Manyika	va-
		1. In M. very many animals are found in Class 1a. 2. Plurals are expressed with composite prefixes: **vadzi**- (Cl 2), **vana**- (Cl 2) or **madzi** (Cl 6).		
3	MU-	munda (*garden*)	Especially trees, plants	u-
4	MI-	minda (*gardens*)	and vegetable matter	i-
5	(ri-)	badza (*hoe*)	Many voiced consonants.	ri-
6	MA-	mapadza (*hoes*)	Miscellaneous nouns	a-
7	CHI-	chinhu (*thing*)		chi-
8	ZVI-	zvinhu (*things*)	Usually inanimate things	zvi-
9	(i-)	mhou (*cow*)	Many animals, birds,	i-
10	(dzi-)	mhou (*cows*)	nasalized nouns etc.	dzi-
11	RU- (Plurals in Cl 6 or 10)	ruoko (*arm*)	Long, thin things and abstract nouns	ru-
12	KA-	katiyo (*chicken*)	Diminutives	ka-
13	TU-	tutiyo (*chickens*)	tukomana (*little boys*)	tu-
14	U-	uipi (*evil*)	Usually abstract nouns	hu-
15	KU-	kurwara (*illness*)	Infinitives: to ail	ku-
16	PA-	pamba (*at the house*)	Locatives: **at** or **on**	pa-
17	KU-	kumba (*at home*)	Locatives: **at** or **to**	ku-
18	MU-	mumba (*in the house*)	Locatives: **inside**	mu-
21	ZI-	zirori (*large lorry*)	Augmentatives	ri-

A

Aardwolf *nocturnal beast like a dog which feeds almost exclusively on termites. Height about 50 cm.* n mbizimumwena 9 (LHHLH); mwena 3 (LH)

abandon *leave behind* vb -siya t (HH); -rega t (LL)

abandon hope *lose heart* vb -rasa mwoyo i (HH HL)

abate (of rain) *cease raining* vb -gasa i (HH)

abdomen *belly* n dumbu 5, matumbu 6 (LL); nhumbu 9 (LL); harwe 9 (HL)

able *be competent, have ability* vb -gona i (LL); -kwanisa i (HHH)

abolish a law vb -pfudza mutemo (HH LHH)

abominate *hate, loathe* vb -sema i & t (HH)

abort *(animals) cause premature delivery* vb -svodza i (LL); *a. (humans)* vb -pfukudzika i (HHHL)

abound *be abundant* vb -rura i (LL); -wanda i (LL) *(stative vb)*

about *approximately* adv -nge (L) + noun or noun clause *(to seem)*; Akanga **enge** masikati. *(It was about midday.)*; -karo- infix vb; Kwaiva navanhu v**aikaro**svika chiuru. *(There were about a thousand people.)*; *concerning* prep nezva — (HL); Anoziva **nezv**emiti yesango. *(He knows about wild trees.)*; *be about to* -va + infin — Chando **chava** kuda kupera/ **chava** kupera. *(Winter is about to end.)*

above *(high above)* prep pauzuru 16 (LLHL); kuuzuru 17 (LLHL); Gondo rinobhururuka **pauzuru**. *(The eagle flies high above.)*; *(on top)* prep pamusoro pa- 16 (LLHH); kumusoro 17 (LLHH); Pamusoro pegomo. *(On top of the hill.)*; *(above all)* prep pana zvose (LH LL); kupinda zvose (LLL HH)

abreast *be level with* vb -ererana i (LLLL) (stative vb)

abscess *boil, suppurating tumour* n mota 5, mamota 6 (LL); pute 5, mapute 6 KM (LL)

abscond *run away* vb -tiza i & t (HH)

absent *be permanently a., go away for good* vb -rova i (LL); *be a. temporarily* vb -rovha i & t (LL)

absolutely *very much* adv kwazvo (HL); chaizvo (LHL)

absolve *forgive wrong* vb -regerera t (LLLL)

abstain from (*mutupo*), *hold certain things as sacred. In Shona society this means not eating the meat of the animal the tribe holds sacred.* vb -era t (LL)

abstruse *be profound, deep* vb -dzama i (LL); -dzika i (LL)

abundant *plentiful* adj -zhinji (HH); vb -wanda i (LL) (stative vb); Ane mari ya**kawanda**. (*He has a lot of money.*)

abuse *insult, revile* vb -tuka i & t (HH); -nyomba i & t (HH); *a. in public, shout at* vb -shaudha i & t (HHH) cf Eng.

abuse *harsh accusation* n rupaumbo 11 (LLLL) cf -paumba (LLL) *a word of a.* n chituko 7 (LHH) cf -tuka (HH)

acacia *mountain a., redwood tree* n muunze 3 (LLL); *winter a.* n munzungu 3 (LLH)

accelerate *increase the speed of* vb

-mhanyisa i & t (HHL); -fangura t MZ (LLL); -faira t (HHH) cf Eng.

accent *manner of speaking* n mutauriro 3 (LLHHH) cf -taura (LLL)

accept *receive* vb -gashira i & t MZ (LLL); -gamuchira i & t (LLLL); -tambira i & t (HHH); *agree, believe* vb -tenda i & t (LL); -bvuma i & t (LL)

accident *chance disastrous event* n njodzi 9 (LL); tsaona 9 (HHL)

accompany *go with* vb -perekedza t (HHHL); -enda na- t (LL)

accomplish *complete* vb -pedza i & t (HH) cf -pera (HH)

according to adv maererano na- (LLLLL); Munhu anopiwa basa maererano noruzivo rwake. (*A person is given work according to his knowledge.*) *according to, in accordance with, in proportion to, in relation to* adv zvakaenzanirana rel cf -enzana (LLL)

accordingly *therefore* conj naizvozvo (LHLH)

account *statement of a.* n akaunzi 9 (LHLL) cf Eng.

account *give an a., explain* vb -tsanangura i & t (LLLL)

accumulate *gather together* vb -unganidza t (HHHL) cf -ungana (HHH)

accuse *give blame* vb -pa mhosva t (HL); *a. falsely* vb -pomera mhosva t (HHL HL); -nenedzera t (HHHL); -revera nhema t (HHH LH); Ndakapomerwa mhosva yokutora mari, asi handina. (*I was accused of taking the money, but I didn't.*)

accustomed *be used to* vb -jaira i & t (HHH); -zivira i & t (HHH); **Ajaira** kusevenza navatema. (*He is accustomed to working with Africans.*)

ache *cause pain* vb -rwadza i (HH); *of a headache* vb -tema i (HH); Musoro wangu uri kutema. (*My head is aching.*)

acknowledge *admit something is true* vb -bvuma i & t (LL); -tenda i & t (LL); *thank* vb -tenda i & t (LL)

acquainted *be a., know* vb -ziva i & t (HH)

acquire *have, find* vb -va na-; -wana t (LL); Ndichava nemari zhinji. (*I shall have a lot of money.*)

acquit *deliver someone from blame* vb -pembedza t (HHH); -chenura t (LLL)

acre *measure of land (4 840 square yards or about 4 000 square metres)* n eka 9 (HL); hakiri 9 (HLL) cf Eng.

across *on the opposite side (usually treated as a Cl. 17 noun, with latent concord* **ku**- n mhiri 9 (LL); Mombe dziri mhiri **kworwizi**. (*The cattle are on the opposite bank.*); *go a.* (*a street*) vb -dimbura t (HHH) -bira (HH); *go a.* (*a ford*) vb -yambuka t (LLL) -bira (HH)

across *place a.* vb -piyanisa t (HHHL)

act *behave, do* vb -ita i (LL); *action, act* n chiito 7 (LLL) cf -ita (LL)

activity *energetic doing* n batapata 5 (LLLL) *sing only*; chipatapata 7 (LLLLL)

actually *in fact, in reality* adv zvazviri (LHL)

Adam's apple *projection of the larynx holding vocal chords* n garahuro 5, magarahuro 6 (LLLL)

add (*the same ingredient*) vb -pamhidzira t (LLLL); (*another ingredient*) *mix* vb -sanganisa t (LLLL) cf -sangana (LLL); *add to, increase* vb -pamhidzira t (LLLL)

adder *viper, sp of poisonous snake* **general name** n chiva 7 (LL); bvumbi 5 (LH)

addition *in a.* conj -zve KM; dzoke K (LH); pakare (LHL); Handimuzivi, **pakare** handisati ndambomuona. (*I don't know him; in addition I have never seen him before.*)

address *place where a person can be written to* n adhiresi 9 (HLLL); kero 9

(HL) cf c/o Eng.

adequate *enough* adj & vb -kwana i (HH) (*stative vb*); Ndine mari yaka**kwana**. (*I have enough money.*)

adhere *stick* vb -tsvetera i (LLL); -namatira i (LLLL)

adjacent *be neighbouring, touching* vb -batana i (HHH) (stative vb); Misha yavo yaka**batana**. (*Their villages are adjacent; i.e. they live in neighbouring villages.*)

adjective *word which names a quality possessed* n chipauro 7 (LHHL)

adjoin *conjoin to* vb -batana na- i (HHH) cf -bata (HH)

adjust *put right* vb -ruramisa t (LLL) cf -rurama (LLL); Ndibatsirewo **kururamisa** cheni dzebhasikoro rangu. (*Help me to adjust the chain of my bicycle.*)

admire *appreciate* vb -yemura t (LLL)

admit *consent, a. something is true* vb -bvuma i & t (LL); -tenda i & t KM (LL)

admit entry *cause to enter, pay admission fee for someone* vb -pinza t (LL) cf -pinda (LL); Aka**pinza** mombe mudanga. (*He drove the cattle into the kraal.*); *admit light, be translucent* vb -njenjemera i (LLLL)

admonish *warn, tell* vb -komera t (HHH)

adopt an orphan vb -tora nherera t (HH HLL)

adore *worship* vb -pfugamira t (*kneel*) (HHHL); -rumbidza t (*praise*) (LLL); -namata i & t (*pray*) *(LLL)*

adorn *put on ornaments or clothing* vb -shonga i (LL); *put on ornaments or clothing* vb -shongedza t (LLL) cf -shonga (LL)

adult *grown up* n munhu mukuru 1 (LL LHH)

adulterate *make poorer in quality* vb -ipisa t (HHH) cf -ipa (HH)

adulterer *One who breaks marriage bond* n mhombo 9 (LL); gomba 5 (LL); mhombwe 9 (LL); ***adulteress***, *prostitute* n hure 5, mahure 6 (HL); pfambi 9 (HH)

adultery *fornication, sins of the flesh* n upombwe 14 (LLL) cf -pomba (LL); *comit a.* vb -pomba i (LL)

advance *proceed ahead, go ahead* vb -enda mberi i (LL LH); *a. culturally, succeed* vb -budirira i (HHHL); -fambira mberi (HHH LH)

advantage *profit, help* n chimuko 7 (LLL); chipundutso 7 (LLLL); yamuro 9 (LLL) cf -yamura (LLL)

adversity *difficulty, affliction* n dambudziko 5, matambudziko 6 (LLLL); nhamo 9 (HH)

advice *opinion of what to do* n zano 5, mazano 6 (LL)

advise *give advice* vb -rayira i & t (LLL); -pa zano (H HL)

advocate *mediator, one who speaks in one's favour* n murevereri 1 (LHHHL) cf -reverera (HHHL)

adze *instrument with a handle for shaping wood* n mbezo 9 (LL) cf -veza (LL)

aeroplane *aircraft* n ndege 9 (HL); furaimachina 9 (LHLLHL) cf Eng.

affection *love* n rudo 11 (LH) cf -da (H)

afflict *with trouble, worry* vb -tambudza i & t (LLL); *affliction, trouble, adversity* n dambudziko 5, matambudziko 6 (LLLL) cf -tambudzika (LLLL); nhamo 9 (HH)

aflame *be a.* vb -bvira i (LL); -pfuta i (LL); Imba yaka**bvira**. (*The house was aflame.*); *set aflame* vb -ngandutsa t MZ (LLL)

afraid *be a. of, fear* vb -tya i & t (H); -bweza i & t (LL)

afresh *anew* adv patsva 16 (LH)

African *belonging to Africa or the people of Africa* adj e.g. tsika dzavatema (*African customs*)

African black wood tree *Rhodesian*

wattle n mupumhamakuva 3 (LLLLHH); musambanyoka 3 (LLLHH); mujisa 3 (LHL); *African beech tree* n mutsatsati 3 (LHHL); *African mangosteen tree* n munhinzwa 3 (LHL); *African sandalwood tree* n munhiti 3 (LLL); *African walnut tree* n mutondochuru 3 (LLLLL)

African golden oriole *sp of bird* n chidzvururu 7 (LLLL) R520

African piano n mbira 9/10 (LL)

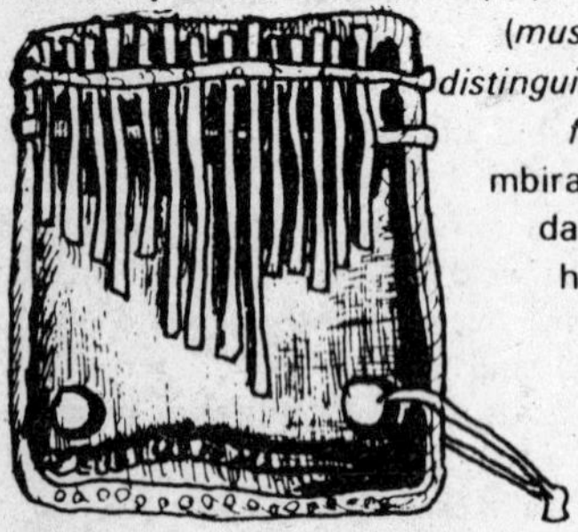

(*must be distinguished from:* mbira (HL) dassie, hyrax)

Afrikaaner *Afrikaâns speaking person* n Bhunu 5, maBhunu 6 (LH)

Afrikaans *language of the Afrikaaner people or South African Dutch* n chiBhunu 7 (LLH)

after adv pashure pa- (LHL); mushure 18 (LHL); Akasvika mushure mechinguvana. (*He arrived after a short time.*); prep mumashure 18 (LLHL); Ari mumashure. (*He is in the rear.*)

after that cf "*and then*"

afternoon (*12.00 a.m. — 3.00 p.m.*) n & adv masikati 6 (LHLH); (*after 3.00 p.m.*) manheru 6 Z (LLH); madekwana 6 K (LHLH); mauro 6 (LLH); madeko 6 (LHL)

afterwards *later* adv pashure 16 (LHL); mushure 18 (LHL)

again *in addition, moreover* adv pakare 16 (LHL); zvakare (LHL); -zve (H)

agama *rock lizard usu with blue head* n chidhambakura 7 (LLLHH); chiguyakuya 7 (LLHH) *cf illustration p. 93*

age *grow old* vb -kwegura i (HHH); *-chembera i (LLL); years of a.* n makore okuberekwa/okuzvarwa; Ini ndiri musikana ane makore 19 okuzvarwa. (*I am a girl, 19 years of age.*)

age group n zera 5, mazera 6 (LLL); zero 5, mazero 6 (LLL)

aggravate *make more serious* vb -sembura i & t (HHH); -svotesa i & t (HHH)

agitated *be apprehensive* vb -rohwa nehana i (HL HLL); Akarohwa nehana paakaona mupurisa. (*He was agitated at the sight of a policeman.*)

ago *some time ago* adv kare (LL); *long a.* adv kare kare (LL HH). Akaberekerwa kuZambia makore 24 akapera. (*He was born in Zambia 24 years ago.*)

agree *a. with, acknowledge, assent* vb -bvuma i (LL); -tenda i & t (LL); *a. with one another* vb -bvumirana i (LLLL) cf -bvuma (LL); -tenderana i (LLLL) cf -tenda (LL); *agreement, testament* n chitenderano 7 (LLLLL) cf -tenderana (LLLL); chibvumirano 7 (LLLLL) cf -bvumirana (LLLL)

ahead *in front* prep mberi 16 (LH); pamberi 16 (LLH)

aid *help, assist* vb -batsira t (HHH); -yamura t (LLL); *aid, help, assistance* n rubatsiro 11 (LHHL); ruyamuro 11 (LLLL) cf -yamura (LLL)

ail *be ill, be sick* vb -rwara i (HH)

aim *(e.g. a gun), point in a direction -ereka i & t (LLL); head in a direction, make for* vb -nanga i & t (HH)

aim *aspiration, ambition, purpose, objective, something aimed at* n vavariro 9 (HHHL) cf -vavarira (HHHL); chinangwa 7 (LHL) cf -nanga (HH)

aimlessly *wander a.* vb -tuuruka i (LLLL)

air *breath, bad smell* n mweya 3 (LH)

air *hang out to air or to dry* vb -yanika t (HHH); Yanika magumbeze. (*Air the blankets.*)

aircraft *aeroplane* n ndege 9 (HL); furaimachina 9 (LHLLHL) cf Eng.

alarm *frighten* vb -tyisa i & t (HH); -vhundutsa i & t (LLL); *alarmed, be frightened* vb -vhunduka i (LLL); *alarmingly, in a way which causes alarm* adv zvinovhundutsa (LHLLL) rel

albino *African lacking pigmentation of the skin (usu having pink skin and yellowish hair)* n musope 1 (LLL); sope 5, masope 6 (LL)

albizia

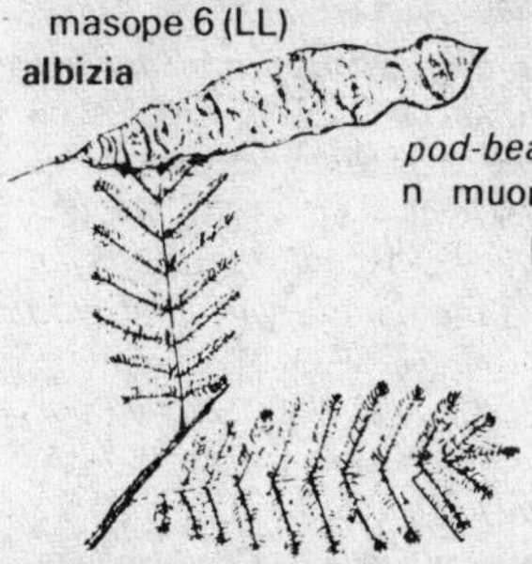

pod-bearing tree n muora 3 (LLL) B. Bk 1,16

alcoholic *drunkard* n chidhakwa 7 (LLH); dhakwa 5, madhakwa 6 (LH) cf -dhakwa (LL)

alert *be on your guard against, be on the a., be careful of* vb -chenjerera i & t (HHHL); -ngwarira i (LLL)

alight *land, perch* vb -mhara i & t (LL)

alight *be aflame* vb -bvira i (LL); -pfuta i (LL); -nganduka i (LLL); Motokari yakanganduka. (*The motor car was a mass of flames.*); *set a.* vb -tungidza t (HHH); -batidza t (HHH)

alike *be of like appearance* vb -fanana i (HHH) (stative vb); -todzana i (HHH); Taka**fanana**. (*We are alike.*); *be of equal size* vb -enzana i (LLL) (stative vb); Mukufuta taka**enzana**. (*We are equally fat/in fatness we are equal.*)

alive *living* adj -penyu (LH), benyu 5 (LH); mhenyu 9 (LH)

all adj -se (H) cf Quantitative prons. p. 188 e.g. vanhu vose (vese M) (*everybody*); *all together* adv pamwe chete (LH LH) **all day long** *all day* infix vb -swero-

all right *right ho!* inter zvakanaka (HHHL) vb *It is well.* ndizvozvo (HLH) cop vb

alleviate pain *calm, comfort* vb -nyaradza t (HHH) cf -nyarara (HHL); -podza t (HH) cf -pora (HH)

allot *divide, distribute* vb -gova i & t (LL)

allow *permit* vb -bvumira i & t (LLL); -bvumidza t (LLL) cf -bvuma (LL); -regera t (LLL); -tendera i & t (LLL) cf -tenda (LL); *allowed, it is allowed* vb zvinobvumirwa (HLLLL)

allow *let, permit (that)* vb Imperative: Rega + Subjunctive: **Rega** ndivate! (*Let me go to sleep!*)

almost adv -karo- (LL); Infix vb; Akagarako mazuva ano**karo**svika gumi. (*He stayed there for almost ten days.*)

aloe *plant with fleshy leaves, sharp spikes and bitter juice* n gavakava 5 (LLLL) B. Bk. 1,50

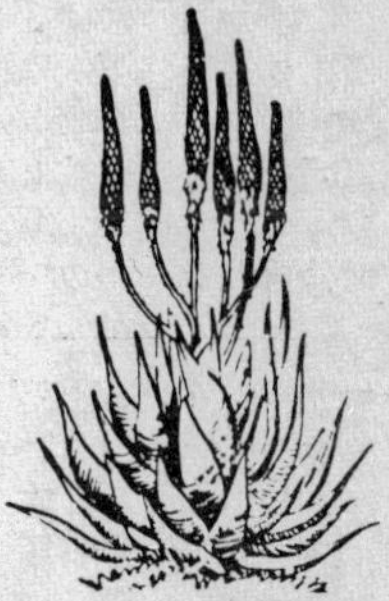

alone adv -ga (H) cf *Quantitative prons. p. 188*

alongside *at the side of* adv munyasi ma-18 (LLH); parutivi pa-16 (LLLL)

already *beforehand, by this time* adv *-to- infix vb; tenge* + Partic; -tonga M + Partic; Baba vakasvika **tatorara**. (*Father arrived when we were already in bed.*) Paunodzoka ndine**tenge** ndaenda. (*When you return I shall already have gone.*)

also *again* adv -wo suff; zvakare (LHL); -zve KM; conj uye (HL)

altar *communion table* n atari 9 (HLL) cf Eng.

alter *make tighter, tuck in* vb -dzora t (LL) cf -dzoka (LL)

although *though* conj kunyangwe (ŁLL); nyangwe (LL); kunyange (LLL); kunyangova (LLLH); kanapo (LLH) + Partic; Ndinomuda, kanapo andinyepera. (*I love him, although he has lied to me.*)

altogether adv kwazvo (HL); chose K (HH)

always *at all times* adv mazuva ose 6 (LHH HH); nguva dzose 10 (HL HH); -garo- (LL) infix vb; *always, habitually* adv -gara (LL) + Partic

am vb Ndiri mukomana. (*I am a boy.*) Ndiri kukura. (*I am growing.*)

amaze *astonish, cause wonder* vb -shamisa i & t (HHH) cf -shama (HH); katyamadza i & t (HHHL); *amazed, be filled with surprise* vb -shamiswa i (HHH) cf -shama (HH)

ambition *aspiration, aim* n vavariro 9 (HHHL) cf -vavarira (HHHL); chinangwa 7 (LHL) cf -nanga (HH)

ambulance *motor vehicle for carrying the sick* n amburenzi 9 (HLLL) cf Eng.

amidst *among, in the midst of* prep pakati pa- 16 (LLH)

ammunition *bullet* n bara 5, mabara/mapara 6 (LH)

amniotic sack *membrane enclosing foetus before birth* n shupa 9 (HH)

among *in the midst of* prep pakati pa- (LLH)

amount to *reach* vb -svika t (LL); Mari yangu ino**svika** makumi mana amadhora. (*My money amounts to $40.*)

amputate *cut in two, cut off* vb -dimura t (HHH); -cheka t (HH)

amulet *charm worn around arm, wrist, or waist* n chitumwa 7 (LHL); zango 5, mazango 6 (LL)

amuse *cause smiles or laughter* vb -fadza i & t (HH) cf -fara (HH); -setsa i & t (LL) cf -seka (LL)

ancestor *senior deceased relative* n tateguru 1a (LHLL); teteguru 1a (LHLL); *ancestral spirit, spirit of the ancestors e.g. grandfather* n mudzimu 1 & 3 (LHH)

ancient *long ago* adv chinyakare 7 (LLLL); mapfekero echinyakare (*the dress of long ago*)

and conj na- (*adverbial formative*) na + a = na (navanhu); na + i = ne (nebasa); na + u = no (nomunhu); *Tonal influence of na:* **1**) Na = *low tone nouns: raises the first syllables and itself is low* (nomunda LHL); **2**) Na + *high tone nouns: depresses high tone syllables and itself is high* (nejira HLL); **3**) Na + LH or LHH or LHHL *nouns: effects no change on the noun but is itself high* (norubatsiro) (HLHHL); **4**) Na + 1a *nouns effects no change on the noun and is itself low* (nababa LLH). *In* M ne- *is used for 1, 2 & 3*

and also *also* conj uye (HL); -wo

and in addition *and also, and furthermore* conj uyezve (HLH)

and (*story telling*) conj *use of consecutive form:* Ndakatsvaga **ndika**tsvaga, asi ndakamushaya. (*I searched and searched, but I could not find him.*) Ndauya **ndika**mushaya. (*I came and I did not find him.*) Infix vb -go-; Akadzima mwenje aka**go**rara pamubhedha. (*He put out the light and lay on his bed.*)

and so *and therefore* conj nokudaro (HLHL); kudaro (LHL); *and that is the reason why* conj saka + partic

and then (*immediately*) conj -bva (L) auxiliary vb + Partic; Vanhu vose vakasimuka **vachibva** vaparara. (*All the people rose up and immediately dispersed.*)

and then (*story telling*) conj ndokubva (HLL) + Partic; Akapinda mumotokari ndokubva aenda. (*He got into the motor car and then left.*); kubvezvo + Indicative (*unconnected events*) Akatamba bhora masikati kubvezvo akaenda kubhaiskopo. (*He played football in the afternoon and then went to the cinema.*)

and then conj ndo + Infinitive; Akamutarisa ndokutanga kutaura. (*He looked at him and then began to speak.*) Akahotsira ndokuisa hengechepfu pamuromo wake. (*She sneezed and raised her handkerchief to her mouth.*)

and when (*story telling*) adv kuzoti (LLL) + Participial (*usually at the beginning of a sentence*); Kuzoti vanhu vapedza kudya, muenzi akasvika. (*And when the people had finished eating, the stranger arrived.*)

anew *afresh* adv patsva 16 (LH)

angel *angelic spirit* n angere 1a (HLH) cf Eng; ngirozi 9 (LHL)

anger *make angry, annoy* vb -shatirisa i & t (HHHL); -tsamwisa i & t (LLL)

anger *rage, fury* n hasha 10 (HH)

angry *be furious* vb -shatirwa i (HHH); -tsamwa i (LL); -va nehasha; -viruka nehasha i (LLL HLL); *make a., annoy* vb -shatirisa i & t (HHHL); -tsamwisa i & t (LLL); Ticha ane hasha. (*A teacher who has anger i.e. an angry teacher.*)

animal *wild a.* n mhuka 9 (LH); *domesticated a.* n chipfuyo 7 (LHH); chipfuwo 7 (LHH) cf -pfuya (HH); *beast of prey* n chikara 7 (LLL)

ankle *chief joint of the foot* n chiziso chegumbo 7 (LHH LHL)

announce *preach* vb -paridza (HHH)

announcement *matter for information* n chiziviso 7 (LHHL) cf -ziva (HH)

announcer *radio a.* n mushamarari 1 (LHHHL) cf -shamarara (HHHL)

annoy *anger* vb -netsa i & t (LL); -sembura i & t (HHH); -shatirisa i & t (HHHL); -netsiwa (LLL)

annoyed *be angered* vb -shatirwa i (HHH); *become a.* vb -gumbuka i (LLL) cf -gumbura (LLL)

anoint *apply oil* vb -zora mafuta t MZ (LL LHH); Mai vakazora mwana mafuta. (*Mother anointed the child with ointment.*)

another adj -mwe cf Enumerative pron p. 186 *precedes the noun*

answer *give reply* vb -pindura i & t (LLL); -davira i & t (HHH); *reply* n mhinduro 9 (LLL) cf -pindura (LLL)

ant *small black a.* n svosve 5, masvosve 6 (LH); svesve 5 (LH) MZ; *white a.* cf *termite; small red-brown a.* n gadzijava 5 (HLHH); *sugar a.* sikana-dzvuku (HHH LH)

antbear *aard vark* n hwiribidi 9 (HHHH); gwiribidi 5 (HHHH); gweru 5,

magweru 6 (LH); dikita 5, matikita 6 (LLL); gwerekwete 5, magwerekwete 6 (LLLL)

African animals

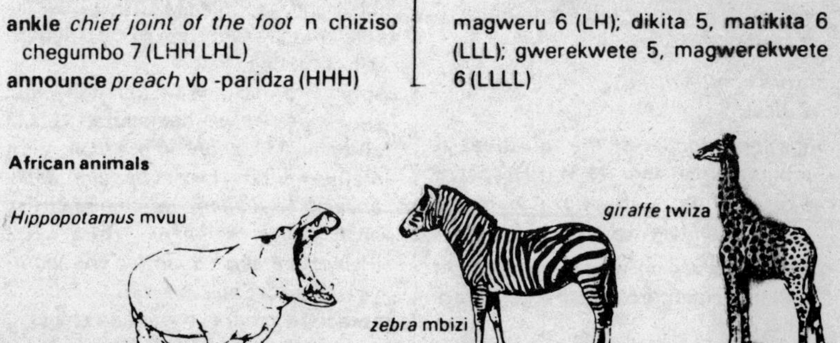

ant-eater *pangolin or scaly a.* n haka 9 (LH)

antelope *buck* n mhuka 9 (LH) *general term for animals*

antenna *feeler of an insect* n nyanga 9 (LH) *the same word as horn*

ant-hill *termite structure or mound* n churu 7 (LL)

ant-lion *kind of insect whose larva makes a conical pit in loose sand; in the adult stage it is rather like a dragon fly* n imbwa yegunguo 9 (LH HLLL); inda yegunguo 9 (LH HLLL)

anthis beetle *black b. with white stripes; nimble b. appearing in early summer* n dundira 5, matundira 6 (LLL)

anthrax *cattle disease* n chigwadara 7 Z (LLLL)

anus *lower outlet of the intestines* n mhata 9 (HH); horo 9 KM (HH) *course expressions;* mupedzazviyo 3 (LHHLH) *polite expression*

anvil *iron block on which smith works metal* n chipfuriro 7 (LHHL) cf -pfura (HH)

anyone *anyone at all* pron ani nani (LH LH)

anything (*meaning: anything in particular*) pron chese chese (HH HL); chose chose (HH HL) etc.

anywhere adv kwose kwose 17 (HH HL)

apart *come a.* vb -kwachuka i (LLL) cf -kwachura (LLL)

apart from *except for* adv kunze kwa (LH)

aperient *opening medicine* n mushonga wokupanza 3 (LLH HLHH)

aperture *hole* n buri 5, mapuri 6 (HL)

aphid *plant louse* n inda 9 (LH) *the same word as for body louse*

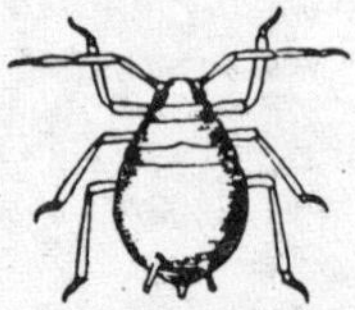

apostle *one who is sent* n mupostori 1 (LHLL) cf Eng.

appear *show oneself* vb -zvionesa i (HLLH); reflex cf -ona (HH)

appear to be *seem to be* vb -nge; -nga M; -tarisika i (LLLL); Imwe mhuka yainge imbwa. (*One of the animals seemed to be a dog.*)

appearance *physical a., build of living things* n chimiro 7 (LHH) cf -mira (HH)

appease spirit elders vb -pfupa t (LL)

appetite *hunger* n nzara 9 (LL)

applaud *with hands* vb -ombera i & t (LLL); -ridza manja t MZ (LL LL)

apple *kind of fruit* n apuro 5, maapuro 6 (HLL) cf Eng.

apply *put on* vb -isa t (LL); *apply glue, stick together* vb -namatidza t (LLLL) cf -nama (LL); *apply ointment* vb -zora mafuta i & t (LL LHH) *cf anoint; apply oneself, be diligent* vb -shinga i (HH); *apply polish, smear* vb -dzira i & t (HH); *make application for* vb -apuraya i (LLLL) cf Eng.

appreciate *admire* vb -yemura t (LLL)

apprehensive *be alarmed, be agitated* vb -rohwa nehana i (HL HLL)

approach *move close* vb -swedera i (LLL)

approve *give permission* vb -bvumidza t (LLL) cf -bvuma (LL); -tendera t (LLL) cf -tenda (LL)

approve of *be happy with* vb -farira t (HHH) cf -fara (HH); *consent to* vb -bvumira t (LLL)

approximately adv -nge + noun or noun clause. Muno muZimbabwe mune vanhu vanenge 10 000 000. (*There are approximately 10 000 000 people here in Zimbabwe.*)

apron n fasikoti 9 (HLLL); fasikoto 9 (HLLL); hapureni 9 (HLLL) cf Eng.

argue *propose arguments* vb -ita nharo i (LL LL)

argumentative adj musikana ane nharo (*an argumentative girl*)

arise (*from sleep*), *get up* vb -muka i (LL); *a.* (*from sitting*) vb -simuka i (HHL) — PT *arose*; PP *arisen*

arithmetic *science of working with numbers* n nhamba 9 (LL); samhu 9 (HL); svomhu 9 K (HL) cf Eng.

arm *upper limb* n ruoko 11, maoko 6 (LHH); muoko 3 M (LHH); *elbow* n gokora 5, makokora 6 (HHL); *shoulder blade* n bendekete 5, mapendekete 6 (HHLH); *shoulder* n pfudzi 5, mapfudzi 6 (HL); fudzi 5, mafudzi 6 (HL); *wrist* n chipfundo choruoko 7 (LHH HLHH); *armpit, hollow under arm at shoulder* n hapwa 9 (LH)

arms *weapons* n zvombo 8 (LL)

army *large detachment of soldiers* n hondo 9 (HH); pfumo 5 (HH) (sing only)

around *cf approximately*

around *in the vicinity of* prep kwa- PC Cl 17 (*Place names of people*); Ku- + Noun Cl 17 (*Most cities and mountains.*) Anogara kuInyanga. (*He lives at Inyanga.*)

arouse *wake up, awaken* vb -mutsa t (LL) cf -muka (LL)

arrange *put straight, put in order* vb -gadzira t (LLL); -ruramisa t (LLLL) cf -rurama (LLL)

arrange *make plans* vb -ronga t (LL)

arrest (*law-breaker*) vb -bata t (HH); -sunga t (HH)

arrival *on a.* adv pakusvika (LLLL); -sviko- (LL) infix vb; **Pakusvika** akawana imba ichibvira. Aka**sviko**wana imba ichibvira. (*On arrival he found the house in flames.*)

arrive *reach* vb -svika i (LL); -uya i (HH); *a. first, beat* vb -tangira t (HHH) cf -tanga (HH)

arrogant *be conceited* vb -virima i (HHH); -zvikudza i (HLH) *reflex* vb

arrow *missile shot from a bow* n museve 3 (LLL)

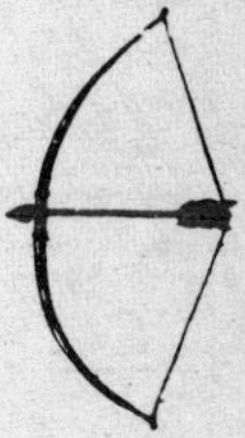

artefact *something fashioned by man* n chiumbwa 7 (LHL) cf -umba (HH)

artery *vein* n tsinga 9 (HH); rutsinga 11 (LHH) *same words for muscle*

as *like* adv sa- + a = sa- (Anoita **sava**mwe.); sa- + i = se- (Anomhanya **se**mhepo.) sa- + u = so. (**So**kufunga kwangu ...); *Same tone rules as* Na- cf *and; as, since, for the reason that* conj zva- PC Cl 8; **Zva**waramba, ndiudze chaunoda. Indirect Rel (*Since you have refused, tell me what you want.*)

as far as *I know* adv sokuziva kwangu

as if adv kunge (LL) + noun or noun clause. Anotaura **kunge** akapfuma (*He talks as if he is rich.*); *as though;* Anotaura **sokunge** ndiye munhu mukuru. (*He talks as though he is the important one.*)

as soon as adv **-ngo-** infix vb; Ndamuóna pandangosvika. (*I saw him as soon as I arrived.*); -chango- cf -ngo- infix vb; Achangosvika akatanga kurwara. (*He began to feel ill as soon as he arrived.*)

asbestos *soft mineral substance which does not burn* n chinda 9 K (LL); shinda 9 MZ (LL)

asbestos bush *guarri b., evergreen shrub* n muchekazani 3 (LHLHH); mutsatsakunaka 13 (LLLLLL)

ascend *climb up* vb -kwira i & t (HH)

ascent *slope going up* n makata 6 (LLL); mukwidza 3 (LHL) cf -kwira (HH)

ash *false a. tree B.Bk. 1,8* n mukarati 3 (LHHL); *caterpillar that feeds on and inhabits the mukarati tree:* harati 9 (HHL)

ash-heap *waste heap* n durunhuru 5, madurunhuru 6 (LLLL)

ashamed *be a.,* vb -nyara i & t (HH); -tsveruka i & t (HHH)

ashes *powder left after something is burnt* n dota 5, madota 6 (LL)

ask *a question* vb -bvunza i & t (LL); *ask for, request, beg* vb -kumbira i & t (HHH)

ask *searching questions* vb -bvunzisisa i & t (LLLL) cf -bvunza (LL); *investigate* vb -feya-feya i & t (HH HL)

asleep *be a.;* vb -kotsira i (LLL) (stative vb); -rara i (HH) (stative vb) *can also mean: lie down;* Mukomana akarara/arere. (*The boy is asleep.*); *be sleepy, feel the need of sleep* vb -batwa nehope (HH HLL)

asparagus fern *cultivated and used as greenery by florists* n rukato 11 (LLL)

assegai *spear, missile that is hurled* n pfumo 5, mapfumo 6 (HH)

assegai wood tree *mangwe t., yellow wood t.* n mususu 3 (LHL); mukonono 3 (LLLL); mutabvu 3 (LLL)

assemble *gather together* vb -ungana i (HHH); -unganidza t (HHHL)

assembly *gathering* n gungano 5, makungano 6 (HHL) cf -ungana (HHH)

assent *agree* vb -bvuma i & t (LL)

assent *consent, permission* n mvumo 9 (LL) cf -bvuma (LL)

assist *help* vb -batidza t (HHH); -batsira t (HHH); -betsera t K (HHH); -yamura t (LLL); *assistance, help* n rubatsiro 11 (LHHL) cf -batsira (HHH)

association *society* n nzanga 9 (LL); chita 7 (LH); sangano 5, masangano 6 (LLL); ruwadzano 11 (LLLL) cf -wadzana (LLL)

asthma *disease of the lungs* n asima 9 (HLL) cf Eng.

astonish *greatly surprise* vb -shamisa i & t (HHH) cf -shama (HH); *astonished, be surprised* vb -shamiswa i (HHH); -katyamadzwa i (HHHL)

astray *go a., get lost* vb -rasika i (HHH) cf -rasa (HH)

at (*time & place*) prep pa- PC 16; kwa- PC 17; also locative nouns: kumusha (LLH) *at home/village* Cl 17; **kumba** (LH) *at home/village* Cl 17; *at first, to begin with* adv pakutanga (LLHH); *at last, finally* adv pakupedzisira (LLHLHL); *at mid-day, at noon* adv masikati 6 (LHHL); *at night* adv usiku 14 (LHH); *at once, immediately, this minute* adv zvino uno (HH HL); iko zvino (HL HH); *at that point* adv ipapo (HLH); *at the side of* prep parutivi pa- (LLLL) pa- (LLLL)

ate *cf eat*

attack *provoke, start a fight* vb -vamba t (LL); -denha t (LL)

attempt *tempt* vb -edza t (LL); idza t K

(LL); *attempt* n chiedzo 7 (LLL) cf -edza (LL) chiidzo 7 K (LLL)

attend *pay attention, follow* vb -teerera i & t (HHHL)

attitude *of mind, thought* n pfungwa 9 (LH) cf -funga (LL)

attract *draw attention* vb -kwezva t (LL)

audible *be loud enough to be heard* adj nzwika (HH) cf -nzwa (H)

auger *tool for boring holes* n bhora 5, mabhora 6 (HL) cf Eng.

aunt *paternal a.* n vatete 2a (HLH); *maternal a.* n maiguru 1a (HLHH)/mainini 1a (HLHL) *term used depends on seniority of age compared to my mother.*

authority *power* n simba 5 (LH); chiremera 7 (LLLL)

avarice *greed of gain* n udyire 14 (LHL); udyi 14 (LH)

avenge *seek revenge* vb -tsiva i & t (LL); -dzorera i & t (LLL)

avoid *escape notice* vb -nyenyeredza t (HHHL); *dodge, evade* vb -nzvenga i & t (HH)

await *wait for* vb -mirira t (HHH) cf -mira (HH)

awake *be conscious, come a., wake up* vb -pepuka i (LLL); *get up* vb -muka i (LL); *awake another* vb -mutsa t (LL) cf -muka (LL) — PT awoke; PP *awaked, awoke*

awhile *a short time* adv kashoma (LLL)

awl *tool for pricking holes* n mutsunda 3 (LLH)

awry *be crooked, lop-sided* vb -tsveyama i (HHH) (stative vb); Denga remba raka**tsveyama** (*The roof of the house is lop-sided.*)

axe *chopper, tool for chopping wood* n demo 5, matemo 6 (HH) cf -tema (HH) dimuro 5, matimuro (HHL); *ceremonial axe* n gano 5, makano 6 (HH)

axle *spindle upon which wheel revolves* n ekisero 9 (HLLL) cf Eng.

B

baboon gudo

babbler *Jardine's b.* n dywedywe 5, madywedywe 6 (HL); zhongozho 5 Z (LHL)

babiana *wild flower-bearing plant* n hwenya 9 Z (HL); hwena 9 K (HL)

baboon n gudo 5, makudo 6 (LL); bveni 5, mapfeni 6 (LL); diro 5, matiro 6 (LL); dede 5 M, matede 6 (LH); *large male b.* n horomba 9 (LLH); *female b.* n gonyn'o 5, magonyn'o 6 (LH); *baby b.* n shokorana 5, mashokorana 6 (LLLH)

baby *babe-in-arms* n mucheche 1 (LLL); *recently born b.* n rusvava 11

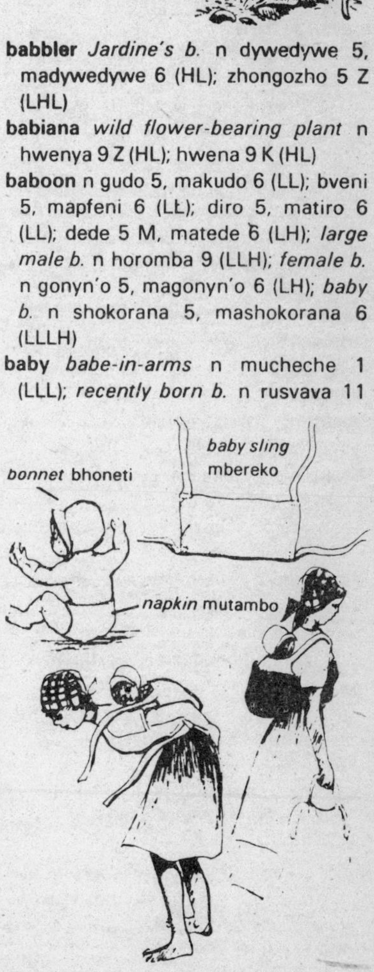

(LLL), tusvava 13 (LLL); *b. sling* n mbereko 9 (LLL) cf -bereka (LLL); *babyhood* n ucheche 14 (LLL) cf mucheche (LLL)

baby-sit *tend a baby* vb -rera t (LL)

bachelor *unmarried man* n pfunda 9 (LL); *confirmed b., elderly b.* n tsvimborume 9 (HHHL)

back *upper hind part of the body* n musana 3 (LHH)

back *come b.* vb -dzoka i (LL); *give b.* vb -dzosera i & t (LLL); -dzorera i & t (LLL); -dzokesa i & t (LLL) cf -dzoka (LL); *go b., turn back, return* vb -dzokera i (LLL) cf -dzoka (LL); *look b.* vb -cheuka i (HHH); *move b., recede, withdraw* vb -suduruka i (LLLL); *turn b. turn around* vb -tendeuka i (HHHL); *turn one's back on someone* vb -furatira t (HHHL)

back *place or direction behind one's back, in the rear* adv shure 17 (HL); mushure 18 (LHL); mumashure 18 (LLHL)

backbite *gossip uncharitably* vb -ita makuhwa (LL LLL)

backbone *spine* n muzongoza 3 (LHLH); zongoza 5 (HLH)

backside *bottom (of human person)* n matako 6 (LHH)

backward *be unprogressive* vb -sarira shure i (HHH HL)

backward *walk b.* vb -dududza i (HHH); -famba namadududu i (HH HLHHH)

bad *be objectionable* adj & vb -ipa i (HH); -shata i (HH) (stative vbs); Vane tsika dzakaipa/dzaka**shata**. (*They have bad manners.*)

bad *be rotten* adj & vb -ora i (LL) (stative vb); Mazai aya aka**ora**. (*These eggs are bad.*)

bad omen *sign suggesting forthcoming disaster, e.g. the sight of a chameleon crossing the path* n shura 5, mashura 6 (LH)

badge *something worn to show rank, position etc.* n bheji 5, mabheji 6 (HL) cf Eng.; chikwangwani 7 (LHLL)

badly *in a way which is bad* adv zvakaipa (LHLL) rel. Haatauri **zvakaipa** pana vakuru. (*He does not talk badly in the company of grown-ups.*) cf excessively

bad-mannered *be rude* vb -shaya tsika/unhu (LL LL/LL)

badness *moral b.* n uipi 14 (LHH) cf -ipa (HH)

bag *flexible container for carrying* n

bhegi 5, mabhegi 6 (HL) cf Eng.; homwe 9 (HH)

bake (*bread*) vb -bheka i & t (HH) cf Eng.

bakery *place where bread is baked* n bheka 5 (HL) cf Eng.

balance *weigh, measure* vb -era t (LL); -pima t (LL); *b. and carry something on the head* vb -dengezera i & t (HHHL)

bald *be b., be lucky* vb -va nemhanza i (HLL); -ne mhanza

bald head *bald patch on head* n mhanza 9 (HH); mhazha 9 K (HH)

bale *scoop out water* vb -kupa t (HH)

ball *solid or hollow sphere* n bhora 5, mabhora 6 (HL) cf Eng.

balsam tree *turpentine t., Rhodesian iron wood t.* n musaru 3 (LHL); musharu 3 (LHL)

bambara groundnut *the flower appears above the ground, then droops to the ground and the pod with one seed develops under the soil* n nyimo 9 (LL); nzama 9 Ko (LL)

bamboo plant n mushenjere 3 (LLLL); musengere 3 M (LLLL)

ban *prohibit* vb -bhana t (HH) cf Eng.

banana plant n muhovha 3 (LLL); mubhanana (LLHL) cf Eng.; *fruit of b. plant* n bhanana 5, mabhanana 6 (LHL) cf Eng.; hovha 5 K (LL)

bandage *material for putting around wounds* n bhandeji 5, mabhandeji 6 (HLL) cf Eng.; mucheka 3 (LHL)

bang *a door* vb -rovera gonhi (HHL HL); 2-kwatidza gonhi (HHL HL)

banish *send someone away, esp out of the country* vb -tanda t (HH); -dzinga -kwatidza gonhi (HHL HL)

bank *firm established for custody of money* n bhangi 5, mabhangi 6 (HL) cf Eng.; bhan'a 5, mabhan'a 6 K (HL) cf Eng.

bank *of a river or lake, shore line* n hombekombe 5, mahombekombe 6 (LLLL)

banner *flag, standard* n mureza 3 (LHL)

baobab tree *cream of Tartar t.* n muuyu 3 (LLH) B.Bk. 1,34

baptism *Christian rite of initiation* n rubhapatidzo 11 (LHHHL) cf -bhapatidza (HHHL); ruombeko 11 (LLLL) cf -ombeka (LLL)

baptize *make person Christian, christen* vb -ombeka t (LLL); -bhapatidza t (HHHL) cf Eng.

bar *close, shut* vb -zarira t (LLL); *closing barrier* n zariro 5, mazariro 6 (LLL) cf -zarira (LLL)

bar *wooden beam* n bango 5, mapango 6 (LL)

bar *pub* n bhawa 5, mabhawa 6 (HL) cf Eng.

barbed wire n waya ine minzwa 9 *wire which has thorns*

barbel *sp of cat-fish* n muramba 3 (LHH); ramba 5, maramba 6 (HH); hokota 9 (HHL); mukokota 3 (LHHL); *electric b.* n nhetemedzi 9 (HHHL); *butter b.* n chinyamudande 7 (LLLHL)

barber *one who cuts hair* n mugeri 1 (LLL) cf -gera (LL)

barbet *sp of bird which uses an excavated cavity for its nest in the*

branches of trees n chimutowegodo 7 (LLLHLL); chikweguru 7 (LHLL); chikondogara 7 (LLHLH); mukohodza 3 (LHHL); chimukohodza 7 (LLHHL); chikumegumbo 7 (LLHHL); *crested b.* n chikodoga 7 (LHHL)

bare the teeth *menace* vb -nyinura i (LLL)

bark (*of a baboon*) vb -homura i (HHH); (*of a dog*) vb -hukura i & t (HHH)

bark *of a tree (dry)* n gwati 5, makwati 6 (LH); *bark fibre, bast with the hard outer cover removed* n rwodzi 11 (LH); gavi 5, makavi 6 (LH)

bark a tree *debark, remove the bark — first stage of collecting bark fibre* vb -ponora t (HHH)

barren animal *a. unable to bear young* n mhanje 9 (HL)

barrow *wheel-barrow* n bhara 5, mabhara 6 (HL) cf Eng.

base *underpart, support* n garo 5, magaro 6 (LL) cf -gara (LL)

bash in *smash in, disfigure (metal surface)* vb -fonyedza t (LLL)

bashful *be shy* vb -nyara i & t (HH); *bashfulness, shyness* n manyadzo 6 (LHH); nyadzi 10 (HH) cf -nyara (HH)

basin *wash-b.* n dhishi 5, madhishi 6 (HL) cf Eng.

bask in the sun *sun-bathe* vb -zambira zuva i (HHL HH)

basket *woven fibre carrying container* n tswanda 9 MZ (LL); swanda 9 MZ (LL); *large b.* n dengu 5, matengu 6 (LH); *flat b. for winnowing* n rusero 11 (LLL) *Plur: tsero 10*

bass *voice, v. low in tone* n bhesi 5 (HL) cf Eng.

bast *bark fibre* n rwodzi 11 (LH); gavi 5, makavi 6 (LH)

bastard marula tree n mubvumira 3 (LLLL) B.Bk. 1

bat *warm-blooded animal that flies by night* n muremwaremwa 3 MZ (LHHHL)

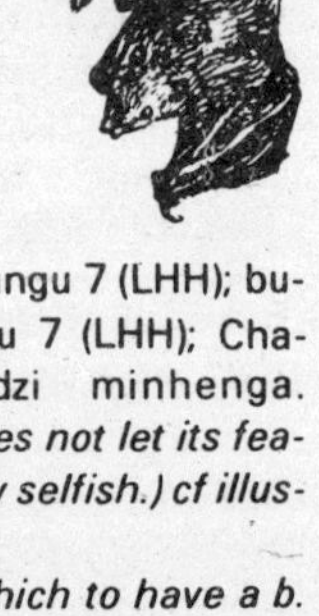

bateleur eagle n chapungu 7 (LHH); bungu 5 (HH); chipungu 7 (LHH); Chapungu hachidonhedzi minhenga. Prov (*The b. eagle does not let its feathers fall. i.e. It is very selfish.) cf illustration p. 48*

bath *large vessel in which to have a b.* n bhavhu 5, mabhavhu 6 (HL) cf Eng.

bathe *wash (usu whole body)* vb -shamba i & t (LL); -geza i & t (LL); -ngura i & t K (LL)

Batoka plum tree *kaffir plum t.* n munhunguru 3 (LLLH)

batter *smash in, dent in (usu metal surfaces)* vb -fonyedza t (LLL)

battery *electric cell* n bhatiri 5, mabhatiri 6 (HLL) cf Eng.

battle *war* n hondo 9 (HH)

battle *fight* vb -rwa i (L)

battle-axe *ceremonial axe* n gano 5, makano 6 (HH)

bauhinia *flowering tree with flowers of a brick-red colour* n mupondo 3 (LLL); munando 3 (LLL) B.Bk. 1,5

bayonet *short knife fixed to a rifle* n bheneti 5, mabheneti 6 (HLL) cf Eng.

be *(vb to be) may be expressed in a variety of forms:* Ndiri mupfumi. (*I am a rich man.*) Ndaiva netsoka. (*I was on foot.*) Ndiri kunzwa zvakanaka. (*I am feeling well.*) Ndava kuenda. (*I am going.*) *Compound forms: Future:* Ndinenge ndiri kunzwa zvakanaka. (*I shall be feeling better.*) *Past:* Ndakanga ndiri mupfumi. (*I was a rich man.*) — PT *was, were;* PP *been.*

bead *(sing & plur)* n chuma 7 (LH)

beak *hard, horny part of a bird's mouth* n muromo weshiri 3 (LLL LHL)

beam *wooden pole* n bango 5, mapango 6 (LL); danda 5, matanda 6 (HH)

beam *sunbeam* n museve wezuva 3 (LLL HLL) *lit: arrow of the sun.*

bean *vegetable* n nyemba 9 (LL); bhinzi 5 & 9 (HL) cf Eng.

bear *carry* vb -takura i & t (LLL); *b. a child, give birth* vb -sununguka i & t (HHHL); -zvara i & t (HH); -ita mwana i (LL LH); *b. fruit, b. young* vb -bereka i & t (LLL) — PT *bore;* PP *borne, born*

beard *growth of hair on chin* n ndebvu 9 (LL)

bearing *build, aspect* n chimiro 7 (LHH) cf -mira (HH)

beat *(of the pulse, heart-beat) b. by hammering* vb -pfura i (HH); *b. an egg* vb -rova-rova t (HHHL); *strike, hit* vb -rova i & t(HH) passive: -rohwa (HH); *b. with fists* vb -dhonora i & t (HHH); arrive first vb -tangira t (HHH) cf -tanga (HH); *surpass, do better than* vb -kunda t (HH); -pinda t (LL); *b.severely, thrash, flog* vb -pura i & t (HH); -zvinda i & t (LL); *b. a drum, sound a drum* vb -ridza ngoma (LL LL) — PT *beat;* PP *beaten*

beautiful *be pretty* adj & vb -naka i (LL) (*stative vb*); Ane musikana akanaka. (*He has a beautiful girl-friend.*) *b. girl* n tsvarakadenga 9 (LLLHL)

beautify *make beautiful* vb -nakisa t (LLL) cf -naka (LL)

beauty *good looks* n runako 11 (LLL) cf -naka (LL)

because conj nokuti (LHL); sokuti (LHL); pamusana pa- (LLHH); ngekuti M (LHL); *as, since* conj zva- PC Cl 8 Indirect rel construction

becium *flowering plant* n chikomamatadza 7 (LHHHLL) B.Bk. 1,79

beckon *call attention (by signalling)* vb -daidza t (HHH); -shevedza t (HHH)

become *come or grow to be* vb -va i (H) *often used in association with formative* na-. Aiva nemari zhinji. (*He used to have a lot of money.*) cf *be — PT became;* PP *become*

become scarce *grow rare, be few* vb -shomeka i (LLL)

becoming *be worthy, proper* adj & vb -kodzera i (LLL) (stative vb)

bed *furniture for sleeping on* n mubhedha 3 (LHL) cf Eng.; *bed of a river* n mugero 3 (LHL)

bed-bug *flat, blood-sucking insect infesting beds* n tsikidzi 9 (LHL)

bee *honey b.* n nyuchi 9 (HH); *drone, male b.* n donganyuchi 5 (LLHH) *queen b.* n zimai renyuchi 21 (LHL HLL); *larva* n zana 5, mazana 6 (LH); *carpenter b.* n zingizi 5, mazingizi 6 (LHL); *bee-sting* n rumborera 11 (LLLL); *beeswax* n namo 9 (LL); mhora 9 KM (HL)

bee-eater *sp of bird* n gamanyuchi 9 (LLHH); bonganyuchi 5, maponganyuchi 6 (LLHH); fukarusheshe 9 (HHHLL); *European b.* n pfukepfuke 9 Z (LHLL) R404

bee-hive *home for bees (man-made from a cylinder of bark)* n mukoko 3 (LLH) pfari 9 KM (LH)

beechwood tree *heartwood similar to that of the European beech* n mutsatsati 3 (LHHL) B.Bk. 1,2

been *cf be*

beer *(African)* n hwahwa 14 (LH); doro 5 (LL) (*must be distinguished from* doro (LH)) *(rice field); European b.* n bhiya 5 (HL); hwahwa hwechiRungu 14 (LH LHLL); *sweet b. (non alcoholic)* n maheu 6 (LHL); *beer-dance, feast* n bira 5, mabira 6 (HL); zhana 5, mazhana 6 (LH); *beer hall, beer garden* n bhawa 5, mabhawa 6 (HL) cf Eng.

beetle *insect with hard, shiny, wing-covers* n ngoko 9 (LL) *There appears to be no general term.*

beetroot *sp of veg* n bhitiruti 5 & 9 (HLLL) cf Eng.
before (*place and time*) adv pamberi 16 (LLH); *before* adv SC + -sa-ti + past partic Akafa **ndisati ndasunungukwa.** (*He died before I was born i.e. I not yet having been born.*); *do b.* adv -tangira t (HHH) cf -tanga (HH); Ndaku**tangira** kusvika pano. (*I arrived here before you.*)
beforehand adv -sano- (LL); -fano- Z (LL) Infix vbs
beg *ask for* vb -kumbira i & t (HHH); *beseech, entreat* vb -teterera i & t (HHHL); *beg by singing or dancing* vb -pemha i & t (LL)
beggar *poor person who begs* n murombo 1 (LLH); murombe 1 (LLL)
begin *originate* vb -tanga i & t (HH); -vamba i & t (LL); -yamba i & t Z (LL); *begin before others* vb -tangira t (HHH) cf -tanga (HH); Ndinomu**tangira** kushanda. (*I begin work before him.*) — PT *began; PP begun*
beginner *instigator* n muvambi 1 (LLL) cf -vamba (LL)
beginning n kutanga 15 (LHH); kuvamba 15 (LLL); mavambo 6 (LLL); *in the b.* adv pakutanga (LLHH) cf -tanga (HH)
begrudge *deny* vb -nyima i & t (HH)
beguile *deceive* vb -nyengedza t (HHH)
behave like *conduct oneself like, be like* vb -ita sa- (LL); Rega **kuita** seusingazivi. (*Don't behave as if you don't know.*); -nge; Rega **kunge** benzi. (*Don't behave like a fool.*)
behave oneself vb -zvibata i (HLH) cf -bata (HH) reflex vb
behind (*one's back*) adv mushure 18 (LHL); shure 17 (HL)
behind *an object which is facing* adv seri 17 (HL); sure 17 K (HL); snure 17 MZ (HL)
belch *growl, bring up wind into the mouth, send out air* vb -dzvova i & t (LL)
belch *emission of air from the mouth* n nhururu 9 (LLL)
belief *religious b.* n chitendero 7 (LLLL) cf -tendera (LLL)
believe *give assent to* vb -bvuma i & t (LL); -tendera i & t (LLL); *believer, one who believes* n mutendi 1 (LLL); mutenderi 1 (LLLL)
bell *cup-shaped metal instrument made to give a musical sound when struck* n dare 5, matare 6 (HL); bhero 5, mabhero 6 (HL) cf Eng.
bellow *make noise of cow or bull* vb -kuma i (HH); -dzvova i (LL)
bellows *apparatus for blowing air into a fire* n mvuto 9 (LL)
belly *stomach, abdomen* n dumbu 5 (LL); nhumbu 9 (LL)
belongings *possessions* n nhumbi 10 (LH)
beloved *loved one* n mudiwa 1 (LHL); mudikani 1 (LHHL); mudikanwi 1 (LHHL); mudikanwa 1 (LHLH) cf -da (H)
below *at or to a lower level* prep adv pazasi 16 (LLH); nyasi 17 (LH); pasi 16 (LH); *underneath, beneath* prep & adv kutsi 17 (LH)
belt *band around waist* n bhandi 5, mabhandi 6 (HL) cf Eng.; bhanire 5, mabhanhire 6 (LHL)
bench *long, hard seat* n bhenji 5, mabhenji 6 (HL) cf Eng.
bend *b. down, b. over* vb -kotama i (LLL); cause to become curved or at an angle vb -kombamisa t (HHHL) cf -kombama (HHH); -bhenda t (HH) cf Eng.; *b. at an angle, flex (joint)* vb -gonya i (HH); -gonyesa t (HHH); *bent, be crooked* adj & vb -kombama i (HHH) (stative vb); Bango iri raka**kombama.** (*This pole is bent.*) — PT *bent;* PP *bent, bended*

beneath *below* prep adv pasi pa- 16 (LH); pazasi 16 (LLH)

benefit *advantage* n chimuko 7 (LLL); yamuro 9 (LLL) cf -yamura (LLL); batsiro 9 (HHL) cf -batsira (HHH)

bereaved person *one whose relative has died* n mufirwi 1 (LHH) cf -firwa (HH); mufirwa 1 (LHL); musiyiwa 1 (LHLH) cf -siyiwa (HHH)

beseech *beg, ask for, plead for* vb -teterera i & t (HHHL) — PT & PP *besought*

beside *at the side of* prep adv parutivi pa- 16 (LLLL); Akagara parutivi paAnna. (*He sat down beside Anna.*)

besides *in addition* conj -zve KM; dzoke K (LH)

besiege *surround* vb -komba t (HH); -komberedza t (HHHL)

besmirch *spoil, make dirty* vb -nyangadza t (HHH); -svipisa t (LLL); -svibisa t (LLL) cf -sviba (LL)

best *cf good*

bestow *give, give away* vb -pa t (H)

bet *risk money on the result e.g. of a race* vb -bheja i (LL) cf Eng. — PT & PP *bet, betted*

bet *money used to bet* n mapike 6 K (LLH); bheji 5 (HL) cf Eng.

betray *be disloyal by informing on* vb -chera t (LL)

better adv nani 1a (HL); Ava kunzwa zviri **nani.** (*He is feeling better.*) *get b., get well, recover health* vb -pora i (HH) *better* adj cf *good*

between *in the middle* prep pakati 16 (LLH)

beware! *look out!* inter hokoyo! (HLL)

bewilder *confuse greatly* vb -kangaidza t (HHHL)

bewitch *cast a spell* vb -roya i & t (LL) *passive form:* -royiwa

beyond *ahead and in front of* prep pamberi 16 (LLH); *outside the limit of* adv kunze 17 (LH)

bias *preference or prejudice for or against* n rusaruro 11 (LLLL) cf -sarura (LLL)

Bible *Sacred Scripture* n Bhaibheri 5 (HLLL) cf Eng.

bicycle *two-wheeled vehicle* n bhasi-

koro 5, mabhasikoro 6 (HLLL); bhizautare 5 (LHLHL)

big *large* adj -kuru (HH), guru 5 (HH); huru 9 (HH); *bigger* adj -kuru pana; Motokari yako ihuru pane yangu. (*Your motor car is bigger than mine.*); *biggest* adj Motokari iyi ihuru pane dzose dzandakaona. (*This is the biggest car I have seen.*)

bile *brownish-yellow, bitter fluid used by the body to digest food* n nduru 9 (HH); nyongo 9 KM (LL)

billy-goat *male goat* n gotora 5, magotora 6 (HHL); hotora 9 (HHL)

biltong *sun-dried meat* n chimukuyu 7 (LLHL)

bin *rubbish b.* n bhini 5, mabhini 6 (HL) cf Eng.

bind *tie* vb -sunga t (HH) — PT & PP *bound*

Bindura bamboo n mushenjere 3 (LLLL)

bioscope *cinema* n bhaiskopu 5, mabhaiskopu 6 (HLLL) cf Eng.

bird *winged, feathered animal that lays eggs* n shiri 9 (LL) *b. of prey* n *largest: eagle* gondo 5, makondo 6 (LH); *somewhat smaller bird of prey:* rukodzi 11 (LHL); owl n zizi 5, mazizi 6 (LL)

bird-cage *c. for fowls* n dendere 5, matendere 6 (LLH) *same word as for nest*

bird-lime *sticky, gluey substance to catch birds* n urimbo 14 (LLL)
birth *action of being born* n kuzvarwa 15 (LHH); kuberekwa 15 (LLLL)
birthday *day of birth* n zuva rokuzvarwa 5 (HH HLHH); zuva rokuberekwa 5 (HH LHLLL)
biscuit *kind of thin, crisp flat cake* n bhisikiti 5, mabhiskiti 6 (HLLL) cf Eng.
bishop *clergyman of high rank* n bhishopi 1a (HLL); mubhishopi 1 (LHLL) cf Eng.
bishop bird (red) *sp of gregarious seed-eater that nests in long grass* n chikenya 7 (LHL); nyamafuro 9 M (LLLL) R808; *yellow b.b., cape widow-bird* n chinyamupondera 7 (LLLHLL); nyamapfuro 9 (LLLL) R811

bit *portion, piece, fragment* n chimedu 7 (LHL) cf -medura (HHH); chidimbu 7 (LHL) cf -dimbura (HHH)
bit of bridle n tomhu 5, matomhu 6 (HL)
bitch *female dog* n imbwa hadzi 9 (LH HH); mbwakadzi 9 K (HLL)
bite vb -ruma i & t (HH); *b. one's tongue* vb -rumira i (HHH) — PT *bit;* PP *bitten, bit*
bitter *be sharp, unpleasant to the taste* vb -vava i (HH)
black *b. coloured* adj -tema (LH); dema 5 (LH), nhema 9 (LH)
black *be dark* adj & vb -sviba i (LL); -svipa i (LL) (stative vb); Mumba makasvipa. (*The house is dark inside.*)
black-jack *common weed with black seeds that cling to clothing* n mhuu 9 (HL); mhuvuyu 9 (HHH)
blacksmith *iron-worker* n mhizha 9 (LH); mupfuri 1 (LHH) cf -pfura (HH)
blackwood *tree or shrub which has almost black heartwood* n murwiti (LLL)
bladder *skin bag in body in which waste liquid collects* n dundira 5, matundira 6 (LLL); furidzo 5, mafuridzo 6 Z (HHL)
bladder bush *shrub bearing copious milky sap* n mufuramvuu 3 (LLLLH); musasasa 3 Z (LLLL)
blade *of knife* n chisvo 7 (LH); *b. of grass* n ruswa 11 (LH); *shoulder b.* n bendekete 5, mapendekete 6 (HHHH)
blame *find fault with* vb -pa mhosva t (HL)
blanket *thick, woolen cloth used as a bed-covering* n gumbeze 5, magumbeze 6 (LHH); jira 5, machira 6 (HH); bhurangeti 5, mabhurangeti 6 (LHLL) cf Eng.
blaspheme *cry out against God* vb -tuka Mwari (HH LH)
blaze *burn with bright flames* vb -bvira i (LL); -pfuta i (LL)
blazer *coloured jacket* n bhureza 5, mabhureza 6 (LHL) cf Eng.
bleat *of a goat* n kumeedza 15 (LHHH); *b. of a sheep* n kubararadza 15 (LHHHL)
bleed *lose blood* vb -buda ropa i (HH HL) — PT & PP *bled*
bleeding *of the nose* n mhuka 9 (LH)
bless *ask God's favour for* vb -komborera t (HHHL); -ropafadza i & t (LLLL); — PT & PP *blessed, blest; blessing, favour* n chikomborero 7 (LHHHL) cf -komborera (HHHL)
blew *cf blow*
blind *be b.* vb -pofomara i (LLLL); *cause blindness* vb -pofomadza t (LLLL)
blind person *one who has lost the power of sight* n bofu 5, mapofu 6 (LL)
blindness *lack of the power to see* n upofu 14 (LLL) cf -bofu (LL)
blink *shut and open the eyes quickly* vb -bhwaira i (HHH)

blister beetle *a common, flying, garden beetle; C.M.R. beetle (Cape Mounted Rifle Brigade)* n chinyamudzunge 7 (LLLHL); nyamudzunge 9 (LLHL)

blister *from friction* n mhoni 9 (LL); *b. from heat* n duhwani 5, maduhwani 6 (LLL); dubwani 5, madubwani 6 (LLL)

bloated *be uncomfortably full from over-eating* vb -zvimbirwa i (HHH)

block the way *make movement difficult or impossible* vb -dzivira t (LLL)

blood *red liquid flowing throughout the body* n ropa 5 (LL); gazi 5 (LH); murombe 3 Ko (LLL)

blood flower n ngarazuva 9 (LLHH)

bloodwood tree *mukwa, kiaat* n mubvamaropa 3 (LLLLL); mukwa 3 (LL) B. Bk. 1,21

blossom *open into flowers* vb -tumbuka i (LLL)

blouse *female outer garment from neck to waist usu covering the arms* n bhurauzi 5, mabhurauzi 6 (LHLL) cf Eng.

blow *the nose, discharge mucus* vb -fura dzihwa t (HH LH)

blow away *in the wind* vb -pupuruka i (HHHL); *blow a breeze* vb -vhuvhuta i (HHH); *drive away with a breath* vb -furidza t (HHH) — PT *blew;* PP *blown*

blow up *pump up, inflate* vb -pombera t (HHH); -vhuta t (LL); Pombera mavhiri angu. (*Pump up my tyres.*)

blue *colour* n 9 bhuruu (LHL) cf Eng.

blue waxbill *sp of small, common, seed-eating bird* n kadhiidhii 12 (LHLHL) R839

blue bottle fly n tunzi 5, matunzi 6 (HH)

bluff *deceive, joke* vb -nyengedza i & t (HHH)

blunder *make a mistake* vb -kanganisa i & t (HHHL)

blunt *be without sharp edge* vb -gomara i (HHH); -gomedzeka i (HHHL) (stative vbs); Ndine banga raka**gomedzeka**. (*I have a blunt knife.*)

blush *be embarrassed* vb -nyara i & t (HH)

boar *male pig* mukono wenguruve 3 (LHH LHLL)

boarding school n bhodhingi 5 (HLL) cf Eng.

boast *brag, speak boastfully* vb -virima i (HHH); -zuwa i MZ (LL)

boastful person n mbirimi 9 (HHL) cf -virima (HHH); *boastfulness, praise of oneself* n umbirimi 14 (LHHL); uvirimi 14 (LHHL) cf -virima (HHH)

boat *(small), canoe* n igwa 5, magwa 6 MZ (LL); gwa 5 K, magwa 6 (L)

bob *up and down (e.g. fisherman's float)* vb -dzoira i Z (HHH)

body *the whole physical structure of a man or an animal* n muviri 3 (LLL)

body odour *stale and offensive smell of the body* n gundu 5 (LH); hunzi 9 K (LH)

bog *muddy patch* n jahwi 5, majahwi 6 (LH)

boil *the action of liquid reaching boiling point* vb -vira i (LL); -fanza i (HH); -vhaira i (LLL); -fashaira i (HHHL); *cause to reach boiling point* vb -vhaidza t (LLL); -vidza t (LL) cf -vira (LL)

boil *abscess, suppurating tumour* n mota 5, mamota 6 (LL); pute 5 M (LL)

bolt *metal fastening for a door or window* n chihuri 7 (LHL); *bolt with*

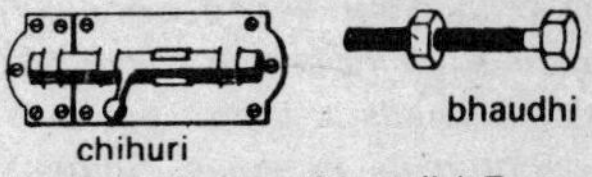

thread and nut n bhaudhi 5, mabhaudhi 6 (HLL) cf Eng.

the human body

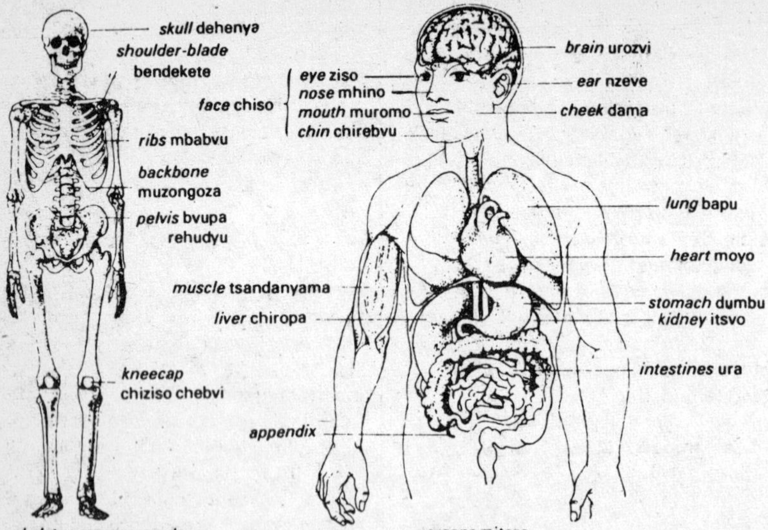

skeleton marangwanda

organs mitezo

bomb *high explosive weapon of war* n bhambu 5, mabhambu 6 (HL) cf Eng.

bond together *e.g. to weld or solder* vb -namatidza t (LLLL)

bone *any one of the parts of the hard frame-work of the animal body* n bvupa 5, mapfupa 6 (HH); godo 5, makodo 6 KM (HH); fupa 5 K, mafupa 6 (HH).

bonnet *hat usu tied under chin, worn by women and babies* n bhoneti 5 & 9 (HLL) cf Eng. cf p. 11

book *bound pages* n bhuku 5, mabhuku (HL) cf Eng.

boomslang *sp of green tree-snake, back-fanged and very poisonous. The female is a light-brown colour. When angry it swells at the throat with air to frighten its enemies. Sometimes confused with the green mamba, which is a front-fanged snake. Length about 1,5 m.* n mhangara 9 (LLL)

boot *shoe* n bhutsu 9 (HL) cf Eng.

border *hem* n mupendero 3 (LLLL); mucheto 3 (LLL)

border *boundary, limit* n muganhu 3 (LHL)

bore *cf bear*

bore *weary by tedious talk* vb -finha i & t (HH); *be fed up* vb -finhwa i (HH)

bore *a hole, drill* vb -boora t (LLL); *done by borer beetles* vb -pfukuta i & t (LLL)

borne *born* cf *bear*

borrow *receive on loan* vb -kwereta i & t (HHH); -posha i & t (HH) — *can also mean lend*

bosom-friend *very close f.* n shamwari yapamwoyo 9 (HLH LHLL)

boss *supervise* vb -foroma t (LLL) cf foromani (LHLL) Eng.

bother *annoy, disturb* vb -netsa i & t (LL); -pfuvisa t (HHH)

bother *annoyance* n nhamo 9 (HH)

bothered *I am not bothered about* vb; Handina hanya/mhosva na....

bottle *usu glass enclosed container for liquids* n bhotoro 5, mabhotoro 6 (HLL); bhodyera 5, mabhodyera 6 (HLL), cf Eng.; *bottle-opener, tin-opener* n chivhuro 7 (LLL) cf -vhura (LL)

bottom *base of a thing* n garo 5, magaro 6(LL) cf -gara (LL); *back-side (of human)* n magaro 6 (LHH)

bought *cf buy*

bounce up (*usu ball*) vb -dauka i (HHH)

bound *cf bind*

bound *be b. to, obliged to* vb -fanirwa i (HHH); -sungirwa i (HHH)

boundary *border* n muganhu 3 (LHL)

bow *arched weapon* n uta 14 (LH); dati 5, madati 6 (LL); *cf illustration p. 9*

bow down *bend over* vb -kotama i (LLL)

bowels *intestines, guts* n ura 14 (LL); matumbu 6 (LLL)

box *container made of cardboard or wood* n bhokisi 5, mabhokisi 6 (HLL) cf Eng.

boxing *fighting with gloves* n bhokiseni 5 (HLLL) cf Eng.; tsiva 9 (LL); *boxing ring* n dariro 5, madariro 6 (HHL)

boy *immature human male* n mukomana 1 (LHLH); *boyhood, years of b.* n ukomana 14 (LHLH) cf mukomana

brace and bit *drilling instrument* n chibooreso 7 (LLLLL) cf -boora (LLL)

bracelet *metal b.* n ndarira 9 (LHL)

braces *straps over the shoulders to hold up the trousers* n makurusibhandi 6 (LLLLHL) cf Eng.

brag *talk boastfully* vb -virima i (HHH); -vhaira i (LLL)

braid *plait* vb -ruka i & t (LL)

brain *mass of soft, grey matter in the head* n uropi 14 (LLH); urozvi 14 (LLH) *cf p. 20*

brake *apparatus to control speed* n bhureki 5, mabhureki 6 (LHL) cf Eng.; *apply brakes* vb -bopa mabhureki

branch *limb of tree* n bazi 5, mapazi 6 (HL); davi 5 K, matavi 6 (LL); nhavani 9 M (LLL); *cut b.* n sanzu 5, masanzu 6 (HH); *fork of pole, river or plant* n mhaswa 9 (LH)

branch off *turn off* vb -tsauka i (HHH)

brand *mark, stamp* n chidhindo 7 (LLL) cf -dhinda (LL); muchiso 3 (LHH) cf -chisa (HH)

brave *be courageous* adj & vb -shinga i (HH) (stative vb); Mukomana uyu aka**shinga** kwazvo. (*This boy is very brave.*)

bravery *courage* n ushingi 14 (LHH) cf -shinga (HH); umhare 14 (LLL)

bread *food made by baking flour with water and yeast* n chingwa 7 (LL); zingwa 5 M, mazingwa 6 (LL)

breadth *distance across* n upamhi 14 (LLH)

break *cause a thing to divide into two or more pieces* vb -tyora t (HH); -vhuna t (HH); *b. off, fracture* vb -dimbuka i (HHH); -tyoka i (HH); *b. anything brittle, smash, shatter* vb -punza t (HH); -pwanya t (LL); *b. off mealie-cob from stalk* vb -svodogora t (HHHL); *b. in oxen* vb -pingudza t (LLL) — PT *broke;* PP *broken*

break down (*mechanically*) *come to a stop* vb -njomba i (HH)

break through *b. out, escape* vb -poya i (LL)

breakfast *first meal a.m.* m chisvusvuro 7 (LHHL) cf -svusvura (HHH)

bream *tilapia, sp of fish* n gwaya 5, magwaya 6 (LH); *red-breasted b.* n mbanje 9 (LH)

breast *female b.; mammary gland* n zamu 5, mazamu 6 (HH); *nipple, teat* n munyatso 3 (LLL)

breast feed *suckle young* vb -yamwisa t (HHH); -mwisa t (HH)

breath *air* n mweya 3 (LH)

breathe *take air into the body and send it out* vb -fema i & t (LL); *b. quickly vb -femereka i (LLLL) cf -fema (LL)*

bred *cf breed*

breed *race, kind, tribe species* n rudzi 11, marudzi 6 (LL); ndudzi 10 (LL)

breed *raise domestic animals* vb -pfuya t (HH); -pfuwa t (HH) — PT & PP *bred*

breeze *wind* n mhepo 9 (HH)

brew *prepare by cooking or boiling* vb -bika t (LL)

bribe *offer or tempt someone with money to do something wrong* vb -pfumba t (LL)

brick *baked unit of clay used for building* n chidhina 7 (LHL); chitina 7 (LHL); *brick-mould, form for moulding bricks* n foroma 9 (LHL) cf Eng.

bride *woman on her wedding day, daughter-in-law* n muroora 1 (LHHL) cf -roora (HHH); mwenga 1a K (LL)

bride-groom *man on his wedding day* n muwani 1 (LLL) cf -wana (LL)

bridge *construction for crossing river* n bhiriji 5, mabhiriji 6 (LHL) cf Eng.

bridge of nose n mutandamhuno 3 (LHHHL)

bright *be clear* vb -chena i (LL); Kunze kwakachena. (*It is bright outside.*)

bring *come with something* vb -uyisa t (HHH); -uya na- t (HH); -unza i & t (HH) cf -uya (HH) — PT & PP *brought*

bring about *cause* vb -sakisa t (LLL) cf -saka (LL); konzera t (HHH) cf -konza (HH)

bring up *look after* (*children*) vb -rera t (LL)

bring upon *b. about* vb -uyisa t (HHH) cf -uya (HH)

broad *wide in extent* adj -pamhi (LH); bamhi 5, mhamhi 9

broadcasting station *radio s.* n nhepfenyuro 9 (LLLL)

broaden *make broad* vb -fadza t (HH); -pamhamisa t (LLLL)

broke *be without cash* (*slang*) vb -tsva i (H) (*slang*)

broke, broken *cf break*

brood (*as a hen*) *sit on eggs* vb -vhumbamira t (HHHL) cf -vhumbama (HHH); -rarira t (HHH) cf -rara (HH)

broom *brush for sweeping floors* n mutsvairo 3 (LHHL) cf -tsvaira (HHH)

brooms and brushes *flowering plant with mauve white flower* n pfeyo 9 (LL) B.Bk. 1,55

brother *elder b. of a boy* n mukoma 1 (LHL); *younger b. of a boy* n munun'una 1 (LHHL); munin'ina 1 (LHHL); *b. of a girl* n hanzvadzi 9 (HHL); hanzvadzikomana 1 (HHLLLL); *b.-in-law of a man* n tezvara 1a (HHL); *b.-in-law of a woman* n muramu 1 (LHH)

brought *cf bring*

brown *light b. colour* adj -shava (HH); shava 5 & 9

browse *graze* vb -fura i & t (LL)

bruise *give injury to the flesh without breaking the skin* vb -kuvadza i & t (HHH) (*hurt*)

brush past *touch lightly* vb -nzvenzvera t (HHH)

brush n bhuracho 5, mabhuracho 6 (LHL) cf Eng.; *b. for sweeping floors, broom* n mutsvairo 3 (LHHL) cf -tsvaira (HHH)

bucket *deep, hollow container with a*

handle for holding liquids n bhagidhi 5, mabhagidhi 6 Z (HLL); bhakete 5 K (HLL), cf Eng.

buffalo *sp of wild ox weighing up to 680 kg.* n nyati 9 (HH) — *mutupo: nhari*

buffalo thorn tree n muchecheni 3 (LHHL) B.Bk. 1,31

bug catcher shrub n rutapatsikidzi 11 (LHHLHL)

build *of the body, aspect, bearing* n chimiro 7 (LHH) cf -mira (HH)

build *construct* vb -vaka i & t (HH) — PT & PP *built*

builder *one who builds* n muvaki 1 (LHH) cf -vaka (HH); bhiridha 1a (HLL) cf Eng.

bulbul *black-eyed Layard's b., sp of fruit-eating and insect-eating bird, popular name* = toppie n chigwenhure 7 (LLHL); gwenhure 5, magwenhure 6 (LHL); gweture 5 M, magweture (LHL); sakambuya 9 (HLHL) R545

bull *male of the ox family* n handira 9 (LLH); ngunzi 9 (LL); mukono 3 (LHH); hando 9 (LL); bhuru 5, mabhuru 6 (HL) cf Eng.

bullet *missile discharged from a rifle* n bara 5, mapara 6 (LH) cf Eng.

bullfrog n dzetse 5, madzetse 6 (LL)

bullock *ox, male calf* n nzombe 9 (HH)

bully *persecuting husband* n mushushi 1 (LLL) cf -shusha (LL)

bump into (*a person*) vb -dhuma t (LL); -gumana i (LLL); *b. into a thing* vb -guma t (LI)

bun *small, round, sweet cake* n bhanzi 5, mabhanzi 6 (HL) cf Eng.

bunch *cluster* n bumha 5, mabumha 6 (HL); bumbu 5 (LL)

bundle *of grass* n chiswa 7 (LL); mwanda 3 (LL); *b. of wood, faggot* n svinga 5, masvinga 6 MZ (HH)

bunting *sp of seed-eating bird* n chidhindiri 7 (LHLH)

burden *heavy load* n mutoro 3 (LHH); mutwaro 3 KM (LHH)

burial place *graveyard* n makuva 6 (LHH) (cf grave)

burn *consume with fire, set light to, b. up* vb -pisa t KM (HH); *be alight* vb -tsva i (H) — PT & PP *burnt, burned*

burrow *made by mice and small animals, hole* n mwena 3 (LH)

burst *explode* vb -putika i (HHH); *b. out laughing* vb -pwatika kuseka i (HHH HLL) — PT & PP *burst*

bury *put a dead body in a grave* vb -viga t (HH)

bus *large vehicle for carrying passengers* n bhazi 5, mabhazi 6 (HL) cf Eng.

bush *shrub* n gwenzi 5, magwenzi 6 (LH)

bush-baby *the larger of two sp of galago occurring in Rhodesia.* n gwee 5, magwee 6 (HL)

bushbuck *sp of antelope, weight about 90 kg* n dzoma 5, madzoma 6 M (LH); tsoma 9 (LH); soma 9 (LH) goho 5 (HL); *cf illustration p. 89*

bushman n mandionerepi 1a (LHLLLH); chimandionerepi 7 (LLHLLLH); *b. paintings* n zvainyorwa navamandionerepi

bush pig *wild p.* n humba 9 (LL); nguruve yomudondo 9 (LLL LHLL)

business n bhizimisi 5, mabhizimisi 6 (HLLL) cf Eng; basa 5, mabasa 6 (LL)

bustard *korhaan, sp of large insect and seed-eating ground bird* n gaudya 5, magaudya 6 (LHL)

Bustard

Korhaan

bustle *move about quickly and excitedly* vb -ita chipatapata i (LLLLL)

busy *be busily active* vb -shena-shena i (HHHL); -ita bishi i (LL LH)

but conj asi (LH); kasi (LH); bva K (L); *but for, except for* conj dai + neg partic; Dai pasina izvi ndingadai ndisina kupona. (*If it were not for these things I would not have escaped.)*

butcher bird *fiscal shrike* n korera 9 (LHH); chikorera 7 (LLHH); chisemaura 7 (LHHHL); nyamatunge 9 M (LLHL) R 707 *cf illustration p. 58*

butchery *slaughter house* n siraha 9 (LHL); bhucha 5, mabhucha 6 (HL) cf Eng.

butt *cigarette-end, stompie* n chigusvani 7 (LLHH); chistompi 7 (LHL) cf Afrik.

butter *fatty food made from cream* n bhata 5 (HL) cf Eng.; peanut b. n dovi 5 (LH); *b. fat* n ruomba 11 (LLL)

butterfly *insect with coloured wings* n shavishavi 5, mashavishavi 6 (LLLL)

buttock *bottom (polite term)* n garo 5, magaro 6 (LL) cf -gara (LL); *one half of the rump or behind* n dako 5, matako 6 (HH) (*impolite term*)

button *small usu round object for fastening articles of clothing* n ngopero 9 (HHL) cf Afrik.; bhatanisi 5 (HLLL) cf Eng.; konobho 9 (HHL); ndoro 9 (LL)

button *fasten buttons* vb -kopera i & t (HHH); -konopera i & t (HHHL)

buy *purchase* vb -tenga i & t (HH) — PT & PP *bought*

buzz *make humming noise like flying insect (bee, wasp, etc.)* vb -ziririka i (HHHL)

buzzard *small bird of prey, augur b.* n nyamudzura i Z (LLLL); *lizard b.* n chikondomatsvinyu 7 Z (LLHHLH) (*also applied to steppe b.*)

by prep na- + a = **navanhu** (LHL) (*by people*); na- + i = **nebhazi** (HLL) (*by bus*); na- + u = **noutsi** (HLH) (*by smoke*)

by and by *before long, presently* adv gare gare (LH LH); mbaimbai (LHLH) cf Eng.

by now *by this time* adv pari zvino (LH LL)

by the way! inter gara zviya! (LL HL)

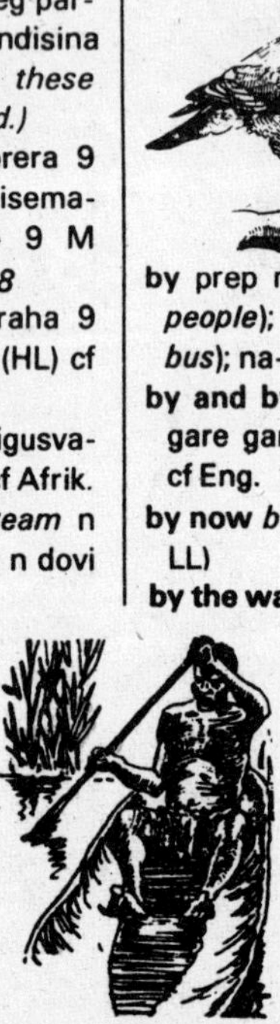

canoe igwa

C

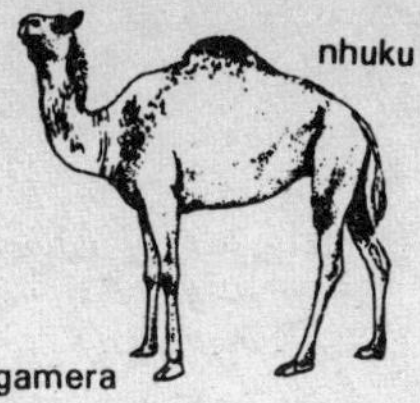

camel ngamera

cabbage *plant with thick, green leaves used as veg* n kabichi 5, makabichi 6 (HLL) cf Eng.

cabbage tree *umbrella tree* n mufenje 3 (LHH) B.Bk. 1,39, 40

cable *electric c.* n tambo yegetsi 9, waya yegetsi 9

cackle *make noise as done by a hen after laying an egg* vb -kerekedza i MZ (HHHL)

cadge *meals, sponge* vb -kwata i (LL)

cage *for fowls, bird-cage* n dendere 5, matendere 6 (LLH)

cajole *use flattery or deceit to persuade* vb -nyengetedza i & t (HHHL); -tsvetera i & t (LLL)

cajolery *flattery* n ruvhevho 11 (LLL) cf -vhevha (LL)

cake *sweet mixture of flour, eggs, etc. baked in oven* n keke 5, makeke 6 (HL) cf Eng.

calabash *gourd* n dende 5, matende 6 (HH); mudende 3 Z (LHH); *very small c. to put oil in* n chinu 7 (LH)

calamity *misfortune, disaster* n rushambwa 11 (LLH); nhamo 9 (HH); dambudziko 5, matambudziko 6 (LLLL) cf -tambudzika (LLLL)

calf *young of cattle and large antelopes* n mhuru 9 (LH)

calf *of leg, muscle behind the shin* n tsapfu 9 MZ (LL); chitumbi 7 (LLH)

call *summon, beckon* vb -daidza t (HHH); -dana t K (HH); -shevedza t (HHH); -danidza t (HHH)

call of bird n kurira kweshiri 15 (LLL LHL); utyirityiri hweshiri 14 (LLHLH LHL); *c. of a jackal* n kuhwaura kwegava 15 (LHHH HLL)

calm *quiet, untroubled* adj & vb -dzikama i (LLL) (stative vb); *make c.* vb -nyaradza t (HHH); *c. off, cool off* vb -pora i (HH); podza t (HH)

calumniate *slander* vb -nenedzera t (HHHL)

calumny *slander, false charge* n guhwa 5, makuhwa 6 (LL); nhema 10 (LH)

came *cf come*

camel *animal of the desert with large hump* n ngamera 9 (LHL); gamera 9 (LHL) cf Eng.; *cf illustration*

camera *apparatus for taking photographs* n kamera 9 (HLL); pikicha 9 (HLL) cf Eng.

camp *district police c.* n kamba 9 (HL) cf Eng.

camp shelter *temporary shelter of branches* n musasa (LLH)

can *be able* vb -gona i & t (LL)

canary *kind of small seed-eating bird (general name)* n nzvidya 9 K (LH)

cancer *serious, diseased growth* n gomarara 5 (HLLL); nhuta 9 Z (LL); nhukusa 9 K (LLL)

candelabra tree *euphorbia ingens* n mukonde 3 (LLL) B.Bk. 1,27 *cf illustration p. 53*

candle n kandyera 5 & 9 (HLL); kanduru 5 & 9 (HLL) cf Eng.

cane *rod used for punishment* n shamhu 9 (LH)

cane-rat *member of rodent family* n tsenzi (LH) *cf illustration p. 132*

canoe *in Africa a hollowed out tree-trunk, usu of the palm tree* n igwa 5, magwa 6 (LL); hwato 9 (LL); bwato 5, mabwato 6 (LL)

cap *soft head-covering without brim*

worn by boys and men n kepisi 9 (HLL); chikepisi 7 (LHLL); chipepe 7 (LLL) cf Eng.

capable *having the ability (usu ability of mind)* adj -va nenjere (HLL); -gona i & t (LL)

capable person *expert* n nyanzvi 9 (LH)

Cape fig tree *wild fig t.* n mukuyu 3 (LHL); muonde 3 (LLH)

Cape mahogany tree *white m. t.* n muchichiri 3 (LLLL)

capsize *overturn (a boat)* vb -kutuka i (HHH)

captive *captured person* n mubatwa 3 (LHL) cf -batwa (HH); *captivity, state of being held captive* n ubatwa 14 (LHL) cf -batwa (HH); utapwa 14 (LHL) cf -tapwa (HH)

caracal *African lynx; large, red, wild cat* n twana 9 Z (HL); hwana 9 K (LL); *cf illustration p. 50*

carcass *dead body of an animal* n mutumbi (LLH); mutumbo 3 KM (LLL)

card *playing c.* n kasi 5, makasi 6 (LL) cf Eng.

card-board box n kadhibhokisi 5, makadhibhokisi 6 (HLHLL) cf Eng.

care n hany'a 9 (LL); mhosva 9 (HL); Handina hany'a nazvo/ Handina mhosva nazvo. (*I don't care about it.*)

care for *provide for* vb -riritira t (HHHL); -kotsvera t M (HHH)

carefully *done with care* adv -nyatso-; -chano- KoZ *infix vbs*

caress *a child, give a loving touch to* vb -rezva t (HH)

carpenter *one who works in wood* n muvezi 11 (LLL) cf -veza (LL)

carried *cf carry*

carrion flower *which emits a strong carrion-like smell which attracts the flies which effect pollination* n chikondepasi 7 (LLLLH) B.Bk. 1,74

carrot *veg. with yellow or orange root* n karotsi 9 (HLL) cf Eng.

carry *move from one place to another* vb -takura t (LLL); -senga t KM (LL); *c. on the back* vb -bereka i & t (LLL); *c. under the arm* vb -pakatira t (HHHL)

cartilage *firm, elastic substance covering the joints in animal bodies* n shwashwa 5 Z (LL)

cartridge (*empy bullet case*) n nyere 9 (LL); rutanga 11 K (LLH)

carve *fashion something usu out of wood* vb -veza i & t MZ (LL)

cascade *waterfalls* n bopoma 5, mapopoma 6 (LLL) cf -popoma (LLL)

case *judicial c.* n mhosva 9 (HL)

cassava *manioc (originating in S. America)* n mufarinya 3 MZ (LLHL)

cassia *long-pod c. tree* n murembarembe 3 (LLLLL); muvheneka 3 (LLHH); *peanut c., peanut-butter c. shrub* n munwahuku 3 (LHLL); mudyahuku 3 (LHLL)

cast a spell *bewitch* vb -roya i & t (LL); *c. a shadow, make a. s. fall* vb -kanda mumvuri i (LL LHL); *c. off skin, slough* vb -vhunura i (HHH) — PT & PP *cast*

castrate *make a male animal useless for breeding* vb -cheka t (HH); -gadzira t (LLL); -sunura t (LLL)

cat *domestic c.* n katsi 9 (HL) cf Eng.; mangoi 1a & 9 M (LLH); *wild c.* n nhiriri 9 (LLL); bonga 5, mabonga 6 (LL)

cataract *disease in the eye causing partial blindness* n tsanga 9 MZ (HH); shanga 9 K (HH)

catch *c. hold, grasp* vb -bata t (HH); *c. a thrown object* vb -gama t (LL); *c. in the act, c. red-handed, find out, discover* vb -dimbura t (LLL); -tumba t

M(LL); *c. fish with a hook* vb -raura i & t (HHH); -vedza i & t (HH); -redza i & t K (HH) — PT & PP *caught*

catechism *book of questions and answers about religion* n katekisimo 9 (LLHLL) cf Eng.; *c. lesson* n katekasi 9 (LLLL) cf Eng.

catechize *teach religion* vb -fundisa katekisimo i & t (HHH HHHLL)

catechumen *one who is being instructed in the catechism* n mukwashi 1 K (LLL)

caterpillar *grub (general term)* n gonye 5, makonye 6 (LL)

cattle *one or more head of c.* n mombe 9 (LL); n'ombe 9 KM (LL); *cow* n mhou 9 (HL); *heifer* n tsiru 5, matsiru 6 (HL); *calf* n mhuru 9 (LH); *young bullock* n gondora 5, magondora 6 (LLH); *hornless animal* n njuma 9 (HL); nzuma 9 KM (HL)

cattle-dung *wet or dry c.* n ndove 9 (LL); *dry c.d. (used as fuel)* n hundwa 9 (LH); ndohwa 9 K (LH)

cattle egret *sp of white insect-eating bird often seen with cattle* n fudzamombe 5, mafudzamombe 6 (LLLL) R61

cattle kraal *c. pen, herd of c.* n danga 5, matanga 6 (LH)

cattle melon n shamba 5, mashamba 6 (LH)

caught *cf catch*

cauliflower *kind of veg* n konifurau 9 (HLLLL) cf Eng.

cause *make something happen, produce an effect* vb -konzera t (HHH); -sakisa t (LLL); -itisa t (LLL); *cause, something that brings about a result* n chikonzero 7 (LHHL); chisakiso 7 (LLLL)

cause abortion *terminate pregnancy* vb -bvisa nhumbu/pamuviri i & t (LL LL /LLLL)

cautious *be careful* vb -chenjera i & t (HHHL); -ngwarira i (LLL) cf- ngwara (LL)

cave *among rocks* n bako 5, mapako 6 (LL); mhako 9 M (LL)

cave-in *collapse* vb -ondomoka i (HHHL)

cavity *in tooth* n mhango 9 (LL)

cease *desist from* vb -rega ku- (LL); *c. aching, heal* vb -pora i (HH); *c. raining, abate, clear up* vb -gasa i (HH); -kasa i (HH); *Stop doing!* (*Imperative*) vb Chimboregera!

ceiling *roof, sky* n denga 5, matenga 6 (HL)

celebrate a wedding vb -tamba muchato (HH HLL)

cell *jail-cell* n chitokisi 7 (LHLL) cf Eng.

cement *grey powder used in building which, after being wetted, becomes hard like stone* n semende 9 (LHL) cf Eng.

cemetery *graves* n makuva 6 (LHH)

cent *small copper coin* n sendi 5, masendi 6 (HL) cf Eng.

centipede *poisonous creature with numerous legs* n mhani 9 (LL); bonambo 5, mabonambo 6 M (HHL)

centre *heart, core* n mwoyo 3 (LL)

certain adj -mwe cf p. 186

certain *be confident, sure* vb -va nechokwadi i (HLLH); -ne chokwadi i (HLH)

certainly *truly* adv zvechokwadi (HLLH); zviro kwazvo (LL HL)

certificate of registration n chitupa 7 (LLL); *c. of juvenile registration n* chitikinyani 7 (LLHLL)

chafe *become sore by rubbing* vb -kwiza t (LL); -svuura t (LLL)

chafer beetle n ndere 5, mandere 6 (LL)

chain *number of rings or links going through one another to make a line* n ngetani 9 (HLL); cheni 9 (HL) cf Eng.

chair *movable seat with a back* n chigaro 7 (LLL) cf -gara (LL); cheya 9 (HL)

cf Eng. *chairman* n sachigaro 1a (HHHL); mubati wechigaro 1 (LHH LHLL)

chalk n choko 9 (HL) cf Eng.

chamber pot *night vessel* n chemba 9 (HL) cf Eng.

chameleon *sp of slow-moving, tree-climbing reptile* n rwavhi 11 (HL); rwaivhi 11 (LHL); ruwavhi 11 (LHL); mbavhi 10 plur (HL)

champion *one who has conquered rivals* n shasha 9 (LL); mbirimi 9 (HHL)

chance *opportunity* n chanzi 9 (HL) cf Eng.

change *take or put one thing in place of another* vb -pindura t (LLL); -sandura t (LLL); -chinja t (LL) cf Eng.; *c. money* vb -chinja mari (LL LH) cf Eng.

change *money given back after a purchase* n chinji 9 (HL) cf Eng.

channel *for irrigation* n mugero 3 (LHL); mukoronga 3 (LLHL)

chant *song, psalm* n rwiyo 11 (LH), nziyo 10 (LH)

chap *skin crack* n in'a 5 MZ (LL); n'a 5 K (L); man'a 6 (LL)

chapter *division of a book* n chikamu 7 (LHL); chitsauko 7 (LHHL)

character *good qualities of c.* n unhu 14 (LL) cf munhu (LL)

charcoal *wood c.* n tsito 5 & 9 (HH); simbe 5, masimbe 6 (LL)

charge a gun *load* vb -paka pfuti t (HH HL)

charitable *be kind* vb -va nomwoyochena i (LHLHL)

charity *(theological virtue) love* n rudo 11 (LH); chido 7 (LH) cf -da (H)

charm *please, make happy* vb -fadza t (HH) cf -fara (HH)

charm *worn round arm or neck* n zango 5, mazango 6 (LL); dumwa 5, matumwa 6 (HL); chitumwa 7 (LHL)

chase away *drive away, frighten off* vb -tanda t (HH); -dzinga t (HH); *c. after, chase with the intention to capture, run after* vb -tandanisa t (HHHL) cf -tanda (HH); -dzinganisa t (HHHL) cf -dzinga (HH)

chastise *punish* vb -ranga i & t (LL)

chastity *purity* n utsvene 14 (LLH)

chat *talk in friendly fashion* vb -kurukura i & t (HHHL); -tandara i (HHH)

chat *insect-eating bird, mocking c.* n nharire 9 (LLL)

chatter teeth *from cold* vb -gedegedesa mazino t (HHHLL LHH)

chatter-box *one who talks a lot* n muzavazi 1 (LLLL) cf -zawaza (LLL)

cheap *be inexpensive* vb -chipa i (LL) cf Eng.; -sadhura i (LHH) cf -dhura (HH); *cheapen, reduce the price* vb -chipisa t (LLL)

cheap *worthless, poor quality* adj Noun + PC + mutowenyemba: Gumbeze **romutowenyemba**. (*A cheap blanket.*)

cheat *deceive* vb -nyengedza i & t (HHH)

cheat *by copying* vb -kopa i & t (HH) cf Eng.

cheek *side of face* n dama 5, matama 6 (HH)

cheek-bone *(upper or lower)* n rushaya 11 (LLH)

cheeky person n Munhu ane waya. (slang) (*He is a cheeky person*)

cheer *applaud* vb -ombera i & t (LLL); -ridza manja t (LL LL)

cheerful *be happy* vb -faranuka i

(HHHL) (stative vb); Aka**faranuka** pameso. (*He has a cheerful face.*)

cheese *solid food made from milk curds* n chizi 9 (HL) cf Eng.

cheetah *spotted member of the cat family and fastest of our beasts of prey* n dindingwe 5, madindingwe 6 (LLL); dindiringwe 5 (LLLL)

chest *upper front part of human body* n dundundu 5, matundundu 6 (HHH); chipfuva 7 (LHH)

chew *work food about between the teeth in order to crush it* vb -tsenga i & t (HH); *chew the cud like cows, goats etc* vb -zeya i & t (LL)

chewing gum n chingamu 9 (HLL) cf Eng.

chick *young bird, nestling* n nyn'ana 5, manyn'ana 6 (LH)

chicken *young fowl* n hukwana 9 (HLH) huku (HH); *young of other ground-birds* n nhiyo 9 (HL)

chicken-pox contagious disease esp. of children n chibhokisi 7 (LHLL) Eng.

chief n mambo 1a (LL); ishe 1a (LH); she 1a K (H)

chiefly *especially* adv kunyanya (LLL); zvikuru (LHH); Motokari dzinosevenzesa peturu *kunyanya*. (*Motors cars chiefly use petrol.*)

chieftainship *kingdom* n umambo 14 (LLL) cf mambo (LL); ushe 14 (LH) cf ishe (LH)

child n mwana 1 (LH) *my child* n mwanangu (LHL); *c. of 1 — 3 years* n mucheche 1 (LLL); *c. of 4—12 years* n pwere 9 (HH); mupwere 1 (LHH); *first-born child* n dangwe 5, matangwe 6 (LH); *last-born child* n gotwe 5, magotwe 6 (LH); *childishness* n chana 7 (LH) cf mwana (LH); *childhood, time of being a child* n upwere 14 (LHH) cf pwere (HH)

childish *behave like a child* vb -ema i (LL)

chilli *red pepper* n mhiripiri 9 (LLLL); *c. plant* n mumhiripiri 3 (LLLLL) cf mhiripiri

chilly *be rather cold* vb; (Kunze) kuri ku**tonhora**. (*The weather is chilly.*) Ndiri kunzwa **chando.** (*I am feeling cold.*)

chimney *structure to lead away smoke* n chimini 9 (HLL) cf Eng.

chin *part of the face under the mouth* n chirebvu 7 (LLL)

Chinese lantern tree n mupangara 3 (LLLL) B.Bk. 1,17

chip *(with adze or axe)* vb -gagadza t (HHH)

chisel *tool with sharp edge for cutting wood* n nhemo 9 (HH); chizera 9 (HLL) cf Eng.

choir *group of persons who sing together esp. in church* n kwaya 9 (HL) cf Eng.

choke *stop somebody's breathing by pressing the windpipe from outside* vb -dzipa t (HH); *be choked by eating in a hurry* vb -dzipwa i (HH); -kachidzwa i (HHH)

choose *select, pick out* vb -sarudza t (LLL); -sarura t (LLL) — PT *chose;* PP *chosen*

chop *cut off, cut up with axe* vb -dimura t (HHH); -tema t (HH); *chopper, axe, tool for chopping wood* n demo 5, matemo 6 (HH) cf -tema (HH); dimuro 5, madimuro 6 (HHH) cf -dimura (HHH); *chop up finely* vb -cheka-cheka t (HHHL)

chose *chosen ct choose*

Christ *the Redeemer and Saviour of mankind* n Kristo 1a (HL); Kristu 1a (HL)

christen *baptize, ceremony of making into a Christian* vb -bhapatidza t cf Eng.; -ombeka t (LLL)

Christian *a believer in Christ* n muKristo 1 (LHL); muKristiyani 1 (LHLLL) cf Eng.; *C. conduct* n uKristo 14 (LHL); *Christianity, the religion of a Christian* n chiKristo 7 (LHL)

Christmas *yearly celebration of the birth of Christ (25th December)* n Krisimasi 9 (HLLL) cf Eng.

christmas beetle *cicada* n nyenze 9 (HH)

church *ecclesiastical body* n chechi 9 (HL) cf Eng.; kirike 5 & 9 (LHL) cf Afrik.; *c. building* n chechi 9 (HL) cf Eng.; *c. service* n svondo 5 & 9 (LL) cf Eng.

cicada *christmas beetle* n nyenze 9 (HH)

cigarette *shredded tobacco rolled in thin paper for smoking* n mudzanga wefodya 3 (LLL HLL); *c.-lighter* n gwenya 5, magwenya 6 (LH); *cigarette-end, butt* n chigusvani 7 (LLHH); chistompi 7 (LHL) cf Afrik.

cinder *piece of wood or coal partly burnt, not yet ash* n dzito 5, matsito 6 (HH)

cinema *bioscope, public building where films are shown* n bhaiskopu 5, mabhaiskopu 6 (HLLL) cf Eng.

circle *perfectly round outline* n denderedzwa 5, matenderedzwa 6 (HHLH) cf -tenderera (HHHL); *c. of people* n dariro 5, matariro 6, (HHL)

circumcise *perform a minor operation on males* vb -dzingisa t (HHH)

cisticola *warbler, very small insect-eating bird living mainly in grassland* n dhimba 9 (LH); timba 9 (LH)

city *large town* n guta 5, maguta 6 (LL)

civet cat n jachacha 5, majachacha 6, (LLL); *illustration p. 50*

clamour *make noise* vb -nyaudza i & t (HHH)

clan *large family group* n dzinza 5, madzinza 6 (HH); rudzi 11, marudzi 6 (LL)

clap hands *in greeting* vb -uchira i & t (HHH); -ombera i & t (LLL); *clap, hit* vb -rova i & t (HH)

clap *of the hands to one in authority with loud, hollow sound* n gusvi 5 (LH)

clap of thunder n bhanan'ana 5, mabhanan'ana 6 (LLLL)

clasp *hold tightly* vb -pfumbata t (HHH)

claw *pointed nail of animal or bird* n nzara 9 (LH) *same word for finger nail*

clay *soft, sticky earth* n rondo 5 (HH); dongo 5 (LH); ivhu 5, mavhu 6 (LH)

clean *be spotless* adj & vb -chena i (stative vb) (LL); Mumba umu maka**chena**. (*This room is clean.*); *tidy, be c.* adj & vb *-shambidzika i (stative vb); Mukomana uyu aka***shambidzika**. (*This boy is well turned out.*); *make white* vb -chenesa t (LLL) cf -chena (LL); *c. a wound* vb -kusha t (HH) *c. a yard, sweep* vb -kura t (LL)

cleanliness *habitual cleanness* n utsanana 14 (LLLL)

clear *site of a garden or field* vb -parura t (HHH)

clearly *plainly, openly, without concealment* adv pachena 16 (LLL)

clench the fist vb -pfumba chibhakera t (HH); -kunga chibhakera t (HH)

clergy *priests of the church* n vapristi 2 (LHL) cf Eng.

clerk *office worker* n mabharani 1a (LHLL)

clever *be bright* adj & vb -chenjera i

(HHH) (stative vb); Vane mwana aka**chenjera**. (*They have a bright child.*)

cleverness *mental ability* n njere 10 (HH); uchenjeri 14 (LHHL) cf -chenjera (HHH); ungwaru 14 (LLH) cf -ngwara (LL)

climb *ascend* vb -kwira i & t (HH)

cling *hold tight to* vb -namatira t (LLLL) — PT & PP *clung*

clinic *where medical treatment is given* n kiriniki 9 (LHLL) cf Eng.

clock *instrument for telling the time* n wachi 9 (HL) cf Eng.

clod *lump of earth* n vhinga 5, mavhinga 6 (LL)

close *nearly* adv pedyo/padyo 16 (LL)

close *be touching* vb & adj -batana i (HHHH) (stative vb); Mbeu dzaka**batana** hadzikuri zvakanaka. (*Crops which touch one another do not grow well.*)

close *a door, bar* vb -pfiga t (HH); -vhara t (LL); -zarira t (LLL); *close the eyes* vb -tsinzinya i (HHH); *c. the mouth* vb -pfumbira t (LLL); *closing barrier, bar* n zariro 5, mazariro 6 (LLL) cf -zarira (LLL)

cloth *piece of woven material* n jira 5, machira 6 (HH); mucheka 3 (LHL)

clothe oneself vb -pfeka i & t (LL); *c. another* vb -pfekedza t (LLL) cf -pfeka (LL) — PT & PP *clothed*

clothes *clothing* n mbatya 10 (LL); nguo 10 (LL); hanzu 10 (LH); hazu 10 K (LH)

cloud *visible vapour n gore 5, makore 6 (LH)*

cloudy *It is c./overcast.* vb (Kunze kwakatibikira; kuna makore.)

club *association* n nzanga 9 (LL); chita 7 (LH); kirabhu 9 (LHL) cf Eng.

clump of trees *growing close together* n chidzotsa 7 (LLL); chitondo 7 (LLL); rusango 11 (LHH); jokocho 5 (LHL)

clung *cf cling*

cluster *number of things close together e.g. grapes, bees* n bumha 5 Z (HL)

clutch *take tight hold of something usu in fear* vb -pfumbatira t (HHHL)

coal *black mineral found below earth's surface used for burning* n marasha 6 (LLL); masimbe 6 (LLL)

coarse meat *gristle* n runda 5, marunda 6 (LH)

coarse *rough, be physically r. (like a blanket)* vb -vava i (HH)

coat *jacket* n bhatye 5, mabhatye 6 (HL); bhachi 5, mabhachi 6 (HL) cf Afrik.; *overcoat, heavy c.* n jazi 5, majazi 6; jasi 5, majasi 6 (HL)

coax *encourage with patience and kindness* vb -nyengetedza t (HHHL)

cob *of corn, mealie-cob* n muguri 3 (LLL); *c. devoid of grain* n guri 5, maguri 6 (LL); muguri 3 MZ (LLL)

cobra *sp of poisonous, hooded snake which, when approached, raises its head and expands its hood in defensive attitude. Average length 5 ft. or 150 cm. Egyptian cobra, a common c. in Rhodesia, occurring in two distinct varieties:* 1) *banded c.* n nyamafingu 9 (LLHL); nyamafungu 9 (LLHL); 2) *a slate-grey, almost black variety* n mhungu 9 (HH); *Mocambique spitting cobra* n mhakure 9 (HLH)

cock *male fowl* n jongwe 5, machongwe 6 (LH); gukurume 5 (HHLL); *cock's comb, fleshy crest of cock* n muchochororo 3 (LLLLL); *cock's spur* n chimbi 7 (LH)

cockroach *insect which comes out at night where food is kept* n bete 5, mapete 6 (LH)

cocoa pan *trolley, small railcart* n ngorovhani 9 (LHLL)

coffee *popular hot drink* n kofi 9 (HL) cf Eng.
coffee bean tree *chocolate berry* n muhubva 3 (LHL); mutsubvu 3 (LHL)
coffin *a box to hold dead person* n bhokisi 5, mabhokisi (HLL) cf Eng.
coil *wind, twist* vb -mona i & t (HH); *coil round, twist round* vb -moneredza t (HHHL); -monerera i & t (HHHL)

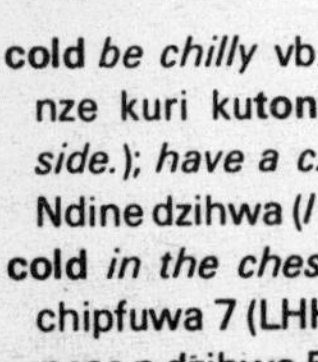

cold *be chilly* vb -tonhora i (HHL); Kunze kuri **kutonhora**. (*It is cold outside.*); *have a c.* vb -va nedzihwa KZ; Ndine dzihwa (*I have a cold*)
cold *in the chest* n chipfuva 7 (LHH); chipfuwa 7 (LHH); *common c., mild illness* n dzihwa 5 (LH)
cold weather *winter, c. season* n chando 7 (LL)
collapse *cave in* vb -ondomoka i (HHHL)
collar *part of garment that fits around the neck* n chipika 7 MZ (LLL)
collar bone n bendekete 5, mapendekete 6 (HHLH); ruchechete 11 (LLLL)
collect *gather together* vb -kokorodza t (HHHL); -unganidza t (HHHL)
collide *bump into another* vb -gumana i (LLL); *collide (motor vehicles)* vb -ita simashi i (LL LHL) cf Eng.
colour *e.g. green, red, etc.* n ruvara 11 (LHH)
Coloured *person of mixed race* n murume wechiKaradhi (*a Coloured man.*)
coly *mousebird, sp of gregarious fruit-eating bird with a long tail* n chiyovhovho 7 (LLLL); shirapopo 9 (LHHL)

comb *instrument for tidying the hair* n kamu 9 (HL) cf Eng.; pfeturo 9 (HHL)
comb *act of using a comb* vb -kama t (HH) cf Afrik.; -petura t (HHH)
combine *join together* vb -sangana i (LLL); *join* vb -sanganisa t (LLLL)
combretum *river c., small tree that favours river banks and water courses* n mutepe 3 (LHL); mupuma 3 (LHL); *mouse-eared c.* n murovamhuru 3 (LHHLH) *red c., burning bush, very ornamental when in flower* n mupfururа 3 (LLLL); *soft-leaved c.* n mugodo 3 (LLL); *large fruited c. tree* n muruka 3 (LLL)

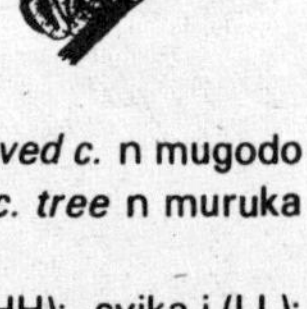

come *arrive* vb -uya i (HH); -svika i (LL); *c. back, return* vb -dzoka i (LL); *c. down, alight from* vb -dzika i (LL); -buruka i (LLL); -jikita i (LLL); *c. from, derive from, begin at, leave* vb -bva i (L);

c. in, enter vb -pinda i (LL); *c. out, emerge* vb -buda i (HH); *c. near, move close* vb -swebera i (LLL); -sebera i (LLL); *c. up, ascend* vb -kwira i (HH); *c. out, sprout* vb -tungira i (HHH); *c. to an end, finish, terminate* vb -pera i (HH); -guma i (HH); *c. together, meet* vb -sangana i (LLL); *c. to oneself, be conscious* vb -pepuka i (LLL); -dzidziuka i (LLLL); *c. undone (stitching)* vb -rudunuka i (LLLL); *c. undone (knot)* vb -sungunuka i (HHHL); -sununguka i (HHHL) cf -sunga (HH); *c. up, germinate* vb -mera i (LL) — PT *came;* PP *come*

comfort *console, soothe* vb -nyaradza i & t (HHH) cf -nyarara (HHL); *comfort (in sorrow or distress)* n runyaradzo 11 (LHHL) cf -nyaradza (HHH)

comical *be amusing* vb -setsa i & t (LL) cf -seka (LL)

command *instruct* vb -rayira t (LLL)

commandment *law* n mutemo 3 (LHH) cf -tema (HH)

commelina *blue, a flowering plant* n chidyahumba (LHLH) B.Bk. 1,48

commence *begin* vb -tanga i & t (HH); -vamba i & t (LL)

commit *a crime or sin* vb -para mhosva t (LL HL); *c. sin* vb -ita rutadzo i (LHH); *c. suicide, cause own death* vb -zvisunga Reflex (HLH)

committee *group of persons appointed to discuss or do a special work* n komiti 9 (HLL) cf Eng.

commotion *noise* n ruzha 11 (LH)

communion *sacrament of c.* n komuniyone 9 (LHLLL) cf Eng.

communism *belief of a Communist* n komonizimu 9 (HHHLL) cf Eng.

Communist *one who believes in communism* n mukoministi 1 (LHHHL) cf Eng.

companion *on a journey* n muperekedzi 1 (LHHHL) cf -perekedza (HHHL)

compare *judge how far things are similar* vb -enzanisa t (LLLL) cf -enzana (LLL)

compared with *more than (comparative form of adj or adv)* pana (LH); *Upenyu hukuru pana zvose. (Life is more important than all things.)*

compartment *room separated by partitions* n mupanda 3 (LLL)

compassion *pity* n tsitsi 10 (LH); ngoni 10 (LL); nyasha 10 (LL)

compel *force* vb -manikidza t (HHHL)

compensate for *make suitable payment* vb -ripa i & t (LL); *compensation, suitable payment* n muripo 3 (LLL) cf -ripa (LL)

compete *take part in a race* vb -ita mapitse (LL LLH)

competent person n mugoni 1 (LLL) cf -gona (LL)

competition *race, contest* n mapitse 6 (LLH); makwikwi 6 (LLH); makundano 6 (LHHL)

complain *grumble* vb -popota i (HHH); -nyunyuta i (HHH); *c. about the food* vb -popota pamusana pezvokudya

complain *formally, lodge a complaint* vb -mhan'ara i (LLL)

complaint *cause of dissatisfaction* n mhosva 9 (HL), mhaka 9 (LH)

complete *finish off, accomplish* vb -pedzisa t (HHH) cf -pedza (HH)

completely *entirely* adv chose (HH)

compost *manure made from decayed vegetable matter* n komposti 9 (HLL) cf Eng.

compound *living quarters, usu on private property* n komboni 9 (HLL) cf Eng.

compress *press out e.g. for juice* vb -svina t (LL)

compulsion *constraint* n chimanikidzo 7 (LHHHL) cf -manikidza (HHHL)

comrade *friend* n shamwari 9 (HLH)

concave *object* n fombwe 9 (LH)

conceal *hide* vb -viga t (HH); -vanza t (HH); -svisa t KoM (HH)

conceited *be self-opinionated* vb **-zvi**kudza i (HLH); **-zvi**da i (HL); **-zvi**tutumadza i (HLLLH); -vhaira i (LLL); -dada i (LL)

conceive *a plan* vb -funga zano t (LL LL); *c. physically, become pregnant* vb -va nenhumbu i (LHL); -bata pamuviri i (HH LLLL)

concentrate mentally vb -chama i (LL)

concern *care for* n hanya 9 (LL); hanyn'a 9 Z (LL)

concerned *be bothered about* vb -ne hanya/hanyn'a *usu in the neg.*

concerning *about* nezva-, zva-; Akataura **nezvo**mudzimai wake. (*He spoke about his wife.)*

conciliate *reconcile* vb -wadzanisa t (LLLL) cf -wadzana (LLL); -yananisa (LLLL)

conclude *finish* vb -pera i (HH); -pedza t (HH)

concurrently *meanwhile, simultaneously* -nguno-; -sano- *infix vbs*

condole *offer condolence (lit. shake hands)* vb -bata maoko i & t (HH LHH); -purura t (LLL)

conduct *behaviour, manner of behaving* n maitiro 6 (LLHH)

confetti tree n chizhozho 7 (LLL); chizhuzhu 7 (LLL)

confidence *trust* n chivimbo 7 (LLL) cf -vimba (LL)

confluence *meeting place of two rivers* n madiro 6 (LLL) cf -dira (LL)

confuse *muddle, puzzle, bewilder* vb -vhiringa i & t (HHH); -kangaidza i & t (HHHL)

congress *big meeting* n musangano 3 (LLLL); kongiresi 9 (HLLL) cf Eng.

conscience *inward knowledge to do right and avoid wrong* n hana 9 (HH)

conscious *be, come to oneself, wake up* vb -pepuka i (LLL)

consent *permission* n mvumo 9 (LL) cf -bvuma (LL)

consequence *advantage, importance* n maturo 6 (LHH) (usu in the neg: *Of no c*). Zvisina maturo.

consequently *therefore, in consequnce, as a result* conj naizvozvo (LHLH); kudaro (LHL); ndosaka (HLL); saka (LL)

consider *think about, deliberate* vb -funga i & t (LL)

console *comfort* vb -nyaradza 6 (HHH) cf -nyarara (HHL)

constitution *laws and principles according to which a state is governed* n chisungo 7 (LHH) cf -sunga

contest *race, competition* n mapitse 6 (LLH); mujahwo 3 (LLL)

continence *keeping the laws of chastity and purity* n utsvene 14 (LŁH)

continue *keep on* vb -ramba + partic Ramba uchinwa mapiritsi. (*Continue taking the pills.*)

conversation *talk, chat* n hurukuro 9 (HHHL) cf -kurukura (HHHL)

converse together vb -taurirana (LLLLL); *chat* vb -kurukurirana i (HHHLLL)

convert morally *adopt a new way of life* vb -pinduka i (LLL); *cause somebody to c.* vb -pindutsa t (LLL) cf -pinduka

convert physically *turn round* vb -tendeutsa t (HHHL) cf -tendeuka (HHHL)

convict *prison inmate* n bhanditi 5, mabhanditi 6 (LHH) cf Eng.

convince *satisfy* vb -gutsa t (HH) cf -guta (HH)

coo *of a dove* n kugururudza kwenjiva 15 Z

cook *one who cooks food* n mubiki 1

(LLL) cf -bika (LL); *prepare food (usu with heat)* vb -bika i & t (LL)

cooked *ripe, be ready to eat* vb -ibva i (HH)

cooking *household c. utensil* n mudziyo 3 (LHH)

cool *be lukewarm* vb -pora i (HH); Tii yapora. (*This tea is cold.*); *be c. (of the weather)* vb -tonhorera i (HLHL); Kuri kutonhorera. (*It is cool outside.*) *c. off (temperature or feelings)* vb -podza t (HH); *make cold* vb -tonhodza t (HHH) cf -tonhora (HHL); -tuvidza t (HHH)

cooperate *work with* vb -batsirana t (HHHL) cf -batsira (HHH)

coot *red-knobbed c.; a common black water-bird with white face, flesh-oender* n hukurwizi 9 (HHLH) (*general term: water-fowl*)

copper *a red metal* n kopa 9 (HL) cf Eng.

copulate *mate (animals)* vb -dzinga t (HH); -tanda t (*chase*) (HH); -kwira t (HH)

copy *cheat by copying* vb -kopa i & t (HH) cf Eng

cord *band* n musungo 3 (LHH) cf -sunga (HH); mukosi 3 (LHL) cf -kosa (HH)

core *centre, heart* n mwoyo 3 (LL)

cork *stopper* n chidzivo 7 (LLL) cf -dziva (LL); chivharo 7 (LLL) cf -vhara (HH)

cork *stop up* vb -dzivira t (LLL); -vhara i & t (LL)

corkwood tree or shrub n mubvuka 3 (LLL); muchabobo 3 (LLLL)

cormorant *diver, sp of bird* n shambira (LLH) 5 *general name*

corner n kona 5 & 9 (HL) cf Eng.

corpse *human c.* n chitunha 7 (LLH)

corpulent *be fat (humans)* vb -futa i (LL)

correct *put right* vb -ruramisa t (LLLL) cf -rurama (LLL)

correctly adv nomazvo (HLH)

corrugated iron n marata 6 (LH)

corrupt *diminish goodness* vb -ipisa t (HHH); *rot* vb -ora i (LL); *cause to r.* vb -odza t (LL) cf -ora i (LL)

cost *price* n mubhadharo 3 (LLLL); cf -bhadhara (LLL); mutengo 3 (LHH); cf -tenga (HH)

costly *be c.* vb -dhura i (HH)

cotton *unprocessed c.* n donje 5 (LL); *c. thread* n shinda 9 (LL)

coucal *black c., insect-eating bird* n murenda 3 Z (LLL)

couch grass a common weed n tsangadzi 9 (HHL) B.Bk. 1,103

cough vb -kosora i (HHH); *illness causing a person to c. much* n chikosoro 7 (LHHL) cf -kosora (HHH)

could *cf can*

council *group of people chosen to give advice* n kanzuru 9 (HLL) cf Eng.

counsel *advice* n zano 5, mazano 6 (LL)

counsellor *adviser* n gurukota 5, makurukota 6 (HHLH)

count *enumerate* vb -verenga t (LLL); -kaunda t (HHH) cf Eng.

counter *long table at which customers are served in a shop* n kaunda 9 (HLL) cf Eng.

couple *link together* vb -kochekedzanisa t (LLLLLL)

courage *bravery* n ushingi 14 (LHH) cf -shinga (HH)

courageous *be brave* vb -shinga i (HH)

course *series of instruction talks* n kosi 9 (HL) cf Eng.

court *make love, win favour* vb -nyenga i & t (HH) (*in M: have sexual relations*); -pfimba i & t MZ (HH); -gadza Ko (HH)

court *(tribal), meeting place* n dare 5, matare 6 (LL); *magistrate's c.* n koti 9 (HL) cf Eng.

courtyard *patio, yard* n chivanze 7 (LHL); ruvazhe 11 K (LHL)

cousin *relative of my generation related through my parents. cf page 212*

covenant *make a c., solemn agreement* vb -tenderana i (LLLL); -bvumirana i (LLLL); *covenant, solemn agreement* n chitenderano 7 (LLLLL); cf -tenderana (LLLL)

cover over *with a blanket or cloth* vb -fukidza t (HHH); *c.o. with earth* vb -fusira i & t (LLL); -fushira i & t (LLL)

cover *put lid on* vb -kwidibira t (HHHL); -pfidigira t Z (HHHL)

cover up *conceal the truth, be evasive (of personal fault)* vb -nzvengeredza i (HHHL); *cover up for another* vb -tsikatsika t (LL LL)

covet *desire eagerly to possess* vb -chiva t (HH)

covetousness *avarice* n ruchiva 11 (LHH) cf -chiva (HH)

cow *full grown f. of the ox family* n mhou 9 (HL); *barren c.* n mhanje 9 (HL); *milking c.* n mhou yomukaka 9 (HL LHLL); *c. dung* n ndove 9 (LL); *old c.* n dore 5, matore 6 (LL)

cow pea *which develops in the earth* n nyemba 9 (LL)

coward *one who runs away from danger* n mbwende 9 (HH); bere 5, mapere (LL); bete 5, mapete 6 (LH) *euphemisms*

cowardice *behaviour of a coward* n umbwende 14 (LHH) cf mbwende (HH) (HH)

crab *ten-legged shell-fish* n gakandye 5, makakandye 6 (LLL); ngoro 9 (LH)

crack *line of division where something is broken but not into separate parts* n mutswi 3 (LL); muswe 3 K (LH)

crack *receive or make a c.* vb -tsemuka i (LLL); *c. an egg* vb -putsa t (zai) (HH)

craftsman *blacksmith* n mhizha 1a (LH)

crake *black water-bird* n nhapata 9 (LLL); chinyamukukutu 7 (LLLHHH)

cramp *painful tightening of the muscles* n chinyamunhari 7 MZ (LLLLH)

crane *(general name), type of tall bird* n horiori 9 (LLHH); *crowned c.* n ewoni M 1a (LHH) R214

crave *desire strongly* vb -panga t (LL); *c. for meat* vb -va nenhomba i (LHL)

craving *strong desire for something, longing for* n havi 9 (LH)

crawl *on all fours like a baby* vb -kambaira i (HHHL); -gwambaira i (HHHL)

crazy *be mad* vb -penga i (HH)

cream *fatty part of milk* n ruomba 11 (LLL); kirimu 9 (LHL) cf Eng.

cream of Tartar tree *baobab t.* n muuyu 3 (LLH)

crease *line made in cloth* n mupono 3 (LLL); mutanda 3 (LHH)

creased *be crumpled* vb -unyana i (LLL)

create *make something exist out of nothing* vb -sika t (LL); *Creator, one who creates* n Musiki 1 (LLL); *creature, something created* n chisikwa 7 (LLH) cf -sika (LL)

credit *money on loan* n chikwereti (LHLL) cf -kwereta (HHH)

creed *religious belief* n chitendero 7 (LLLL) cf -tendera (LLL)

creep *crawl, move with the body close to the ground* vb -nanaira i (HHHL) — PT & PP *crept*

creep up unobserved *stalk* vb -nyangira t (HHH)

crew *cf crow*

cricket *sp of insect which makes a shrill noise* n wishuwishu 9 (HLHL); *mole cricket* n jenya 5, majenya 6 (LH); *black c.* n chikokororo 7 (LLLLL); gurwe 5, makurwe 6 (HL)

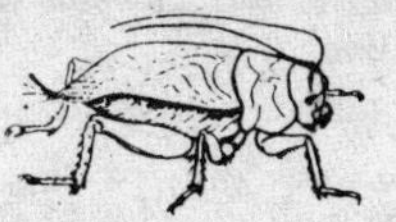

cried *cf cry*

crime *offence* n mhosva 9 (HL), mhaka 9 (LH); *commit c.* vb -para mhosva t (LL HL)

cripple *deformed or lame person* n chirema 7 (LHH); chidai 7 (LLH); *someone with involuntarily folded limbs* n mhetamakumbo 9 Z (LLLLL)

crippled *be lame* vb -remara i (HHH) (stative vb); harahwa yaka**remara** *(a crippled old man)*

criticise *unfavourably, find fault* vb -shoropodza t (HHHL); -tsoropodza t (HHHL)

croak *of a frog* vb -kororodza i (HHHL)

crochet *knit with one hooked needle* vb -kirosha (LLL) cf Eng.

crocodile *large man-eating reptile* n garwe 5, makarwe 6 (HL); goko 5 M (HH); ngwena 9 KKoM (LL)

crocodile bark tree n mutakuranhere 3 (LLLLHH)

crooked *be bent* adj & vb -tsveyama i (HHH); -dzvongama i (HHH)

crop *yearly or season's produce* n mbesanwa 10 (HLH)

cross *crucifix, two beams fastened, usu at right angles* n chipiyaniso 7 (LHHHL); muchinjiko 3 (LHHL)

cross *go across* vb -dimura i & t (HHH); *c. a road* vb -dimura mugwagwa t (HHH LLH); vb -bira (HH); *c. a river or a ford* vb -yambuka i & t (LLL); *c. the arms* vb -gumbata maoko (HHH LHH)

cross *be angry* vb -shatirwa i (HHH); *make c., make angry* vb -shatirisa t (HHHL)

crossing *river c., ford* n zambuko 5, mazambuko 6 (LLL)

cross-member *of a roof* n mbariro 9 (LLL)

cross-roads *road intersection* n mhararano 9 (LLLL) cf -parara (LLL)

crouch *on haunches, sit on one's heels (usu done by men)* vb -chochomara i (HHHL)

crow *of a cock* vb -kukuridza i (HHHL); — PT & PP *crowed*

crow *black c., sp of carrion-eating bird* n chikunguobaya 7 (LHHLLH) R523;

pied c. n gunguo 5, makunguo 6 (HHL); savara 5 M, masavara 6 (HHL) R522

crowd *of people* n mhomho 9 (HH); dumbu 5, matumbu 6 (HH) *to be distinguished from* dumbu 5 (LL): *stomach*

crowed *cf crow*

crown *head-dress of gold, jewels etc. usu worn by a king* n ndaza 9 (LH)

crucify *fasten on a cross* vb -roverera pachipiyaniso t K (HHHL LLHHHL); -rovera pamuchinjiko (HHH LLHHL)

cruel *be hard-hearted* vb -va noutsinye i (LHLL)

cruelty *quality that inflicts pain or shows no pity* n utsinye 14 (LLL); tsinye 9 (LL); *cruel* adj munhu ano utsinye (*a cruel person*)

crumb *tiny, broken-off piece usu of bread* n fufu 5, mafufu 6 (HL)

crumble *break into pieces* vb -pfupfunyuka i (HHHL); -mepfura t (HHH); -pfupfunyura t (HHHL)

crumpled *be creased* vb -unyana i (LLL); -funyana i (LLL) (stative vbs) bhatye rakaunyana (*a crumpled jacket)*

crunch *with the teeth of the mouth* vb -bubuna t (HHH)

crush *press to destruction* vb -tswanya t (LL); -dzwanya t (LL); *c. corn in a mortar* vb -tswa i & t (H); -dzvura i & t (HH)

crust *pot scrapings* n goko 5, makoko 6 (HH)

cry *mourn* vb -chema i & t (HH)

cuckoo *sp of bird whose chief characteristic is to lay eggs in the nests of other birds and to have its young brought up by them* n haya 9 (LH); hwaya 9 K (LH); hwishori 9 (HLH); *red-chested c., pietmyvrou, is the commonest*

cucumber *wild c.* n gaka 5, magaka 6 (HL)

cucumber tree *sausage t.* n mumve 3 (LH); mubvee 3 (LHL)

culpable *be guilty* vb -va nemhosva i (HLL)

cultivate *plough, till* vb -rima i & t (LL)

cultivator *instrument for breaking up ground* n karuvheti 9 (HLLL) cf Eng.; chikoforo 7 (LHLL)

cunning n njere 9 (HH); *cleverness at deceiving, guile* n muzvambarara 3 (LLLLL)

cup *drinking vessel* n gaba 5, magaba 6 (LH); komichi 9 (HLL); kapu 9 (HL) cf Eng.

cupboard *furniture for storing things* n kabati 9 (HLL) cf Eng.

curdled milk n mukaka wakakora 3 (LLL LHHL)

cure *bring back to health* vb -rapa i & t (LL)

curl up (*like a millipede: zongororo*) vb -gonyana i (HHH); *cause to c. up* vb -gonyanisa t (HHHL)

curtain *piece of cloth hung up in front of a window* n keteni 5, maketeni 6 (HLL) cf Eng.

curved *follow part of outline of a circle, be bent* adj & vb -kombama i (HHH); Shiri ine muromo **wakakombama**. (*This bird has a curved beak.*)

cushion *small bag filled with soft padding* n kusheni 5 & 9 (HLL) cf Eng.

custom *general behaviour* n tsika 9 (LL)

cut *with knife* vb -cheka i & t (HH); *c. with axe, c. down* vb -tema i & t (HH); *c. off, amputate vb -dimura t (HHH); c. cards* vb -gwanda i (LL); *c. grass* vb -mweta uswa t (LL LH); *c. hair* vb -gera i & t (LL); *c. meat from carcass* vb -svaura t (LLL); *c. meat into strips* vb -vedzenga t (LLL); *c. teeth, teethe* vb -buda mazino i (HH LHH) — PT & PP *cut*

cycle *travel on a bicycle* vb -famba nebhasikoro i (HH HLLL); *pedal* vb -chovha t (LL) *lit push*

cynical *person, one who sees no good in anything and has no belief in human goodness* n tsoropodzi 9 (HHHL); *cynicism, inability to see right intentions in actions or persons* n utsoropodzi (LHHHL) 14 cf tsoropodzi 9 (HHHL)

D

dog imbwa

daft *be crazy, silly, mad, insane* vb -penga i (HH)

dagga *wild hemp, marijuana* n mbanje 9 (LH)

dagger *knife* n banga 5, mapanga 6 (HH) cf Hindustani

daily *everyday* adv mazuva ose 6 (LHH HH)

dairy *shop or firm selling milk products* n dheri 5 (HL) cf Eng.

daisy *aspilia, yellow veld d.* n mukushamvura 3 (LHLHH); *sun d.* n nyakashinda 9 (LLLL)

dally *delay, be late* vb -nonoka i (LLL)

dam *man-made reservoir of water* n dhamu 5, madhamu 6 (HL) cf Eng.

damage *(animate or inanimate things) bruise, hurt, cause d.* vb -kuvadza i & t (HHH); *damaged, be hurt, injured* vb -kuvara i (HHH)

damage *fine paid to the father of a girl to compensate for the unlawful pregnancy in his daughter* n dhemeji 5 (HLL) cf Eng.

damp *be wet, moist* vb -nyorova i (HHH) (stative vb); Pasi pakanyorova. (*The ground is damp.*) *dampen, mosten* vb -nyatisa t (LLL) cf -nyata (LL)

dampness *softness* n unyoro 14 (LHH); mwando 3 (LL)

dance *celebrate* vb -tamba i (HH)

dance *rhythmic movement of the feet* n dhanzi 5 (HL) cf Eng.

dandruff *flaky skin on the head* n makwene 6 (LHH)

danger *misfortune, harmful accident* n ngozi 9 (LL); njodzi 9 (LL)

dangle from *hang down, overhang* vb -rembera i (LLL)

dark *be black* adj & vb -svipa i (stative vb) (LL); Kunze kwakasvipa. (*It is dark outside.*)

darkness *lacking light* n rima 5 (HL)

darn *mend, esp a hole in something knitted (socks, jerseys, etc.)* vb -runda t (LL)

darter *snake bird; sp of water-bird with long, slender neck, cormorant* n shambira 5, mashambira 6 (LLL); sambira 5, masambira 6 (LLL); chigwikwi 7 (LLL) R52 *cf illustration p. 146*

dassie *rock-rabbit, hyrax* n mbira 9 (HL) (*must be distinguished from: mbira 10 (LL): African piano) cf illustration under rodent.*

date *the day of a happening or event* n dheti 5 (HL) cf Eng.

date *palm, false d.p., palm with a few tufted stems* n muchindwi 3 (LHH)

daughter *female child* n mwanasikana 1 (LHLLL); *d. of sister of girl's mother i.e. daughter of her maternal aunt* n mukoma 1 (LHL); munun'una 1 (LHHL); *d. of brother of girl's mother i.e. daughter of her maternal uncle* n mainini 1a (HLHL); amainini 1a (LHLHL); *d. of sister of boy's mother i.e. daughter of his maternal aunt* n hanzvadzi 9 (HHL); *d. of brother of boy's mother i.e. daughter of his maternal uncle* n mainini 1a (HLHL); amainini 1a (LHLHL); *d. of brother of girl's father i.e. daughter of her paternal uncle* n mukoma 1 (LHL); munun'una 1 (LHHL); *d. (or son) of sister of girl's father i.e. daughter of her paternal aunt (tete)* n mwana 1 (LH); *d. of brother of boy's father i.e. daughter of his paternal uncle* n hanzvadzi 9 (HHL); *d. of sister of boy's father i.e. daughter of his paternal aunt (tete)* n **muzukuru 1 (LHH)**

daughter-in-law *young woman related by marriage* n muroora 1 (LHHL)

dawdle *be late* vb -nonoka i (LLL)

dawn *be daylight* vb -edza i (HH)

dawn *at d., very early* adv -fumo- (HH) infix vb; *at d.,* adv mavambakuedza 6 (LLLLHH); mambakwedza 6 (LLLL)

day *period of light from sunrise to sunset* n zuva 5, mazuva 6 (HH); musi 3 (LH); *bright, clear d.* n mhare 9 M (LL)

day after tomorrow adv kusweramangwana (LLLLHH); hwedza M (HL)

day before yesterday adv marimwezuro 6 Z (LLLLL); *day by day, day after day* adv zuva nezuva (HH HLL); *by d., usu mid-day* adv masikati 6 (LHHL); *day and night,* adv siku nesikati (HH HLLL)

daylight *be d., dawn* vb -edza i (HH)

dazzle *shine, be brilliant* vb -penya i (LL)

deaf person *one who cannot hear* n matsi 1a (LH)

deal out *distribute, share out* vb -govera t (LLL) — PT & PP *dealt*

dear *be wanted, necessary* vb -diwa i (HH); -dikana i (HHH) cf -da (H)

dear *be costly, expensive* vb -dhura i (HH)

death *funeral* n rufu 11 (LH) cf -fa (H)

debark *strip bark from a tree* vb -svuura t (LLL)

debt *payment which must be made* n chikwereti 7 (LHLL) cf -kwereta (HHH)

decay *be rotten, go bad* adj & vb -ora i (stative vb) (LL); Mazino ake aka**ora**. (*His teeth are rotten.*)

deceased person *one who has died* n mushakabvu 1 (LLHH); *body of d.p., corpse* n chitunha 7 (LLH)

deceive *deliberately mislead, beguile* vb -nyengedza t (HHH); *deception, act of deceiving* n unyengedzi 14 (LHHL) cf -nyengedza (HHH)

decide *make a decision* vb -funga i (LL) *decide a case, judge* vb -tonga mhosva (HL HL); *decision* n sarudzo 9

declare *speak openly* vb -taura pachena i (LLL LLL)

decline *refuse* vb -ramba i & t (LL); Aka**ramba** kuenda. (*He refused to go.*)

declivity *downward slope* n materu 6 (LHL)

decompose *rot, go bad* vb -ora i (LL)

decorate *adorn* vb -shongedza t (LLL) cf -shonga (LL)

decrease *be scarce, few, inadequate, get less* vb -shomeka i (LLL)

deep *be profound* adj & vb -dzama i (LL); -dzika i (LL) (stative vbs); Gomba iri raka**dzika**. (*This ditch is deep.*)

defecate *go to the lavatory for a bowel motion* vb -enda kunze i (LL LH); -ita tsvina (LL LL)

defeat *overcome* vb -kurira i & t (HHH); -kunda i & t (HH)

defect *fault, moral imperfection* n chinana 7 MZ (LHH); chinongo 7 K (LLH)

defend *protect* vb -dzivirira t (LLLL)

deficient *be wanting, lacking* vb -shaya t (LL)

defile *spoil, make dirty* vb -svipisa t (LLL)

deformed *be lame* vb -remara i (HHH)

deformed person *p. badly shaped* n chirema 7 (LHH) cf -remara (HHH)

defraud *deceive* vb -nyengedza t (HHH)

defrost *raise above freezing point* vb -bvisa chando (LL LL)

dejected *be downcast* adj & vb -tsamwa i (stative vb) (LL); Iye zvino baba vangu vaka**tsamwa**. (*Right now my father is dejected.*)

delay *be late* vb -nonoka i (LLL); *make someone late* vb -nonotsa t (LLL)

deliberate *consider, think over* vb -funga i (LL)

deliberately *with intent, knowingly* adv (*usu partic of the verb*) -ziva i (HH)

Akaita izvi **achiziva**. (*He did it deliberately.*)

delighted with *be happy with* vb -fadzwa i (HH); -farira t (HHH) cf -fara (HH)

deliver *release, save* vb -nunura t (LLL); -sunungura t (HHHL) -ponesa t (HHH)

deliverer *saviour* n mununuri 1 (LLLL); -nunura (LLL); muponesi 1 (LHHL) cf -ponesa (HHH)

demolish *pull down, destroy* vb -paza t (LL)

demon *devil, evil spirit* n mweya wakaipa 3 (LH LHLL); dhimoni 5 (LHL); dhiyabhori 1a (HLLL)

demonstrate *take part in a demonstration* vb -ratidzira i (LLLL)

dent *make a hollow in a hard surface* vb -fondora t (LLL)

deny *say that something is not true* vb -ramba t (LL); *deny oneself, fast* Reflex vb -**zvi**nyima i (HLH); -**zvi**rambidza i MZ (HLLH)

depart *go away, go* vb -enda i (LL); *leave, go from* vb -bva i & t (L)

depend on *rely on* vb -vimba (LL) na-i; -nyinda i M (LL)

deportment *behaviour* n chimiro 7 (LHH)

depressed *be downcast* vb - suruvara i (HHHL); - tsamwa i (LL)

deprive *take away from* vb -torera t (HHH) cf -tora (HH); -shayisa (LLL) cf-shaya

depth *measure from top to bottom* n udzami 14 (LLL); udzamo 14 (LLL); kudzama 15 (LLL)

descend *come down from, alight from, go down* vb -dzika i (LL); -buruka i (LLL)

describe *explain* vb -tsanangura i & t (LLLL); *d. fully, detail* vb -donongora t (HHHL)

desert *barren country; desolate, treeless country* n gwenga 5, magwenga 6 MZ (HL); renje 5, marenje 6 (HH)

desert *run away, flee* vb -tiza i & t (HH)

deserted *kraal or village* n dongo 5, matongo 6 (LL); *d. field* n gura 5, makura 6 (LL)

deserve *be worthy of* adj & vb -kodzera (stative vb) i (LLL); **Akakodzera** kupiwa mubayiro. (*He is worthy of a prize.*)

desire *wish for, want* vb -da i & t (H) *long for* vb -panga t (LL); -suwira t (HHH)

desire *wish, purpose* n chido 7 (LH) cf -da (H)

desist *stop doing, cease from doing* vb -regera + Infinitive (LLL)

desolate *be d., feel lonely, be sad* vb -suruvara i (HHHL)

despair *lose heart* vb -rasa mwoyo i (HH HL)

despatch *kill, finish off* vb -kohovedza t (LLLL)

despatch *send off* vb -tuma t (HH)

despise *feel contempt for* vb -shora t (LL); -zvidza t (LL)

despite *cf although*

destroy *kill* vb -uraya i & t (HHH); *destroy (wantonly), devastate* vb -paradza t (LLL); *demolish, pull down* vb -paza t (LL)

detach *untie, unfasten* vb -sunungura t (HHHL); *unstick* vb -kwatura t (LLL)

detail *give details, describe fully* vb -donongora t (HHHL)

detective *person whose business is to detect criminals* n mutikitivha 1, matikitivha 6 (LLHLL); mufeyi 1 (LHH) cf -feya (HH)

deteriorate *decline in quality, go down* vb -dzikira i (LLL); -derera i (LLL)

determined *be resolute* vb -tsunga i (HH); *be persevering* vb -shinga i (HH) + Infinitive, -shingirira (HHHL) + Infinitive

detest *hate* vb -sema i & t (HH)

detestable *be revolting, hateful, repulsive* vb -semesa i & t (HHH); Mazai akaora anosemesa. (*Rotten eggs are detestable.*)
detour *make a d.* vb -nyenyeredza t (HHHL)
devastate *destroy* vb -paradza t (LLL)
deviate *diverge, branch off* vb -tsauka i (HHH)
devil *evil spirit* n dhiyabhori 1a (HLLL) cf Eng.
devil's thorn n feso 5, mafeso 6 (LL); *devil's thorn creeper* n mufeso 3 (LLL) cf feso (LL)
dew *deposit of moisture on the ground usu in the morning* n dova 5 (LH)
dewlap *loose skin below the throat of cattle* n rembe 5, marembe 6 (HH)
dialect *language* n mutauro 3 (LLLL) cf -taura (LLL); rurimi 11 (LHH)
diaper *nappy* n mutambo 3 (LLL) *cf illustration p. 11*
diarrhoea *tummy upset causing dysentery and stomach ache* n manyoka 6 (LHH); *severe dysentery stool* n rupanzo 11 (LHH) cf -panza (HH)
die *come to the end of life* vb -fa i (H); -shaya i (LL); -tandadza (LLL)
diesel oil *fuel of diesel engines* n dhiziri 5 (HLL) cf Eng.
did *cf do*
dictionary *word book* n duramazwi 5 (LLLH); dhikishinari 5 (LLHLL) cf Eng.
differ *vary from, be different* vb -siyana i (HHH); -tsaukana i (HHHL)
difference *variation* n siyano 9 (HHL) mutsauko 3 (LHHL)
different *be unlike* adj & vb -siyana i (HHH) (stative vb); Tine motokari dzakasiyana. (*We have different kinds of motor cars.*)
difficult *be hard* adj & vb -rema i (LL); -oma i (HH); Basa iri rakaoma. (*This is difficult work.*) *more difficult;* Basa rangu rakaoma kupinda rako. (*My work is more difficult than yours.*) *most d.;* Basa iri rakaoma kupinda ose. (*This work is the most difficult.*)
difficulty *adversity* n dambudziko 5, matambudziko 6 (LLLL) cf -tambudzika (LLLL)
dig *remove soil* vb -chera i & t (LL); *d. deep to loosen the soil* vb -timba t (HH); *d. out* vb -fukunura t (LLLL) — PT & PP *dug*
digging blade *instrument* n nzope 9 (HH)
dignified behaviour *good disposition, good quality of human behaviour* n unhu 14 (LL) cf munhu (LL)
dignity *true worth* n chiremera 7 (LLLL)
diligence *hard work* n ushingi 14 Z (LHH)
diligent *be hard working* vb -shinga i (HH)
dilute *strength of a liquid, water down* vb -tuvidza t (HHH); -isa mvura t (LHHH)
diminutive *tiny* adj 1) usu Classes 12/13:2) kadiki or kadikidiki (LHLHL)
din *long, confused noise* n ruzha 11 (LH); bongozozo 5 (LLLL); *make noise or d.* vb -nyaudza t (HHH); -ita ruzha i (LL LH)
dining room n imba yokudyira 9 (LH HLHH); dhanduru 5 (HLL) cf Eng.
dinner *evening meal* n chirariro 7 (LHHL) cf -rarira (HHH)
dip *submerge in liquid* vb -nyika t (HH); *dip cattle* vb -tivisa t (LLL); -dhibhisa t (HHH) cf Eng.; *dip sadza (into flavouring dish)* vb -seva t (LL); -tonha t MZ (LL)
dip attendant n mudhibhisi 1 (LHHL)
dip fluid *or d. tank* n dhibhi (HL) cf Eng.
direction *often expressed with the help of class 17 concords* Enda nokukuku! (*Go in this direction!*)
directive *instruction* n murayiro 3 (LLLL); cf -rayira (LLL)
dirt *filth, rubbish* n tsvina 9 (LL); mara-

ra 6 (LLL); svina 9 K (LL); *dirty* adj hembe ine tsvina (*a dirty shirt*); maoko akasvipa (*dirty hands*); *dirtiness, uncleanliness* n uyanga 14 MZ (LHH)

dirty *make d., soil* vb -svibisa t (LLL)

disappoint *cause displeasure, offend* vb -tsamwisa i & t (LLL); *disappointed, be depressed, down-cast* adj & vb -tsamwa i (LL) (stative vb); Nhasi John akatsamwa. (*Today John is downcast.*)

disarrangement *disorderliness* n uyanga 14 (LHH)

disaster *calamity* n dambudziko 5, matambudziko 6 (LLLL); nhamo 9 (HH); rushambwa 11 (LLH)

discard *throw away* vb -rasa t (HH)

discharge *from imprisonment* vb -buritsa mujeri t (HHH LHL); *discharge from work* vb -buritsa basa t MZ (HHH HL)

discoloured *be muddy* vb -bvunduka i (LLL)

discover *see* vb -ona t (HH); -wana t (LL)

discrimination *favouritism* n rusaruro 11 (LLLL) cf -sarura (LLL); *racial d.* n rusaruraganda 11 (LLLLHH)

discuss *chat* vb -taurirana i (LLLLL); -kurukurirana i (HHHLLL)

discussion *chat, friendly dialogue* n hurukuro 9 (HHHL) cf -kurukura (HHHL)

disease *illness* n chirwere 7 (LHH) cf -rwara (HH)

disembark *get out, get off a vehicle* vb -buruka i (LLL)

disembowel *remove intestines* vb -tumbura i & t (LLL)

disentangle *unravel, unwind* vb -mononora t (HHHL) cf -mona (HH)

disgrace *put to shame* vb -nyadzisa i & t (HHH) cf -nyara (HH)

disgust *cause strong displeasure vb* -sembura i & t (HHH);-semesa i & t (HHH); -nyanyasa M i & t (HHH); *disgusting, be revolting* vb -misa mwoyo i (HH HL)

dish *wash-basin* n dhishi 5, madhishi 6 (HL) cf Eng.

dish out *serve food* vb -pakura i & t (HHH)

dishonest *be d., cheat* vb -nyengedza t (HHH); -chengedza t (HHH)

dislocate *put out of joint* vb -svodogora t (HHHL); -minyura t (LLL); *be dislocated, be out of joint* vb -minyuka i (LLL); -svodogoka i (HHHL)

dismantle *take to pieces* vb -gurunura t (HHHL)

dismiss *drive away* vb -tanda t (HH); -dzinga t (HH)

dismount *alight from* vb -buruka i (LLL)

disobedience *habit of* n musikanzwa 3 (LHLH); *disobedient* adj mwana anomusikanzwa (*a disobedient child*)

disorder *put in d.* vb -bvonganyisa t (HHHL); *be scattered and disorderly* vb bvururu (ideo) (LLL); Akasiya zvinhu zvakati bvururu mumba. (*He left the room in disarray.*)

disperse *scatter* vb -parara i (LLL)

displeased *be downcast, be sad* vb -tsamwa i (stative vb) (LL); Anenge akatsamwa. (*He seems to be displeased.*)

disposition *good d.* n unhu 14 (LL); *benevolent d.* n mwoyochena 3 (LLHL); *bad d.* n tsika dzakaipa 10 (LL LHLL)

dispute *argue* vb -itirana nharo i (LLLL LL)

disregard *despise* vb -zvidza t (LL)

dissolve *the action of a solid becoming part of a liquid surrounding it* vb -nyangadika i (LLLL); -nyongodeka i (LLLL); *make a liquid absorb a solid* vb -nyangadisa t (LLLL)

distance *measure of space between two points* n chinhambwe 7 Z (LLL); chinhambo 7 KM (LLL)

distort the truth *exaggerate, add on* vb -pamhidzirai (LLLL); -nyonganisa (HHH)

distress *worry* vb -baya mwoyo i & t (LL LL); *cause alarm and tears* vb -chemedza i & t (HHH); *be dejected, sad* adj & vb -tsamwa i (LL); Nhasi mwana wake aka**tsamwa**. (*Today her child is dejected.*)

distribute *divide, allot* vb -gova t (LL)

district *region* n ruwa 5 & 11 (LL); dunhu 5, matunhu 6 (HH); dhistrikiti 5 (HLLL) cf Eng.; *d. commissioner* n mudzviti 1 (LHH)

disturbed *be alarmed* vb -vhunduka i (LLL); -netsiwa (LLL)

ditch *narrow channel dug to carry away water* n goronga 5, makoronga 6 (LHL)

dive *go head-first into water* vb -dhaivha i (HHH) cf Eng.

divide *break up into parts* vb -kamura t (HHH)

divine *cause of misfortune (as witch-doctors do)* vb -shopera i & t (LLL)

diviner *witch-doctor, medicine man* n n'anga 9 (LL); *diviner's "bones"* n hakata 10 (HHL)

divorce *leave one another* vb -siyana i (HHH); -rambana i (LLL)

dizziness *giddiness* n dzungu 5 (HL) (*sing only*)

dizzy *be giddy* vb -va nedzungu i (HLL); -batwa nedzungu (HH HLL)

do *make, behave* vb -ita i & t — PT *did;* PP *done*

do in this way *do like this* vb -dai i & t (HL); *do in that way, do like that, do so, say so* vb -daro i & t (HL)

doctor *one who heals* n chiremba 1a (LLH); murapi 1 (LLL) cf -rapa (LL); dhokotera 1a (LLLL) cf Eng.; *diviner* n n'anga 9 (LL); *female diviner* n nyahana 1a (LHH)

dodge *side-step, evade, elude* vb -nzvenga i & t (HH)

doek *headkerchief* n dhuku 5, madhuku 6 (HL) cf Afrik.

dog n imbwa 9 MZ (LH); mbwa 9 K (H); ingwa 9 Ko (LH); *wild d., w. hunting d.* n bumhi 5 (LH); mhumhi 9 (LH)

doll *model of a baby or a child* n mudhori 3 (LLH)

dollar *unit of money* n dhora 5, madhora 6 (HL) cf Eng.

domestic *animal (herbivorous)* n chipfuyo 7 MZ (LHH); chipfuwo 7 (LHH) *cf illustration p. 45*

domesticate *keep d. animals* vb -pfuya t MZ (HH); -pfuwa t (HH)

donate *contribute* vb -pa i & t (H)

donation *gift* n chipo 7 (LH) cf -pa (H)

done *cf do*

donga *erosion gully* n goronga 5, makoronga 6 (LHL)

donkey *ass* n dhongi 5, madhongi 6 (LH); mbongoro 9 (LLL)

donkey berry shrub *bears yellow flowers and edible fruit* n mubura 3 (LLL); munjiri 3 (LHL) B.Bk. 1,32; mutongoro 3 (LHHL)

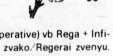

don't . . . (Imperative) vb Rega + Infinitive Regera zvako/Regerai zvenyu. (*Don't bother, don't do it.*)

door *hinged exit opening* n gonhi 5, makonhi 6 (HL); musuo 3 (LHL); musio 3 (LHL); dhoo 5, madhoo 6 (HL) cf Eng.; *doorway* n musuo 3 (LHL); musio 3 (LHL)

dormouse *sp of small mouse with bushy tail* n chisindireva 7 (LHHLL); chisindimbeva 7 (LHHLL)

dose *of medicine* n mushonga 3 (LLH); muti 3 (LH)

double over *fold o.* vb -peta t (LL)

doubt *be in d.* vb -konona i (HHH)

dove *general term* n njiva 9 (LH); *Cape turtle d.* n gukutiwa 5, magukutiwa 6 (HHLH); *small, long-tailed Namaqua d.* n nzembe 9 (LL); nhondoro 9 (LLL); dzembe 9 (LL) R318; *laughing d.* n tagurukutana 9 (LHLLLL); mhetura 9 (HHL); kanjivamutondo 12 (LLHHLL) R317

down *on the ground* adv pasi 16 (LH)

downward direction n nyasi 17 (LH); dzasi 17 (LH); zasi 17 (LH)

doze *nap, fall asleep* vb -dzimwaira i (HHHL); -tsimwaira i (HHHL)

drag *pull along* vb -zvuva t MZ (LL); -kweva t (LL)

dragon fly n mukonikoni 3 MZ (LLLLL); mukonekone 3 (LLLLL)

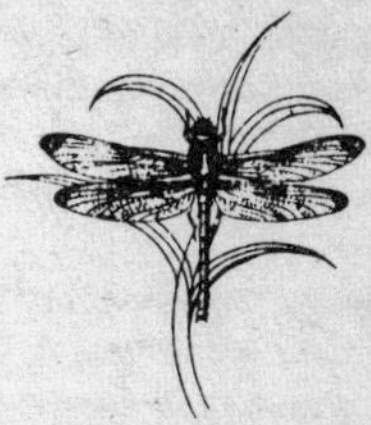

drain *water channel for drainage* n mugero 3 (LHL)

drank *cf drink*

draw *a line* vb -tara mutsetse i (HH LHL); *d. a picture* vb -ita/-nyora mufa-

domestic animals

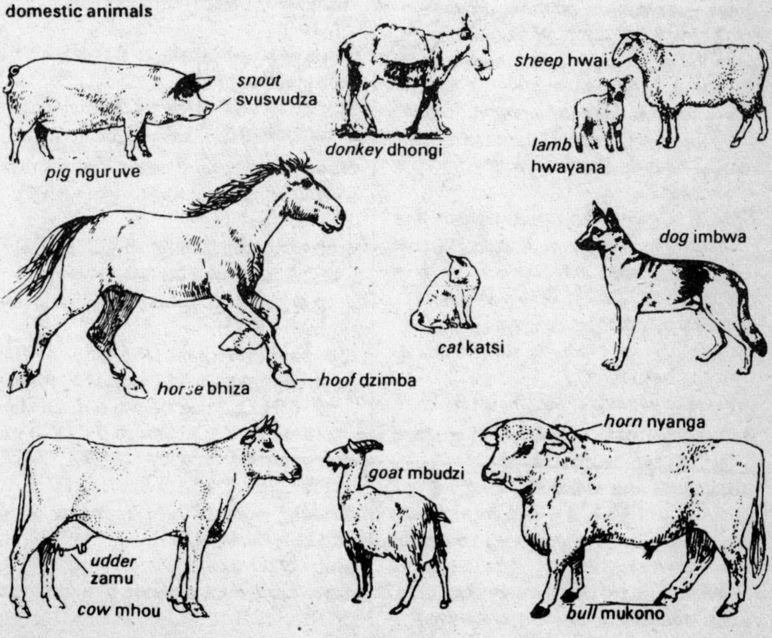

nanidzo i (LL/HH LHHHL) — PT *drew;* PP *drawn*

draw away from *withdraw from* vb -suduruka i (LLLL)

draw water vb -chera mvura (HL HH); -teka (HH)

drawer *moving receptable in furniture* n dhiroo 5, madhiroo 6 (LHL) cf Eng.

dread *fear* vb -tya i & t (H); *dreadful, be frightening* vb -tyisa i & t (HH); cf -tya (H)

dream *an imagined experience during sleep* vb -rota i & t (HH) — PT & PP *dreamed, dreamt*

dream *something which one seems to see or experience during sleep* n chiroto 7 (LHH) cf -rota (HH); hope 10 (HH)

dreamed *dreamt cf dream*

dregs of beer *worthless matter which sinks to the bottom* n masese 6 (LLL)

dress *female outer clothing* n rokwe 5, marokwe 6 (HL) cf Afrik.; dhirezi 5, madhirezi 6 (LHL) cf Eng. *maternity d.* n mateneti 6 (LHLL)

dress oneself *put clothes on* vb -pfeka i & t (LL); (stative vb); Akapfeka zvichena. (*She is dressed in white.*)

drew *cf draw*

dribble *allow saliva to pass out of the mouth* vb -buritsa masiriri (HHH LHHH); -buritsa rute i (HHH LH); *d. a football* -nzvengesa bhora (HHL HL)

dried up *be parched* vb -pwa i (H)

drift *ford, river crossing* n zambuko 5, mazambuko 6 (LLL)

drill *make a hole* vb -boora i & t (LLL)

drill *tool for making holes* n chibooreso 7 (LLLLL) cf -boora (LLL)

drink *consume liquid* vb -nwa i & t Z (H); -mwa i & t KM (H); *d. from spring or stream with the mouth (humans) vb -tsinatira i (HHHL); d. to excess* vb -nwisa i & t (HH);-nwa zvakapfurikidza; *something to d.* n chokunwa 7 (HLH) cf -nwa (H) — PT *drank;* PP *drunk*

drinking vessel *cup, tin, mug, etc.* n chinwiro 7 (LHH)

drip *drop* vb -donha i (LL)

drive *(motor car, team of oxen)* vb -tyaira i & t (LLL); -chaira i & t (LLL); *d. cattle* vb -tinha mombe t (LL LL) — PT *drove.* PP *driven*

drive away *d. out, chase out* vb -dzinga (HH); -tanda t Z (HH); *d. away flies, swot flies* vb -nina t (LL)

driven *cf drive*

driver *(vehicle)* n mutyairi 1 (LLLL); muchairi 1 (LLLL); mutekenyi 1 (LLLL); dhiraivha 1a (LHLL) cf Eng.

driver ant *(The male only is winged and sausage-like)* n dumbwi 5, matumbwi 6 (LL); gadzishava 5 (HLHH)

drizzle *wet mist* n guti 5 (LL); *drizzling rain* n mubvumbi 3 MZ (LLH)

drone *male bee* n donganyuchi 5 Z (LLHH)

drone *of an aeroplane or bus* n kudhirima kwendege 15

drongo *black, fork-tailed d., sp of bird* n nhengure 9 (LHL); nhengu (LH) R517

droop *dangle, hang down, hang limply* vb -dembera i (LLL), -rezuka i (HHL); -rembera i (LLL)

drop *fall to the ground* vb -donha i (LL); *let fall* vb -donhedza t (LLL)

drop *of liquid* n donhwe 5 MZ (LH); domhwe 5 K (LH)

dropping *excrement (of fowl or bird)* n doto 5, matoto 6 (LL); dororo 5, madororo 6 (LLL); dhokonoro 5 (LHLL); dhokororo 5 Z, madhokororo 6 (LHLL) *excrement of duikers, hares, mice, caterpillars, etc.* n nhoko 9 (LH)

drought *want of rain* n mauni 6 M (LLL), mhare 9 (LL)

drove *cf drive*

drove *herd, flock* n danga 5, matanga 6 (LH)

drown *die in water* vb -nyura i (HH); -mwira i (HH); *cause death in water, suffocate under water* vb- nyudza t (HH)
drowsy *be sleepy* vb -va nehope i (HLL)
drum *musical instrument* n ngoma 9 (LL); *the very large variety* n mutumba 3 (LLL)

drum *metal d. for holding liquids* n mugomo 3 (LHL); dhiramu 5, madhiramu 6 (LHL) cf Eng.
drunk *cf drink*
drunk *be inebriated* adj & vb -dhakwa i (LL); -raradza i (LLL) (stative vb); Murume uyu aka**dhakwa**. (This man is drunk.)
drunkard *a person who is always drunk* n chidhakwa 7 (LLH) cf -dhakwa (LL)
dry *be hard, difficult, free of moisture* adj & vb -oma i (HH) (stative vb); huni dzakaoma (*dry firewood*); *be dried up, parched* vb -pwa i (H); *make d., d. out* vb -omesa t (HHH) cf -oma (HH); *spread out in order to d., hang out* vb -yanika t (HHH)
dry season *extremely hot weather before the rains* n chirimo 7 (LLL)
duck *(general term), water fowl* n dhadha 5, madhadha 6 (LL); *small d.* n sekwe 5 (LH); *goose* n hanzi 9 (LH)
due to *owing to, because of* adv pamusana pa- (LLHH)
dug *cf dig*
duiker *sp of common small antelope, weight about 18 kg* n mhembwe 9 (LL); *blue d. (E. districts only) height 30 cm* n ndundu 9 M (LL); *cf illustration p. 89*
duiker tree *duiker berry t.* n mudyamhembwe 3 (LHHL); mutsonzowa 3 (LHLH); mukuvazviyo 3 (LHHLH) B.Bk. 1,25

dumb person *one who is unable to speak* n chimumumu 7 (LHHH); mbeveve 9 (HHH); mumumu 9 (HHH)
dung *excrement of cattle* n ndove 9 (LL); *excrement of smaller creatures* n nhoko 9 (LH), *dung beetle, scarab b.* n nyamututa 1a (LLLL); ngoko 9 (LL); *rhinoceros or rhino d.b.* n nyangare 9 (LLL); *larva of d.b.* n gonye romudanga 5 (LL LHLH)
dusk *twilight, half-light before night* n rufuramhembwe 11 (LLLLL); rubvunzavaenzi 11 (LLLLLH); rukunzvikunzvi 11 (LHHLH)
dust *very fine grit* n huruva 9 (HHL); guruva 5 (HHL); *dusty* adj e.g. shangu dzine huruva (*dusty pair of shoes*)
dust pan n gwati 5, magwati 6 (LH); zengwete 5 Z, mazengwete 6 (LLL)
dust *wipe, remove dust* vb -pukuta i & t (LLL)
Dutchman's pipe *wild D. p.* n chividze 7 (LHL)
duty *moral or legal obligation* n basa 5, mabasa 6 (LL); faniro 9 (HHL) cf -fanira (HHH)
dwarf *person much below the usual size* n chidhoma 7 (LLL); chimandionerepi 7 (LLHLLLH) (*same name as for Bushman*)

dwell *stay, live* vb -gara i (LL) — PT & PP *dwelt*

dwelling *house, hut* n imba 9 (LH); *deserted buildings* n dongo 5, matongo 6 (LL)

dwelt *cf dwell*

dynamite n dharameti 5 (LLHL) cf Eng.

dysentery *bowel disorder, loose bowels* n manyoka 6 (LHH)

E

eagle gondo

each adj & pron; Mwana **mumwe no-mumwe** ngaapiwe bhuku. (*Let each child be given a book.*) Murume **oga oga** ngaazvionere. (*Let each man see for himself.*)

eagle *large bird of prey (general term) cf illustration* n gondo 5, makondo 6 (LH); hondo 9 K (LH) *fish e.* n hungwe 9 (LH) R149; *bateleur e.* n chapungu 7 (LHH); chipungu 7 (LHH); bungu 5 (HH) R 151; *black e.* n gwamuramakwande 5 (LLLLLH) R 133; *martial e.* n chinyamudzura 7 Z (LLHHH); mudzurambudzana 3 K (LLLHLH); dorambudzi 5, matorambudzi 6 (HHHH) (*terms shared with the crowned eagle*)

ear *hearing organ* n nzeve 9 MZ (LH); zheve 9 K (LH); *e. drum* n ruve 11 Z (LL); *e. wax* n mafunzi 6 (LHH); mafunzu 6 K (LHH)

ear ring n mhete 9 MZ (LH)

early adv -chimbidzo- infix vb; -chimbidza + Infin; -kurumidza + Infin; *e. in the morning* adv mangwananingwanani 6 (LHHHLLL); rungwanangwana 11 (LHHLH); *do e. in the morning* vb -fumo- Infix vb

earn *work for* vb -sevenzera t (HHHL)

earnings *wages, reward* n mubayiro 3 (LLLL)

earth *this world* n pasi 16 (LH); pasi 5 M (LH) e.g. pasi rose

earth *lair, hole made by burrowing animals e.g. ant-bear* n guru 5 MZ, maguru 6 (LL)
(must be distinguished from: guru 5 (LH) *stomach; and* guru 5 (HH) *polygamous union)*

earth *soil* n ivhu 5 MZ (LH); vhu 5 K (H), mavhu 6 (LH); *potter's clay* n rondo 5 (HH); dongo 5 (LH)

earth-worm n honye 9 (LL); gonye 5, makonye 6 (LL)

east *where the sun rises* n mabvazuva 6 (LLHH)

Easter *anniversary of the Resurrection* n Pasika 9 (HLL); Isita 9 (HLL) cf Eng.

eastern border kaffir boom *tree* n murungu 3 (LLH)

easy *be light in operation* adj & vb -reruka i (HHH) (stative vb); Basa iri inyore. Basa iri raka**reruka**. (*This work is easy.*) *easier* adj -reruka pana; Basa rangu rakareruka pane rako. (*My work is easier than yours.*); *easiest* adj; Basa iri rakareruka pana ose. (*This is the easiest work of all.*)

eat *consume food* vb -dya i & t (H); *e. breakfast* vb -svusvura i (HHH); *e. lunch* vb -swerera t (LLL); *e. plain sadza* vb -temura t (HHH); *e. supper*

birds of prey

bateleur eagle chapungu

kite ngavira

sparrow-hawk rukodzi

fish eagle hungwe

African hawk eagle gondo

secretary bird hwata

martial eagle chinyamudzura

lesser beasts of prey

caracal hwana

wild dog mhumhi

serval cat nzunza

civet jachacha

otter mbiti

beasts of prey

cheetah dindingwe

leopard ingwe

lion shumba

vb -rarira t (HHH); -raira t K (HHH); — PT *ate;* PP *eaten*

eaves *space beneath overhanging roof* n berevere 5, maperevere 6 (HHHH); berere 5, maperere 6 (HHH)

ebony *tree, large evergreen t.: heart-wood almost black and very hard* n mushuma 3 (LHL); mushenje 3 (LLL) B.Bk. 1,41

eccentric *be odd; be given to strange behaviour* vb -penga i (HH)

echo *sound sent back from a wall or hill-side* n maun'ira 6 (LLLL); maungira 6 (LLLL)

edge *boundary* n mucheto 3 (LLL); mhendero 9 (LLL); *e. (of water), bank* n hombekombe 5 & 9 (LLLL); *e. of clothing, hem* n mupendero 3 (LLLL) cf -pendera (LLL); *e. of a solid surface* n mugumo 3 (LHH) cf -guma (HH)

edible *be fit to eat* vb -dyika i (HH) cf -dya (H)

educate *teach* vb -dzidzisa i & t (HHL) cf -dzidza (HH); -fundisa i & t (HHH) cf -funda (HH); *education, schooling* n dzidzo 9 (HL); fundo 9 (HH)

eel *long, snake-like fish* n hunga 9 (LH); mukunga 3 M (LHH); *mottled e.* n nyamatsatsi 9 Z (LLHL)

effervesce *give off gas bubbles* vb -vira i (LL); -fanza i (HH)

egg n zai 5, mazai 6 (HL); zanda 5 M, mazanda 6 (LH); *e. shell* n gekenya 5, makekenya 6 (HLH); *infertile e.* n shupa 9 (HH)

egret *cattle e., small sp of white stork* n fudzamombe 5, mafudzamombe 6 (LLLL) R61

Egyptian cobra *banded c.* n nyamafungu 9 (LLHH) cf cobra; *E. goose R89* hanzi 9 (LH) *general name*

eight adj -sere (HH); tsere 10

either . . . **or** . . . conj kana . . . kana . . . (LL LL)

eland *the largest of our antelopes, weight up to 600 kg* n mhofu 9 (HL); nhuka 9 (LL); *person of the e. clan* n shava 1a (HH) (*mutupo*); *cf illustration p. 88*

elastic *be e., stretch* vb -dhadhanuka i (LLLL); -tatamuka i (LLLL)

elbow *middle joint of the arm* n gokora 5, makokora 6 (HHL)

elderly person *usu a woman* n chembere 9 (LLL); *a man* n harahwa 9 (LLL)

electric light bulb n bhoni 5 & 9 (HL); girobhu 5 (LHL) cf Eng.

electricity *e. current* n magetsi 6 (LHL) cf Eng. (gas)

elephant *the largest of our animals, sometimes reaching 6 000 kg in weight* n nzou 9 MZ (LL); zhou 9 K (LL)

elephant orange tree *monkey apple tree, sp of klapper apple producing sweet fruit, the size of an orange, August to December* n muzhumu 3 (LLH); muzhuni 3 (LLH); muzhimi 3 (LLH); muzimi 3 (LLH)

elephant shrew *jumping s., a small insect-eating animal the size of a small mouse* n mudune 3 (LLH); *cf illustration p. 79*

elevate *lift up, raise up* vb -simudza t (HHL)

elope *run away with a girl, enter marriage unlawfully* vb -tizisa mukumbo 6 (HHH HLL); *run away with a boy* vb -tiza mukumbo i (HH HLL)

eloquent *be fluent* vb -taura zvakanaka (LLL LHHL) (*speak well*)

elsewhere adv kumwe 17 (LL)

elude *evade, dodge* vb -nzvenga i & t (HH)

emaciated *be thin* adj & vb -onda i (HH) (stative vb); Ane mombe dzakaonda. (*He has thin cattle.*)

embarrass *cause shame* vb nyadzisa t (HHH); *be embarrassed, be shy, blush* vb -nyara i (HH)

ember *small piece of burning wood or coal in a dying fire* n vhunze 5, mavhunze 6 (LH); gara 5 M (LL); simbe 5, masimbe 6 MZ (LL)

embezzle *steal money left in one's care* vb -ba i & t (H)

embrace *with affection* vb -mbundira t (LLL)

emerge *come out, go out* vb -buda i (HH)

eminence *greatness* n ukuru 14 (LHH)

employ *make use of (things)* vb -sevenzesa t (HHHL) cf -sevenza (HHH)

employee *worker* n musevenzi 1 (LHHL) cf -sevenza (HHH) cf Zulu

employer *one who is worked for* n murungu 1 (LLL)

employment *work* n basa 5, mabasa 6 (LL)

empty out *pour out* vb -durura t (LLL); *empty* adj e.g. bhotoro risina chinhu (*a bottle which has nothing i.e. an empty bottle*)

enable *make able* vb -gonesa t (LLL)

encircle *surround* vb -poteredza t (HHHL); -komberedza t (HHHL); -tenderedza t (HHHL)

enclosure *fence* n rutsito 11 (LHH); *wall* n rusvingo 11 (LLL)

encourage *urge* vb -kurudzira t (HHHL)

end *come to an e.* vb -guma i (HH); -pera i (HH); *endless, unending* adj e.g. nhamo dzisingaperi (*endless trouble*)

end *terminus* n mugumo 3 (LHH); magumo 6 (LHH)

end up vb -pedzisira i (HLHL)

endeavour *try* vb -edza t (LL); -vavarira i (HHHL)

endure *suffer, bear, put up with* vb -shivirira i Z (LLLL); -shiva i MZ (LL)

enemy *foe, one who hates* n mhandu 9 (LH); musemi 1 (LHH) cf -sema (HH); muvengi 1 (LHH) cf -venga (HH)

energetic *be e., be healthy* vb -gwinya i (HH) (*stative vb*)

engage *someone in work, employ* vb -pinza basa t (LL LL)

engine *machine producing power* n injini 9 (HLL) cf Eng.

English *usu the E. language* n chiRungu 7 (LLL); chiNgezi 7 (LLL)

engrave *fashion out of wood* vb -senda i & t (LL); -veza i & t (LL)

enjoy *be happy* vb -fara i (HH)

enlarge *make larger* vb -kudza t (HH)

enlighten *inform, tell* vb -zivisa i & t (HHH) cf -ziva (HH)

enormous *very large* adj -kurukuru (HHLH); guruguru 5, huruhuru 9

enough *have, have e. to eat, be sufficient* vb -kwana i (HH) (stative vb); Tine zvitina zvaka**kwana**. (*We have enough bricks.*)

enquire *ask* vb -bvunza i & t (LL); *e. by asking a lot of questions* vb -feyafeya i & t (HHHL)

ensnare *trap* vb -teya t (HH)

enter *go in* vb-pinda t (LL) *usu followed by locative Cl 18.*

entertain *with conversation* vb -tandadza t (HHH); *entertaining, be interesting* vb -nakidza i & t (LLL)

entice *attract* vb -kwezva (LL)

entirely *completely* adv kwazvo (HL); chose K (HH)

entrails *bowels, intestines* n ura 14 (LL); matumbu 6 (LLL) *cf illustration p. 20*

entrance *door* n musuo 3 (LHL)
entrap *ensnare, catch in a trap* vb -teya t (HH)
entreat *beg, beseech* vb -teterera i & t (HHHL)
enumerate *count* vb -verenga i & t (LLL)
envelope *paper wrapper or covering* n emvuropu 9 (HLLL); hamvuropu 9 (HLLL) cf Eng.

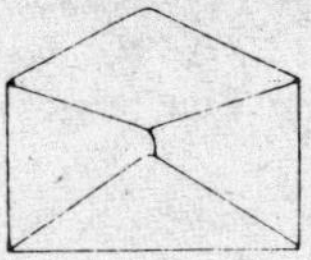

envious *be jealous, envy* vb -va neshanje i (LHL)
envy *desire of better fortune (of another)* n shanje 9 (LL)
epilepsy *fainting fit, nervous disease causing a person to lose consciousness* n tsviyo 10 (HL); pfari 10 (LH); zvipusha 8 K (LLL)
epistle *letter* n tsamba 9 (LL)
equal *be the same in number, size, value, etc.* vb -enzana i (LLL); Vanopiwa zvaka**enzana**. (*They are given the same.*)
erase *rub out (writing)* vb -dzima t (HH)
eraser *rubber* n rabha 9 (HL) cf Eng.
erect *be upright* adj & vb -twasuka i (LLL) (stative vb); Mapango aya aka**twasuka**. (*These poles are upright.*)
erect *set upright* vb -misa t (HH) cf -mira (HH)
erode *(of the soil), wear away by rain water* vb -kukura t (HHH)
err *make a mistake* vb -kanganisa i & t (HHHL); -tadza i & t (HH); *error, slip, mistake* n chikanganiso 7 (LHHHL) cf -kanganisa (HHHL)
escape *evade, run away* vb -punyuka i (LLL); *e. by force* vb -poya i & t (LL); -puya i & t (LL); *e. notice, avoid being seen by evasive action* vb -nyenyeredza t (HHHL); *break free from an enclosure* vb -paza t K (LL)
escort *one who accompanies* n muperekedzi 1 (LHHHL) cf -perekedza (HHHL)
especially *particularly, mostly* adv kunyanya (LLL); zvikuru (LHH)
establish *set up* vb -misa i & t (HH); -dzika i & t (LL)
eternity *for ever* adv narini narini (LHL LHL); nokusingaperi (HLHLHL)
eucalyptus *tree, blue gum* n mupuranga 3 (LLHL)
Eucharist n Yukaristiya 9 (LLHLL) cf Eng.
euphorbia ingens *candelabra tree* n mukonde 3 (LLL); *e. matabelensis,*

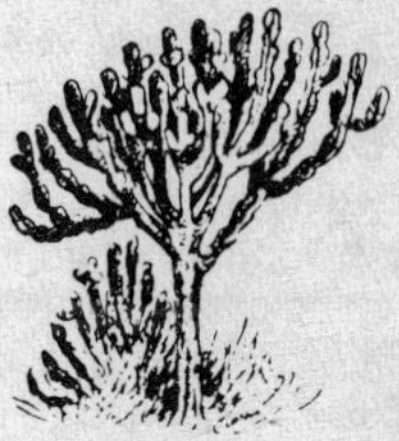

shrub or small tree whose latex is used as bird-lime n chitatarimbo 7 (LLLLL)
European *any white person* n muRungu 1 (LLL); *European* adj muti wechiRungu (*European medicine*)
evade *dodge, elude, side-step* vb -nzvenga i & t (HH)
evangelist *preacher of the Gospel* n muvhangeri 1 (LLHL) cf vhangeri 5 & 9 (LHL); mubvuvi 1 KM (LLL)
evaporate *dry up* vb -pwa i (H)
evasive *be unwilling to give a straight answer* vb -nzvengeredza i (HHHL)
even conj kana (LL); *even though* kunyange (LLL); nyange (LL) + Partic; *or even* adv kana (LL); *even if* conj kana + consecutive form
even *make e.* vb -enzanisa i & t (LLLL); *evenly, squarely (in a way which is even)* adv zvakaenzana (LHHLL) rel

even today adv nanhasi (LHL)

evening *afternoon (after 3.00 p.m.)* n mauro 6 (LLH); manheru 6 (LLH); *this e.* manheru ano 6 (LLH HL)

eventually *finally* adv -zo- Akazobuda basa. (*He eventually left his work.*)

ever *(neg), not ever* infix vb -mbo-

ever since *from the time of* adv kubvira (LLL)

every day adv mazuva ose 6 (LHH HH)

everyone adj munhu wose (LL HH)

everywhere adv kwose kwose 17 (HH HL)

evidence *facts that support belief* n uchapupu 14 Z (LLHH); ufakazi 14 (LLLL); umboc 14 MZ (LLH)

evidence *give testimony* vb -fakaza i (LLL)

evil *wickedness* n uipi 14 (LHH) cf -ipa (HH); *do wrong* vb -tadza i (HH)

evil spirit *devil* n dhiyabhori 1a (HLLL) cf Eng.; *avenging spirit* n ngozi 9 (LL)

evolvulus *plant with blue flower* n kaparuramhanje 12 (LHHLHL) B.Bk. 1,78

ewe *female sheep* n nhunzvi yehwai 9 (LL LHL)

exaggerate *distort the truth* vb -pamhidzira i (LLLL)

examination *test* n bvunzo 9 (LL); zamanishoni 5, mazamanishoni 6 (LLHLL) cf Eng.

examine *small object, scrutinize* vb -penengura t (HHHL); *examine, go into the matter, observe* vb -ongorora i & t (HHHL)

example *person or thing to be imitated* n muenzaniso 3 (LLLLL) cf -enzanisa (LLLL)

exasperate *bully* vb -shusha i & t (LL)

exceed *excel* vb -pfuura t (HHH); -pinda t (LL); -kunda t (HH)

exceedingly *very much* adv -isvo- Z; -nyanyo- Z; samare (LHL); chaizvo (LHL)

except *e.for, apart from* conj kusiya (LHH); kunze kwa- Hapana waakataurira izvi kusiya ini. (*He told nobody this except me.*)

excess *be in e.* vb -raudza i (HHH)

excessive *be e.* vb -nyanya i (LL) (stative vb)

excessively *very much* adj zvakaipa (*slang*) (LHLL) *rel; excessively, beyond due limit* adv zvakapindiridza (LHHLLL) rel

exchange *one thing for another* vb -tsinhana i (LLL)

excrement *human e., dirt* n tsvina 9 (LL) (*polite term*)

excuse *reason* n chikonzero 7 (LHHL)

excuse me *(a request for permission)* Pamusoroi (LLHHHH).; *I beg your pardon.* Ndino urombo (*lit. I have sorrow*)

exhausted *be tired* vb -neta i (stative vb) (LL); Iko zvino nda**neta**. (*Right now I am tired.*)

exhibit *show* vb -ratidza t (LLL); -onesa t (HHH) cf -ona (HH)

exile *drive away* vb -dzinga t (HH)

exist *be present* vb -vapo i. Kubvira pakutanga Mwari ai**vapo**. (*God existed from the beginning.*)

expand *with heat* vb -futa i (LL); *expand what is elastic* vb -tatamura t (LLLL)

expect *hope for* vb -tarisira i & t (LLLL)

expel *drive or send out by force* vb -tanda t (HH); -dzinga t (HH)

expensive *be dear, costly* vb -dhura i (HH)

expert *person with special skill or knowledge* n shasha 9 (LL); nyanzvi 9 (LH); *expertise, special ability* n ushasha 14 (LLL) cf -shasha (LL); unyanzvi 14 (LLH) cf nyanzvi (LH)

explain *detail one's meaning* vb -tsanangura i & t (LLLL)

explanation n tsananguro 9 (LLLL) cf

-tsanangura (LLLL); tsanangudzo 9 *(LLLL)*
explode *burst* vb -putika i (HHH)
express *juice or fluid from fruit, squeeze* vb -svina i (LL)
extend *make larger* vb -pamhidzira t (LLLL)
extensive *be wide* vb -fara i (HH)
exterminate *kill* vb -uraya i & t (HHH)
extinguish *put out* vb -dzima i & t (HH)
extortion *robbery* n upambi 14 (LHH) cf -pamba (HH)
extract *a thorn* vb -tumbura munzwa (LLL LH); *e. a tooth* vb -gura (HH); -bvisa zino (LL HH)
extremely *very much* adv kwazvo (HL); chaizvo (LHL)
eye n ziso 5, maziso 6 (HH); *eyebrow, eyelash* n tsiye 9 MZ (HL); *eyelid* n chikope 7 (LHH); *eye discharge* n maranga 6 (LLL); *pupil* n mboni 9 (HH); *red eyes i.e. angry eyes* n meso matsvuku 6 (LH HLH); meso azere ropa (LH LHH HL)

F

falls bopoma

fable *story, folk-tale* n rungano 11 (LLL); ngano 9 (LL)
face *eyes, cheeks and mouth* n chiso 7 (LH); uso 14 (LH)
face towards *look at* vb -tarisa t (LLL)
factory *place where things are manufactured* n fekitari 9 (HLLL) cf Eng.
fade *lose colour* vb -puma i (HH)
faggot *bundle of firewood* n svinga 5, masvinga 6 (HH)
fail *not succeed* vb -kundikana i (HHHL); -tadza i (HH); -kona i (LL)
faint *swoon* vb -fenda i (HH) cf Eng.; *f. from want of food* vb -ziya i (HL)
fainting fit *of epilepsy* n tsviyo 10 (HL); pfari 10 (LH)
fairly *in a fair manner* adv zvakanakisisa (LHHLLL)
faith *religious belief* n chitendero 7 (LLLL) cf -tendera (LLL); *faithful, one of the f., believer* n mutenderi 1 (LLLL) cf -tendera (LLL)
faithful *be trustworthy* vb -tendeka i (LLL); -vimbika i (LLL)
falcon *kestrel* n rukodzi 11 (LHL)
fall *f. off* vb -punzika i (HHH); -wa i (L); *f. down, f. to the ground* vb -wira pasi i (LL LH); *f. (of leaves and fruit)* vb -donha i (LL) — PT *fell;* PP *fallen*
fall asleep vb -kotsira i (LLL); -batwa nehope (HH HLL)
fall silent vb -nyarara i (HHL); -ti zi-i ideo (HL)
fallen *cf fall*
falls *natural cascade of water* n bopoma 5, mapopoma 6 (LLL); *Victoria Falls* n Bopoma reVictoria. *cf illustration above*
false witness *bear f. w.* vb -nenedzera t (HHHL); -pomera mhosva (HHL HL)

false witness n munenedzeri 1 (LHHHL) cf -nenedzera (HHHL)

falsehood *untruth* n nhema 10 (LH); manomano 6 (LLLL); kunyepa 15 (LLL)

fame *glory, renoun* n mbiri 9 (HH); mukurumbira 3 (LHHLH); *famous* adj tateguru ane mbiri (*a famous ancestor*)

family *parents and children* n mhuri 9 (LL)

famine *hunger* n nzara 9 MZ (LL); zhara 9 K (LL)

famished *starve, be very hungry* vb -ziya i (HL); -fa nenzara i (H LHL) *lit. die with hunger*

famous *be well-known* adj & vb -kurumbira i (stative vb) (HHHL); Baba vake vaka**kurumbira**. (*His father is famous.*)

far *a long way off* adv kure 17 (LL); kurefu 17 (LLH); *very f. away* adv kure kure 17 (LL HH); *f. from* adv kure kwa- (LL); kure na- 17 (LL)

farewell *bid f., say goodbye* vb -oneka i & t (LLL)

farm *land for growing crops, raising animals* n purazi 5 & 9 (LHL) cf Afrik.; famu 9 (HL) cf Eng.

farmer *one who cultivates* n murimi 1 (LLL) cf -rima (LL)

farther *beyond* adv pamberi (LLH); mberi 16 (LH)

fashion *plane, shape, form (wood)* vb -veza i & t (LL); *f., mould, form (e.g. clay)* vb -umba i & t (HH)

fashion *behaviour* n tsika 9 (LL) (plur *good manners*)

fast *abstain from food* vb -tsanya i (HH); **-zvinyima** i (HLH) Reflex.

fast *be f., hurry, hasten* vb -kurumidza i (HHHL); -chimbidza i (HHH); *fast* adv nokukurumidza (HLHHHL)

fasten *tie up* vb -sunga t (HH); *make fast, tie fast* vb -sungisa t (HHL) cf -sunga (HH); *fasten buttons, button up* vb -konopera t (HHHL); -kopera t (HHH)

fat *oil, grease* n mafuta 6 (LHH)

fat *be stout (of humans)* adv & vb -futa i (LL) (stative vb); Munhu aka**futa** haamhanyisi. (*A fat person does not run fast.*); *fat, be plump (of animals)* adj & vb -kora i (LL) (stative vb); Mombe dzedu dzaka**kora**. (*Our cattle are plump.*)

father *male head of family* n baba 1a (LH); *father (a priest)* n baba 1a (LH); fata 1a (LL) cf Eng.

father-in-law *of man* n tezvara 1a (HHL); mukarabwa 1 K (LLLL); tsano 1a KKo (LL); *father-in-law of woman* n tezvara 1a MZ (HHL); sazawani 1a M (HHHH)

fatigue *tiredness* n kuneta 15 (LLL)

fatigued *be tired* vb -neta i (LL) (stative vb); **Ndaneta.** (*I am tired.*) **Ndakaneta.** (*I am tired.*)

fatten (*farm animals*) vb -kodza t (LL) cf -kora (LL)

fatty *be f.* adj & vb -nuna i (LL) (stative vb); Nyama iyi yaka**nuna**. (*This meat is fatty.*)

fault *sin* n murandu 3 (LLH)

favour *prefer* vb -da t (H)

favouritism *special favour to one party* n rusaruro 11 (LLLL) cf -sarura (LL)

fawn *newly born buck* n tsvana 9 (HL)

fear *be afraid of* vb -tya i & t (H)

feast n mabiko 6 (LLL) cf -bika (LL); mutambo 3 (LHH); cf -tamba (HH); *marriage f.* n muchato 3 (LLL) cf -chata (LL); *beer dance* n bira 5, mabira 6 (HL); zhana 5, mazhana 6 (LH)

feat *extraordinary trick or achievement* n pipi 5, mapipi 6 (HH)

feather n munhenga 3 (LLH)

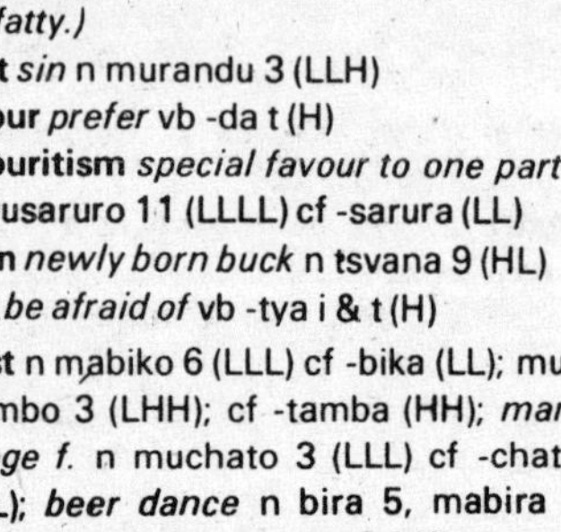

fed *cf feed*

fed up *be bored* vb -finhwa i (HH) cf -finha (HH)

feed *give food to* vb -pa zvokudya t (HLH); *f. poultry* vb -posha t (HH); *put food into a child's mouth* vb -paka t (HH); *breast f.* vb -yamwisa t (HHH) — PT & PP *fed*

feel *(well, cold, etc.) hear, understand* vb -nzwa i & t (H)

feel contempt for *despise* vb -shora t (LL); -zvidza t (LL)

feel lonely *be desolate* vb -suruvara i (HHHL)

feeler *antenna of an insect* n nyanga 9 (LH)

fell *cf fall*

felt *cf feel*

female *(human)* n munhukadzi 1 (LLLL) woman, wife n mukadzi (LHH); *big, fat woman* n gadzi 5 (HH); *f. animal* n hadzi 9 (HH); *fowl, pullet* n tseketsa 9 (LHL); sheche 9 K (LL); sheshe 9 MZ (LL); *hen* n nhunzvi 9 (LL)

fence *wire enclosure* n fenzi 9 (HL); waya 9 (HL) cf Eng.; *fence-strainer* n makako 6 (LHL)

ferment *effervesce, give off gas/bubbles* vb -vira i (LL); -tutuma i (LLL)

fern *flowerless plant that grows in damp places* n mumvuri webwe 3 (LHL LH)

ferocious *man, savage person* n gandanga 5, magandanga 6 (LLL)

fertile *be able to produce* adj & vb -orera i (LLL) (stative vb); **Ivhu iri rakaorera** kwazvo. (*This soil is very fertile.*)

fertility *ability to produce* n rubereko 11 (LLLL); ruzvaro 11 (LHH)

fertiliser *agricultural f., chemicals to add to the soil for greater fertility* n fetiraiza 9 (HLHLL) cf Eng.

fetch *go for and bring back, come with* vb -tora t (HH); -uya na- t (HH); -unza t (HH)

fever *condition of the human body with temperature higher than normal* n denda 5, matenda 6 (HL); hosha 9 (LL); fivha 9 (HL) cf Eng.

fever-tree *big leaf f. t.* n mugopogopo 3 (LLLLL)

few *little* adj -shoma (LL); *very f., little* -shomanana (LLHH); -shomashoma (LLHH)

fib *small lie* n manomano 6 (LLLL)

fibre *of bark, bark fibre, bast* n gavi 5, makavi 6 (LH); rwodzi 11 (LH)

fibre *in meat, sweet potato and vegetable matter* n dzira 5, madzira 6 (LH)

fibre tree *wild violet t.* n mufufu 3 (LLH)

fidget with *handle with curiosity* vb -bata-bata t (HH HL)

field *garden* n munda 3 (LL); *virgin f.* n gombo 5, makombo 6 (HH)

fierce *be frightening* vb -tyisa i (HH) cf -tya (H)

fifth *(of a series)* chishanu (LHL)

fifty n makumi mashanu 6 (LHH LHL) *lit: five tens*

fig *(fruit)* n guyu 5, makuyu 6 (HL); onde

5, maonde 6 (LH); *f. tree* n mukuyu 3 (LHL); muonde 3 (LLH) B.Bk. 1,1

fight *battle* vb -rwa i (L); *set upon angrily* vb -rwisa t (LL) cf -rwa (L) — PT & PP *fought*

file of men *single f.* n mudungwe 3 (LHL); rundaza 11 (LLH)

file *blacksmith's tool* n rima 5 (HL); faera 5 (HLL) cf Eng.

file snake n mhunzamusha 9 (HHLH); ndara 9 (LL)

fill *f. up, add to completion* vb -zadza t (HH); *f. with earth, cover, f. up* vb -fusira t (LLL); -futsira t (LLL); *fill up, stuff inside* vb -paka t (HH)

film *for camera* n firimu 9 (HLL) cf Eng.; *f., cinema picture* n bhaiskopu 5 (HLLL); firimu 9 (HLL) cf Eng.

filth *dirt, rubbish* n tsvina (LL); marara 6 (LLL)

finally *at length* adv -zo- infix vb

finch *hooded f., very small seed-eater* n ndirendire 9 (LHLL); *melba f.* n njekedya 9 (HHL); zazo 5 (LL)

find *discover* vb -ona t (HH); -wana t (LL); *pick up* vb -nonga t (HH); -nhonga t MZ (HH) — PT & PP *found*

find fault with *blame* vb -pa mhosva t (HL)

find out *discover by observation* vb -tarisa i & t (LLL); -ona i & t (HH); *discover by question* vb -bvunza t (LL)

fine *be pretty* adj & vb -naka (stative vb) (LL); Nhasi kwakanaka. (*The weather is fine today.*); Maruva akanaka anofadza. (*Pretty flowers give pleasure.*); Zvitsvene. (*That's fine*)

fine *penalty payment* n muripo 3 (LLL); faindi 9 (HLL) cf Eng.

finger n munwe 3 MZ (LL); little f. n kasiyanwa 12 MZ (LHLH); *f.-nail* n nzara 9 (LH); *thumb* n chigunwe 7 (LLL); chara 7 (LH)

finish *complete* vb -pedza i & t (HH); *finish off* vb -pedzisa t (HHH) cf -pedza (HH); *kill something that is about to die* vb -korovedza t (LLLL); -pfuudza t (HHH)

finished *be completed* vb -pera i (HH); **Basa rapera.** (*The work is finished.*)

fire n moto 3 Z (LH); mwoto 3 KM (LH); *flame of f.* n rimi 5, marimi 6 (HH); *make a f.* vb -kuhwidza moto t (LLL LH); *set on f.* vb -tungidza t (HHH); *be on f., catch, f.* vb -tsva i (H); -psva i M (H)

firebrand *piece of wood on fire* n tsiga 5, matsiga 6 (HL)

firebush *very conspicuous shrub early in the dry season when the leaves are vivid red* n chiwirowiro 7 (LHLHL); mururamapfeni 3 (LLLLLL)

firefinch *red waxbill, sp of small seed-eating bird* n kandirendire 12 (LLHLL); tondondo 9 (HHH)

firefly *fly that glows by night* n chidwaidwai 7 M (LLLLL); chidzimamuriro 7 (LHHHLL); chitaitai 7 (LLLLL); chin'ain'ai 7 (LLLLL)

fireplace *hearth* n choto 7 (LH)

firewood *heavy or light wood for the fire-place* n huni 9 (HH); *bundle of f., faggot* n svinga 5, masvinga 6 (HH)

firm *business undertaking* n femu 9 (HL) cf Eng.

firm *be strong* adj & vb -simba i (LL) (stative vb); Akasunga mbatya zvakasimba. (*He tied up his belongings firmly — in a way which is firm.*) rel

first (*of a series*) n chiposhi 7 (LLH)

first *at f.* adv pokutanga 16 (HLHH); *be f.* vb tanga i (HH); Ndatanga kusvika pano. (*I was here first.*); *first* adj chidzidzo chokutanga (*the first lesson*); *be f. to* vb -tangira t (HHH); Ndatangira vamwe kusvika pano. (*I was the first to arrive.*)

first-born n dangwe 5, matangwe 6 (HL); nevanje 1a K (HLH)

first of all *in the first place* adv -tanga + Rec PP; **Tanga wabatidza moto.** (*First of all light the fire.*); Pokutanga Mwari akasika pasi. (*To begin with God made the world.*)

fiscal shrike *butcher bird* n korera 9 (LHH); chikorera 7 (LLHH) R707

fish *cold-blooded animal living in the water* n hove 9 (HH); tsomba 9 M (LL); *minnow, very small f.* n sinde 5, masinde 6 (LL)

fish *catch fish with hook and line* vb -raura t (HHH); -vedza t M (HH); -redza t K (HH)

fish eagle n hungwe 9 (LH); *cf illustration p. 49*

fishhook n chirauro 7 (LHHL) cf -raura (HHH); chivedzo 7 M (LHH) cf -vedza (HH); chiredzo 7 K (LHH) cf -redza (HH); *fishing net* n usvasvi 14 (LLH); *fishing basket made with reeds, fish trap* n duwo 5, matuwo 6 (LL)

fist *hand when tightly closed* n chibhakera 7 (LLLL); tsiva 9 (LL)

fit *be healthy* adj & vb -gwinya i (HH) (stative vb); Mucheche uyu aka**gwinya**. (*This is a healthy baby.*)

fit *be worthy* adj & vb -kodzera i (LLL) (stative vb); Aka**kodzera** kurangwa. (*He is fit to be punished.*)

fit *of epilepsy* n tsviyo 10 (HL); pfari 10 (LH)

fit to eat *be edible* vb -dyika i (HH)

five adj -shanu (HL); shanu 10

fizz *effervesce* vb -tutuma i (LLL)

flag *ensign, standard* n mureza 3 (LHL)

flake off *peel off as skin or paint* vb -funuka i (LLL)

flame *visible tongue of fire* n rimi 5, marimi 6 (HH); murazvo 3 K (LHL); marazvo 6 Z (LHL)

flame lily *sp of flower* n jongwe 5 (LH) B.Bk. 1,51

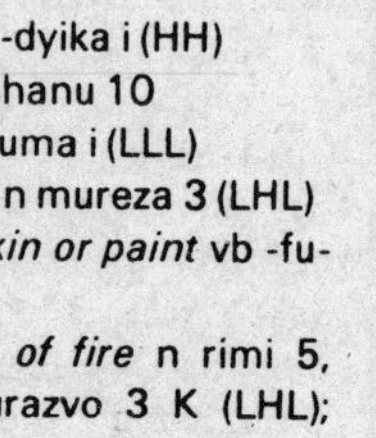

flank *of an animal (meat)* n rumbabvu 11 (LLL); mbabvu 9 (LL)

flank *on one's side (locat)* parutivi 16 (LLLL)

flap *wings* vb -bhabhama i (LLL); -papama i (LLL)

flash *shine, glitter* vb -penya i (LL); *flash of lightning* n kupenya 15 (LLL)

flat *suite of rooms as residence* n furati 9 (LHL) cf Eng.

flat *be f.* vb -ti sandara (LLL) ideo

flatter *praise insincerely in order to gain something* vb -bata mumwe kumeso t

flattery *guile* n muzvambarara 3 (LLLLL)

flaw *physical or moral defect* n chinana 7 (LHH); chinongo 7 (LLH)

fledgeling *young bird just able to fly* n nyn'ana 5 Z (LH); nyana 5 MZ, manyana 6 (LH)

flea *very tiny insect that bites* n nhata 9 (HL); *fowl or dog f.* n utata 14 (LHL); *chicken f.* n data (HL) *cf illustration p. 124*

fled *cf flee*

flee *run away, take to flight* vb -tiza i & t (HH) — PT & PP *fled*

flesh *meat* n nyama 9 (LL)

flew *cf fly*

flexible *be pliable* vb -tepuka i (HHH)

flight *take to f., run away* vb -tiza i & t (HH)

fling *throw* vb -kanda t (LL) — PT & PP *flung*

flint *very hard stone that produces sparks* n gwenya 5, magwenya 6 (LH)

float *lie on the surface of a liquid* vb -yangarika i (LLLL)

float *of a fishing line* n nheme 9 MZ (LH); chinheme 7 (LLH); chituba 7 K (LHL)

flock (*of domestic animals*) n danga 5, matanga 6 (LH)

flog *beat severely with rod or whip* vb -pura t (HH); -zvinda t (LL); -rova t (HH)

flood *excessive rainfall, great quantity of water* n mafashama 6 (LLLL)

floor *on the ground* n pasi 16 (LH), uriri 14 MZ (LLL); *threshing floor* n ruware 11 (LLH); buriro 5, mapuriro 6 (HHL)

flour *ground meal (usu mealie meal)* n upfu 14 (LL); wheaten f. n furawa 9 (LHL) cf Eng.

flow *move with the current* vb -erera i (LLL)

flow over *the side of a container, overflow by being overfilled* vb -deura t (HHH); -deuka i (HHH); *flow over by boiling* vb -tutuma i (LLL)

flower *coloured part of plant from which fruit or seed is later developed* n ruva 5, maruva 6 (LL)

flower *come into f.* vb -tumbuka i (LLL)

flu *influenza* n furuwenza 9 (LLHL) cf Eng.

flung *cf fling*

flush *(game) cause to get up* vb -mutsa t (LL) cf -muka (LL)

flute *musical instrument* n nyere 9 (LL)

flutter *(of birds), move the wings hurriedly but without flying* vb -pupuruka i (HHHL)

fly *move through the air, move by aeroplane* vb -bhururuka i (LLLL) — PT *flew;* PP *flown*

fly *two-winged insect* n nhunzi 9 (HH); tsetse-fly n mhesvi 9 (HL); *large f.* n chitunzi 7 (LHH); *horse-fly, blood-sucking f.* n mbuo 9 (LL); *small sp* chin'ono 7 (LLL)

flying ant *(black and edible)* n tsambarafuta 9 (LLLHH)

fly-catcher *paradise f.* n kateredemu 12 Z (LLLHL); zvigone 9 (HLH); cf p. 113

foal *young donkey* n dhongana 5, madhongana 6 (LHH); *young horse* n mwana webhiza 3 (LH HLH)

foam *froth* n furo 5, mafuro 6 (HH)

foe *enemy* n mhandu 9 (LH); musemi 1 (LHH) cf -sema (HH); muvengi 1 (LHH) cf -venga (HH)

fog *mist, water vapour in the air* n mhute 9 (LH); *light drizzle* n guti 5 (LL)

fold *double over* vb -peta t (LL); *f. the arms* vb -gumbata i (HHH); *something folded* n mheto 9 (LL) cf -peta (LL)

folk tale *story* n ngano 9 (LL); rungano 11 (LLL)

follow vb -tevera t (LLL); *f. the scent* vb -bvumba i Z (LL); *pay attention* vb -teerera i & t (HHHL); *follow spoor or tracks, track* vb -ronda t (LL); *follow suit* vb -tevedzera t (LLLL); following adj & vb. Usiku hwakatevera . . . (*On the following night* . . .)

folly *stupidity* n urema 14 (LHH); upenzi 14 (LHH)

fontanelle *soft space on top of infant's head* n nhova 9 (LL)

food *nourishment for eating* n chokudya 7 (HLH); kudya 15 (LH) cf -dya (H); *f. for a journey* n mbuva 9 (LL); mpako 3 M (HH)

fool *stupid person* n rema 5, marema 6 (HH); benzi 5, mapenzi 6 (HH); *foolishness, stupidity* n urema 14 (LHH); upenzi 14 (LHH)

foolish *be stupid* vb -pusa i (LL)

foot *footprint of humans* n tsoka 9 MZ (LL); rutsoka 11 MZ (LLL); *ankle* n ziso regumbo 5 (HH LHL); *toe* n chigunwe 7 (LLL); *big t.* n gunwe 5 (LL); *foot of hill* n jinga 5, majinga 6 (LH); *footprint of animals* n dzimba 5 MZ, matsimba 6 (LL)

football game n nhabvu 9 (LH); bhora 5 (HL) cf Eng.

footpath n nzira (LL)

footstep *audible f.* n mutsindo 3 (LHH)

foot-rot *in sheep* n chiodzanzondo 7 (LLLLL)

for *a period of time, for a distance* prep PC kwa-. Cl 17; forever adv narini (LHL); *for example, namely* adv sokuti

(LHL); *for nothing, without charge* adv pachena (LLL); *for this reason, therefore* conj saka (LL)

forbid *prohibit, order not to do something* vb -rambidza t (LLL) — PT *forbade, forbad;* PP *forbidden*

force *compel* vb -manikidza t (HHHL)

force *strength, power* n simba 5, masimba 6 (LH)

ford *river crossing* n zambuko 5, mazambuko 6 (LLL)

ford *cross a river* vb -yambuka i & t (LLL); -bira i & t MZ (HH)

forefather *ancestor* n tateguru 1a (LHLL), vadzitateguru 2a (LLLHLL)

forehead *part of the face above the eyes* n huma 9 (LL); mhanza 9 KoZ (HH)

foreign coin *c. from another country* n zuda 5, mazuda 6 (HL)

foreigner *person from another country* n mubvakure 1 (LLLL); murudzi 1 (LLL)

foreman *man in charge* n foromani 1a (LHLL) cf Eng.

forever adv nokusingaperi (HLHLHL); narini wose (LHL HH); narini narini (LHL LHL)

forest *thick f.* n dondo 5, matondo 6 (LL); *savanna f. with scattered trees, veld* n sango 5, masango 6 (HH)

foretell *guess* vb -fembera i & t (HHH) — PT & PP *foretold*

forget *fail to remember* vb -kanganwa i & t (HHH) — PT *forgot,* PP *forgotten*

forgetfulness n hanganwa 10 (HHH)

forgive *pardon, absolve* vb -regerera i & t (LLLL); *forgiveness* n ruregerero 11 (LLLLL) cf -regerera (LLLL) — PT *forgave,* PP *forgiven*

fork n forogo 9 (HLL) cf Eng. *f. of branch, pole or river* n mhaswa 9 (LH)

fork-tailed drongo n nhengure 9 (LHL)

form *class at secondary school* n fomu 5 & 9 (HL) cf Eng.

form *mould, fashion e.g. from clay* vb -umba i & t (HH)

fornicate *break the commandments of purity* vb -ita choupombwe i (LHLL); *fornication, adultery, impurity* n choupombwe 7 (LHLL); upombwe 14 (LLL)

forsake *leave behind* vb -siya t (HH) — PP *forsaken,* PT *forsook*

fortitude *power to endure under difficulties* n usimbarari 14 (LLLLL)

fortunate *be lucky* vb -va nemhanza yakanaka ?

forward *ahead* adv pamberi 16 (LLH)

foster *bring up children* vb -rera t (LL)

fought *cf fight*

found *cf find*

foundation *ground-work of building* n fandesheni 9 (LHLL) cf Eng.

four *the number 4* adj -na (L); ina 10 (LL)

fourth *(of a series)* n -china 7 (LL)

fountain *water spring, well* n tsime 5, matsime 6 (HL)

fowl n huku 9 (HH); *male f., cock* n jongwe 5 (LH); *hen, female f.* n nhunzvi 9 (LL); *chicken* n hukwana 9 (HHH); *pullet* n tseketsa 9 (LHL); *fowlhouse* n chizumbu 7 (LLL); chitata 7 (LLL); chirugu 7 (LLL); zumbu 5 (LL); chikwere 7 M (LLL)

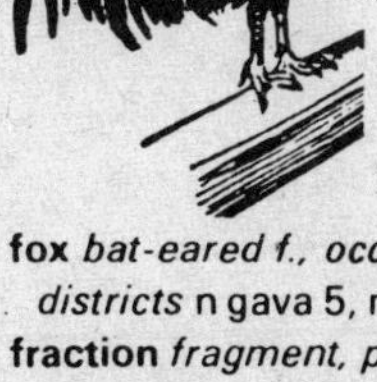

fox *bat-eared f., occurs in the western districts* n gava 5, makava 6 (HH)

fraction *fragment, portion broken off* n chimedu 7 (LHL) cf -medura (HHH)

fracture *break* vb -dimuka i (HHH) cf -dimura (HHH); -tyoka i (HH) cf -tyora (HH)

frame *of a bicycle* n mutanda 3 (LHH)

fruit

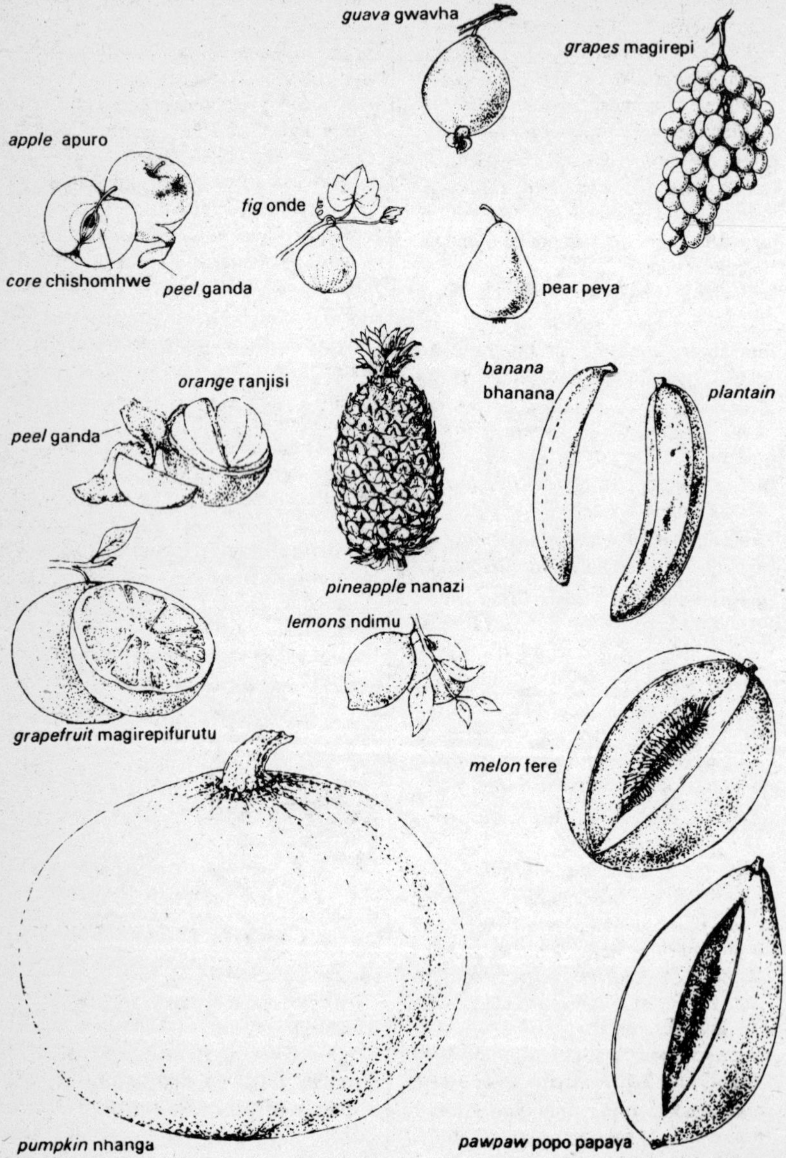
guava gwavha
grapes magirepi
apple apuro
fig onde
core chishomhwe
peel ganda
pear peya
banana
bhanana
plantain
orange ranjisi
peel ganda
pineapple nanazi
lemons ndimu
grapefruit magirepifurutu
melon fere
pumpkin nhanga
pawpaw popo papaya

francolin *sp of game bird, "pheasant"* n hwari 9 (LH); gwari 5 K (LH); gwarimutondo 5 (LHHLL); hwerekwere 9 (LLLL); *Swainson's f.* n gorwe 5 (LH); horwe 9 (LH) R185; *Shelley's f.* n renge 5, marenge 6 (HH) R177. *cf illustration p. 64*

frayed *be ragged, worn out* adj & vb -sakara i (LLL) (stative vb); Ane hembe yaka**sakara**. (*He has a ragged shirt.*)

free *untie, loosen* vb -sunungura t (HHHL); -sungunura t (HHHL) cf -sunga (HH)

free *be at liberty* vb -sununguka i (stative vb); Nhasi ndaka**sununguka**. (*Today I am free.*); *freedom* n rusununguko 11 (LHHHL) cf -sununguka (HHHL)

free of charge *for nothing* adv mahara (LHL); pachena (LLL)

freeze *make cold* vb -tonhodza t (HHH) -tonhora (HHL); *f. solid* vb -gwamba i (HH)

frequently *habitually* adv -garo- infix vb

Friday *fifth day of the week after Sunday* n Chishanu 7 (LHL)

friend *someone whose company one enjoys* n shamwari 9 (HLH); *friendship* n ushamwari 14 (LHHH) cf shamwari (HHH)

friendly *be on good terms* vb -shamwaridzana i (HHHLL)

frighten *alarm* vb -tyisa t (HH); -vhundutsa t (LLL); *be frightened, alarmed* vb -vhunduka i (LLL); *frightening, be fierce* vb -tyisa i & t (HH) cf -tya (H)

frog *tail-less, four-legged swimming reptile* n dafi 5, matafi 6 (HL); datya 5, matatya 6 (HL); chura 7 (LH)

from *come f., derive f.* vb -bva (L) **Simba rokutonga rinobva kuna Mwari.** (*Authority to judge comes from God.*)

from . . . to . . . prep kubvira . . . kusvikira . . . (LLL LLL)

front *in f.* adv mberi 17 (LH)

frost n chando 7 (LL)

froth *foam* n furo 5, mafuro 6 (HH)

frown *draw the eyebrows together causing lines on the forehead* vb -finyama i (HHH)

froze *cf freeze*

fruit *edible product of tree or plant containing seeds* n muchero 3 (LLL)

fruits of effort n zvibereko 8 (LLLL) (usu plur); *outcome, result* n chimuko 7 (LLL); *wage, reward* n mubayiro 3 (LLLL)

fry *cook in boiling fat* vb -kanga t (HH)

frying pan n pani 9 (HL) cf Eng.

fulfil *complete a task, duty, promise, etc.* vb -zadzikisa t (HHHL)

full *be filled to capacity* adj & vb -zara (HH); Bhagedhi ri**zere** nemvura. (*The bucket is full of water.*)

full moon *complete m.* n jenaguru 5 (LLHH)

full stop *punctuation mark* n furustopi 9 (HLLL) cf Eng.

fully *entirely* adv chaizvo (LHL)

funeral *burial of a dead person* n rufu 11 (LH); mariro 6 (LLL)

funny *be comical, cause laughter, be amusing* vb -tsetsa i (LL)

fur *body hair* n mvere 9 (LL)

furious *be wild and angry* vb -ipa i (HH)

furniture n fanicha 9 (HLL) cf Eng.

furrow *man-made channel for water* n mugero 3 (LHL); *furrow left by a plough* n muforo 3 (LHL); foro 9 (HL); cf Eng.

further *ahead* adv pamberi 16 (LLH)

furthermore *and in addition* conj zvakare (LHL)

fury *anger* n hasha 10 (HH) (plur)

G

galago gwee

gaboon viper *sp of adder* n bvumbi 9 (LH)

gain *obtain, find* vb -wana i & t (LL)

gait *manner of walking* n mufambiro 3 (LHHH) cf -famba (HH)

galago *There are 2 sp in Rhodesia: bush-baby, night-ape cf illustration*

gale *very strong wind* n dutu 5 (LL); bupu 5 M (LL)

gall-bladder *bile* n nduru 9 (HH)

gallop *run at fastest pace of a horse* vb -rimbinyuka i (HHHL)

gambol *frolic, play* vb -tamba i (HH)

game (*recreation*), *contest played* n mutambo 3 (LHH) cf -tamba (HH)

game animal *wild a. of any kind* n mhuka 9 (LH)

game bird

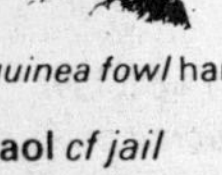

guinea fowl hanga

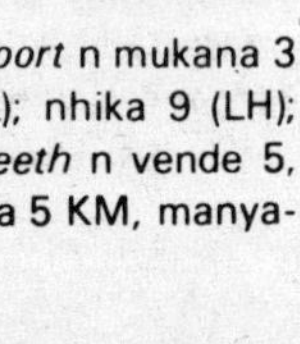

francolin horwe

gaol *cf jail*

gap *in the hills, pass, poort* n mukana 3 (LLL); mupata 3 (LLL); nhika 9 (LH); *gap left by missing teeth* n vende 5, mavende 6 (LL); nyada 5 KM, manyada 6 (LL)

gape *open the mouth* adj & vb -shama i (HH) (stative vb); Ari kutarisa akashama. (*He is looking with mouth agape.*)

garden *agricultural land* n munda 3 (LL); *vegetable g.* n bindu 5, mabindu 6 (LH); gadheni 5, magadheni 6 (HLL) cf Eng.; *rice g.* n deka 5, mateka 6 (LL); doro 5, matoro 6 (LH); *strip of cultivated land* n ndima 9 (LH)

gardenia *erect deciduous shrub or small tree* n mutara 3 (LLL)

garment *article of clothing* n hanzu 9 (LH)

gasp *pant* vb -takwaira i (HHHL); -femedzeka i (LLLL); -femereka i (LLLL)

gate *goalpost* n gedhe 5, magedhe 6 (HL) cf Eng.

gather *round up* vb -kokorodza t (HHHL); *collect together* vb -unganidza t (HHHL) cf -ungana (HHH)

gather together *assemble* adj & vb -ungana i (HHH) (stative vb); Vanhu vakaungana nhasi. (*The people are assembled today.*); *gather together, collect, assemble into a container (e.g. scattered things)* vb -dyorera t (LLL); -horera (LLL)

gathering of people *crowd* n gungano 5, makungano 6 (HHL); *g. of Christians, Church* n sangano 5 (LLL)

gave *cf give*

gaze *look fixedly, stare* vb -dzvokora i & t (LLL)

gecko *small lizard which likes to inhabit human dwellings. There are many sp of gecko between 75 mm to 200 mm in length.* n chifurira 7 (LHHL)

generally *usually* adv -garo- infix vb

generation *people of the same age* n chizvarwa 7 (LHL)

generosity *kindness* n mwoyochena 3 (LLHL)

generous *be kind* vb -va nomutsa i (HLH)

generous person *kind p.* n munhu ano mutsa 1

genet *small, spotted carnivore. There are 2 sp in Rhodesia: large-spotted g.* n nyongo 9 (LL); *rusty, small-spotted g.* n simba 9 (LL); tsimba 9 (LL)

large-spotted nyongo

small-spotted tsimba

gentle *be good natured* adj & vb -pfava i (LL)

gentleness *manner of being good-natured* n rupfave 11 (LLH) cf -pfava (LL)

gently *softly* adv zvinyoronyoro (LHHLH)

genuflect *kneel* vb -pfugama i (HHH); -fugama i K (HHH)

genuine *good* adj *cf pronouns p. 196*

germ *micro-organism* n jemusi 5 (HLL) *cf Eng.;* utachiona 14 (LLHLL)

German *coming from Germany* adj e.g. banga rechiJerimani (*a German knife)*

germinate *sprout* vb -mera i (LL)

game animals

hippo mvuu

rhino (white) fura

rhino (black) nhema

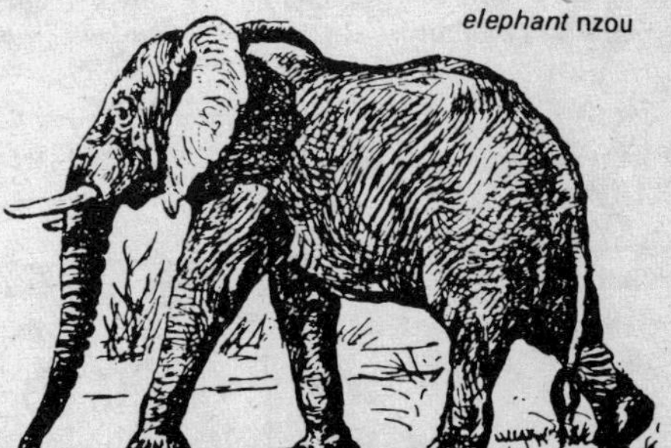

elephant nzou

buffalo nyati

get *take, accept, fetch* vb -tora t (HH); *g. away, run away, escape* vb -tiza i & t (HH); -punyuka i & t (LLL); *g. better, g. well* vb -pona i (HH); -va nani (HL); *g. down, descend, disembark e.g. from a bus* vb -buruka i (LLL); -dzika i (LL); -jitika i (LLL); *g. hurt* vb -kuvara i (HHH); *g. in, enter* vb -pinda i & t (LL);

g. well vb -pona i (HH); -va nani (HL); -naya (LL); *g. down, descend, disembark e.g. from a bus* vb - buruka i (LLL); -dzika i (LL); -jitika i (LLL); *g. hurt* vb - kuvara i (HHH); *g. in, enter* vb -pinda i & t (LL); *g lost, go astray* vb -rasika i (HHH); *g. on, agree mutually* vb -wirirana i (LLLL); *g. some fresh air* vb -furwa nemhepo i (HL HLL); *g. stuck in mud* vb -nyura i (HH); *g. to the side, move aside* vb -peuka i (HHH); *g. up, rise* vb -simuka i (HHL); -muka i (LL); *g. worse (sickness)* vb -nyanya kurwara (LL LHH); — PT & PP *got*

ghost *visible spirit of the dead* n chipoko 7 (LHL) cf Afrik.

giddiness n dzungu 5 (HL); *giddy, be dizzy* vb -batwa nedzungu i; -ita dzungu i

gift *something given without desire of return* n chipo 7 (LH) cf -pa (H)

giggle *silly laugh (as schoolgirls do)* vb -kekedza i MZ (HHH); -pfipfidza i (HHH)

gimlet *tool for making a small hole in wood* n chibooreso 7 (LLLLL) cf -boora (LLL); muururo 3 (LHHL) cf -urura (HHH)

giraffe *the tallest of our animals. It grows up to 18 ft high (5,4 m)* n twiza 9 (LL); swiza 9 (LL); furiramudenga 9 MZ (LLLLHL)

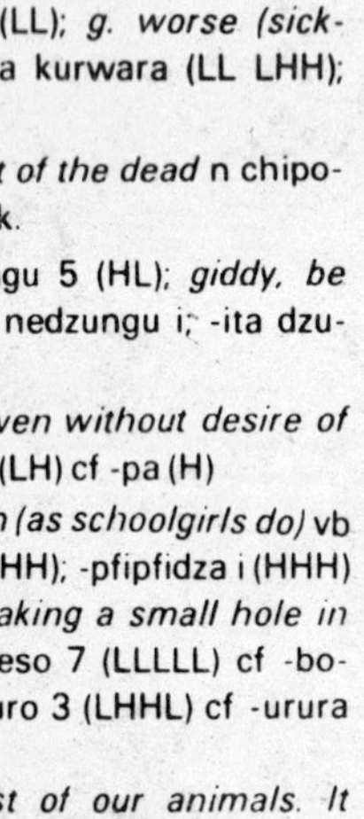

girdle *waist band* n bhandi 5, mabhandi 6 (HL) cf Eng.

girl *young g. (until age of 15), g. friend* n musikana (LHLH); *attractive g.* n tsvarakadenga 9 (LLLHL); chibhamu 7 (LLL); chiwawa 7 (LLL); *full-grown unmarried g.* n mhandara 9 (LLL); *girlhood* n usikana 14 (LHLH) cf musikana (LHLH)

give *grant, g. away* vb -pa t (H); *g. advice, advise* vb -pa zano t (H HL); -rayira i & t (LLL); *g. an account* vb -rondedzera t (LLLL); - zvidavirira *g. an explanation, explain* vb -tsanangura t (LLLL); *g.back, return* vb -dzorera t (LLL); -dzokesa t (LLL); -dzosa t (LL); *g. birth to, bear a child* vb -sununguka i & t (HHHL); -pona i & t (HH); *be on the pont of giving birth* vb -kurirwa i (HHH); *g. birth to (animals)* vb -bereka i & t (LLL); *g. blame, accuse* vb -pa mhosva t (HL);*g. details, describe fully* vb -donongora t (HHHL); *g. false testimony, tell lies about* vb -nyepera t (LLL); *g. grudgingly* vb -konora t (HHH); *give in, g. up* vb -regera i & t (LLL); *g. a lift to, carry* vb -takura t (LLL); g. *permission to, allow* vb -bvumira t (LLL); *g. pleasure* vb -fadza i & t (HH) cf -fara (HH); *g. up, surrender* vb -tera i (LL); -sarenda i (LLL)cf Eng.; *g. up hope, despair* vb -rasa mwoyo i (HHHL); PT *gave,* PP *given*

gizzard *edible second stomach of a chicken* n chihururu 7 (LLLL); chikanganwahama 7 (LHHLHH)

glad *be happy* vb -fara i (HH); *gladden, make happy* vb -fadza i & t (HH)

gladiolus *parrot-beak flower* n hwenyanguruve 9 (HLLLL) B.Bk. 1,56

gladly *happily* adv nokufara (HLHH)

gladness *joy, happiness* n mufaro 3 (LHH); rufaro 11 (LHH) cf -fara (HH)

glandular swelling n mwambabvu 3 (LHH)

glare at *stare at* vb -dzvokora t (LLL)

glass *hard, clear substance that one can see through, drinking vessel of*

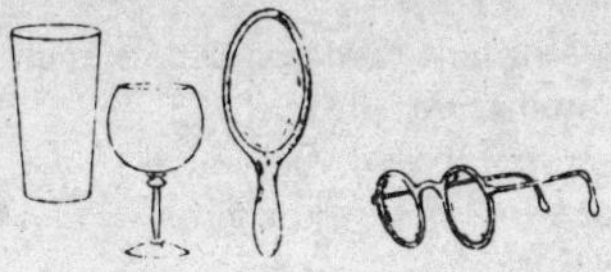

this material n girazi 5, magirazi 6 (LHL) cf Eng.

gleam *shine brightly* vb -taima i (LLL); -n'aima i MZ (LLL)

glee *joy, happiness* n rufaro 11 (LHH); kufara 15 (LHH)

glitter *glisten, dazzle* vb -penya i (LL); -bwinya i (LL); -taima i (LLL); -vaima i (LLL)

glorify *praise* vb -rumbidza t (LLL); -tunhidza t (LLL)

glory *renoun* n mbiri 9 (HH); mukurumbira 3 (LHHLH)

glow red *as iron in fire* vb -tsvuka i (LL)

glow-worm *worm that glows by night* n chitaitai 7 (LLLLL); chin'ain'ai 7 (LLLLL); *same word for fire-fly*

glue *sticky substance* n guruu 5 (LHL) cf Eng.

glutton *for meat* n muruti 1 (LLL) cf -ruta (LL)

gluttony *greed for food* n nhafu 9 Z (LH); mbayo 9 MZ (LL)

gnash teeth *grind the t. together* vb -gedegedza t (HHHL); -gedegedesa t (HHHLL); -geda-geda (HHHL)

gnat *midge, tiny fly* n unyunyu 14 (LLH)

gnaw *continue biting (as mice do)* vb -tetena t (HHH); -n'en'ena t (HHH); -n'un'una t (HHH)

go *g. away, depart, leave* vb -enda i (LL); -inda i K (LL); *g. about for pleasure, g. for a quick walk* vb -bvakacha i (HHH); *g. across a stream, ford* vb -yambuka i & t (LLL); -bira t (HH); *g. across a street* vb -dimura mugwagwa t (HHHHLL); *g. ahead, proceed, g. in front* vb -fanoenda i (LLLL); -tungamira i (HHHL); *g. ahead, make progress* vb -enderera mberi i (LLLL LH); -budirira (HHHL); *g. around, walk around -poterera i & t (HHHL); cf -pota (HH);* -tenderera i & t (HHHL); *g. aside, move away* vb -suduruka i (LLLL); -tsauka i (HHH); *g. astray, get lost* vb -rasika i (HHH); *g. away, come from* vb -bva i (L) Ibva ! (*Go away!*); *g. away for good* vb -rova i (LL); *g. bad, rot* vb -ora i (LL); *g. back, return (to place of departure* vb -dzokera i (LLL); *g. by, pass through* vb -pfuura na- i (HHH); *g. down, descend, alight* vb -dzika i (LL); -buruka (LLL); *g. down, subside (river or swelling)* vb -serera i (LLL); *g. into investigate* vb -ongorora t (HHHL); *g. faster, speed up, run hard* vb -mhanyisa i & t (HHL) cf -mhanya (HH); *g. walking backwards* vb -dududza i (HHH); *g. on hands and knees, crawl* vb -kambaira i (HHHL); *g. on, continue* vb -ramba + Partic (LL); *g. beyond a point* vb -pfuurira i (HHHL); *g. in, enter* vb -pinda i (LL); *g. near, move near, draw near* vb -swedera i (LLL); *g. out (fire or light)* vb -dzima i (HH); *g. round* vb -tenderera i & t (HHHL); -poterera i & t (HHHL) cf -pota (HH); *g. straight (morally)* vb -rurama i (LLL); *g. to meet, g. and meet* vb -chingura t (HHH); *g. too far (in joking or playing)* vb -pindiridza i (LLLL); *g. up, climb* vb -kwira i & t (HH); *g. with a person, accompany* vb -perekedza t (HHHL); PT *went,* PP *gone*

go-away bird *grey lourie, turaco* n kuwe 9 MZ (HL); pfunye 9 (LL) *cf illustration 94*

go-between *in marriage negotiations* n munyayi 1 (LLL); dombo 1a (LH); sadombo 1a (HLH)

goal-post *gate* n gedhi 5 (HL) cf Eng.

goat *small, horned, domestic animal* n mbudzi 9 (HH); *see p. 45; he g.* n gotora 5, magotora 6 (HHL); *she g.* n nhunzvi 9 (LL)

God *creator, Supreme Spirit* n Mwari 1a (LH) cf *spirit*

goitre *usu swollen gland in the neck, enlargement of the thyroid gland in the throat* n humbu 9 (LL); sokorodzi 5 M (HHHL); dukumuriro 5 (HHHLL)

gold *precious metal* n ndarama 9 (LLH) cf Arabic; goridhe 5 (HLL) cf Eng.

gone *cf go*

good *be nice* adj & vb -naka i (stative vb); Ticha wedu aka**naka**. (*Our teacher is good.*); *g. looks, beauty* n runako 11 (LLL) cf -naka (LL); *g. luck* n rombo rakanaka 5; mhanza yakanaka 9; *be on good terms* vb -fambidzana i (HHHL)

goodbye *say g., take leave* vb -oneka i & t (LLL)

good-looking *be handsome* adj & vb -naka i (stative vb)

good-mannered *be well-behaved* vb -va netsika i (LHL); -va nounhu i (LHL)

goodness *(physical)* n kunaka 15 (LLL); runako 11 (LLL) cf -naka (LL)

goods *possessions, love-token given by a girl* n nhumbi 9 (LH)

goose *large sp of duck (general name)* n hanzi 9 (LH) cf Afrik.

gore *damage with horns* vb -tunga i & t (HH); -baya i & t (LL)

Gospel *the life and teaching of Jesus Christ as recorded in the New Testament* n vhangeri 5 (LHL) cf Latin

gossip n guhwa 5, makuhwa 6 (LL); *g. uncharitably, idle talk* vb -ita makuhwa i

got *cf get*

gourd *calabash* n dende 5, matende 6 (HH)

govern *administer, judge, rule* vb -tonga i & t (HH)

government *ruling body of a country* n hurumende 9 (LLHH)

grab *snatch* vb -bvuta i & t (LL)

grace *(theological)* n girasiya 5 (LHLL) cf Eng.

grade a road vb -kura mugwagwa t (LL LLL)

gradually *little by little* adv kashoma nakashoma (LLL LHLL)

grain of maize n tsanga 9 (HH); shanga 9 K (HH); *grain of sand* n tsanza 9 (LL)

grammar *structure of a language* n girama 5 (LHL) cf Eng.

granadilla *a fruit produced by a climbing plant* n girandera 5, magirandera 6 (LHLL) cf Eng.

granary *storage house for grain* n hozi 9 (HL); *granary compartment of a hut* n dura 5, matura 6 (HL)

grandchild *nephew, niece* n muzukuru 1 (LHHL)

grandfather *father of my parent* n sekuru 1a (LHL) *the same term is used for maternal uncle or any of his male line.*

grandmother *mother of my parent* n ambuya 2b Z (LHL); mbuya 1a KM (HL) *Note: Terms for grandmother:* ambuya (LHL) *and mother-in-law:* ambuya (HLL) *differ only tonally.*

grant *give* vb -pa i & t (H)

grape *wild g. (edible)* n tsambatsi (LLH); *fruits from which wine is made* n magirepi 6 (LLHL)

grapple *wrestle* vb -ita tsimba i (LL LH)

grasp *hold* vb -bata i & t (HH); *grab, snatch* vb -bvuta i & t (LL)

grass *common plants whose leaves provide the main food of cattle, sheep, goats, etc.* n uswa 14 (LH); *blade of g.* n ruswa 11 (LH); *rapoko g.*

n mombe 9 (LL) B.Bk. 1,97; *Natal red top g.* n bhurakwacha 5 (LHLL) B.Bk. 1,98; *spear g.* n tsine 9 (LH) B.Bk. 1,100; *couch g.* n tsangadzi 9 (HHL) B.Bk. 1,103; *Bindura bamboo* n muchenjere 3 (LLLH) B.Bk. 1,04; *water g., yellow nut-g.* n pfende (HH); *blue g.* n vatasoma 5 (HHLH); *bottle brush g.* n shavahuru 9 (HLHH); *bristle g.* n mutsvairo 3 (LHHL); *autumn g.* n chiraramhene 7 (LHHLH); *brachiaria; black-footed, densely-tufted perennial g.* n chidyashana 7 (LHLH)

grass warbler *small bird which inhabits grass-land* n dhimba 5, madhimba 6 (LH)

grasshopper *insect with long hind-legs, capable of flight* n hwiza 9 Z (HL); chitototo 7 (LHHH); chitota 7 (LHL)

grate *rub into small bits, usu against a rough surface or grater* vb -para t (HH); -kwesha t (HH)

grateful *be thankful* vb -tenda i (LL); *gratitude, desire to thank* n rutendo 11 (LLL) cf -tenda (LL)

gratis *freely, for nothing* adv pachena 16 (LLL)

grave *resting place of dead* n guva 5 MZ, makuva 6 (HH); rinda 5 KM, marinda 6 (LH); hwiro 5 MZ, mahwiro 6 (LL); *graveyard, burial ground* n makuva 6 (LHH)

gravy *juice which comes from meat while cooking* n muto 3 (LL); girevhi 5 (LHL) cf Eng.

graze *touch lightly* vb -nzvenzvera t (HHH); *g. the surface of the skin* vb -svuura t (LLL)

graze *and browse* vb -fura i & t (LL); *pasture cattle* vb -fudza mombe t (LL LL); *grazing area, pasture* n mafuro 6 (LLL); ufuro 14 (LLL) cf -fura (LL)

grease *fat, oil* n mafuta 6 (LHH); girisi 5 (LHL) cf Eng.; *greasy* adj maoko ana mafuta (*greasy hands*) *i.e. hands which have grease*

great *large, big* adj -kuru (LHH), guru 5, huru 9; *greatness, eminence* n ukuru 14 (LHH)

greatly *very much* adv zvikuru (LHH)

greed for food n makaro 6 Z (LHH); ukari 14 (LHH) cf -kara (HH); *greediness, desiring more than is right* n nhafu 9 (LH); *greedy* adj pwere ine nhafu (*greedy child*)

greed for wealth *covetousness* n ruchiva 11 (LHH)

green *unripe, uncooked (vegetable or fruit)* adj -mbishi (HH)

green *be luxuriant g.* adj & vb -svibirira i (LLLL) (stative vb)

greet *say words of or make signs of greeting* vb -kwazisa t (HHH); -mhoresa t (HHH); -mhorosa t (HHH); *g. one another* vb -kwazisana i (HLHL) cf -kwazisa (HHH); *greeting, sign or word of salutation* n kwaziso 9 (HHL) cf -kwazisa (HHH)

grew *cf grow*

grey *colour which is a blend of black and white* adj -girei (LHL)

grievance *ground of complaint* n chigumbu 7 (LLH)

grind *crush into powder, usu grain into flour* vb -kuya i & t (LL); *grinding machine for grain, mill* n chigayo 7 (LHH) cf -gaya (HH); *grind-stone, large, lower g.* n guyo 5, makuyo (LL) cf -kuya (LL); *smaller, upper g.* n huyo 9 (LL) cf -kuya (LL); *grind-stone for sharpening* n chirodzero 7 (LLLL) cf -rodza (LL); noro 9 Z (LH)

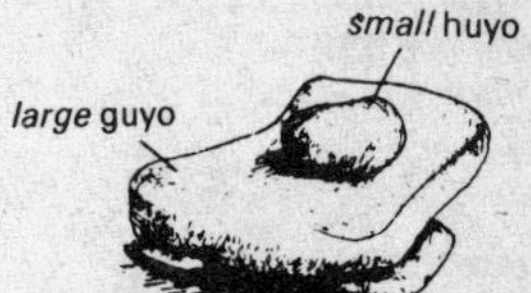

grip *grasp, hold* vb -bata i & t (HH); *close hand on* vb -pfumbata (HHH)

gristle *tough tissue in coarse meat* n runda 5, marunda 6 (LH); *soft, elastic substance in animal bodies* n mashwaushwau 6 (LLLLL)

groan *make deep sounds of despair or pain* vb -gomera i (HHH)

grocery store *grocer* n girosa 5, magirosa 6 (LHL) cf Eng.

groom *trim fabrics or grass* vb -kuruza t (LLL)

ground *cf grind*

ground *on the ground* adv pasi 16 (LH)

groundnut *peanut, monkey nut* n nzungu 9 (LH); *peanut butter* n dovi (LH); *groundnut shell* n gekenya 5, makekenya 6 (HHL); *uproot g.* vb -dzura t (LL); *shell g.* vb -menya t (HH); *roast g.* vb -kanga t (HH);*grind g. into a paste for peanut butter* vb -kuya t (LL)

group *flock, drove* n boka 5, mapoka 6 (LL)

grow *get bigger, or older* vb -kura i (HH); *g. old, age* vb -chembera i (LLL); -kwegura i (HHH) — PT *grew;* PP *grown*

growl *make a threatening sound like a dog* vb -hon'a i (LL); -nguruma i (LLL)

growl/roar *of a lion* n kudzvova kweshumba 15 (LL HLL); *g. of a leopard* n kuomba kwengwe 15 (LLL LH)

grown-up *adult* n mukuru 1 (LHH); *g.u. girl* n mhandara 9 (LLL); *g.-u. boy* n jaya 5, majaya 6 (LH)

grub *maggot, larva, caterpillar* n honye 9 (LL); gonye 5, makonye 6 (LL)

grudge *feeling of ill-will against someone* n daka 5 (LL); chigumbu 7 (LLH)

grumble *complain* vb -popota (HHH); -nyunyuta i (HHH)

grunt *make a low, rough sound like that of a pig* vb -omba i (LL)

grysbok *Sharpe's; sp of small antelope, weight about 9 Kg.* n deke 5 K (LL); mhiti 9 Z (LL); timba 9, nhimba 9 Z(LL) *cf illustration p. 89*

guard *keep g.* vb -chengeta t (LLL); *person who guards and protects* n muchengeti 1 (LLLL); *g. against, use care to prevent* vb -dzivirira t (LLLL)

guava *sp of fruit* n gwavha 5 (HL) cf Eng.

guess *foretell* vb -fembera i & t (HHH)

guest *lit a visitor* n mweni 1 (LL); muenzi 1 (LLH)

guide *lead* vb -tungamira i & t (HHHL)

guild *association* n nzanga 9 (LL)

guile *flattery* n muzvambarara 3 (LLLLL)

guilt *culpability of a crime* n mhosva 9 (HL); mhaka 9 (LH); *guilty, be culpable* vb -va nemhosva i (HLL)

guinea fowl *helmeted g.* n hanga 9 (HH); *crested g.* n hangatoni 9 Z (HHLH) *cf illustration p. 64*

guitar *musical instrument with strings* n gitare 5, magitare 6 (LHL) cf Eng.

gully *channel formed by rain water* n goronga 5, makoronga 6 (LHL)

gums *flesh around the teeth* n matadza 6 (LLL); *toothless g.* n manyada 6 (LLL)

gun *firearm that fires bullets* n pfuti 9 (LL); *machine g.* n chigwagwagwa 7 (LLLL); *gunpowder, explosive powder* n unga 14 (LL); *rifle bullet, cartridge* n bara 5, mabara 6 (HL)

gusty *be windy* vb Kunze kune mhepo. (*It is gusty out-of-doors.*)

guts *intestines, bowels* n ura 14 (LL); matumbu 6 (LLL)

gutter *channel to carry rain water* n gata 5 (HL) cf Eng.

H

hare tsuro

habit *way of acting* n tsika 9 (LL); muitiro 3 (LLHH)

hack-saw *saw usu for cutting metal* n hwandisi 9 (LLL)

had vb *past tense of vb to have:* -na; Ndakanga ndiino mukadzi. (*I used to have a wife.*); *Past Perfect Tense.* Mwana akanga apiwa jekiseni. (*The child had been given an injection.*)

hail *frozen raindrops* n chimvuramabwe 7 (LHHHL); chimvuramahwe 7 (LHHHL)

hair *of the head* n vhudzi 5 (LL) (sing only); *h. on human body or animals* n mvere 9 (LL); *tuft of h. in front* n zhumu 5, mazhumu 6 (LH)

hair *cut h.* vb -gera i & t (LL); *dress hair, comb h.* vb -petura t (HHHL); -kama t (HH) cf Eng.

half *a whole divided into two equal parts* n chimedu 7 (LHL); hafu 9 (HL) cf Eng.

half-full *short measure* n gasva 5, makasva 6 (LH)

half-wit *fool* n rema 5, marema 6 (HH); fuza 5, mafuza 6 (LL)

hall *large, long, open room* n horo 9 (HL) cf Afrik.

halt *stop moving, stand still* vb -mira i (HH); *bring to a halt, cause to stand still* vb -misa t (HH) cf -mira (HH)

halve *make the parts equal* vb -enzanisa t (LLLL) cf -enzana (LLL); *divide into halves* vb -dimura napakati t (HHH LHLH)

hammer *tool for beating in nails* n nyundo 9 (LL)

hammerhead *hamerkop, sp of semi-water bird* n kondo 9 (HH) R 72

hamstring *muscle behind the knee* n datira 5 (LLH); hadyambu 9 (LLH)

hand *right hand* n rudyi 11 (LH); *left hand* n ruboshwe 11 (LLH); runzere 11 M (LLH); *finger* n munwe 3 (LL); *palm* n chanza 7 (LL); *wrist* n chipfundo choruoko 7 (LHH HLHH)

handbag *bag used by ladies for carrying small things* n hendibhegi 9 (HLLL) cf Eng.

hand-cuffs *pair of metal rings joined by a chain, placed on a prisoner's wrists* n kechemu 9 (HHL); simbi 9 (LH)

handkerchief *square piece of cotton cloth used for wiping the nose* n hengechefu 9 (HLLL) cf Eng.

handle *part of a tool by which it is held* n mubato 3 (LHH) cf -bata (HH); *handle of bucket, cup, etc.* n mupakato 3 (LHHL); *handle of a hoe* n mupinyi 3 (LHH); mupini 3 MZ (LHH)

handle *hold, grasp* vb -bata i & t (HH)

handsome *be good-looking* adj & vb -naka i (LL) (stative vb); Mukomana wake akanaka. (*Her boyfriend is handsome.*)

hang *execute a person by hanging* vb -sunga t (HH)—PT & PP *hanged, hung*

hang up *stack, put objects one on top of another* vb -turika t (HHH)

hang down *droop d.* vb -rembera i (LLL); -rezuka i (HHH); *h. down* vb -rembedza t (LLL) cf -rembera (LLL)

hang clothes out *to dry, put out to dry* vb -yanika t (HHH)

hangover *ill-feeling after drinking beer* n bhabharasi 5 (LHLL)

happen *take place* vb -itika i (LLL)

happy *be pleased* vb -fara i (HH); *h. with, be delighted with* vb -farira t (HHH) cf -fara (HH); *happiness, joy* n rufaro 11 (LHH); mufaro 3 (LHH) cf -fara (HH)

harass *worry repeatedly, trouble* vb -netsa t (LL)

hard *be difficult* adj & vb -oma i (HH); -rema i (LL) (stative vbs); Zvaka**rema** kuramba baba. (*It is difficult to refuse father.*) *harder* adj -oma kupinda i; Ivhu iri raka**oma kupinda** iro. (*This soil is harder than that.*) *hardest* adj; Ivhu iri rakaoma kupinda ose. (*This is the hardest soil of all.*); *h. to touch* adj -kukutu (HHH), gukutu 5, hukutu 9; *hardness, quality of being hard* n ukukutu 14 (LHHH); *be dry* adj & vb -oma i (HH) (stative vb); Huni iyi yaka**oma**. (*This firewood is dry.*) Pasi paka**oma**. (*The ground is dry.*)

hare *animal that gnaws, rodent* n tsuro 9 (LL); shuro 9 K (LL); *young of h.* n nhohwa 9 (LH); *red rock -h.* n guhwe 5, maguhwe 6 (LL) *cf illustration p. 71*

harm *hurt, injure* vb -kuvadza t (HHH)

harrow *break up and smooth out ploughed land with a h.* vb -hara t (HH) cf Eng.

harrow *machine to break up the ground after ploughing* n hara 9 (HL) cf Eng.

hartebeest *Lichtenstein's weight 140 Kg.* n hwiranondo 9 Z (HHHL); nondoshava 9 (LLHH) *cf illustration p. 88*

harvest *reap crop* vb -kohwa t (LL)

hasten *hurry* vb -kurumidza i (HHHL); -chimbidza i (HHH); *h. movement, nudge, prod* vb -dyunga t (HH)

hasty action *devoid of caution* n chivhurumukira 7 (LHHHLL)

hat *head-wear* n nguwani 9 (LHH); heti 9 (HL) cf Eng.

hatch *emerge from the egg* vb -chechenya i (HHH); -sosodza i M (HHH)

hatchet *chopper, axe* n dimuro 5, matimuro 6 (HHL); bheura 5, mabheura (HHL)

hate *have violent dislike for* vb -venga t (HH); *hatred, violent dislike* n ruvengo 11 (LHH); daka 5 (LL)

haughty *be arrogant* vb -virima i (HHH)

have *be with* vb -va na-; *Present:* Ndino mukadzi. (*I have a wife.*); *Future:* Ndichava nomukadzi. (*I shall have a wife.*); *Past:* Ndaiva nomukadzi. (*I had a wife.*); *h. mercy on* vb -nzwira tsitsi t (HH LH); -itira tsiye nyoro; PT & PP *had*

hawk *bird of prey (general term); small h. sparrow hawk* n kakodzi 12 (LHL); gayisa 9 M (LHL); rusvosvera 11 (LLLL); rukodzi 11 (LHL); ruvangu 11 (LLH); nyamarimbira 9 M (LLHHL); *eagle and larger hs.* n gondo 5, makondo 6 (LH) *cf illustration 49.*

hawker *person who moves about looking for buyers of his wares* n mushambadzi 1 (LHHL) cf -shambadza (HHH)

hay *cut grass for animal food* n hei 9 (HL) cf Eng.

head *part of body containing mouth, brain, eyes, etc.* n musoro 3 (LHH); *bald h.* n mhanza 9 (HH); *ear* n nzeve 9 (LH); zheve 9 K (LH); *hair on the h.* n vhudzi 5 (LL); *back of the h.* n gotsi 5, makotsi 6 (LL); *forehead* n huma 9 (LL); mhanza 9 (HH)

head-ache *have a h.* vb -temwa nomusoro (HH HLHH); -va nomusoro i (HLHH); Ndino musoro. (*I have a h.a.*)

head in a direction *aim for* vb -nanga i (HH)

head-over-heels *turn h.* vb -ita mhidigari i (HHLH)

heading *title* n musoro 3 (LHH)

headkerchief *doek* n dhuku 5, madhuku 6 (HL) cf Afrik.

headman of a village n sabhuku 1a (HLL)

heal *recover from ill health, deliver a child* vb -pona i (HH); *return to normal health* vb -pora i (HH); *heal, give medicine to h.* vb -rapa i & t (LL)

healthy *be fit* vb -gwinya i (HH); -simba i (LL)

healthy person n mutano 1 (LHH)

heap *mass of material piled up like a small hill* n murwi 3 MZ (LL)

hear *understand, feel* vb -nzwa i & t (H) — PT & PP *heard*

heart *organ that pumps the blood* n mwoyo 3 (LL)

heartburn *a burning feeling of the stomach, indigestion* n chirungurira 7 (LLLLL)

hearth *fireplace* n choto 7 (LH); *hearthstone* n pfihwa 5, mapfihwa 6 (HL)

heartwood tree n muremberembe 3 (LHHLH)

heat to boiling point vb -virisa t (LLL); *heat up, warm up* vb -dziyisa t (HHH)

heathen *pagan* n muhedheni 1 (LHLL) cf Eng.

heave a sigh *take a deep breath that can be heard (indicating tiredness etc.)* vb -tura mafemo (HH HLL)

heaven *roof, ceiling, sky* n denga 5, matenga 6 (HL)

heavy *be weighty* vb -rema i (LL); *heavier* adj -rema kupinda (LL LLL); Jongwe rangu rinorema kupinda rako. (*My rooster is heavier than yours.*) *heaviest* adj Jongwe iri rinorema kupinda ose. (*This rooster is the heaviest.*)

hedge *fence of branches, poles, etc.* n rutsito 11 (LHH); rusvingo 11 (LLL)

hedgehog *small carnivorous and insect-eating creature covered with sharp spines* n tyoni 9 (LL); shoni 9 M (LL); sandawana 9 (LHLH) *cf illustration p. 79*

heel *rear joint of foot* n chitsitsinho 7 (LHHL)

heifer *female calf* n tsiru 5, matsiru 6 (HL)

height *distance from top to bottom* n urefu 14 (LLH)

heir *person who inherits when the owner dies* n mugari wenhaka 1

held *cf hold*

hell *everlasting fire* n moto usingaperi 3 (LH LHLHL)

help *assist* vb -batsira t (HHH); -yamura t (LLL)

help *assistance* n rubatsiro 11 (LHHL); ruyamuro 11 (LLLL) cf -yamura (LLL); *advantage, profit* n chimuko 7 Z (LLL) cf -muka (LL); yamuro 9 (LLL) cf -yamura; *helper, assistant* n mubatsiri 1 (LHHL) cf -batsira (HHH); muyamuri 1 (LLLL) cf -yamura

helpless person *half-wit* n fuza 5, mafuza 6 (LL)

hem *to fold over and sew layers together* vb -pendera t (LLL); *edge of clothing* n mupendero 3 (LLLL) cf -pendera (LLL); *h. in, surround* vb -komba t (HH); -komberedza t (HHHL)

hemp *dagga, marijuana* n mbanje 9 (LH); *decan hemp, flower-bearing common weed* n sosoori 5, masosoori 6 (HHLH)

hen *female fowl* n nhunzvi 9 (LL); *h. house, fowl house* n chitata 7 (LLL); chizumbu 7 (LLL)

hence *therefore* conj kudaro (LHL); naizvozvo (LHLH)

herald snake *red-lipped sp of back-fanged snake* n chiatsi 7 (LLL)

herb *natural remedy* n muti 3 (LH)

herbalist *seller and healer of medicinal herbs* n murapi 1 (LLL)

herd *look after grazing cattle* vb -fudza t (LL); *herdsman, person who herds cattle* n mufudzi 1 (LLL) cf -fudza

herd of cattle *or of game* n danga 5, matanga 6 (LH)

here is *locative demonstrative copulative cf p. 192*

heron *long-legged water-bird that*

feeds on frogs and fish n shorechena 9 (LLLL); nyarupani 9 (LLHL)

hesitate *delay before acting* vb -zengurira i (LLLL)

hiccup vb -dikura i (HHH)

hiccups *frequent noisy stopping of breath* n munhikwi 3 (LHL)

hid *cf hide*

hidden *be concealed* vb -hwanda i (HH); -vanda i (HH); *hide oneself* vb -hwanda i (HH); -vanda i (HH); *h. an object* vb -viga t (HH); -vanza t (HH); -hwanza t M (HH) — PT *hid;* PP *hidden, hid*

hide *animal's skin* n dehwe 5, matehwe 6 (LL)

hide-and-seek *a game of hiding* n gwegwe 5 (HL); chihwandehwande 7 M (LHLHL)

hideous *be ugly* adj & vb -nyangara i (HHH) (stative vb); Ari kuvaka imba yakanyangara. (*He is building a hideous house.*)

high *be tall* adj & vb -reba i (LL); *high* adj -refu (LH)

high *above* adv pauzuru 16 (LLHL); kuuzuru 17 (LLHL)

highway *motor road* n mugwagwa 3 (LLL)

hill *mountain* n gomo 5, makomo 6 (LL); *anthill* n churu 7 (LL); *hillock, small h., kopje* n chikomo 7 (LLL)

hinder *obstruct, prevent* vb -tadzisa t (HHH)

hint *(idiomatic) make remarks which suggest or forewarn* vb -nyevera t (LLL); -bayira zanhi t (LLL HH); *mild warning* n nyevero 9 (LLL) cf -nyevera

hip-bone *solid frame at the base of the spine* n hudyu 9 (LH); tsoro 9 (LL)

hippopotamus *large animal, called by the Greeks "water-horse"* n mvuu 9 (LH); hwindi 9 (LL; *cf illustration p. 7*

hire *obtain the use of at a price* vb -haya t (HH) cf Eng.

hiss *the sound of SSS or the sound made by an angry snake* vb -shinyira i (LLL)

hissing sand snake *olive grass snake* n dzvoti 9 (LH); svoti 9 (LH)

hissing tree *mobola plum* n muhacha 3 (LLL) B.Bk. 1,3

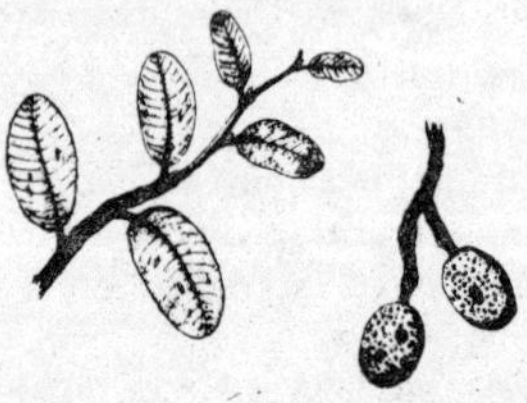

hit *beat, strike a blow* vb -rova i & t (HH); -nera KoM (LL); *hit back, repay, pay back, retaliate* vb -tsiva i & t (LL) — PT & PP *hit*

hive *bee-hive made by man from a cylinder of bark* n mukoko 3 (LLH); *bee-hive in a crevice among rocks* n gonera 5 (LLL)

hoarse *be husky* vb -shoshoma i (LLL)

hoe *hand implement for breaking up the soil* n badza 5, mapadza 6 (LH)

hoe *weeds, cultivate with a hoe* vb -sakura i & t (LLL)

hoist *raise up, lift up* vb -simudza t (HHL)

hold *grasp* vb -bata i & t (HH); Anofamba ak**abata** tsvimbo. (*He walks holding a club.*); *hold by force, press* vb -dzvinya t (LL); *h. firmly* vb -batisa t (HHH); *h. together in both arms* vb -gumbatira t (HHHL) — PT & PP *held*

hold out hands flat vb -tambanudza maoko (HHHL LHH); *h.o. hands hollow* vb -chingidzira t (HHHL)

hole *ditch* n gomba 5, makomba 6 (LH); *h. of rat etc. in the ground* n mwena 3 (LH); *h. of larger creature, burrow, lair* n guru 5, makuru 6 (LL)

hole in a garment n buri 5, mapuri 6 (HL)

hole *shaft in a mine* n mugodhi 3 (LLH)

holiday *rest* n zororo 5, mazororo 6 (HHL); horodhi 9 (HLL) cf Eng.

hollow in a tree n mhango 9 (LL)

holy adj -tsvene (LH); dzvene 5, tsvene 9; *holiness, quality of being pleasing to God* n utsvene 14 (LLH); usande 14 (LHL) cf Lat.

holy *be sacred, be taboo* vb -era (LL)

home *village* n musha 3 (LH)

honest *be trustworthy* vb -vimbika i (LLL); -tendeka i (LLL)

honey *product of the honey-bee* n uchi 14 (LH)

honey badger *ratel* n chitsere 7 Z (LLL); chisere 7 K (LLL); tsere 9 (LL); *cf illustration p. 125*

honey-guide *sp of bird* n mukaranga 1 MZ (LHHH); tsenzi 9 Z (LH); shezhu 9 KM (LH); tsoro 9 (LL)

honour *praise* vb -kudza t (HH); -remekedza t (LLLL)

hoof *horny outer part of the foot of horse, ox, antelope, etc.* n zondo 5, mazondo 6 (LH); nzondo 9 (LL); *hoof-print, spoor, tracks* n dzimba 5, matsimba 6 (LL)

hook *fish h.* n chirauro 7 (LHHL) cf -raura (HHH); chiredzo 7 (LHH); chivedzo 7 (LHH); *hook-thorn tree* n muunga 3 (LLL)

hookworm n hukuwemu 9 (HLLL) cf Eng.

hooligan *rough, disorderly person* n tsotsi 5 & 9 (LH)

hoopoe *sp of bird* n chigubhubhu 7 (LLLL); mhupupu 9 (HHH); *red-billed wood h.* n shavi-shavi 5 (LLLL); *scimitar-bill h.* n shokosha 9 (LLL)

hooter *usu a loud factory horn* n huta 9 (HL) cf Eng.

hop *jump* vb -svetuka i & t (HH); -tauka i & t (HHH)

hope for *long for* vb -tarisira t (LLLL); *hope, feeling of expectation* n chitarisiro 7 (LLLLL)

horizon *the far distant curve of the earth* n jengachenga 5 (LLLL)

horn *tusk, insect-feeler* n nyanga 9 (LH); runyanga 11 (LLH); *horn, medicine h.* n gona 5, makona 6 (LH); *h. to suck blood* n murumiko 3 (LHHL) cf -rumika (HHH)

hornbill *sp of bird, boskraai* n hoto 9 (LH); goto 5 (LH); *ground h.* n dendera 5, matendera 6 (HHL); *trumpeter h.* n mbudzimukume 9 (HHLHL)

horse n bhiza 5, mabhiza 6 (LH); hachi 5, mahachi 6 (HL); *cf illustration p. 45*

hosepipe *flexible pipe for delivering water usu in a garden* n hosipaipi 9 (HLHLL) cf Eng.

hospital *place of cure and care of the sick* n chipatara 7 (LLLL); hosipitari 9 (HLLLL) cf Eng.

hot *be warm* vb -pisa i (HH); *make h., heat up (liquids)* vb -virisa t (LLL); -dziyisa t (HHH); *make h., heat up (solids)* vb -dziyisa t (HHH)

hot season n madziya 6 (LHL)

hotel *lodging house for travellers* n hotera 9 (LHL) cf Eng.

Hottentot god *praying mantis* n jemberebande 5 (LLLLH); mbuyambuya 9 (HLHL); mbuyamuderere 9 (HLLLLH)

hour *measure of time* n awa 9 (HL) cf Eng.

house *dwelling* n imba 9 (LH), dzimba 10 (LH)

house tick *(tampan)* n humba 9 (LL)

household utensil n mudziyo 3 (LHH)

householder *owner of the house* n saimba 1a (HLH)

hover *remain in the air over one place e.g. birds* vb -tapatira i (LLLL)

how? interrog sei? Unotasva bhasikoro **sei?** (*How do you ride a bicycle?*) Ndokutendai **sei?** (*How am I to thank you?*)

however *nonetheless* conj zvisinei (HLHL); *however much, no matter what* conj; Kana ukaita sei, handiendi newe. (*No matter what you do, I am not going with you.*)

how many? adv -ngani? (LH), ngani? 10 (LH); *how many times? how often?* adv kangani? (LLH)

howl (*of a man*), *cry for help* vb -ridza mhere (LL LL); *h. or cry (of a dog)* vb -uura i (HHH); *h. or cry (of a hyena)* vb -rira i (LL)

hubbub *noise, din* n ruzha 11 (LH)

hug *fling arms around* vb -mbundira t (LLL)

huge *large, very big* adj -kuru (HH), guru 5, huru 9 & 10

human *of or belonging to man* adj mwana womunhu (*a human child*)

humble *be gentle* vb -pfava i (LL); -nyorova i (HHH)

humble oneself *be extremely modest* vb -**zvi**dukupisa reflex (HLLLH)

humble person n munhu akapfava 1 (LL LHHL)

humiliate *embarrass, put to shame* vb -nyadzisa i & t (HHH) cf -nyara (HH)

humility *quality of not thinking too highly of oneself* n kuzvidukupisa 15 (LHLLLH)

hump *deformity of humans* n nhuku 9 (LL); *h. of animals, lump above the shoulder* n nyundwa 9 (LL)

humus *compost* n maorera 6 MZ (LLLL); kombosti 9 (HLL) cf Eng.

hundred *the number 100* n zana 5, mazana 6 (LL)

hung *hanged cf hang*

hunger *famine* n nzara 9 (LL)

hungry *be ravenous* vb -fa nenzara i (LHL) (lit *to die of hunger*)

hunt *go after wild animals for food or sport* vb -vhima t (HH); -kwasha Z t (LL); *hunt for, search for* vb -tsvaga t (LL); -tsvaka t KM (LL)

hunter *a person who hunts* muvhimi 1 (LHH) cf -vhima (HH); *successful h.* n hombarume 1a (LLLL)

hurry *hasten, be quick* vb -kurumidza (HHHL); -chimbidza (HHH); *hurriedly, quickly* adv nokukurumidza (HLHHHL); nokuchimbidza (HLHHH)

hurt *give pain, ache* vb -rwadza i (HH)

hurt *be injured* vb -kuvara i (HHH); *hurt, harm, injure* vb -kuvadza t (HHH) — PT & PP *hurt*

husband *man* n murume 1 (LHH)

husky *be hoarse* vb -shoshoma i (LLL)

hut *house, room* n imba 9 (LH)

hyena *carrion and flesh-eating wild animal* n bere 5, mapere 6 (LL); magondo 1a M (LHH) *cf illustration 136*

hygiene *cleanliness to promote health* n utsanana 14 (LLLL)

hymen *vaginal membrane* n rwatahwi 11 (LHL); katahwi 12 (LHL)

hymn *song of praise to God* n rwiyo 11 (LH), nziyo 10 (LH); rumbo 11 (LH), dzimbo 10 (LH)

I

inspan -sunga

I Abs pronoun cf p. 207 ini (LH)

I don't know inter hamheno Z (LHH); hapeno M (LHH)

ice *water made solid by cold* n chando 7 (LL); aizi 9 (HLL) cf Eng.

ice-cream *sweetened frozen food made chiefly from milk or cream* n aizi kirimu 9 (HLL LHL) cf Eng.

idea *advice* n zano 5, mazano 6 (LL)

identical *of the same size* adj & vb -enzana i (LLL) (stative vb); Vana ava vaka**enzana**. (*These children are of the same size.*)

idiocy *stupidity* n upenzi 14 (LHH), ubenzi 14 (LHH)

idiot *fool* n fuza 5, mafuza 6 (LL); rema 5, marema 6 (HH)

idleness *laziness* n nungo 10 (plur) (LL); usimbe 14 (LLL); *idle, be lazy* vb -va nenungo (LHL); -va nousimbe i (LHLL)

if conj kana/kunge + Partic *Realizable condition;* Kana achida ndinouya. (*If he wishes I shall come.*)

if only conj dai + Partic *Unlikely conditions;* Dai ndiine mari, ndaitenga motokari. (*If only I had the money, I would buy a motor car.*); Dai ndakaziva! (*If only I had known!*)

ignite *set light to* vb -pisa t (HH); -tungidza t (HHH); -batidza t (HHH)

ill *be sick, become ill* vb -rwara i (HH)

illegally *not according to law* adv zvisiri pamutemo; zvisiri pamurau

illegitimate child n mwana asina baba 1; nyamuza 1a M (LLL)

illness *sickness* n denda 5, matenda 6 (HH); chirwere 7 (LHH) cf -rwara (HH); hosha 9 (LL)

ill-treat *bully (usu wife)* vb -shusha t (LL)

illuminate *give light* vb -vheneka i & t (LLL)

image *likeness, statue* n mufananidzo 3 (LHHHL); chifananidzo 7 (LHHHL)

imagine *think* vb -funga i & t (LL) ufunge! *just imagine!*

imitate *copy mannerism or behaviour, mimic, follow suit* vb -tevedzera t (LLLL); *ridicule by imitating* vb -edzesera t MZ (LLLL); -idzisira t K (LLLL)

immediately *instantly* adv chiriporipocho M (LHLHLH); bva + Rec Past Partic; Akatsikwa nemotokari aka**bva** afa. (*He was struck by a car and immediately died.*)

immediately after *no sooner than* adj -chango- (infix vb); Ndi**chango**pedza kudya ndakatanga kurwara. (*No sooner had I eaten than I began to feel sick.*)

immense *huge* adj -kuru (HH); guru 5, huru 9 (*often reduplicated*) -kurukuru (HHLH)

immerse *in liquid, plunge in water, soak* vb -nyika t (HH)

immoral act *sin* n chitema 7 K (LLH); rutadzo 11 (LHH); chivi (LH)

immoral person *lecherous p.* n nzenza 9 (HH); *immorality, impurity* n unzenza 14 (LHH) cf nzenza (HH); *immoral, be lecherous* vb -va nounzenza i (HLHH)

impala *sp of swift, graceful antelope, weight 60 Kg (female: 45 Kg)* n mhara 9 (LH) *cf illustration p. 89*

impartial *lacking favouratism* adj mutongi asina rusaruro (*a judge who does not have partiality*)

impatient (*use the vb: be angry*) vb -shatirwa i (HHH)

impede *prevent* vb -tadzisa t (HHH)

impediment *obstacle* n chipingamupinyi 7 (LHHLHH)

imperfection *moral i., defect, fault* n chinana 7 (LHH); chinongo 7 (LLH)

impi *Matabele regiment of warriors* n imbi 9 (HL)

implements *instruments or tools of work, weapons* n zvombo 8 (LL)

implore *beseech, beg* vb -teterera i & t (HHHL)

imply *mean, suggest* vb -reva t (HH)

importance *consequence, advantage* n maturo 6 Z (LHH) (*usu in neg of no i.*)

important *great* adj -kuru (HH); guru 5, huru 9

important *be i.* adj & vb -komba i (LL); -kosha i (LL)

impossible (*use the vbs:* -bvira (LL); -goneka ('LL) = *be possible*) Hazvibvíri. (*It is impossible.*

impoverished land *i. soil* n gura 5, makura 6 (LL)

imprison *put in jail* vb -isa mujeri t (LL LHL)

improve *make good, make better* vb -natsa i & t (LL)

improvidence *wasteful use of possessions* n urombe 14 (LLL)

improvident *person, spendthrift* n rombe 5, marombe 6 (LL)

impurity *fornication, adultery* n upombwe 14 (LLL)

in *inside* prep *loc Cl 18* **mujeri** (*in jail*); *with Cl 1a:* **muna** August (*in August*); *in front* adv mberi (LH); pamberi 16 (LLH); *in here* muno (HH) near precised dem: Uyai nazvo muno. (*Bring them in here.*); *in the middle (time or place)* adv pakati 16 (LLH); *in order that, in order to* conj kuti + subj. Tinokumbira kuti auye. (*We ask for him to come.*); -uya + kuzo- Tauya kuzomuona. (*We came in order to see him.*); -enda + kundo- Taenda kundomuona. (*We went in order to see him.*); *in the vicinity of, around* prep kwa- PC Cl 17; *in this way, in this fashion* adv kudai (LHL) Ita kudai. (*Do it like this.*); *in vain, for nothing* adv pasina (LHH) rel

incense *scented resin for burning in religious worship* n inzenzi 9 (LHL) cf Eng.

incest *sexual relations with a near relative* n makunakuna 6 Z (LLLLL)

inch *small measure of distance, about 2,5 cm* n inji 5 (HL) cf Eng.

incite *rouse trouble* vb -pesva t (HH)

incline *slope, inclined plane, upward i.* n mukwidza 3 (LHL); *downward i.* n materu 6 (LHL)

inclined *be i. at an angle, lean over* vb -rereka i (HHH)

inconvenienced *be put to great trouble* vb -netseka i (LLL)

increase *become greater* vb -wanda i (LL); *add to* vb -wanza t (LL); *increase the price* vb -kwidza mutengo (HH LHH)

incredulous *be unbelieving* vb -pokana i (LLL)

incubate *hatch, sit on eggs, brood* vb -rarira t (HHH); -vhumbamira t (HHHL)

indecisive *be hesitant, be unready to act* vb -zengurira i (LLLL)

indecent *be vulgar (in behaviour)* vb -nyadza i (HH)

indeed *truly* adv chokwadi (HLH); zviro kwazvo (LL HL)

Indian *Asiatic* n muIndia 1 (LHLL); munhu wechiAsia 1 (LL HLHLL); muSami 1 (LLH)

indicate *show* vb -ratidza t (LLL); *point out* -nongedzera t (HHHL); -taridza t

industry *quality of being hardworking* n kushinga 15 (LHH)

inexpensive be cheap vb -chipa i (LL) cf Eng.; -sadhura i (LHH)

infant *baby* n mucheche 1 (LLL)

infect *give disease germs to* vb -zadza t (HH); Mukaka waamai wakazadza mwana chirwere. (*The mother's milk infected the baby with disease.*)

infirm *be sick* vb -rwara i (HH)

inflate *pump up, blow up* vb -pombera t (HHH); -vhuta t (LL)

influenza *a disease* n furuwenza 9 (LLHL); fureza 9 (LHL) cf Eng.

inform *enlighten, tell* vb -zivisa t (HHH); -udza t (HH)

infuriate *make angry* vb -shatirisa i & t (HHHL); -zaridza t (HHH)

ingratitude *lack of gratitude* n tsinda 9 K (LL); kusatenda 15 (LLLL)

inhabitant *occupant of a house* n mugari 1 (LLL)

inherit *receive property from owner at his death* vb -gara nhaka (LL LL)

inject *administer an injection* vb -baya jekiseni (LL HLLL)

injection *liquid medicine administered under the skin by a syringe* n jekiseni 5 (HLLL) cf Eng.

injure *hurt* vb -kuvadza i & t (HHH); *be injured* vb -kuvara i (HHH)

ink *fluid (black, red, etc.) for writing with a pen* n ingi 9 (HL) cf Eng.

ink flower *trailing herb with large white flowers* n chidzimamuriro 7 (LHHHLL) B.Bk. 1,81

innocent *sinless* adj mwana asina mhaka (*an innocent child*)

inoculate *protect (usu by introducing a germ to produce a mild form of disease) against a severe attack* vb -baya nhomba t (LL LH)

inquire *ask, question* vb -bvunza i & t MZ (LL); -vhunza i & t KKo (LL)

insane *be mad, be daft* vb -penga i (HH)

insect (*e.g. ants, flies, beetles, etc.*) n kambuyu 12 (LLH); *flying i. (general name)* n chipembenene 7 (LLLLL)

insect eaters

hedgehog tyoni

shrew dzwitswitswi

elephant shrew mudune

Parts of body

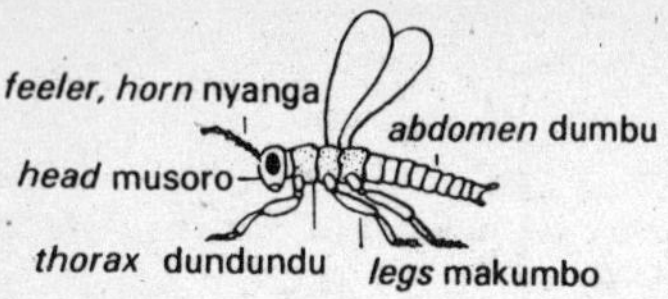

Life cycle

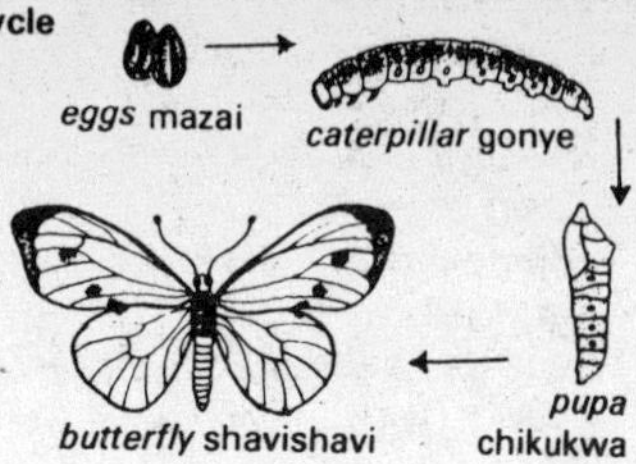

Some insects and other creatures

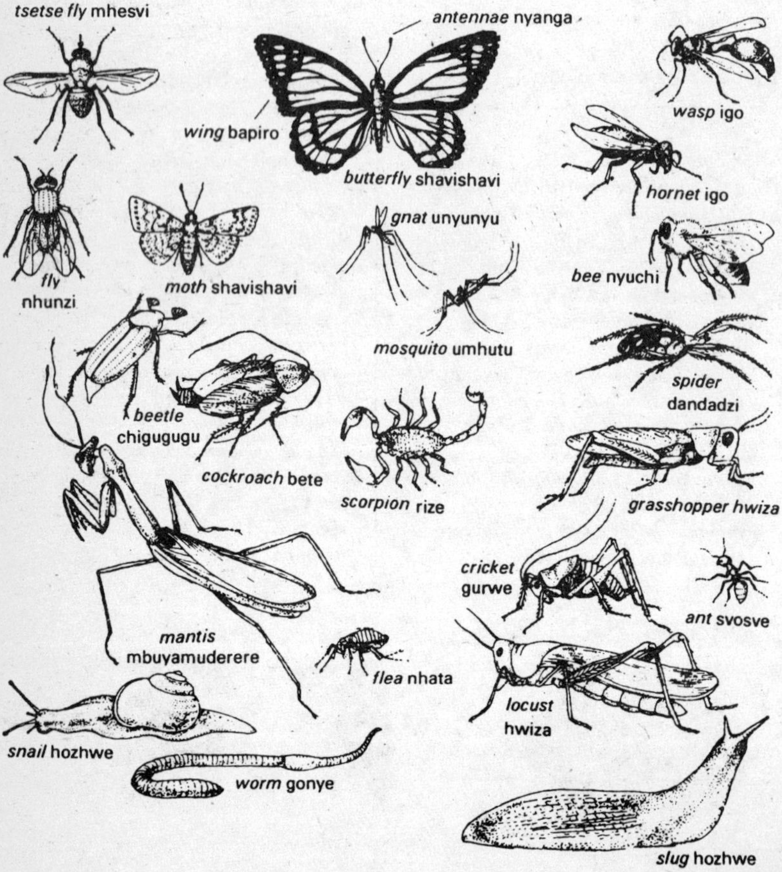

insert *put inside* vb pinza t (LL) cf -pinda (LL)

inside *within* adj & prep mukati 18 (LLH) cf dem pron p. 205

inside out *be the wrong way round* vb -pinduka i (LLL) (stative vb); Hembe yako yakapinduka. (*Your shirt is inside out.*)

insist *urge strongly against disbelief or opposition* vb -simbirira i (LLLL)

insolent *be cheeky* vb -virima i (HHH)

inspan *tie up* vb -bopa t (HH); -sunga t (HH) *cf illustration p. 77*

inspect secretly vb -ongorora i & t (HHHL)

instantly *immediately, at the same moment* adv chiriporipocho (LHLHLH); pakarepo (LHLH)

instead of *in place of* adv panzvimbo pa- (LLL)

instigator *beginner* n muvambi 1 (LLL) cf -vamba (LL)

instruct *teach* vb -dzidzisa i & t (HHL); -fundisa i & t (HHH); *give an order* vb -rayira t (LLL); -dzidzisa t (HHL); *instructor, teacher* n mudzidzisi 1 (LHHL); mufundisi 1 (LHHL)

insult *abuse* vb -tsvinya i (HH); -tuka i & t (HH); -nyomba i & t (HH)

insufficient *be in short supply* vb -shomeka i (LLL)

intellect *mental ability* n njere 9 (HH); *intelligence, wisdom, cleverness* n ungwaru 14 (LLH) cf -ngwara (LL)

intelligent *be gifted of mind, be wise* vb -ngwara i (LL)

intelligible *able to be understood* vb -nzwika i MZ (HH); -nzika i K (HH) cf -nzwa (H)

intercede *ask in favour of someone* vb -reverera t (HHHL); *intervessor, advocate* n murevereri 1 (LHHHL) cf -reverera (HHHL)

interest *be interesting, be entertaining* vb -nakidza i & t (LLL)

interested in *be pleased with* vb -farira t (HHH) cf -fara (HH)

interfere *disturb* vb -kanganiso i & t (HHHL)

interlace *place across* vb -piyanisa t (HHHL)

intermediary *in marriage negotiations* n munyai 1 (LLL); samutume 1a MZ (HLHL); sadombo 1a MZ (HLH)

interpret *translate* vb -turikira i & t (HHHL); *interpreter, translator* n muturikiri 1 (LHHHL) cf -turikira (HHHL)

interrupt *speak to somebody while he is talking* vb -dzivaidza t (HHHL)

intersection *cross-roads* n mhararano 9 (LLLL) cf -pararana (LLLL)

intestine *(usu plur) bowels, guts* n ura 14 (LL); matumbu 6 (LLL); *large intestine, colon* n ura ukuru/ukobvu 14 (LL LHH/LLH); *small intestine* n ura udiki/utete 14 (LL LHL/LLL)

intimidate *frighten* vb -tyisidzira i & t (HHHL)

into *(motion)* prep mu- locative Cl 18 Akapinda mumba make. (*He walked into his house.*)

intoxicate *make drunk* vb -dhaka i & t (LL); -kora i & t Ko (HH); *intoxicated, be drunk* vb -dhakwa i (LL); -raradza i M (LLL); -batwa nehwahwa i (HH HLH)

invalid *sickly person or animal* n ndonda 9 (LL)

invert *turn upside down* vb -pindura t (LLL); -sandura t (LLL)

investigate *question closely* vb -feyafeya i & t (HHHL)

invigorate *stengthen* vb -simbisa t (LLL)

invite *ask someone for social occasion* vb -koka t (HH)

inyala *sp of antelope* n nyara 9 Ko (LL); *cf illustration p. 88*

irascible *be irritable* vb -va nehasha i (HLL)

iron *general term:* simbi 9 (LH), *i. ore* n utare 14 (LHL), mhangura n 9 (LLH)

iron *instrument for ironing clothes* n simbi 9 (LH); aini 9 (HLL) cf Eng.

iron clothing vb -chisa t (HH); -aina t (HHH) cf Eng.

ironheart tree *snake bean t.* n mucherechese 3 (LLLHL); mucherekese 3 (LLLHL)

iron-wood tree n muvanga 3 (LLH)

irrigate *apply water to soil to maintain growth* vb -diridza i & t (LLL)

irritable *be irascible* vb -va nehasha i (HLL); *irritate, make angry* vb -shatirisa i & t (HHHL); -netsa i & t (LL); *tease (creatures)* vb -svosva t (LL); *irritate the skin, itch* vb -vava i (HH); -swinya i MZ (HH); *irritate with noise* vb -nyaudza i & t (HHH)

is that so? *really* interj nhai? (HL / HH)

island *land surrounded by water* n chitsuwa 7 MZ (LHL)

isn't it? is it not so? vb handiti? (LHL)

itch *have a feeling of irritation in the skin causing a desire to scratch* vb -vava i (HH); -nyeredza i & t MZ (LLL); -swinya i & t MZ (HH)

it is Impersonal Copulative cf p. 190

it is better vb zviri nani (HH HL)

it is so vb ndizvo (HL); ndizvozvo (HLH)

ivory *white bone-like substance forming the tusks of elephants* n nyanga yenzou 9 (LH LHL)

ivory *pink i. tree, possesses pinkish heartwood used for carving ornaments and curios* n muvhunambezo 3 (LHHHL); musukachuma 3 (LLLLH)

J

jackal hungubwe

jacana *lily trotter, sp of riverine bird* n katewetewe 12 (LLLLL) R228

jack *mechanical jack for raising motor car* n jega 5, majega 6; jeki 5 (HL) cf Eng.

jack up *raise with a jack* vb -jega (HH) cf Eng.

jackal *African fox (general name, which covers side-striped j. and bat-eared fox)* n gava 5, makava 6 (HH); hava 9 (HH); *black-backed j.* n hungubwe 9 (HHL); hunguhwe 9 (HHL)

jacket *short coat* n bhachi 5, bhatye 5, mabhachi 6 (HL) cf Afrik.

jail *gaol* n jere 5, majere 6 (HL) cf Eng.; tirongo 5, matirongo 6 (LHL) cf Afrik.; *jail-cell* n chitokisi 7 (LHLL) cf Eng.; *prisoner* n bhanditi 5, mabhanditi 6 (LHH) cf Eng.

jam *fruit boiled with sugar and preserved* n jamu 5 (HL) cf Eng.

jaw *one or other of the bone structures containing the teeth* n shaya 9 (LH); rushaya 11 (LLH)

jealous *be envious* vb -va neshanje i (LHL); *jealousy, suspicious fear* n shanje 9 (LL); *jealous* adj mukadzi ane shanje (*a jealous wife*)

jeer *mock, laugh rudely* vb -seka i & t (LL) -shora i & t (LL)

jerk *give a sudden pull* vb -gwinha i & t (LL)

jerrymunglum *hunting spider* n dzvatsvatsva 5, madzvatsvatsva 6 (HHH)

jersey *pullover (sleeved or sleeveless)* juzi 5, majuzi 6 (HL) cf Eng./Afrik.

Jew *Israelite* n muJuta 1 (LHL); muYudha 1 (LHL)

job of work n mushando 3 (LHH) cf -shanda (HH)

jockey *person who rides horses in races* n joki 5, majoki 6 (LH) cf Eng.

join *meet with* vb -sangana na- (LLL); *be joined to* vb -batana na- (HHH); *j. two pieces together* vb -batanidza t (HHHL); *j. by binding, j. by tying together* vb -sunganidza t (HHHL) cf -sunga (HH); *j. by sewing* vb -sonanidza t (LLLL) cf -sona (LL); *j. by hooking together* vb -kochekedza t (LLLL)

joint of the body *knot* n pfundo 5, bvundo 5, mapfundo 6 (HH); *joint and ligament* n chipfundo 7 (LHH)

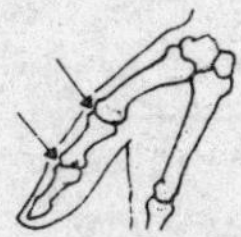

joke *jest, play the fool* vb -tamba i (HH); -seka i (LL)

joke *something said or done to cause amusement, romancing, exaggerated talk, practical joke, playful threat, playful talk* n nyn'ambo 9 MZ (LL); musara 3 (LLL); jee 5 (HL)

jolt *give someone a jerk or sudden shake* vb -gujùra i & t (HHH)

journey *distance of travel* n rwendo 11 (LL); *journey, make a j.* vb -famba rwendo i (HH HL)

joy *great pleasure* n mufaro 3 (LHH); rufaro 11 (LHH) cf -fara (HH)

judge *decide a case* vb -tonga i & t (HH); *judge, one who judges* n mutongi 1 (LHH)

judicial case n mhosva 9 (HL)

jug *deep vessel for liquids* n jagi 5 (HL) cf Eng.

jugular *vein, prominent v. in the neck* n uzhwa 14 (LH)

juice *liquid part of fruits, vegetables, meat, etc.* n muto 3 (LL)

jump *leap, hop, j. over* vb -svetuka i (HHL) (stative vb);

junction *cross-roads* n mhararano 9 (LLLL)

just adv -ngo- infix vb Zvaka**ngo**fanana. (*It is just the same.*) **Ingo**nwa mushonga kuti upone. (*Just drink the medicine to get better.*)

just *be upright* adj & vb -rurama i (LL) (stative vb); Murume uyu **akarurama**. (*This man is just.*)

just now adv iye zvino (HL HH); zvino zvino (HL HL); iko zvino KoK (HL HH)

justice *moral quality of being right and fair* n ururami 14 (LLLL); ruenzaniso 11 (LLLLL)

jut out *protrude, project, stick out* vb -chanjamara (HHHL)

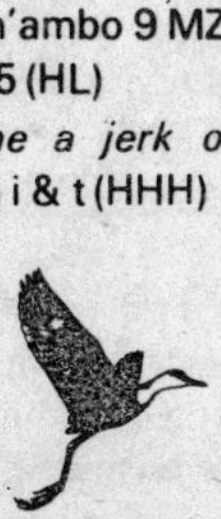

jacana **katewetewe**

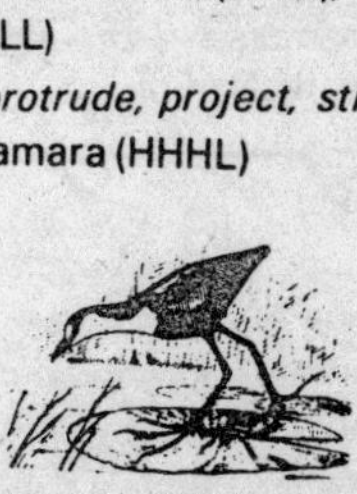

K

kopje chikomo

kaffirboom *lucky-bean t.* n mutiti 3 (LLL); *eastern border k. b. tree* n murungu 3 (LLH); *kaffir plum tree, Batoka plum t.* n munhunguru 3 (LLLH)

karreeboom *bastard willow* n mufokosiana 3 (LLLHLL); mutepe 3 (LHL) B.Bk. 1,29

keep *preserve, look after* vb -chengeta i & t (LLL); *keeper, guardian* n muchengeti 1 (LLLL) cf -chengeta (LLL) — PT & PP *kept*

keep on *continue* vb -ramba (LL) + Partic

keep silent *be quiet* **adj &** vb -nyarara i (HHL) (stative vb); Anoruka aka*nyarara*. (*She knits in silence.*)

kei apple tree n munhunguru 3 (LLLH); mutsvoritsvoto 3 (LLHLL)

kept *cf keep*

kestrel *a common small hawk* n rukodzi 11 (LHL); ruvangu 11 (LLH) *cf illustration p. 49*

kettle *metal vessel for boiling water* n ketero 9 (HLL) cf Eng.

kew weed *gallant soldier weed* n teketera 5 (LLLL)

key *metal instrument for opening and closing* n kiyi 9 (HL) cf Eng.

khaki bush *Mexican marigold, stinking roger* n mbanda 3 (LL)

khaki weed n chibayamahure 7 (LLLLHL)

khat *evergreen tree* muzvaravashava 3 (LHHLHH); mutsvahari 3 (LHLL)

kick *(by an animal)* vb -pfura i & t (HH); (*by a person*) vb -kwipura i & t (LLL); *k. ball* vb -banha t (LL)

kid *young goat* n mbudzana 9 (HLH)

kidney *one of a pair of organs in the body which separates waste liquid from the blood* n itsvo 9 MZ (LH); tsvo 9 KM (H); svo 9 K (H)

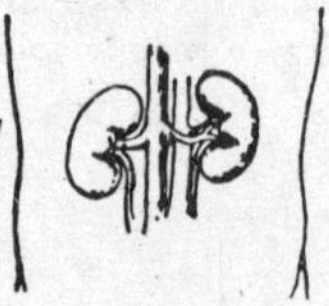

kill *murder* vb -uraya i & t (HHH); *passive forms:* -urayiwa & -urawa KM; -ponda i & t (LL); *killer, murderer* n mhondi 9 (LL) cf -ponda (LL); muurayi 1 (LHHL) cf -uraya (HHH)

kill *slaughter (animal)* vb -baya t (LL); uraya t (HHH) *cf above*

kilometre *measure of distance* (1 000 metres) n kiromita 5, makiromita 6 (HHHL) cf Eng.

kind *be merciful* vb -va nomwoyochena i (LHLHL); -va netsitsi i (HLH)

kind *variety, sort* n rudzi 11 (LL), mhando 9 MZ (LL)

kindheartedness n mwoyochena 3 (LLHL)

kindle a fire vb -kuhwidza moto (LLL LH)

kindness *mercy* n mutsa 3 KoMZ (LH); tsitsi 10 (LH); ngoni 10 (LL); *kind* adj Harahwa ino mutsa. (*A kind old man.*)

kindred *relative* n hama 9 (HH)

king *royal ruler of the land* n mambo 1a (LL); *kingship* n umambo 14 (LLL); ushe 14 (LH)

kingfisher *sp of bird which dives for fish* n kanyururahove 12 (LHHLHH); nyururahove 9 (HHLHH); *Malachite k.* n chinderera 7 (LHLL) R397; chinyururahove 7 (LHHLHH)

kinsman *relative* n hama 9 (HH)

kiss *touch with the lips to show affection* vb -tsvoda i & t (HH)

kitchen *room used for cooking* n kicheni 9 (HLL) cf Eng.; imba yokubikira 9 (LH LHLLL)

kitchen-kaffir *fanigalo* n chirapara-pa 7 (LHLHL)

kite *sp of bird of prey* n ngavira 9 (LHL); ngavi 9 Z (LH) *cf illustration p. 49*

klapper apple tree *general name for the tree producing hard-skinned fruit the size of an orange* n mutamba 3 (LLH); *klapper apple fruit* n damba 5; matamba 6 (LH)

klipspringer *diminutive antelope dwelling in rocky regions, weight about 16 kg* n ngurudu 9 (LHL) *cf illustration p. 89*

knead *mix a solid with a liquid* vb -kanya t (LL)

knee *joint between the upper and lower leg* n ibvi 5, mabvi 6 KoMZ (LH); bvi 5 K (H)

kneel *genuflect* vb -pfugama i (HHH) — PT & PP *knelt*

knew *cf know*

knickers *female underwear* n nika 9 (HL) cf Eng.

knife *instrument with sharp edge for cutting* n banga 5, mapanga 6 (HH)

knit *make an article of clothing from wool and with the aid of two needles* vb -ruka i & t (LL) — PT & PP *knitted, knit*

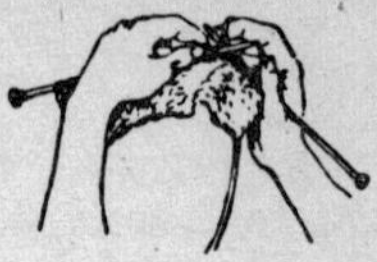

knobkerrie *throwing stick* n nduni 9 (LL); tsvimbo 9 (HH); ndonga 9 M (LL)

knock *against each other, bump into another* vb -gumana i (LLL); knock at *the door* vb -gogodza i & t (HHH); -gugudza i & t (LLL); *knock to the ground* vb -rovera pasi t (HHH LH); *knock off (slang) cease work* vb -chayira basa i (LLL LL)

knock over *push o., upset* vb -punza t (HH); -ngundumura t (HHHL)

knot *in string* n pfundo 5, mapfundo 6 MZ (HH); fundo 5 K, mafundo 6 (HH);

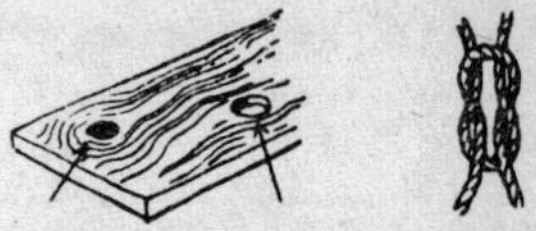

knot in rope, k. in wood, lump n bundu 5, mapundu 6 (HH)

know *be acquainted with (a person)* vb -ziva i & t (HH); -ziya i & t KoM (HH); *know by heart* vb -ziva nomusoro (HH HLHH); *know thoroughly, k. all about* vb -zivisisa t (HHHL) cf -ziva (HH); *understand* vb -nzwisisa i & t (HHH) cf -nzwa (H) — PT *knew*, PP *known*

know-all *someone who thinks he knows all the answers and does not want to be told* n zanondoga 1a (LLHH); marambakuudzwa 1a (LLLLHH)

knowledge *(acquired)* n ruzivo 11 (LHH); zivo 9 K (HH) cf -ziva (HH); *knowledge, understanding* n nzwisiso 9 (HHL) cf -nzwa (H); *knowledgeable person, expert* n nyanzvi 9 (LH)

know *cf know*

known *be well-known* vb -zivikanwa i (HHHL); -zikanwa MZ i (HHL)

knuckle *bone at finger joint* n chipfundo chomunwe 7 (LHH LHL)

kopje *small hill, granite outcrop* n chikomo 7 (LLL) *cf illustration p. 84*

korhaan *bustard, large sp of ground bird* n gaudya 5 Z (LHL); guhwi 5 (LH) *cf illustration p. 24*

kraal *village, home* n musha 3 (LH)

kraal *closed-in pen for cattle, sheep, goats, etc.* n danga 5, matanga 6 (LH)

kudu *koedoe, sp of large, brousing antelope, males have spiral horns and weigh up to 250 kg.* n nhoro 9 (LH) *cf illustration p. 88*

L

leopard ingwe

labour *work* n basa 5, mabasa 6 (LL)

labour *work* vb -sevenza i & t (HHH); -shanda i & t (HH); *labourer, worker* n musevenzi 1 (LHHL) cf -sevenza (HHH)

lace of a shoe *shoe l.* n ruhanda 11 (LLL); tambo yebhutsu 9 (LL HLL)

lack *be short of, not find* vb -shaya i & t (LL); -shayiwa K (LLL); Ndamutsvaga ndikamu**shaya**. (*I searched and did not find him.*); *lack the proper quantity* vb -shota i (HH) cf Eng.

lad *boy* n mukomana 1 (LHLH)

ladder *device with rungs for climbing* n danho 5 (LL); manera 6 (LHL)

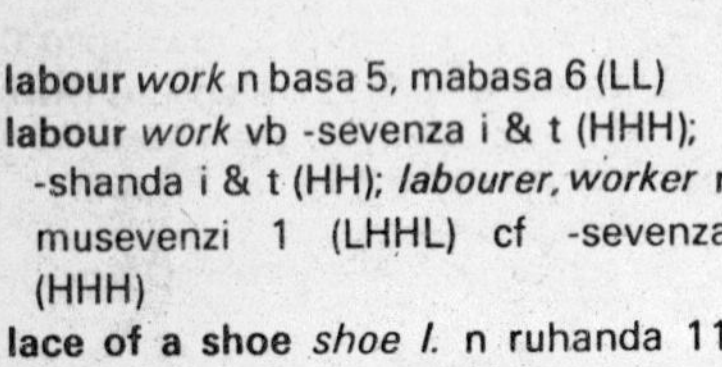

ladle mukombe

ladder manera

ladle *made from gourd for scooping liquids* n mukombe 3 (LHL); ***ladle, large wooden spoon*** n mugwaku 3 (LHL); rugwaku 11 (LLH)

ladle *plunge a l. into a liquid* vb -tubvura t (LLL)

ladle food *serve food onto a plate* vb -pakura t (HHH)

lady's fingers *okra, bears a fruit cooked as a vegetable* n derere 5 (LLH); derere rechipudzi 5 (LLH LHLH)

laggard *one who moves too slowly* n mononoki 1 (LLLL) cf -nonoka (LLL)

laid *cf lay*

lain *cf lie*

lair *burrow of ant-bear* n guru 5, MZ, makuru 6 (LL)

lake *sea* n nyanza 9 (LH)

lamb *young sheep* n hwayana 9 MZ (LLH); gwayana 5 K, makwayana 6 (LLH)

lame *be crippled* adj & vb -remara i (HHH) (stative vb); Amai vangu vaka**remara**. (*My mother is lame.*)

lame person n chikamhi 7 (LLH); chirema 7 (LHH); chidai 7 (LLH)

lament *cry, weep* vb -chema i & t (HH); *lament loudly, sob* vb -huhudza i MZ (HHH)

lamp *instrument for illumination* n mwenje 3 (LL); rambi 5 (HL) cf Eng.

land *come to rest after flying* vb -mhara i & t (LL)

land *territory* n nyika 9 (LL)

land (*agricultural), field, garden* n munda 3 (LL)

language *form of speech used by nation or race* n mutauro 3 (LLLL); rurimi 11 (LHH)

languid *be weak, exhausted* adj & vb -rukutika i (LLL) (stative vb); Nhasi ndafuma ndakarukutika. (*I got up today feeling exhausted.*)

lannea *plant bearing edible fruit* n mutsambatsi 3 (LLLH) B.Bk. 1,67

lantern *lamp* n rambi 5, marambi 6 (HL) cf Eng.

lap water *l. up as a dog* vb -kapa i & t (HH)

lap *on the l., waist to knees* adv pamakumbo 16 (LLLL)

lard *fat* n mafuta 6 (LHH)

large *big* adj -kuru (HH); guru 5, huru 9

lark *sp of small, brown bird* n chitambirambuya 7 Z (LHHHHL); chimbuyavagore 7 (LHLHLH); *clapper l.* n chinyamambure 7 (LLLHL); chibakobwerabwera 7 (LLLHHHL) R468; *rufous-naped l.* n ndondoza 9 (HHL); tsotso 9 M (HH); nhunhudza 9 Z (HHL); tsutsuma 9 (LLL)

larynx *vocal organ in the throat* n garimanyemba 5 (LHHLL)

lash *beat* vb -pura i & t (HH); -rova i & t (HH)

last *final* adj PC + kupedzisira (LHLHL); Munhu wokupedzisira. (*The last person.*) Zuva rokupedzisira. (*The last day.*) Pokupedzisira . . . . (*At last . . . .*); *last year* n makei 6 (LHL); gore rakapera 5 (LH LHLL); *l. month* n mwedzi wakapera 3 (LH LHLL); l. night n usiku hwanezuro 14 (LHH LHHL); *last week* n svondo rakapera 6 (LL LHLL)

last *be l.* vb -gumisira i (HHHL); Anogumisira kurara. (*He is the last to go to bed.*)

last *be durable* vb -gara i (LL); Hembe inodhura inogara nguva ndefu. (*An expensive shirt lasts a long time.*)

last born n gotwe 5, magotwe 6 (LH)

latch *simple fastening for a door or window* n chihuri 7 (LHL)

late *be unpunctual* vb -nonoka + infin (LLL) Anonoka kuuya. (*He came late.*)

later *afterwards* adv pashure 16 (LHL); *later on, by and by* adv gare gare (LH LH); mbaimbai (LHLH) cf Eng.

latex *bird lime* n urimbo 14 (LLL)

lath of a roof *long, thin strip of wood* n mbariro 9 (LLL)

lather *white froth from water and soap* n furo 5 (HH); furu 5 (HH)

lather *form froth e.g. water and soap* vb -pupuma i (LLL)

laugh *laugh at, despise* vb -seka i & t (LL); -nyomba t (HH); *giggle* vb -kekedza i (HHH); -pfipfidza i (HHH); *laugh mockingly, l. to scorn* vb -funa i Z (LL); *laughable, be amusing* vb -setsa i (LL) cf -seka (LL); *laugh out loud in unison (as African women do)* vb -ridza chikwee (LL LHL)

lavatory *latrine* n chimbuzi 7 (LLL); ravhatiri 9 (HLLL) cf Eng.

law *ruling* n mutemo 3 (LHH) cf -tema (HH); murau 3 (LLL); murao 3 (LLL)

larger antelopes

wildebeest mvumba

tsessebe nhondo

kudu nhoro

roan antelope ndunguza

eland mhofu

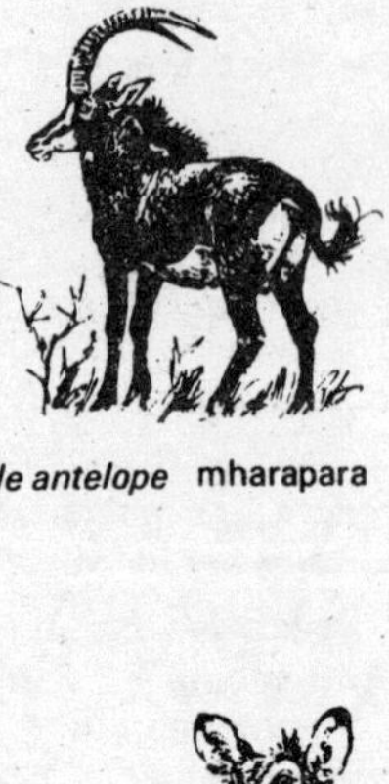

sable antelope mharapara

nyala antelope nyara

Lichtenstein's hartebeest hwiranondo

waterbuck dhumukwa

lesser antelopes

impala mhara

steenbok mhene

oribi tsinza

reedbuck bimha

blue duiker ndundu

bushbuck dzoma

duiker mhembwe

Sharpe's grysbok timba

klipspringer ngururu

lawyer *person who has studied law and advises in matters of law* n gweta 5, magweta 6 (LH)

laxative *opening medicine* n mushonga wokuendesa kunze 3

lay down *take a burden from head and place it down gently, unload* vb -tura t (HH); *lay down on the ground* vb -radzika t (HHH)

lay *produce (eggs)* vb -kandira i & t (mazai) (LLL) — PT & PP *laid*

lay *cf lie*

laziness *idleness* n nungo 10 KoMZ (LL); usimbe 14 (LLL); unyope 14 (LLL); adj musevenzi ane nungo (*a lazy servant*); *lazy, be indolent, idle* vb -va nenungo i (LHL); -va nousimbe i (LHLL)

lazy person n nyope 9 (LL); tsimbe 9 (LL)

lead *heavy, soft, grey metal; solder* n mutobvu 3 (LLL)

lead *go in front* vb -tungamira i & t (HHHL); *leader, one who leads* n mutungamiri 1 (LHHHL) — PT & PP *led*

lead astray *l. into wrong, tempt* vb -runzira t (HHH); -furira t (HHH); -nyengera t K (HHH)

leader *human l. of a span of oxen* n mukokeri 1 (LHHL)

leaf *single segment of foliage* n shizha 5, mashizha 6 (LL); zanhi 5, mazanhi 6 (HH)

leak *let out liquid from a container* vb -bvinza i (LL); -vhinza i (LL); *squirt in a stream* -chucha i (LL); -juja i (LL); *leak through the roof, drip down* vb -donha i & t (LL)

lean *thin* adj -tete (LL); dete 5, nhete 9

lean *become thin* vb -onda i (HH)

lean against vb - zendama i (HHH); - zendamira t (HHHH); *lean over* vb -kotama i(LLL); *lean over* vb -kotamisa t (LLLL); *lean, put against t* vb -sendeka t (HHH) — PT & PP *leant, leaned*

leap *jump* vb -svetuka i & t (HHH); -uruka i & t K (LLL) — PT & PP *leapt, leaped*

learn *gain knowledge* vb -dzidza i & t vb -dzidzira + Infinitive; *learner, disciple* n mudzidzi 1 (LH); cf -dzidza (HH); mufundi 1 (LHH); n mudzidzi 1 cf -dzidza; mufundi 1 (LHH) cf -funda (HH) — PT & PP *learnt, learned*

learning *what is gained by careful study* n dzidzo 9 (HL) cf -dzidza (HH)

leather *skin, hide* n dehwe 5, matehwe 6 (LL)

leave *go from* vb -bva i (L); *l. behind, abandon, forsake* vb -siya t (HH); *l. alone, let go* vb -regera i & t (LLL); *l. off, desist from* vb -rega i & t (LL); *l. one another, part company* vb -siyana i (HHH) — PT & PP *left*

leaven *yeast* n chimera 7 (LLL); mbiriso 9 (LLL) cf -virisa (LLL)

lecherous *be immoral* vb -va nounzenza i (HLHH)

led *cf lead*

ledge *inside a hut* n rukuva (LHH)

left *l. hand* n ruboshwe 11 (LLH); ruboshe 11 Z (LLH); *l. hand side* adv kuruboshwe 17 (LLLH)

left-overs *(food)* n munya 3 (LL)

leg *limb for walking* n gumbo 5, makumbo 6 (LL); *knee* n ibvi 5, bvi 5 K, mabvi 6 (LH); *shin* n mupimbira 3, mupimbiri 3 (LHHL); *thigh* n chidya 7 (LL)

leguaan *two distinct species: monitor water lizard, 2 m. in length* n mupurwa 3 MZ (LHL); *monitor savanna or land lizard, length 1,5 m* n gwava 5 (LL); magwavava 6 (LLL)

lemon tree n mundimu 3 (LHL); *lemon fruit, a sour citrus fruit* n ndimu 9 (HL); remoni 5, maremoni 6 (HLL) cf Eng.

lend *give in the hope of return* vb -kweretesa t (HHHL); -posha t (HH) — *can also mean borrow* — PT & PP *lent*

length *measurement from end to end* n urefu 14 (LLH); kureba 15 (LLL); *lengthen, make longer* vb -rebesa t (LLL) cf -reba (LL)

leopard *large, spotted, carnivorous animal; spotted, shy and cunning member of the cat family* n ingwe 9 KoMZ (LL); mbada 9 (LL); kamba 5 M (HH) *cf illustration p. 86*

leprosy *loathesome and dreadful skin disease* n mapere 6 (LLL); mapere-mbudzi 6 (LLLHH)

lessen *make less* vb -tapudza i & t (HHH)

lesson *something to be learnt* n chidzidzo 7 (LHL); chifundo 7 (LHH)

let go *leave alone, release* vb -regera t (LLL); -regedza t (LLL); *let out, take out drive out* vb -buritsa t (HHH); *let in, allow entry* vb -pinza t (LL); *let down, put down* vb -burutsa t (LLL); *let off, forgive* vb -regerera t (LLLL); -regedza t(LLL) *let loose, outspan (oxen)* vb -sunungura t (HHHL) — PT & PP *let*

letter *note* n tsamba 9 (LL); rugwaro 11 (LLL); *letter of the alphabet* n vara 5, mavara 6 (HH); bhii 5, mabhii 6 (HL); *letters, mail, post* n posti 9 (HL) cf Eng.

lettuce *a leaf veg* n retisi 9 (HLL) cf Eng.

level *be flat* vb -sandarika i (LLLL); -ti sandara (LLL) (ideo); *level, make l. make even* vb -enzanisa t (LLLL)

liar *person who lies* n munyepi 1 MZ (LLL) cf -nyepa (LL)

liberate *release, untie* vb -sunungura t (HHHL); *liberty, freedom* n rusunungu-ko 11 (LHHHL) cf -sununguka (HHHL)

license *written or printed statement giving permission* n raisenzi 5 & 9 (HLLL) cf Eng.; rezenisi 5 (HLLL) cf Eng.

lick *pass the tongue over* vb -nanzva t (HH)

lid *movable top forming part of a container* n hwidibo 9 (HHL)

lie *untrue statement, known as untrue* n nhema 9 (LH); kunyepa 15 (LLL)

lie *deceive, make untrue statement* vb -nyepa i (LL); -reva nhema i (HH LH)

lie down *rest on flat surface* vb -rara i (HH); -enzera i KoM (LLL); *lie full length* vb -zvambarara i (HHHL); *lie in wait for, l. in hiding for* vb -hwandira (HHH) cf -hwanda (HH); -vandira t (HHH) cf -vanda (HH) — PT *lay;* PP *lain*

life *condition of being alive* n upenyu 14 (LLH); rupenyu 11 (LLH); *in my life* adv chizvarirwo (LHLH); Handisati ndambobika sadza **chizvarirwo** changu. (*I have never yet cooked sadza in my life.*)

lift *raise up* vb -simudza t (HHL); -sumudza t (HHL)

ligament *fibrous tissue which joins movable bones* n runda 5 (LH)

light *torch* n mwenje 3 (LL)

light *be daylight* vb -edza i (HH); *first light of dawn* n chiedza 7 (LHL) cf -edza (HH); *light up, give l.* vb -vheneka i & t (LLL); *artificial light* n ruvheneko 11 (LLLL) cf -vheneka (LLL)

light *cause to burn or shine* vb -batidza t (HHH); -tungidza t (HHH); *light in weight, be l.* adj & vb -reruka i (HHH) (stative vb); Bhokisi iri **rakareruka.** (*This box is light.*); *lighter* adj -reruka pana; Bhokisi iri rakareruka pane rako. (*This box is lighter than yours.*); *lightest* adj Bhokisi iri rakareruka kupinda ose. (*This is the lightest box.*) — PT & PP *lighted, lit*

light rain *drizzle* n mubvumbi 3 (LLH)

light-skinned *(African) person* n mutsvuku 1 (LLH) cf -tsvuka (LL)

lightning n mheni 9 (LL); rukore 11 K (LLH); *flash of l.* n kupenya kwemheni 15

like *want, desire,* vb -da i & t (H)

like *be l. to* vb -fanana na- i, -nge i, -nga KoM; *be similar* adj & vb -fanana i (HHH) (stative vb); Vana ava vakafanana. (*These children are alike.*); *likeness, picture, image* n mufananidzo 3 (LHHHL) cf -fananidza (HHHL)

likewise *in like manner, similarly* adv conj saizvozvo (LHLH)

lily *flame l.* n kajongwe 12 (LLH) B.Bk. 1,51; *vlei l.* n durura 5 (LLL) B.Bk. 1,53

lily trotter *jacana* n katewetewe 12 (LLLLL) R228; *cf illustration p. 82*

lime *to trap birds* n urimbo 14 (LLL)

limit *boundary* n muganhu 3 (LHL)

limp *walk as a lame person* vb -kamhina i (LLL); -gamhina i MZ (LLL); -kumhina i (LLL)

line *straight or crooked l.* n mutsetse 3 (LHL); *line, a l. of string* n mukosi 3 (LHL); *line or file of men, queue* n mudungwe 3 (LHL); *line of men abreast* n rundaza 11 (LLH); *line of stitching* n musono 3 (LLL); *washing l.* n mutariro 3 (LHHL); mutariko 3 (LHHL)

linen *cloth* n jira 5, machira 6 (HH)

linger *delay* vb -nonoka i (LLL)

link together vb -kochekedzanisa t (LLLLLL)

lintel *support over doorway* n chikotamo 7 (LLLL) cf -kotama (LLL)

lion *the largest of our beasts of prey and member of the cat family* n shumba 9 (HL); *ancestral spirit is said to enter into a lion and to speak through a human medium* n mhondoro 9 (LLL)

lip *mouth* n muromo 3 (LLL)

lisp *defect of speech* n chirimi 7 (LHH)

listen *hear, obey* vb -teerera i & t (HHHL)

lit *cf light*

litre *measure of capacity, about 1¾ pints* n rita 5 (HL) cf Eng.

little *(in size)* adj -duku (HL); -diki MZ (HL); -doko KM; -nduku 9 MZ (HL); ndoko 9 KM (HL); *little (in quantity)* adj -shoma (LL)

little by little adv kashoma nakashoma (LLL LHLL)

little finger n kasiyanwa 12 (LHLH)

live *dwell* vb -gara i & t (LL); *live in harmony, l. in concord* vb -wadzana i (LLL)

live *be alive* adj -penyu (LH), benyu 5, mhenyu 9

live-long *tree* n mushamba 3 (LLH); mugan'acha 3 B.Bk. 1,30

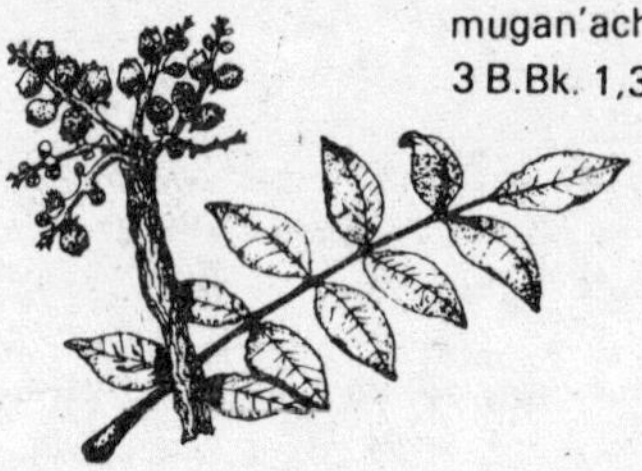

liver *organ in the body which purifies the blood* n chiropa 7 (LLL)

living *alive* adj -penyu (LH), benyu 5, mhenyu 9

living *way of l., manner of l.* n mugariro 3 (LLHH); magariro 6 (LLHH)

lizard *the commonest of our ls. is the striped house skink; small, long-tailed insect-eating, four-legged reptile,* n dzvinyu 5, madzvinyu 6 (LH); dzvombi 5, madzvombi 6 (LH); mukotyo 3 M (LHL); *rock lizard, agama l., with blue head which characteristically bobs up and down* n chidhambakura 7 (LLLHH); chiguyakuya 7 (LLLHH); *spiny agama* n chidhanana (LLLL); *gecko, small l. that is frequently* *found on the interior walls of human dwellings* n chifurira 7 (LHHL); *rock plated (60-90 cm)* n gweshadombo 5, magweshadombo 6 (HHLH); gwereveshe 5 (LLLL); *ornate scrub l.* n demashanga 5, mademashanga 6 (HHHL); dematsanga 5, madematsanga 6 (HHHL); *leguaan; exists in two var:*

agama chidhambakura

skink dzvinyu

monitor water l. n burwa 5, mapurwa 6 (HL); mupurwa 3 (LHL) (*associated in the popular mind, but quite falsely, with stealing milk from cows). Savanna, land l.; square nosed and about 1,5 m in length* n gwava 5, magwava 6 (LL); gwavava 5, magwavava 6 (LLL)

load *put a l. on or in* vb -tutira t (HHH); *l. to excess, overload* vb -remedza t (LLL)

load *that which is to be carried* n mutoro 3 (LHH)

load *a gun, prepare a gun for firing* vb -paka pfuti t (HH HL)

loaf *of bread* n rofu rechingwa 5 (HL LHL); chingwa 7 (LL)

loafer *person who does not like to work* n tsimbe 9 (LL); rovha 5, marovha 6 (LH) cf Eng.

loan *(money given or recieved on loan)* n chikwereti 7 (LHLL)

loathe *hate, strongly dislike* vb -sema i & t (HH)

lobola *bride-price* n roora 5 (HHL); pfuma 9 (HL)

location *large collection of workers' dwellings, usu on a farm* n rukisheni 11 (LHLL) cf Eng.

lock *secure fast with a lock* vb -kiya t (HH) cf Eng.

lock *device for fastening and securing with a key* n chimai chekiyi 7 (LHL HLL)

locust *winged insect like large grasshopper* n hwiza 9 Z (HL); mhashu 9 K (LL); ndongwe 9 M (HL)

lodge a complaint *report to higher authority* vb -mhan'ara i & t (LLL)

log *rough length of a tree trunk* n danda 5, matanda 6 (HH)

lonely *be lonesome* vb -surukirwa i (HHHL)

long *be tall* adj & vb -reba i (stative vb) (LL); Murume uyu akareba kwazvo. (*This man is very tall.*)

long *tall* adj -refu (LH), refu 5, ndefu 9

long ago adv kare kare (LL LL); *from long ago* adv kubvira kare (LLL LL); kubva kare (LH HL); *long ago, olden times* n pasichigare 16 (LHHLH); chinyakare 7 (LLLL)

long for *long to see, pine for* vb -suwa i & t (HH); -panga t (LL); *long for meat* vb -va nenhomba (LHL)

longclaw *sp of bird like wagtails and pipits* n nhonhonho 9 (HHH); *yellow-throated l.* n nyamudzwe 9 (LLL) R704

longing *desire* n shungu 9 (HH); chisuwo 7 MZ (LLL) cf -suwa (HH)

loofah *plant, member of the pumpkin family* n chishambo 7 (LLL). BBk 1,91

look *l. after, l. at* vb -tarisa i & t (LLL); -tarira i & t (LLL); -ringa i & t (HH); *l. about, l. here and there* vb -ringa-ringa i & t (HHHL) cf -ringa (HH);

after, keep safe vb -chengeta i & t (LLL); *l. at one another* vb -tarisana i (LLLL); *l. for, search for, seek* vb -tsvaga t KoMZ (LLL); *l. back, l. around* vb -cheuka i (HHH); *l. like, seem to be* vb -nge + noun or rel. **Rinenge ruva.** (*It looks like a flower.*); Anenge ava nani. (*He seems to be better.*); *l. out for, beware of* vb -chenjerera i (HHHL) cf -chenjera (HHH)

loop *slip-knot in string* n chishwe 7 (LL); chiswe 7 M (LL)

loose *be l., wear l.* vb -sekeneka i (LLLL); *be mal-adjusted (of mechanical things)* vb -ruza i (LL) cf Eng.; *be l., e.g. elastic in clothes* vb -dhamba i (LL); loosen knots vb -sungunura t (HHHL) cf -sunga (HH); *loosen bolts* vb -mononora t (HHHL) cf -mona (HH); *loosened, be undone* vb -sunungúka i (HHHL) cf -sunga (HH); -sungunuka i (HHHL)

lopsided *be inclined at an angle, tilt to one side* adj & vb -tsveyama i (HHH)

loquat fruit n zhanje 5, mazhanje 6 (LL); shuku 5, mashuku 6 K (LL); *loquat tree mahobohobo;* n muzhanje 3 (LLL); B.Bk. 1,26

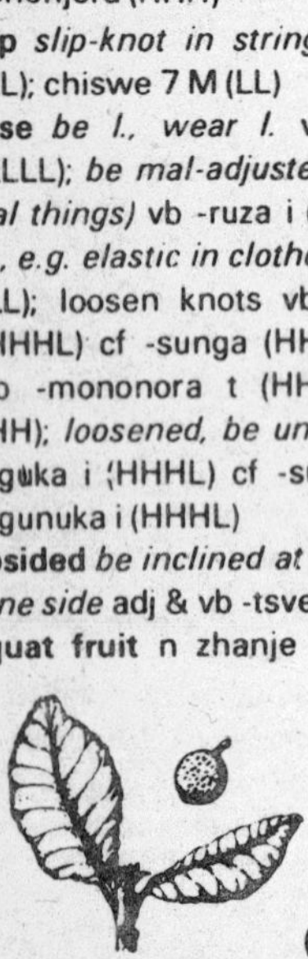

lord *king* n mambo 1a (LL); tenzi 1a (HL)

lorry *very large vehicle for carrying* n rori 9 (HL) cf Eng.

lose *throw away, forsake* vb -rasa t (HH); *squander, be late for* vb -ruza t (LL) cf Eng.; *l. blood, bleed* vb -buda ropa i (HH HL); *l. feathers, moult* vb -unduka i (LLL); *l. heart, abandon hope* vb -rasa mwoyo t (HH HL); *l. weight, get thin* vb -onda i (HH) — PT & PP *lost*

lost *get l., be l.* vb -rasika i (HHH); *be l. never to be found again* vb -tsakatika i (LLLL)

lourie *grey l., go-away bird* n kuwe 9 MZ (HL); pfunye 9 (LL) R339; *Knysna l.* n hurungira 9 (HHLH)

louse *small insect living on the bodies of human beings and other creatures* n inda 9 (LH); *illustration p. 124*

love *like, want* vb -da i & t (H); *l. (human and divine), longing disposition* n rudo 11 (LH); chido 7 (LH) cf -da (H); *l. one another, be in l.* vb -dana i (HH); -danana i (HHH)

love token *given by a girl to a young man as proof of her love* n nhumbi 9 (LH); nduma 9 K (LL)

lover *of a married woman, suitor of unmarried woman* n chikomba 7 (LLL)

low *be l. lying, be l. in price* adj & vb -derera i (LLL)

low *(of a bull)* vb kuma i (HH); -dzvova i (LL); *low (of cattle)* vb -kuma i (HH); -bowa i (HL)

lower *lessen* vb -tapudza i & t (HHH) ; l *physically* —dzikisa (LLL); *l. the price* vb -deredza mutengo t (LLL LHH)

luck *good l.* n rombo 5 MZ (LH); raki 5 (HL) cf Eng.; mhanza yakanaka 9 Z; *lucky* adj e.g. *A lucky man.* (Murume ane mhanza)

luck *bad l. n munyama 3 (LHL). persistant bad l.* n ropa rakaipa 5 (LL LHLL)

lucky *be fortunate, have good luck* vb -va nemhanza yakanaka.

lucky-bean tree *kaffirboom, has bright-red flowers in September* n mutiti 3 (LLL); B.Bk. 1,19; *erythrina* n mutsodzo 3 (LHH)

luggage *baggage* n mukwende 3 (LHH); mutwaro 3 (LHH); nhumbi 9 (LH)

lukewarm *be warm* vb -dziya i (HL); *cool hot water by adding cold* vb -tuvidza t (HHH)

lull to sleep *caress child* vb -rezva t (HH)

lump *swelling* n bundu 5, mapundu 6 (HH)

lump of earth *clod* n vhinga 5, mavhinga 6 (LL); vhungwa 5 M, mavhungwa 6 (LL)

lunatic *madman* n benzi 5, mapenzi 6 (HH); *lunacy, madness* n upenzi 14 (LHH)

lung *breathing organ* n bapu 5, mapapu 6 (LH)

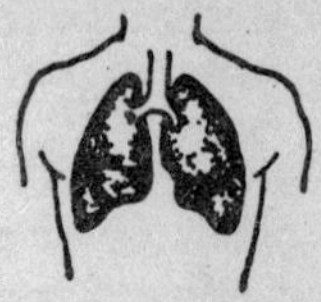

lust after *desire strongly* vb -chiva t (HH); *lust, strong impure desire* n ruchiva 11 (LHH) cf -chiva (HH)

luxury *costly and expensive living* n umbozha 14 (LLL)

M

mamba rovambira

machine *apparatus to provide power or to use power* n muchini 3 (LHL); muchina 3 (LHL) cf Eng.

machine-gun *gun firing a continuous stream of bullets* n chigwagwagwa 7 (LLLL)

mad *be mental* vb -penga i (HH)

made *cf make*

madman *fool, idiot* n benzi 5, mapenzi 6 (HH); *madness, foolishness, stupidity* n upenzi 14 (LHH) cf benzi (HH)

maggot *grub, larva* n honye 9 (LL); gonye 5, makonye 6 (LL)

maggot fly nhunzi 9 (HH)

magistrate *civil officer acting as judge in the lowest courts* n mejastriti 1a (HLHL) cf Eng.

mahogany *pod m. tree* n mukamba 3 (LHH); mungongoma 3 (LLLL); mungwingwi 3 (LLL) B.Bk. 1,4

mail *post, letters* n posti 9 (HL) cf Eng.

maim *mutilate, permanently damage* vb -remadza t (HHH)

maimed person *cripple* n chirema 7 (LHH)

main *great, principal* adj -kuru (HH), guru 5, huru 9

main road *motor road, street* n mugwagwa 3 (LLL)

mainly *especially* adv zvikuru (LHH)

maintain *keep, look after* vb -chengeta t (LLL)

maize *cereal crop* n chibage 7 Z (LLH); chibarwe 7 K (LLH); gwere 5 M (HL);

chibahwe 7 KoZ (LLH); *green and fresh m.* n chibage chinyoro 7 (LLH LHH); *m. flower or stigma* n mucheke-chera 3 (LLLLH); *m. cob with grains* n muguri 3 (LLL); *m. cob without grains* n guri 5, maguri 6 (LL); *green m. stalk* n gunde 5, magunde 6 (HL); *dry m. stalk* n shanga 5, mashanga 6 (LL); *m. tassel (beard)* n rurebvu 11 (LLL); *break off m. cob from the stalk* vb -svodogora t (HHHL); *remove m. grains from the cob* vb -tsvokonyora t (HHHL); *remove leaves around m. cob* vb -furura t (LLL)

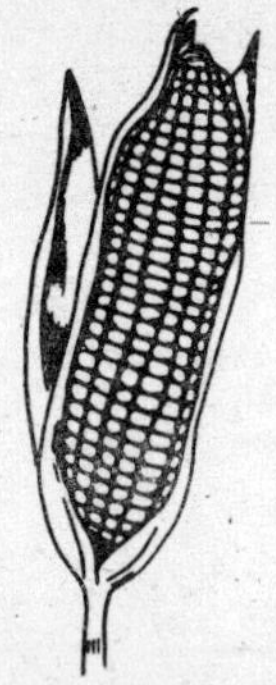

maize meal *mealie meal* n upfu 14 (LL)

majesty *greatness* n ukuru 14 (LHH)

majority *the greater part* n ruzhinji 11 (LHH)

make *do, prepare* vb -ita t (LL); -gadzira i & t (LLL); *m. a bed* vb -waridza mu-bhedha t (LLL LHL); *m. a decision, decide* vb -funga i (LL); *m. a detour* vb -tsauka i (HHH); *m. a fire, kindle a fire* vb -kuhwidza moto t (LLL LH); *m. a mistake, err* vb -kanganisa i (HHHL); *m. a considerable noise, clamour* vb -ita mheremhere (LL LLLL); *m. faces, pull faces* vb -finyamisa pameso (HHHL LLH); *m. fun of, laugh at* vb -se-ka t (LL); *m. for, proceed towards* vb -nanga t (HH); *m. haste, hurry* vb -ku-rumidza i (HHHL); -chimbidza i (HHH); *m. inquiries, investigate* vb -feya-feya i & t (HHHL); *m. up for, compensate for* vb -ripa i & t (LL); *m. known, inform* vb -zivisa t (HHH) cf -ziva (HH); *m. love, court* vb -nyenga i & t (HH) (*impolite term in M*); -pfimba i & t M (HH); *m. off, run away, abscond* vb -ti-za i & t (HH); *m. out, detect, see* vb -ona i & t (HH); *m. up for lost time or money* vb -kuchidza i (LLL); *m. up the mind* vb -funga i (LL); -tsunga i (HH); *m. up to, curry favour, persuade, coax* vb -nyengetera t (HHHL); *m. up weight, increase* vb -pamhidza t (LLL); *m. use of, employ, use* vb -seve-nzesa t (HHHL); *m. way, move out of the way* vb -suduruka i (LLLL); *m. well, restore a person to health* vb -ponesa i & t (HHH) cf -pona (HH)—PT & PP *made*

malaria *disease carried by the anopheles mosquito* n musarara 3 (LLLL); marariya 9 (LHLL) cf Eng.

Malawian *person from Malawi* adj Mu-nhu wechiMalawi.

male *(human)* n munhurume 1 (LLLL); murume 1 (LHH); *male (animal)* n nzo-mbe 9 (HH); mukono 3 (LHH); hono 9 (HH); *male (bird)* n jongwe 5, macho-ngwe 6 (LH)/ majongwe 6 (LH)

malice *active ill will, spite, desire to hurt, vindictiveness* n pfini 9 (HH); chinya 7 (LL); tsinye 10 (LL); *behave maliciously* vb -shinhwa i (LL)

malign *slander, back-bite* vb -ita maku-hwa i (LL LLL); -chera t (LL); -reva mu-mwe (HH HL)

mallet *hammer* n ndovero, nyundo 9 (LL) *cf illustration p. 162*

malt *base for beer-making* n chimera 7 KoMZ (LLL); mamera 6 MZ (LLL)

mamba *much feared and very poisonous sp of snake, whose colour may vary from brown to slate-grey or black. The under-parts are white. When angry it has the habit of swelling (with air) at the throat in order to appear more menacing. Length about 3 m.; black mamba* n rovambira 5 (HHHL); mubobo 3 MZ (LLL); *green mamba, bright green sp often confus-*

ed with the boomslang and referred to by the same Shona name: Mhangara 9 (LLL) *cf illustration p. 95*

man *human male* n murume 1 (LHH); *married m.* n saimba 1a (HLH); murume 1 (LHH); *m. of position* n mukurumukuru 1 (LHHHLL); *old m.* n harahwa 9 MZ (LLL); mutana 1 K (LHH); *unmarried old m., bachelor* n tsvimborume 9 (HHHL); *young m.* (18—21) n jaya 5, majaya 6 (LH); jaha 5, majaha 6 M (LH)

manage to *be able to* vb -kwanisa i & t (HHH); -gona i & t (LL)

mane *of a lion or any animal* n zenze 5, mazenze 6 (LL)

mange *skin disease* n gwembe 5 (LH)

manger *food trough for animals* n chidyiro 7 (LHH) cf -dya (H)

mango *tree* n mumango 3 (LHL); *mango, tropical fruit; plur mangoes* n mango 9 (HL) cf Eng.

mangwe *tree, silver t., yellow-wood tree* n mukonono 3 (LLLL); musuzu 3 (LHL) B.Bk. 1,38

manner of *custom* n mutoo 3 (LLL); tsika 9 (LL)

mannered *be well-behaved* vb; (Ane) tsika dzakanaka (LL LHHL). (*He has good manners / is well-behaved.*)

manners *good m.* n tsika 10 (LL); unhu 14 (LL); *bad m.* n tsika dzakaipa 10 (LL LHLL)

mannikin *sp of bird* n chinjengenja 7 (LHLH); njengenja 9 (HLH)

mantis *praying m., sp of insect* n mbuyamuderere 9 (HLLLLH); mbuyambuya 5 K (HLHL); nyamuputsahari 1a M (LLHLHH) *cf illustration p. 80*

manure *animal waste or other material, natural or artificial, used for making soil fertile* n mupfudze 3 (LHL); manyowa 6 (LLL) cf Eng.

many adj -zhinji (HH); zhinji 10; *how many?* adj -ngani? (LH)

many times *often* adv kazhinji 12 (LHH)

map *chart which describes an area* n mepu 9 (HL) cf Eng.

mar *spoil* vb -nyangadza t (HHH)

marabou *stork, sp of long-legged, carrion-eating bird* n natsure 9 (LLL); shuranyama 9 (LLLL); svorenyama 9 (LLLL) R73 *cf illustration p. 136*

march *walk as soldiers do* vb -fora i Z (HH); -macha i (HH) cf Eng.

margarine *vegetable or animal fat used instead of butter* n majarini 6 (LLHL) cf Eng.

marijuana *dagga, wild hemp* n mbanje 9 (LH) cf Hindustani

mark *make or put a sign* vb -cherechedza t Z (HHHL); -tara t (HH); *mark, sign* n mucherechedzo 3 (LHHHL), cf -cherechedza (HHHL)

market-place n musika 3 (LLL)

marriage *Christian rite of m.* n muchato 3 (LLL) cf -chata (LL)

married *be taken by a husband as a wife* vb -roorwa i (HHH)

marrow *soft interior of a bone* n mwongo 3 (LH); mongo 3 (LH)

marry *by tribal custom, pay bride-price for marriage* vb -roora i & t (HHH); *m. in church or civilly* vb -chata i & t (LL); *promise in marriage* vb -roodza t (HHH)

marsh *water-logged area* n murove 3 (LLH); matope 6 (LLL)

marula *tree, producing a fruit which is a favourite food of the elephant and of very many antelopes* n mupfura 3 (LHL); mutsomo 3 (LHL) B.Bk. 1,28; *bastard m. t.* n mubvumira 3 (LLLL); mutuva 3 (LHL) B.Bk. 1,22

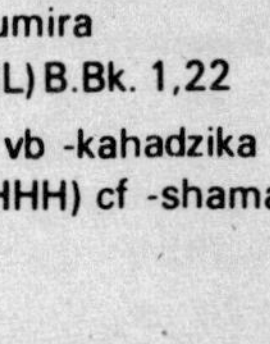

marvel *be surprised at* vb -kahadzika i (LLLL); -shamiswa i (HHH) cf -shama (HH)

mash *crush into a soft, damp mess* vb -pwanya t (LL); -tsonda t (LL)

mason wasp n mbuzambuza 9 (HLHL); mbuzvambuzva 9 K (HLHL)

Mass *Eucharistic sacrifice* n Misa 9 (HL) cf Latin

mass of people *crowd* n mhomho 9 (HH)

master *owner* n muridzi 1 (LLL); tenzi 1a (HL); mwene 1a (LH)

mat *table m.* n meti 9 (HL) cf Eng.; *m. of reeds, sleeping m.* n rukukwe 11 (LHL); rupasa 11 (LLL); bonde 5 (LH); *old sleeping m.* n rutsapata 11 (LLLL)

matches n machisi 6 (LLL) cf Eng.; fofo 9 (HL)

matchstick n nziswa 9 (LH)

mate *copulate* vb -tanda t (HH); -kwira i & t (HH) (euphemisms)

maternity dress *m. ward* n mateniti 6 (LHLL) cf Eng.

matrimony *state of being married* n muchato 3 (LLL) cf -chata (LL)

matter *subject of conversation or of news* n nyaya 9 (LH)

mattress *long, thick pad on which to sleep* n matiresi 9 (HLLL) cf Eng.

maxim *proverb* n tsumo 9 (HH)

may *might, should, would Use Potential Mood*

me pron ini (LH) cf p. 207; object cc -ndi- *cf p. 206*

meal *evening m.* n chirariro 7 (LHHL) cf -rarira (HHH); *mid-day m.* n dhina 5 (HL) cf Eng.; *morning m., breakfast* n chisvusvuro 7 (LHHL) cf -svusvura (HHH)

mealie meal *flour* n upfu 14 (LL); *mechanically ground maize* n mugayiwa 3 (LHLH) cf -gaya (HH)

mealies *cobs of maize* n chibage 7 (LLH); chibahwe 7 (LLH) sing. only; *mealie cob n muguri 3 (LLL); mealie rice, samp* n munyuchu 3 (LHL); *green m.* n chibahwe chinyoro 7 (LLH LHH); *half a m. cob* n chigodo 7 (LHL); *dry m.* n mhandire 9 (LHL)

mean *indicate, explain* vb -reva t, *passive:* -rehwa (HH); -bvira t K (LL); *mean, say, name* vb -ti i & t (LL); Tinomuti John. (*We call him John.*) — PT & PP *meant*

mean *be stingy* vb -nyima i & t (HH); -pomera i (HH); *mean, be m. with money* vb -va norutsuta i (LHLL)

meant *cf mean*

meanwhile *meantime* adv -fano-; -nguno- Z; -sano- *infix vbs*

measles *infectious disease* n gwirikwiti 5 (LLLL); biripiri 5 (LLLL); biripiti 5 (LLLL)

measure *find the size, quantity, degree etc.* vb -pima i & t (LL); -yera i & t (LL)

measure *size, quantity, degree* n chipimo 7 KM (LLL); chiero 7 (LLL)

measurement *due measure* n mwero 3 Z (LL) cf -era (LL)

measuring device *m. instrument* n chiereso 7 (LLLL) cf -era (LL)

meat *flesh* n nyama 9 (LL); *boneless m.* n munyepfu 3 (LLL); *fatty m.* n nyama yakakora 9 (LL LHHL); *sinewy m., gristle* n runda 5, marunda 6(LH); *strip of m., fresh or dry* n mudzonga 3 (LHL)

mechanic *skilled workman who makes or repairs or works machines* n makanika 1a (LHLL) cf Eng.

medal *flat piece of metal with a design stamped on it* n medhuru 9 (HLL) cf Eng.; menduru 9 (HLL)

meddle *interfere* vb -bvonganyisa t (HHHL); -pindira i & t (LLL)

mediate *speak for* vb -reverera t (HHHL); *mediator, advocate* n murevereri 1 (LHHHL)

medicine *remedy* n muti 3 (LH); mushonga 3 (LLH); *opening m., laxative* n mushonga wokuendesa kunze 3

meditate *think deeply, reflect* vb -rangarira i & t (LLLL); *meditation, deep thought, prayerful thought* n chirangariro 7 (LLLLL)

medium *living spirit-m.* n svikiro 5, masvikiro 6 (LLL)

medlar *tree, false m.* n munzvirwa 3 (LHL) B.Bk. 1,46

meek *be gentle* adj & vb -pfava i (LL) (stative vb); Ano murume aka**pfava**. (*She has a kindly husband.*)

meekness *kindness* n unyoro 14 (LHH); rupfave 11 (LLH)

meet *m. up with* vb -sangana na- (LLL); *go to m.* vb -chingura t (HHH) — PT & PP *met*

meeting *a coming together of persons for some purpose* n musangano 3 (LLLL) cf -sangana (LLL); *chance m.* n mahwekwe 6 (LLH)

melon *water m.* n mwiwa 5, mamwiwa 6 (HL); nwiwa 5, manwiwa 6 (HL); vise 5, mavise 6 (HL); *cattle m.* n shamba 5, mashamba 6 (LH)

melt *become unstuck through heat e.g. solder* vb -nanauka i (LLLL); -nanautsa t (LLLL)

melt *dissolve, become a liquid, liquify* vb -nyunguruka i (LLLL); -nyungudika i Z (LLLL) — PT *melted;* PP *melted, molten*

member *of a body or organisation* n mutezo 3 (LHH); nhengo 9 (LL)

memorial *something made or done to remind people of an event or person* n chiyeuchidzo 7 (LLLLL)

menace *frighten, threaten* vb -tyisidzira t (HHHL)

mend *repair, put right* vb -gadzira t (LLL); *sew* vb -sona i & t (LL)

menstruate *have a menstrual discharge* vb -enda kumwedzi (LL LLH); -shamba i (LL)

mental *be mad* vb -penga i (HH)

mentally retarded *simple person* n dandara 5 MZ, madandara 6 (LLL); rema 5, marema 6 (HH)

mention *talk about* vb -taura nezva-

merchant *salesman* n mutengesi 3 (LHHL) cf -tengesa (HH)

mercy *holding oneself back from punishing or causing suffering* n tsitsi 10 (LH); nyasha 10 KKoM (LL); ngoni 10 (LL)

merely *only* adv -to- infix vb; chete (HL)

merry *be happy, be cheerful* vb -fara i (HH)

mess up *disarrange, spoil* vb -bvonganyisa t (HHHL)

Messiah *Saviour* n Mununuri 1 (LLLL); Mesiya 1a (LHL) cf Eng.

message *news* n dama 5, matama 6 (HH); shoko 5, mashoko 6 (LL)

messenger *a person carrying a message* n nhumwa 9 (HL); mutumwa 1 (LHL); nhume 9 (HL) cf -tuma (HH)

messenger *court m.* n chikonzi 7 (LHL)

met *cf meet*

metal *(general term)* n simbi 9 (LH)

method *manner of* n mutoo 3 (LLL)

mew *noise of a cat* vb -n'eura i (HHH)

midday *(10.00 a.m. — 3.00 p.m.)* n masikati 6 (LHLH); *m. meal, lunch* n kudya kwamasikati 15 (LH HLHHL)

middle *at the centre* n pakati 16 (LLH)

midge *gnat, tiny fly* n unyunyu 14 (LLH)

midnight *in the middle of the night* adv pakati pousiku 16 (LLH HLHH)

midst *in the m. of* prep pakati pa- 16 (LLH); mukati ma- 18 (LLH)

midsummer *in the middle of the summer* n masutso 6 (LHH)

midwife *one who helps women in childbirth* n nyamukuta 1a (LLLL)

mile *measure of distance, 1760 yards* n maira 9 (HLL) cf Eng.

milk *liquid food from a female mammal* n mukaka 3 (LLL); *m.-man* n mufambisi womukaka 1; *m. bucket* n hamiro 9 MZ (HHL); kamiro 9 K (HHL) cf -kama (HH); *first m. of a cow* n munamba 3 (LHH); *draw m. from a cow* vb -kama i & t (HH); *release m.* vb -sisa i (LL); *sour m.* n mukaka wakakora 3 (LLL LHHL)

milkwood *shrub, fluted m.s., stemfruit, red milkwood* n mutswatswa 3 (LLL)

mill *grinding machine for grain* n chigayo 7 (LHH) cf -gaya (HH)

miller *one who grinds grain with a machine* n mugayisi 1 (LHHL) cf -gaya (HH)

millet *bulrush grain plant with tiny seeds* n mhunga 9 (LL); *finger m.* n zviyo 8 (LH); rukweza 11 (LHH)

millimeter *very small measure of distance* n mirimita 9 (HLHL) cf Eng.

million *1 000 000* n miriyoni 9 (HLLL) cf Eng.

millipede *creature with numerous legs* n zongororo 5, mazongororo 6 (LHLL); chongororo 7 (*small m.*) (LHLL)

mimic *imitate, follow good or bad example* vb -tevedzera i & t (LLLL); *ridicule by imitating* vb -edzesera i & t (LLLL)

mimosa thorn tree *sweet thorn t.* n muunga 3 (LLL); mubayamhondoro 3 (LLLLLL) B.Bk. 1,15

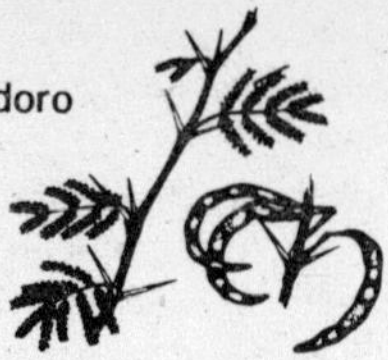

mince *chop finely* vb -cheka-cheka t (HHHL) cf -cheka (HH); *m. by machine* vb -gaya t (HH)

mind *intellect* n njere 9 (HH)

mind *care about* vb -katara i (HHH); *look after* vb -chengeta t (LLL)

mine *hole made in the earth to get out coal, copper, gold etc.* n mugodhi 3 (LLH)

mingerhout tree *wild oleander, redwood t.* n muona 3 (LHH)

minister of religion *missionary* n mufundisi 1 (LHLL) cf -fundisa (HHH)

minnow *very small fish, the young of larger fish* n sinde 5, masinde 6 (LL); musunde 3 (LLL)

minute *small division of time, one sixtieth part of an hour* n miniti 9 (HLL) cf Eng.

minute *very small* adj -duku (HL); duku 5 & 9, nduku 9; diki 5 & 9, ndiki 9 dikidiki (HL HL)

miracle *remarkable or surprising event beyond understanding* n chishamiso 7 (LHHL) cf -shama (HH)

mirage *a false picture that appears before the eyes* n maedzera 6 M (LLLL); dzamaradzimu 5 (LLLHH)

mirror *looking glass* n chiringiro 7 (LHHL) cf -ringa (HH)

misbehave *behave badly or wrongly* vb -shereketa i (LLLL); -ita musikanzwa (LL LHLH)

miscarry *deliver a baby that is dead at birth or soon afterwards* vb -svodza i & t (*animals*) (LL); -pfukudzika (*humans*) (HHHL); -rasa pamuviri (HH HLLL); -tadza i (HH)

mischief *foolish or thoughtless behaviour likely to cause trouble* n musikanzwa 3 (LHLH); Ane misikanzwa. (*He is mischievous.*)

mischievous *be misbehaved, be fond of mischief* vb -shereketa i (LLLL)

miserliness *stinginess* n rutsuta 11 (LLL); *miserly, be stingy* vb -omera i (HHH); -va norutsuta (LHLL)

misery *misfortune* n rushambwa 11 (LLH); nhamo 9 (HH)

miss *aim badly, fail to hit* vb -potsa i & t (LL)

miss *be too late for* vb -ruza i & t (LL) cf Eng.

miss one another *pass by without meeting* vb -pesana i (LLL)

mission *m. station conducted by missionaries; place of instruction in Christian doctrine with school attached* n misheni 5 & 9 (HLL); mishoni 5 & 9 (HLL) cf Eng.

missionary *minister of religion* n mufundisi 1 (LHLL) cf -fundisa (HHH)

mist *fog, water vapour in the air* n mhute 9 (LH); *heavy m., very light rain* n guti 5 (LL)

mistake *make m.* vb -kanganisa i & t (HHHL); -nyangadza i & t (HHH) — PT *mistook;* PP *mistaken; mistake* n chikanganiso 7 (LHHHL)

mistreat *treat cruelly* vb -va noutsinye i (LHLL)

mix *put several things together so that they are no longer separate* vb -vhenga t (HH); *knead* vb -kanya t (LL)

mixture *of different kinds* n masanganiswa 6 (LLHHL); musanganiswa 3 (LLHHL)

mnondo *tree, very similar to the musasa tree* n munhondo 3 (LLL) B.Bk. 1,10

moan *utter a low sound of pain or suffering* vb -uura i (HHH)

mob *multitude, crowd* n mhomho 9 (HH); dumbu ravanhu 5 (HH LHL)

mobola plum *tree, hissing t.* n muhacha 3 (LLL) B.Bk. 1,3

Mocambique rough-scaled sand lizard n demashanga 5, matemashanga 6 (HHHL); *M. spitting cobra* n mhakure 9 (HLH)

mock *laugh at, despise* vb -seka i & t (LL); -nyomba i & t (HH); *ridicule* vb -sveveredza i & t (HHHL)

model *likeness* n chifananidzo 7 (LHHHL) cf -fananidza (HHHL)

moderation *in due measure* n mwero 3 Z (LL)

moist *be damp* adj & vb -nyorova i (HHH) (stative vb); Akapfeka hembe yakanyorova. (*He put on a damp shirt.*)

moisture *dampness* n mwando 3 (LL); munya 3 (LL)

molar tooth *t. used for grinding food* n zeyo 5, mazeyo 6 (LL); dzeyo 5, madzeyo 6 KM (LL)

mole-rat *a blind burrowing rodent, which eats bulbs etc.* n nhuta 9 (LL) *cf p. 132*

molest *annoy* vb -netsa i & t (LL)

Monday *first day of the week* n Muvhuro 3 (LLL)

money *cash* n mari 9 (LH) cf Arabic *(wealth)*

mongoose *meercat, banded m.* n dzvovororo 5, madzvovororo 6 (LLLL); *water m. and dwarf m.* n chidzvororo 7 K (LLLL); *white-tailed m.* n jerenyenje 5, majerenyenje 6 (LLLL); *slender m.* n hovo 9 (LL); kovo 1a M (LL); govo 5 K, makovo 6 (LL) *cf illustration p. 102*

mousebird *coly, gregarious sp of fruit-eating bird* n chiyovhovho 7 K (LLLL); shirapopo 9 Z (LLLL); dzvinyira 5 M (LLL); muchihoho 3 (LHLL)

mouse-trap *device for killing mice* n chikirimbani 7 (LLHLL)

moustache *hair allowed to grow on the upper lip* n usopo 14 MZ (LLL)

mouth *opening through which food is taken* n muromo 3 (LLL); *beak of a bird* n muromo weshiri 3 (LLL LHL); *inside of m.* n mukanwa 18 (LLL); *gums* n matadza 6 (LLL); *tongue* n rurimi 11 (LHH); *tooth* n zino 5, mazino 6 (HH); *palate* n hwavhu-utete 14 (LL LLL)

move *walk, travel* vb -famba i (HH); *m. heavy object, push* vb -sandidzira t (LLLL); *m. apart, give way* vb -taramuka i (HHHL); *move away* vb -bva i (L); -suduruka i (LLLL); *m.away, take away* vb -bvisa t (LL) cf -bva (L); *m. back, recede, make way* vb -suduruka i (LLLL); *m. close, approach, come near* vb -swedera i (LLL); *m. at slow pace, m. slowly* vb -nanaira i (HHHL)

move home *m village* vb -tama i & t (HH)

move to pity *evoke pity* vb -siririsa i & t (HHHL); -pisa tsitsi i & t (HH LH)

mow grass *cut grass* vb -cheka uswa t (HH LH) — PT *mowed*; PP *mown*

Mozambique *cf Mocambique*

Mrs. X n Mai Nhingi 1a MZ (HH LH)

much *a good quantity* adj -zhinji (HH); *very much* adv chaizvo (LHL); kwazvo (HL)

mucus *fluid from the nose* n dzihwa 5, madzihwa 6 (LH) — *same word as for a cold*

mud *mortar* n dhaka 5, madhaka 6 (LL)

mudguard *wheel shield to protect from mud* n madhigadhi 9 (HLLL) cf Eng.

mud-sucker *labeo, a sp of fish with curious rubber-like mouth* n mhumbu 9 (LL)

muddle *bring into confusion* vb -bvonganyisa t (HHHL); -vhiringa t (HHH)

muddy *be discoloured* vb -bvongeka i (HHH); -bvunduka i (LLL) (stative vb); Mvura yaka**bvunduka**. (*The water is muddy.*)

mug *large drinking vessel* n bhikiri 5, mabhikiri 6 (HLH)

mukwa tree *blood-wood t.* n mubvamaropa 3 (LLLLL); mukwa 3 (LL) B.Bk. 1,21

mulberry *fruit* n habhurosi 9 (HLLL); *mulberry tree* n muhabhurosi 3 (LHLLL)

multiply *by natural increase* vb -wanda i (LL); *make numerous* vb -wanziridza t (LLLL)

multitude *of people, mob* n mhomho 9 (HH); dumbu ravanhu 5 (HH LHL)

mumps *contagious disease with swelling of the glands* n mahumunya 6 MZ (LLHL)

municipality *governing body of town or city with local self-government* n menisiparati 9 (HHHHLL) cf Eng.

murder *kill a human being* vb -ponda i & t (LL); -uraya i & t (HHH); *murder, unlawful killing of a human being on purpose* n umhondi 14 (LLL) cf -ponda (LL); *murderer, killer* n mhondi 9 (LL) cf -ponda (LL); mupondi 1 (LLL) cf -ponda (LL); muurayi 1 (LHHL) cf -uraya (HHH)

musasa tree *(also known as msasa)* n musasa 3 (LLH)

muscle *tissue by which movement is effected* n tsinga 9 (HH) *(same word as vein)*

mushroom *fast-growing fungus* n hwohwa 14 MZ (LL); *cf illustration p. 170*

music *melodious, harmonious, plea-*

sant sound n mumhanzi 3 (LLH); musakazo 3 (LLLL)

must *ought to, should* vb -fanira i (HHH)

mustard *hot-tasting sauce* n mastadhi 9 (HLL) cf Eng.; *Indian or Chinese m. (a veg)* n tsunga 9 (HL); ndakupuka 9 (LHHL)

mutilate *maim permanently, damage a living thing* vb -remadza i & t (HHH)

mutton *flesh of the sheep* n nyama yehwai 9 (LL LHL)

mystery *astonishing event* n chishamiso 7 (LHHL) cf -shamisa (HHH)

N

nest dendere

naartjie *tangarine, mandarin* n nachisi 5, manachisi 6 (HLL) cf Afrik.

nail *finger or toe n., hard substance covering the end of a finger or toe* n nzara 9 (LH); runzara 11 (LLH); nzwara 9 (LH)

nail *piece of metal with a point at one end and a hood at the other, for holding things together* n chipikiri 7 (LHHH); *hammer in a nail* vb -rovera t (HHH)

Namaqua dove *small, long-tailed d.* n nhondoro 9 (LLL); nzembe 9 (LL); dzembe 9 (LL)

name *word by which a thing or creature is spoken of* n zita 5, mazita 6 (HH)

name *give a name to* vb -tumidza t (HHH); *be named, be called* vb -nzi i (L) (*Passive Form of vb* -ti)

namesake *person with the same name* n sazita 1a (HLL)

nanny *one who takes care of small children* n mureri 1 (LLL) cf -rera (LL); neni 1a (LH) cf Eng.

napkin *nappy, diaper, towel folded between a baby's legs* n mutambo 3 (LLL); napukeni 9 (HLLL) cf Eng.

narrate *tell a story, speak* vb -taura i & t (LLL)

narrow *thin* adj -tete (LL), dete 5 (LL); nhete 9 (LL)

Natal red top grass n bhurakwacha 5 (LHLL)

nation *people, tribe, race* n rudzi 11, marudzi 6 (LL)

native syringa tree n munhondo 3 (LLL); mutondo 3 (LLL)

navel *belly button, umbilicus* n guvhu 5, makuvhu 6 (HH)

near *close* adv padyo 16 (LL); pedyo 16 (LL); *time and place* padyo na-: padyo nemba yangu (*near my house*)

nearby adv pakarepo 16 (LHLH)

neat *be tidy, be in good order* adj & vb -chena (LL); -tsvinda (LLL); -shambidzika (LLLL); Mumba umu maka**chena**. (*This house is neat inside.*)

necessary *be needful* adj -dikanwa i (HHH) cf -da (H)

neck *part of the body which joins the trunk to the head* n mutsipa 3 (LLL); huro 9 M (LL); *nape or back of the n.* n chikotsikotsi 7 (LLLLL)

necktie n tai 9 (HL) cf Eng.

need *love, like, require, want* vb -da i & t (H); *needed, be required* vb -dikanwa i (HHH) cf -da (H)

needle *sharp, steel instrument with a hole at one end (called an eye) used for sewing* n tsono 9 (LL); tsingano 9 KM (HHL); *sacking n.* n dumbu 5 (LL)

neglect *lack attention for, fail to pay attention to or care for* vb -shaya hanyn'a i (LL LL)

neigh *of a horse, make the cry of a horse* vb -hwihwidza i (HHH)

neighbour *person living close by, next-door n.* n muvakidzani 1 (LHHHL); mubanzi 1 M (LHH)

neighbouring *be touching, be adjacent* vb -batana i (HHH) (stative vb)

neither . . . **nor** . . . conj neg + kana (LL) . . . kana . . . (LL); Haadyi **kana** zviwitsi **kana** shuga. (*He eats neither sweets nor sugar.*)

nephew *of maternal uncle (sekuru)* n muzukuru 1 (LHHL); *of maternal aunt (mainini/maiguru)* n mwana 1 (LH); *of paternal uncle (baba)* n mwana 1 (LH); *of paternal aunt (tete)* n mwana 1 (LH); muzukuru (LHHL)

nervous *be alarmed* vb -vhunduka i & t (LLL)

nest *home made by birds for their young* n dendere 5, matendere 6 (LLH); chitsaki 7 M (LLH) *cf illustration p. 105*

nestling *young bird* n nyn'ana 5, manyn'ana 6 (LH)

net *for fishing* n usvasvi 14 (LLH); *n. for hunting* n mambure 6 (LHL)

never *not ever, not at all* adv -mbo-, -tongo- M infix vbs (*to emphasize a negative vb*); Handimbotsiki pano pamusha zvakare. (*I will never set foot in this village again.*); -fa + Remote PP; Handifi ndakatsika pano pamusha zvakare. (*I will never set foot in this village again.*)

nevertheless *in spite of that, yet* conj zvisinei (HLHL)

new *not existing before* adj -tsva (H); idzva 5 (LH), itsva 9 (LH)

newcastle poultry disease n chibhubhubhu 7 (LLLL)

news *report or account of what has recently happened* n nhau 9 (LH); *newspaper* n pepanhau 5, mapepanhau 6 (LLLH); nyuzipepa 5, manyuzipepa 6 (HLLL) cf Eng.

next *the one following in time* adj mwedzi unouya *(next month)*

nibble *(eating done by mice, rats, etc.)* vb -n'en'ena t (HHH)

nice *be beautiful, pretty* adj & vb -naka i (LL) (stative vb); *nicer* adj -naka kukunda . . . Imba yangu yaka**naka kukunda** yako. (*My house is nicer than yours.*) *nicest* adj Imba yangu yakanaka kukunda dzose. (*My house is the nicest of all.*); *nice to look at, be attractive* vb -yevedza i (LLL)

nicely *well, in a nice way* adv zvakanaka (LHHL) rel

nickname *name given in addition to, or altered from, used instead of, the real name* n zita ramadunhurirwa 5 (HH HLHHLH); zita rokunemera 5 (HH HLHHH)

niece *of paternal uncle (baba)* n mwana 1 (LH); *n. of maternal uncle (sekuru)* n muzukuru 1 (LHHL); *n. of paternal aunt (tete)* n mwana 1 (LH); muzukuru 1 (LHHL); *of maternal aunt (mainini / maiguru)* n mwana 1 (LH)

night *time of darkness* n usiku 14 (LHH); *night and day* adv siku nesikati (HH HLLL); *all n. long* adv -rariro-; -rindo-; -raro- (infix vbs)

night jar *night-flying bird that passes the day resting on the ground* n dahwa 5 MZ, matahwa 6 (LH); dabwa 5 K (LH); *pennant-winged n.j.* n dahwamaringa 5, madahwamaringa 6 (LHHLH)

night ape *nagapie, smaller of our 2 sp of galago* bunha 5 MZ (HL); buna 5 M (HL); chinhavira 7 (LLLL); gwee *cf illustration p. 64*

nine *a number* adj -pfumbamwe (LLL); pfumbamwe 10

ninth *(of a series)* adj -chipfumbamwe (HLLL)

nipple *teat, part of the breast through which milk passes* n munyatso 3 (LLL)

nit *egg of louse or other parasitic insect* n gadzanda 5, magadzanda 6 (LLH); rakadzi 5, marakadzi 6 (LHL)

no *a denial or refusal* interj aiwa (HLL); kwete (HL)

no longer adv Progressive implication; Hapa**sisi**na ronda. (*There is no longer any wound.*); Han**disisiri** kurwara. (*I am no longer ill.*)

no matter how *Kana (LL)* + consecutive form; *no matter what* Kana (LL) + consecutive form. **Kana u**kaita sei handibvumi. (*No matter what you do, I shall not agree.*)

no one *none, nothing* n Copulative vb -n; Kana mumba musina mari ndinokupa. (*If there is no money in the house, I will give you some.*); Hapana achiri kuyeuka. (*There is no one who remembers.*)

nod sleepily, *doze* vb -dzimwaira i Z (HHHL); -guswaira MZ (HHHL); -tsimwaira i K (HHHL)

nod *in agreement, n. the head in recognition* vb -gutsurira i & t (HHHL)

noise *sound, esp loud, unpleasant sound* n mheremhere 9 (LLLL); mhere 9 (LL); ruzha 11 (LH); bongozozo 5 (LLLL); *make n., be noisy* vb -ita ruzha i (LL LH); *noisy* adj munhu ane mheremhere (*a noisy person*); Chii chiri kudaro? *What is making that noise? (What is doing that?)*

noon (*12.00 a.m. — 1.00 p.m.*) adv masikati 6 (LHHL)

noose *loop of rope (with a running knot) that becomes tighter when the rope is pulled* n chishwe 7 (LL)

north *quarter of the compass* n chamhembe (LHH) (*less often:* maodzanyemba (LLLLL))

nose *nostril* n mhuno 9 KoZ (LL); mhino 9 KM (LL); *bridge of n.* n mutandamhuno 3 (LHHHL); *mucus, slimy substance of n.* n dzihwa 5 (LH)

not at all *never, by no means* adv -mbo- infix vb in negation. Handina ku**mbo**muona. (*I never saw him.*)

not yet adv -ti *auxiliary vb in negation.* Handi**sati** ndamuona. (*I have not yet seen him.*) *cf yet*

nothing *for n., for no price* adv mahara (LHL); pachena 16 (LLL)

notice *observe, see* vb -ona t (HH); -cherechedza t (HHHL)

notice-board n chikwangwani 7 (LHLL)

notify *inform, advise* vb -zivisa t (HHH); -udza t (HH)

notwithstanding *though* conj kunyange (LLL), nyange (LL), kanapo (LLL) + Partic: **Kunyange** airwara akaenda. (*He went although he was sick.*)

noun *(grammar) word used as the name of a person or a thing* n zita 5, mazita 6 (HH)

nourish *bring up and educate, nurse* vb -rera t (LL); *provide for, care for, sustain with food* vb -riritira t (HHHL)

nourishment *food* n kudya 15 (LH)

now *at present* adv zvino 1a (HH); *just n.* adv iye zvino 1a (HL HH); iko zvino (HL HH); zvino zvino 1a (HL HL); zvino uno 1a (HH HL); *nowadays* adv mazuva ano 6 (LHH HL)

nudge *prod, hasten movement* vb -dyunga t (HH)

number *individual or collective count* n nhamba 9 (LL) cf Eng.

numerous *many* adj -zhinji (HH); colloq: *a-hundred-and-one* gumi nefararira (HH LHLLL)

nun *dedicated religious woman who lives in a community with others* n sisita 1a (HLL) cf Eng.

nurse the sick *look after carefully* vb -pepa varwere (HH LHH); *nurse, one who tends the sick* n nesi 1a (HL) cf Eng.

nurse children *e.g. nanny* vb -rera vana (LL LH); *one who rears children* n mureri 1 (LLL)

nut *(which screws onto a bolt)* n bhaudhi 5, mabhaudhi 6 (HLL) cf Eng.

nutshell *outer covering of a nut* n deko 5, mateko 6 (HH)

nyala *large antelope which lives in wooded areas; weight approx 135 kg cf inyala* n nyara 9 Ko (LL) *cf illustration p. 88*

O

oribi tsinza

oar *pole with flat blade used in rowing* n gwasvo 5, magwasvo 6 (LL)

oath *solemn promise* n mhiko 9 (LL) cf -pika (LL); *make an o., promise on o.* vb -pika i (LL); -tsidza i (LL)

obedience *readiness to obey* n kuteerera 15 (LHHHL)

obey *do what one is told to do* vb -teerera i & t (HHHL)

object *refuse to do* vb -ramba i & t (LL) + infin

obliged *be bound to* vb -sungirwa i Z (HHH); -fanira i (HHH)

obscure *hinder the view from someone* vb -dzikatira t (HHHL)

observe *examine carefully* vb -ongorora i & t (HHHL); -cherechedza i & t (HHHL)

observe *keep, look after* vb -chengeta t (LLL)

obstacle *impediment* n chipingamupinyi 7 (LHHLHH)

obstinacy *pig-headedness* n nharo 9 (LL)

obstinate *be self-willed, hard to persuade* adj & vb -va nenharo i; -ne nharo
obstruct *hinder, be in the way* vb -pingidza t (HHH)
obtain *find* vb -wana t (LL)
obtainable *be easily o.* adj & vb -booka (LLL) i (stative vb); Kumusha hwahwa hwaka**booka**. (*Beer is easy to obtain at home.*)
obvious *be clear* vb -va pachena: Zviri pachena. (*It is obvious.*) obviously = It is obvious.
occasion *time* n nguva 9 (HH)
occupied *be busy* vb -va nebasa (LHL); -ne basa (LL)
ochna *dwarf o. flower* n muminu 3 (LLH); muminu-mudiki 3 (LLH-LHL)
odd *be strange, be astonishing* vb -shamisa i & t (HHH) cf -shama (HH); *be odd, eccentric* vb -**penga** i (HH)
odour *bad smell* n gwema 5 (LL); kunhuhwa 15 (LLL); *body o., stale smell of perspiration* n hwema 14 (LL); bwema 14 K (LL); chikwembe 7 (LLH); *stink, strong offensive smell* n gwema 5 (LL)
oesophagus *canal leading food from the mouth to the stomach, gullet* n huro 9 (LL) *same word as throat*
off *cut o.* vb -cheka i & t (HH); -dimura t (HHH); *fall o.* vb -punzika i (HHH); -wa i (L); A**kapunzika** pabhasikoro. (*He fell off the bicycle.*); *get o. bicycle or vehicle* vb -buruka i (LLL)
off-load *take off from the head* vb -tura t (HH); *from a vehicle* vb -burutsa (LLL)
off-shoot *side growth of a plant* n dungirwa 5 (HLH) cf -tungira (HHH)
offence *guilt* n mhosva 9 (HL); mhaka 9 (LH)
offend *sin against, wrong* vb -tadzira t (HHH) cf -tadza (HH); *make angry, annoy* vb -shatirisa i & t (HHHL); -gumbura i & t (LLL); -tsamwisa t (LLL) cf -tsamwa (LL); *take offence, be offended* vb -gumbuka i (LLL)
offer *give* vb -pa t (H)
offer sacrifice *make ritual offering* vb - teura i & t (HHH); -pira t (HH)
office *room used as a place of business for clerical work* n hofisi 9 (HLL) cf Eng.
office-worker *clerk* n mabharani 1a (LHLL)
offspring *young of men or creatures* n mwana 1 (LH)
often *frequently* -wanzo- (LL); -garo- (LL); -ziviro- (HHH) infix vbs; Ano**wanzouya** kuno. (*He often comes here.*); -si-; Anosisvika neChitanhatu. (*He usually arrives on Saturday.*)
often *many times* adv kazhinji 12 (LHH); ruzhinji 11 (LHH)
oil *grease, fat, ointment* n mafuta 6 (LHH)
oil calabash *o. container* n chinu 7 (LH) (LH)
old cow n dore 5, matore 6 (LL)
old man n harahwa 9 (LLL); mutana 1 K (LHH); chembere 9 (*usu old woman*)
old vehicle *old crock* n mugweje 3 (LLH)
old woman n chembere 9 (LLL)
old *worn out* adj -tsaru (HL); dzaru 5, tsaru 9
old *grwo o., age* vb -chembera i (LLL); -kwegura i (HHH); -kura i (HH); *grow o. (of things)* vb -sakara i (LLL)
olden times *long ago* adv pasichigare 16 (LHHLH); karekare (LLLL); chinyakare 7 (LLLL); makarekare 6 (LLLLL)
olive grass snake n svoti 9 (LH); dzvoti 5 (LH)
omen *bad o.* n shura 5, mashura 6 (LH); manenji 6 M (LLH); *be of bad o.* vb -shura i (LL)
omit *not to do* vb -rega i & t (LL); *leave out* vb -siya t (HH)

on prep & adv pa- 16 Mari iri **pa**tafura. (*The money is on the table.*) Akauya musi weSvondo. (*He came on Sunday.*); *on account of, for the reason* adv nemhaka ya-; nokuda kwa-; pamusana pa-; pamusoro pa-; *on arrival* adv -sviko- infix vb; Aka**sviko**wana imba ichibvira. (*On arrival he found the house in flames.*); *on condition that, provided that* adv: Use a conditional sentence: *If . . . . ; on the left* adv kuruboshwe 17 (LLLH); *on the other hand, but* conj asika (LHL); *on the other side (of the river)* adv mhiri 17 (LL); *on the right* adv kurudyi 17 (LLH); *on the spot* adv ipapo 16 dem. (HLH); *on top, at a high point* adv pamusoro 16 (LLHH); pauzuru 16 (LLHL); *right on top* adv pamusoroso-ro 16 (LLHHLH)

once *one time* adv kamwe chete (LH LH); kamwe (HH); *at once, immediately* adv zvino uno 1a (HH HL); iye zvino 1a (HL HH); iko zvino (HL HH); *once upon a time, once* adv -mbo- infix vb: Aka**mbo**sevenzera dhokotera. (*He once worked for a doctor.*)

one adj -mwe (H) enumarative *cf p. 186*

onion *vegetable plant with sharp taste and smell* n hanyanisi 9 (HLLL) *cf Eng. illustration p. 170*

only adv chete (HL); bedzi (HL); -ngo- infix vb: **Akaenda kumusha achingo**funga zvemari bedzi. (*He went home thinking only of the money.*)

onward *in front* adv pamberi 16 (LLH); Akaenderera mberi. (*He went on.*)

ooze *describes a liquid substance passing slowly through a small opening* vb -sininika i (LLLL); -finyinya i (LLL)

open *make o.* vb -zarura i & t (LLL); *o. an abscess, cut o.* vb -tumbura t (LLL); *o. a bottle* vb -dziura t (LLL); *o. a box or pot* vb -pfudugura i & t (HHHL); *o. the mouth* vb -shama i (HH); *o. out, unfold* vb -petenura t (LLLL) cf -peta (LL); *o. eyes* vb -svinura i (LLL)

opener *instrument for openning* n chivhuriso 7 (LLLL); cf -vhura (LL); opena 9 (HLL) cf Eng.

opening *hole, orifice* n buri 5, mapuri 6 (HL), maburi 6; mwena 3 (LH); Ndapona napa**buri** retsono. (*I survived through the eye of a needle, i.e. I escaped by the skin of my teeth.*)

opening *doorway* n musuo 3 (LHL)

openly *clearly, publicly* adv pachena 16 (LLL)

operate *work* vb -shanda i (HH); -shandisa t (HHH)

operate *surgically, perform an operation* vb -vhiya t (LL); -vhuya t M (LL)

opinion *advice* n zano 5, mazano 6 (LL); *in my opinion . . .* sokufunga kwangu . . .

opportunity *time* n nguva 9 (HH)

oppose *set oneself against* vb -pikisa i & t (LLL)

oppress *persecute* vb -dzvinyirira i & t (LLLL)

oppressive *be hot* vb (kunze) Kuri kupisa. (*The weather is hot.*)

or conj kana (LL)

or *either . . . or . . .* kana (LL) kana (LL) . . .

orange *citrus fruit* n ranjisi 5, maranjisi 6 (HLL) cf Eng. *cf p. 62*

orchid *bauhinia tree* n chigwendere 7 (LLLL); mupondo 3 (LLL); *leopard o.* n mubatanai-vakuru 3 (LHHHH-LHH)

order *command* n odha 9 (HL) Eng.; murayiro 3 (LLLL) cf -rayira (LLL); *order goods by post, direct merchant to supply* vb -odha t (HH) cf Eng.

order *put in o., arrange* vb -ruramisa t (LLLL); -rongedza t (LLL)

orderly *be neat, tidy* vb -shambidzika i (LLLL)

ore *(iron or copper); raw material (rock,*

earth etc.) from which metal can be extracted n mhangura 9 (LLH)

oribi *sp of small antelope, weight about 18 kg* n tsinza 9 Z (LL); sinza 9 K (LL); *cf illustration p. 108*

origin *beginning* n mavambo 6 (LLL); kutanga 15 (LHH)

original sin *s. of Adam* n rutadzo rwa-mavambo 11 (LHH LHLL)

originate *come from* vb -bva i (L)

oriole *African golden o.* n chidzvururu 7 Z (LLLL); dzvitsvirori 5 (HHLH); *black-headed o.* n gochiwo 5 K (LHL); godowa 5 Z (LLL); mutoweguru 9 Z (LLHLL)

ornament *something designed or used to add beauty or make beautiful* n chi-shongo 7 (LLL) cf -shonga (LL)

orphan *child that has lost its parents* n nherera 9 (LLL)

ostrich *the largest of our birds* n mhou 9 (HL); mhowani M (LLL)

other Enumerative pron, -mwe which precedes the noun *cf p. 186*

otter *clawless o.* n mbiti 9 MZ (HH); nzvidzi 9 Z (LL) *cf illustration p. 50*

ouch! inter *expressive of pain* yowe!

ought to *should, supposed to* vb -fani-ra i & t (HHH)

out of doors *outside* adv kunze 17 (LH); panze 16 (LH)

outcome *end result* n mhedziso 9 (HHL) cf -pedzisa (HHH); mugumisiro 3 (LHHHL) cf -guma (HH)

outdo *surpass, exceed* vb -pinda t (LL); -kunda t (HH); -pfuura t (HHH) — PT *outdid;* PP *outdone*

outspan *unharness oxen* vb -kurura t (HHH); -sunungura t (HHHL) cf -sunga (HH)

ovary *female organ in humans, ani-mals or plants* n chibereko 7 (LLLL); chizvaro 7 (LHH)

oven *heated container for cooking food* n hovhoni 9 (HLL) cf Eng.

over *above, overhead* adv pamusoro 16 (LLHH)

over here dem. kuno 17 (HH); pano 16 (HH)

over there dem. uko 17 (LL); apo 16 (LL)

overalls *working garment worn over ordinary clothes to keep them clean* n hovhorosi 9 (HLLL) cf Eng.

overcome *overpower, get the better of* vb -kunda i & t (HH); -kurira i & t (HHH) — PT *overcame*; PP *overcome*

overflow *flow over* vb -fashamira i (LLLL)

overgrow *stifle other vegetable growth* vb -vhunga t (LL)

overhang *dangle from, hang down* vb -rembera i (LLL) — PT & PP *overhung*

overhead *above, over* adv pamusoro 16 (LLHH)

overload *load to excess* vb -remedza t (LLL)

overlook *miss out, leave* vb -siya t (HH)

overpower *overcome, get the better of* vb -kunda t (HH); -kurira i & t (HHH)

overseas *across or beyond the sea* n mhiri kwamakungwa 17 (LL LHLLL)

overshadow *cast a shadow over* vb -dzikatira t (HHHL)

overtake *catch up with and pass* vb -pfuura t (HHH) — PT *overtook*; PP *overtaken*

overturn *(in a vehicle)* vb -bheuka i (LLL); -kudubuka i (HHHL); Motokari **yakabheuka**. (*The car overturned.*); -pidiguka i (HHHL)

over-coat *long coat worn out of doors over ordinary clothes* n jasi 5, majasi 6 (HL)

over-eat *be bloated* vb -zvimbirwa i (HHH)

over-indulge *pamper, spoil* vb -tunhira t (LLL)

owing to *because of* adv pamusana pa- (LL HH)

owl *night-flying bird that usu lives on mice* n zizi 5, mazizi 6 (LL); *fishing o.* n dinhidza 5, madinhidza 6 (LLL)

own *(emphasising ownership)* Imba iyi ndeyangu **pachangu**. (*This is my own house.*)

own up *acknowledge, agree* vb -bvuma i & t (LL); *speak out* vb -dura i & t (LL)

owner *person to whom something belongs* n muridzi 1 Z (LLH); tenzi 1a (HL); mwene 1a MZ (LH)

ox *male domestic cattle made unsuitable for breeding, often used as beasts of burden; plur oxen* n jon'osi 5, majon'osi 6 (HLL); dhonza 5, madhonza 6 (LL); *hornless ox* n njuma 9 (HL)

ox pecker *sp of bird* n chidyamadari 7 (LHHLH); tsanda 9 (LL); shakahuni 9 (LLHH) R747-8

P

protea mubonda

pace *step* n nhanho 9 Z (LL)

pacify *silence* vb -nyaradza i & t (HHH); *pacify a crying child* vb -rezva t (HH)

pack *arrange* vb -rongedza i & t (LLL)

package *packet, parcel* n mutundu 3 (LHH)

packet *container usu of paper* n pakiti 5, mapakiti 6 (HLL) cf Eng.

pad *to protect the head when carrying* n hata 9 (HH)

paddle *propel canoe by means of paddles* vb -gwasva (LL); *paddle, short oar for propelling a canoe* n gwasvo 5, magwasvo 6 (LL); mukwasvo 33 (LLL); chikwasvo 7 (LLL) *cf illustration under* oar

padlock *removable lock* n chimai chekii 7 (LHL HLL)

page *leaf of paper usu in a book* n peji 9 (HL) cf Eng.

paid *cf pay*

pail *bucket-like container with a handle* n bhagedhi 5 (HLL) cf Eng.

pain *give p., be painful* vb -rwadza i & t (HH); -dzimba i & t Ko (LL); *pain, suf-*

fering of the body n marwadzo 6 (LHH); kurwadza 15 (LHH)

paint *apply a coat of p. usu with a brush* vb -penda t (HH) cf Eng.

paint *colouring matter mixed with oil or other liquid* n pendi 9 (HL) cf Eng.; *painter, person who paints* n penda 1a (HL) cf Eng.

painting *picture* n chifananidzo 7 (LHHHL) cf -fananidza (HHHL)

palate *roof of mouth* n hwavhuutete 14 (LL LLL)

palm *of hand, inner part of the hand* n chanza 7 (LL)

palm tree n muchindwi 3 (LHH); murara 3 (LLL)

palpitate *throb of pulse* vb -pfura i & t (HH)

palsy *paralysis causing shakes* n nhetemwa 10 (LHL)

pamper *over-indulge, spoil (esp a child)* vb -tunhira t Z (LLL)

pan *frying p.* n pani 9 (HL) cf Eng.

pancreas *one of the glands of the body that aid digestion* n rwatata 11 (LHL)

pangolin *scaly ant-eater* n haka 9 (LH); harakabvuka 9 M (LLLLL); hambakubvu 9 K (HHHL) *cf illustration p. 8*

pant *breathe heavily through the mouth* vb -takwaira i (HHHL); -femereka i (LLLL)

panties *knickers* n nika 9 (HL) cf Eng.

paper *thin sheet made from wood pulp* n pepa 5, mapepa 6 (LL) cf Eng.

parable *story with a moral lesson* n muenzaniso 3 (LLLLL); fananidzo 9 K (HHHL)

parachute *apparatus used to slow down the fall from a great height* n parachuti 9 (HLLL) cf Eng.

paradise fly-catcher *sp of long-tailed bird* n kateredemu 12 (LLLHL); zvigone 9 (HLH)

paraffin *liquid fuel* n parafini 9 (LLHL) cf Eng.

parasite *see illustration p. 124*

parcel *thing wrapped and tied in paper* n pasuru 9 (HLL) cf Eng.

parched *be very thirsty* vb -oma pahuro (HH HLL)

pardon *forgive* vb -regerera t (LLLL)

pare *cut away the skin of a veg* vb -senda t (LL)

parent *father or mother of children* n mubereki 1 (LLLL) cf -bereka (LLL)

parish n parishi 9 (HLL) cf Eng.

park *place of recreation* n paka 9 (HL) cf Eng.

park *leave motor car on an open space* vb -paka t (HH) cf Eng.

parliament *highest council of the land* n paramende 9 (HLLL) cf Eng.

parrot *sp of bird with hooked top beak* n chihwenga 7 (LLH)

parry *ward off blow* vb -vhika i & t (LL); -dziva i & t (LL); -tava t (LL)

parsnip *sp of root veg* n pasinipi 9 (HLLL) cf Eng.

parson's nose *fleshy tail of chicken* n chigaramanhenga 7 (LLLLLH)

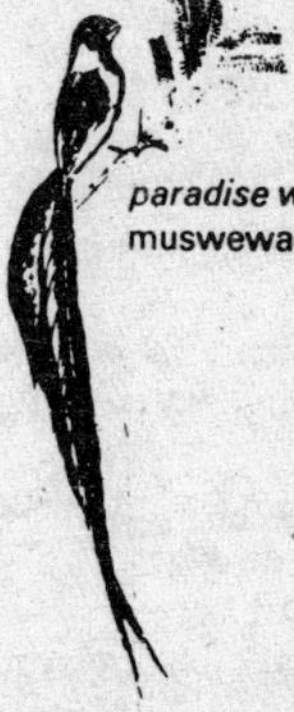

paradise whydha
muswewadepa

paradise fly-catcher
kateredemu

part *section of a thing, portion* n chikamu 7 (LHL); chimedu 7 (LHL)
part company *separate* vb -paradzana i (LLLL)
particular *specific, rendered by the* vb -ti Relative mood. Unofanira kuuya nomusi **wakati**. (*You must come on a particular day.*)
parting *(of the hair)* n dharakishoni 9 (LLHLL); shedhi 9 (HL)
partition *dividing wall* n mupanda 3 (LLL)
partridge *francolin, sp of game bird* n hwarikwari 9 (LHLH); hwerekwere 9 (LLLL); gwari 5 (LH)
pass by *pass through* vb -pfuura na-(HHH); -dimura na-(HHH); *pass water, urinate* vb -ita mvura (LL HH); -ita dope (LL LL); *pass by without meeting, miss each other* vb -pesana i (LLL)
pass *gap between hills, poort* n mupata 3 (LLL); mukana 3 (LLL)
pass *(food), hand, cause to reach* vb -svitsa i & t (LL); *pass an examination* vb -pasa i & t (LL) cf Eng.; -budirira i (HHHL); *pass out of sight with only a glimpse* vb -nyenguka i (HHH)
passage *through a line of hills, pass* n mukana 3 MZ (LLL); mupata 3 (LLL); *passage, path-way* n nzira 9 (LL)
passer-by *person who passes* n mupfuuri 1 (LHHL) cf -pfuura (HHH)
paste *stick* vb -nama t (LL)
pasture *grass-land for grazing* n mafuro 6 (LLL); ufuro 14 (LLL) cf -fura (LL)
pat *caress animal or child* vb -puruzira t (LLLL)
patch *small piece of material or rubber to cover a hole* n chigamba 7 (LLL); chiremo 7 Z (LLL)
patch *a tube* vb -nama t (LL); *patch clothes, mend, sew on a patch* vb -sonera chigamba t (LLL LLL)
path *foot-path* n nzira 9 (LL); gwanza 5 M (HH)
patient *be long suffering* vb -tirira i & t (LLL); *patience, ability to wait or suffer patiently* n rutiriro 11 (LLLL) cf -tirira (LLL)
patient *sick person* n murwere 1 (LHH) cf -rwara (HH)
pattern *something serving as a model for dress-making* n patani 9 (HLL); peteni 9 (HLL) cf Eng.
pause *wait* vb -mira i (HH)
pawpaw *soft tropical fruit, usu with yellow flesh* n popo 5, mapopo 6 (HL) cf Eng. *cf illustration p. 62*
pay *make payment* vb -bhadhara i & t (LLL); *p. back, return, give back* vb -dzorera i & t (LLL); *p. back, take revenge on* vb -tsiva i & t (LL) — PT & PP *paid; pay bride wealth* vb -roora t (HHH); *pay attention, listen, obey* vb -teerera i & t (HHHL); *p. tax or rent* vb -tera i & t (LL); *p. a fine* vb -ripa i & t *p. wages* vb -tambirisa t (HHHL) cf -tambira (HHH); *be fined* vb -ripiswa i (LLL); *pay a visit* vb -shanya i (HH); *pay a visit to* vb -shanyira t (HHH); cf -shanya (HH)
pay ransom *pay a price to recover something* vb -tsikinura t (LLLL)
pay *wages* n mubayiro 3 (LLLL)
payment *price paid* n muripo 3 (LLL) -ripa (LL)
pea *sp of veg* n ndodzi 9 M (LH); pizi 9 (HL) cf Eng. *cf illustration p. 170*
peace *freedom from war and disagreement* n runyararo 11 (LHHL) cf -nyarara (HHH); rugare 11 (LLH)
peace *be at p., be on good terms* vb -wadzana i (LLL); -yanana i (LLL); *peace-maker, one who unites* n muwadz .nisi 1 (LLLLL) cf -wadzana (LLL); muyananisi 1 (LLLLL) cf -yanana (LLL)
peach tree n mupichisi 3 (LHLL) cf Eng. *peach fruit* n pichisi 5, mapichisi 6 (HLLL) cf Eng.

pear *kind of fruit* n peya 5, mapeya 6 (HL) cf Eng. *cf illustration p. 62*

peck *feeding or defensive action of a bird* vb -chobora i & t (HHH); -jobora i & t (HHH)

pedal *a bicycle* vb -chovha t (LL) cf Eng.

pedal *of a bicycle* n pedhuru 9 (HLL) cf Eng.

peel *remove the skin or the peel from* vb -menya t (HH); -funura t (LLL); *lose body skin after surface damage e.g. heat* vb -svauka i (LLL); *p. bark from a tree* vb -svuura t (LLL); *p. off, flake off (of skin or paint)* vb -funuka i (LLL)

peeling-bark ochna tree *brick-red ochna tree* n muminu 3 (LLH); murambambari 3 (LLLLH)

peep *take a short, quick look* vb -dongorera i & t (LLLL)

peer *look closely when not able to see well* vb -sonza i KM (HH)

peg *wooden p. in ground* n hoko 9 (LH)

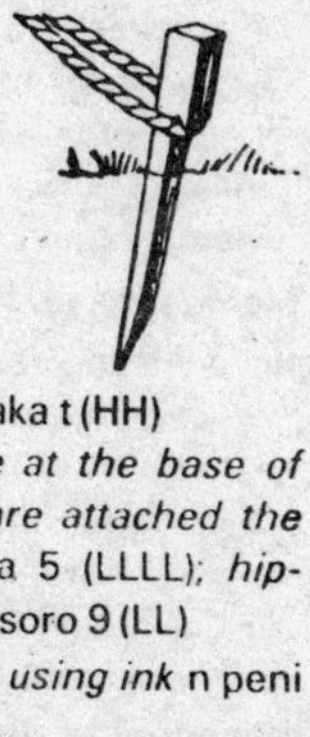

pelt *throw stones* vb -taka t (HH)

pelvis *cradle-like bone at the base of the spine to which are attached the hip-bones* n deyateya 5 (LLLL); *hip-bone* n hudyu 9 (LH); tsoro 9 (LL)

pen *writing instrument using ink* n peni 9 (HL) cf Eng.

pen *enclosure for goats, sheep, calves* n chirugu 7 (LLL); danga 5, matanga 6 (LH)

penance *punishment* n chirango 7 (LLL) cf -ranga (LL); *penance (sacramental)* n chiripiro chamatadzo 7 (LLLL HLHH)

pencil *writing instrument loaded with lead* n penzura 9 (HLL) cf Eng.

penetrate *enter* vb -pinda i & t (LL)

penis *male organ* n mboro 9 (HH); mhuka 9 (LH) *euphemism; foreskin* n nguo yechirema 9 (LL HLHH)

penitent *be repentant* vb -pfidza i (HH); *penitent, one who is sorry for wrong-doing* n mupfidzi 1 (LHH) cf -pfidza (HH)

pension *regular payment made to someone after employment has ended* n penjeni 9 (HLL) cf Eng.

pepper *red p., hot p., cayenne p. made from the red fruit of the chili plant* n mhiripiri 9 (LLLL)

perceive *see, notice* vb -ona i & t (HH)

perceive *understand, feel, taste, hear, smell* vb -nzwa i & t (H)

perch *land, alight* vb -mhara i & t (LL)

perform *do* vb -ita t (LL)

perhaps *possibly* adv zvimwe (LL); kuda (LH); pamwe (LL); zvichida (LHH); musi MZ (LH)

peril *danger* n njodzi 9 (LL); ngozi 9 (LL)

period *time* n nguva 9 (HH); nhambo 9 (LL)

perish *die* vb -pera i (HH); -fa i (H)

permission *consent, statement that permits or allows* n mvumo 9 (LL) cf -bvuma (LL)

permit *allow, give permission* vb -bvumira t (LLL) cf -bvuma (LL); -bvumidza t KoMZ (LLL) cf -bvuma (LL); -tendera t (LLL) cf -tenda (LL)

perpertually *for ever and ever* adv narini narini (LHL LHL); narini wose (LHL HH)

perplex *puzzle, bewilder* vb -shamisa i & t (HHH) cf -shama (HH)

persecute *cause annoyance* vb -tambudza i & t (LLL); -netsa i & t (LL); *scold continuously (by a husband)* vb -shusha i & t (LL); *persecution, continuous scolding by a husband* n rushusho 11 (LLL) cf -shusha (LL)

persevere *go on despite the difficulties* vb -tirira i (LLL); *perseverance, ability* *to keep on* n rutiriro 11 (LLLL) cf -tirira (LLL)

persist *continue* vb -ramba (LL) + Partic i & t: Mvura yaka**ramba** ichinaya. (*The rain persisted / continued.*)

person *man, woman or child* n munhu 1 (LL)

personally adv ini pachangu (LH LHL); *cf p. 198* ini pauzima (LH HLLL)

perspiration *sweat* n dikita 5 MZ (LLH); ziya 5 K (LH)

perspire *give off sweat through the pores due to heat or heavy exertion* vb -tikitira i (HHHL); -buda dikita (HH HLH); -pfundira i M (HHH); -buda ziya K (HH LH)

persuade *(often by guile), coax* vb -nyengetedza t (HHHL)

pester *ask persistently* vb -sembura i & t (HHH)

pestle *instrument used for crushing or pounding in a mortar (usu grain)* n mutswi 3 MZ (LL); musi 3 K (LL)

petition *request* n chichemo 7 (LHH) cf -chema (HH)

petrol *engine fuel* n peturu 9 (HLL) cf Eng.

petticoat *under-garment used by women* n pitikoti 9 (HLLL) cf Eng.

pheasant *francolin, partridge* n hwari 9 (LH); hwarikwari 9 (LHLH); horwe 9 Z (LH) *cf illustration p. 64*

phlegm *thick waste substance brought up by coughing* n gorwa 5, makorwa 6 (HL)

photograph *picture taken with a camera* n pikicha 9 (HLL) cf Eng.; mufananidzo 3 (LHHHL) cf -fananidza (HHHL)

photograph *take a picture with a camera* vb -pikicha t (HHH) cf Eng.; -tora mufananidzo t (HH LHHHL)

physical appearance *a. of the body* n chimiro 7 (LHH)

piano *musical instrument* n piyano 9 (LHL) cf Eng.; *Shona piano* n mbira 10 (LL) (*to be distinguished from:* mbira 9 (HL) *rock rabbit, dassie, hyrax*)

pick *select, p. out* vb -sarudza t (LLL); -keta t (LL); *pick flowers, fruit vegetables; p. off* vb -tanha t (HH)

pick *the ground, break ground surface* vb -timba i & t (HH); *pick up on the way* vb -tora t (HH); *pick up from the ground* vb -nonga t (HH); -nhonga t (HH)

pick on *provoke* vb -denha t (LL)

pickaxe *pick, heavy tool for breaking up the earth* n piki 9 (HL) cf Eng. *illustration p. 162*

picture *man-made likeness* n mufananidzo 3 (LHHHL) cf -fananidza (HHHL); pikicha 9 (HLL) cf Eng.

piece *portion, part* n chimedu 7 (LHL) cf -medura (HHH); *p. of broken gourd or calabash* n demhe 5, matemhe 6 (LH); *p. of broken earthenware* n rwainga 11 (LHL) rwenga 11 (LH); *p. of meat* n nhango 9 (LL); nhindi 9 (LL)

pierce *stab, prick* vb -baya i & t (LL)

pig *domesticated animal whose flesh we call pork* n nguruve 9 (LLL); *bush p., wild p.* n humba 9 (LL); mbeve 9 (HH); ngurungunda 9 (LLLL); *piglet, small p.* n chana chenguruve 7 (LH LHLL); ngurwana 9 (HLH); *pigsty* n danga renguruve 5 (LH LHLL)

pigeon *domesticated bird like a large dove* n hangaiwa 9 (HHLH); *wild speckled rock p., red around the eyes* n bvukutiwa 5 (HHLH); *green p., wild fruit-eating variety* n huriti 9 (LHH); hwiriti 9 (LHH); R 323

pile *heap* n murwi 3 (LL)

pile up *heap one on top of another* vb -turikidza t (HHHL)

pill *medicinal p.* n piritsi 5, mapiritsi 6 (HLL) cf Eng.

pillage *plunder, ransack* vb -kukura t (HHH)

pillow *soft cushion for the head* n piro 9 (HL) cf Eng.; mutsamiro 3 (LHHL) cf -tsamira (HHH); *pillow-case* n pirokesi 9 (HLLL) cf Eng.

pimple *small, hard, inflamed spot on the skin* n mburwa 9 (LH)

pin *short, thin length of metal for holding things together* n pini 9 (HL) cf Eng.; *safety-p.* n chipeneti 7 (LHLL)

pincers *instrument for gripping things and pulling out nails* n pinjisi 9 (HLL) cf Eng.; *cf illustration p. 162 (same word as for pliers)*

pinch *tightly grip the skin, take the skin between thumb and finger* vb -tswinya t (LL); *take a p. of snuff* vb -tsunya t (LL)

pineapple *a fruit covered in spines* n chinanazi 7 (LHLH); nanazi 5 (HLH); *cf illustration p 62*

pink n pingi (HL) cf Eng.

pins and needles *tingling and lack of feeling* n chiveve 7 (LLL)

pipe *water p.* n pombi 9 (LH) cf Eng.

pipe *smoker's p.* n chikwepa 7 (LLL); paipi 9 (HLL) cf Eng.

pipit *sp of bird related to the wagtail* n ndondoza 9 (HHL); ndondodza 9 (HHL)

pit *deep hole in the earth with steep sides* n gomba 5, makomba 6 (LH); *rubbish p.* n durunhuru 5, madurunhuru 6 (LLLL)

pitiful *be p., evoke pity* vb -pisa tsitsi i & t (HH LH)

pity *feelings of sorrow for the troubles of another* n tsitsi 9 (LH); nyasha 9 (LL); ngoni 9 (LL)

place *particular portion of space occupied by something* n nzvimbo 9 (LL)

place across *put across* vb -chinjika t (HHH); -piyanisa t (HHHL)

place close together *join together* vb batanidza t (HHHL) cf -batana (HHH)

place of refuge n diziro 5, matiziro 6 (HHL) cf -tiza (HH)

placenta *bag that contains the unborn baby* n chavakuru 7 (HLHH)

plague *severe infectious disease affecting whole populations* n mukondombera 3 (LLLLL)

plainly *openly, without concealment* adv pachena 16 (LLL)

plait *knit, weave together, braid* vb -ruka i & t (LL)

plan *advice* n zano 5, mazano 6 (LL)

plan to do *make a plan* vb -rangana i MZ (LLL)

plane *instrument for smoothing and*

shaving wood n musendo 3 (LLL); mutsendo 3 Z (LLL); tsendo 9 MZ (LL)

plane *make smooth with a plane* vb -veza i & t (LL)

plank *long, flat piece of wood* n puranga 5, mapuranga 6 (LHL) cf Eng.

plant *put in the earth* vb -dyara t (HH); -dzvara t K (HH)

plant out *transplant* vb -sima t (HH)

plaster *smear a paste of cement, sand and water to conceal rough brickwork* vb -nama t (LL)

plate *dish in which food is served (originally wooden; today china or metal)* n ndiro 9 (HH); *curved, round dish for relish* n mbiya 9 (LH)

play *gambol, floric* vb -tamba i & t (HH); *play pranks, misbehave* vb -shereketa i (LLLL); *p. truant, miss* vb -rovha i (LL); *play an instrument* vb -ridza t (LL)

playfulness *jocular behaviour* n jee 5 (HL)

playing card n kasi 5 KM, makasi 6 (LL); *p. cards (a set)* n mupaka 3 (LLL)
plead *earnestly beg* vb -teterera i & t (HHHL)
please *cause pleasure* vb -fadza i & t (HH) cf -fara (HH)
please *earnest request* Rendered by: -do infix vb: Dondipa mari. (*Please give me some money.*)
pleased *be happy, delighted* vb -fara i (HH); *be p. with* vb -farira t (HHH); -fadzwa na- (HH)
pleasure *feeling of being happy or satisfied* n purezha 9 (LHL) cf Eng.
pleat *fold* n mino 5 MZ, mamino 6 (LL); vuko 5 K (LL)
plentiful *be abundant* adj & vb -wanda i (LL) (stative vb); Ano mukaka wakawanda. (*He has plenty of milk.*)
plenty *many* adj -zhinji (HH)
pleurisy *pneumonia* n chibayo 7 (LLL); mabayo 6 (LLL)
pliable *be flexible* vb -tepuka i (HHH)
pliers *small, scissors-like tool for holding, turning or twisting things* n pinjisi 9 (HLL) cf Eng. *cf illustration p. 162* (same word as for pincers)
plot *make secret plans* vb -rangana i (LLL)
plough *turn over the soil with a plough* vb -rima i & t (LL); *p. in winter time* vb -unda t (HH); -pindura t (LLL); *p. virgin soil* vb -unda t (HH); -tsindikira t K (HHHL)
plough *instrument for turning over the soil* n gejo 5, magejo 6 (LL); *plough-*

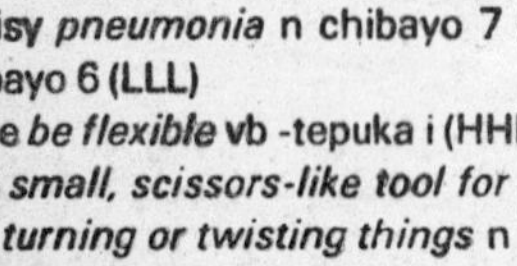

share, blade of a plough n muromo 3 (LLL)
plover *kiewietjie, crowned p., sp of ground-bird* n hurekure 9 (LHLL) R242
pluck *a fowl, take off the feathers* vb -undura i & t (LLL); *p. fruit or vegetables* vb -tanha t (HH)
plug *device for making a connexion with a supply of electric current* n pu-

ragi 9 (LHL) cf Eng.; *plug for bath or washbasin* n chidzivo 7 (LLL); chivharo 7 (LLL)
plunder *pillage, ransack* vb -kukura t (HHH); *take goods by force* vb -paradza i & t (LLL); -pamba t (HH)
pneumonia *pleurisy* n chibayo 7 (LLL); mabayo 6 (LLL)
pocket *purse* n homwe 9 (HH)
pod *spindle p.; sp of wild veg* n mujakari 3 (LHHH); musemwasemwa 3 (LHLHL); mungwingwi 3 (LLL); mungongoma 3 (LLLL)
pod-mahogany *tree* n mukamba 3 (LHH); mugoriwondo 3 (LLHLL)
poem *verse* n detembo 5, madetembo 6 (HHL); detembedzo 5 (HHHL)
point at *indicate* vb -nongedza t (HHH); *p. out, show* vb -ratidza t (LLL); -rakidza t (LLL)
poison *substance causing death or injury* n chepfu 9 (HL); muchetura 3 Z (LHHL)
poison *give poison to, administer p.* vb -pa mushonga wokuuraya
poke *prod (usu with instrument)* vb -svokosva t (LLL); -gofa t (LL)
pole *fencing post* n bango 5, mapango 6 (LL)
polecat *striped p. or zorilla* n chidembo 7 (LLL); *There are two distinct sp which appear to share the same Shona name. cf snake weasel*
policeman *member of the police force* n mupurisa 1 (LHLH) cf Eng.; *police*

station, charge office n chajihofisi 9 (HLHLL) cf Eng.

polish *make shiny by rubbing* vb -kwiza i & t (LL); -pukuta t (LLL)

polish *substance used to obtain a shine* n mushonga 3 (LLH) (*the same word as for medicine*)

polite *be well-mannered* vb -pfava i (LL) (stative vb)

politics *matters of government* n zvamatongerwo enyika 8 (HLHHH LHL)

polled ox *hornless animal* n njuma 9 (HL)

pond *pool* n dziva 5, madziva 6 (LL)

ponder *think deeply, reflect* vb -funga i & t (LL); -rangarira i & t (LLLL)

poor person n murombo 1 (LLH); muchena 1 (LLL); *become p., having little money and few posessessions* vb -va murombo i (LLH)

pop *burst, explode* vb -putika i (HHH)

pope *bishop of Rome* n papa 1a (LH) cf Latin

porcupine *large rodent with spiny quills used for its defence. Weight about 20 kg* n nungu 9 (LH); ngweveve 9 M (LLL); njenje 9 (HH) *cf illustration p.* 133

pork *flesh of the pig* n nyama yenguruve 9 (LL LHLL)

porridge *soft, cooked mixture of meal and water* n bota 5 (HH); parichi 9 (HLL) cf Eng. *N.B. The conventional stiff porridge made from mealie meal (maize meal) is called sadza. It is a staple diet.*

portion *part* n chimedu 7 (LHL); chidimbu 7 (LHL)

Portuguese person *European of P. nationality* n muPutukezi 1 (LLLLL) cf Eng. *P. person or thing* adj mari yechiPutukesi 9 (*Portuguese money*)

possessions *riches* n pfuma 10 (HL); *belongings, goods* n nhumbi 10 (LH)

possible *be capable of attainment* vb -goneka i (LLL) cf -gona (LL); -bvira i (LL); **Zvinobvira here kutaura naye?** (*Is it possible to speak to him?*) **Hazvibviri.** (*It is impossible.*)

possibly *perhaps* adv kuda (LH); zvimwe (LL); zvichida (LHH); musi MZ (LH); pamwe (LL); dzimwe nguva (LL HH)

post *fencing post* n bango 5, mapango 6 (LL)

post *mail, letters* n positi 9 (HLL) cf Eng.

post *a letter* vb -posita t (HHH) cf Eng.

pot *vessel for cooking (earthenware)* n hari (HH); *pot scrapings* n makoko 6 (LHH); *metal vessel for cooking* n poto 9 (LL) cf Eng.; *p. for water* n chirongo 7 (LLH); *potsherd, broken piece of eathenware pot* n rwainga 11 (LHL); rwenga 11 (LH); chainga 7 K (LHL); chaenga 7 Z (LHL); *potter, one who fashions pots* n muumbi 1 (LHH) cf -umba (HH)

potato *a vegetable, plur: potatoes* n mbatatisi 9 (LHLL); dapiri 5, matapiri 6 (HLL); *sweet p.* n mbambaira 9 (LLLL) *cf illustrations p. 170*

poultry *hens, ducks, geese, turkeys, etc.*

poultry

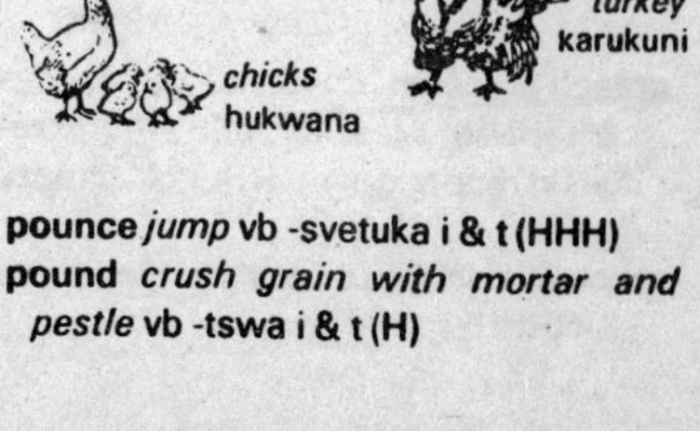

pounce *jump* vb -svetuka i & t (HHH)

pound *crush grain with mortar and pestle* vb -tswa i & t (H)

pour in vb -dira i & t (LL); *p. out* vb -durura i & t (LLL)

poverty *state of being poor* n urombo 14 (LLH); *poor person* n murombo 1 (LLH)

powder *substance that has been crushed to dust* n paudha 9 (HLL) cf Eng.; mupfumbwe 3 (LHL)

power *strength, authority* n simba 5, masimba 6 (LH); *powerful* adj dhonza rine simba (*a powerful draught-ox*) rel; *powerful, be strong* vb -simba i (LL); *powerfully, vigorously (in a way which is strong)* adv zvine simba (LH LH) rel

practise *do something repeatedly in order to become skilful* vb -dzidzira i & t (HHL); -purakitiza i & t (LLLLL) cf Eng.

praise *speak with approval of* vb -rumbidza t (LLL); -tunhidza t MZ (LLL); *praise self* reflex vb -zvikudza i (HLH)

pram *small four-wheeled carriage for a baby* n purema 9 (LHL) cf Eng.

pray *p. to, raise the mind and heart to God* vb -namata i & t (LLL); -nyengetera K (HHHL); *p. for* vb -namatira t (LLLL)

prayer *form of worship or of words used in praying* n munamato 3 (LLLL); chinamato 7 (LLLL) cf -namata (LLL); munyengetero 3 K (LHHHL) cf -nyengetera (HHHL)

praying mantis *Hottentot god* n mbuyamuderere 9 (HLLLLH); jemberebande 5, majemberebande 6 (LLLLH); mbuyambuya 9 (HHHL); nyamuputsaharj 1a M (LLHLHH) *cf illustration p. 80*

preach *proclaim, announce* vb -paridza i & t (HHH); *preacher, one who preaches* n muparidzi 1 (LHHL) cf -paridza (HHH)

precede *lead, go in front* vb -tungamira i & t (HHHL)

precious *be valuable* adj & vb -kosha (LL) (stative vb); Anotsvaga matombo akakosha. (*He searches for precious stones.*)

precipice *very steep face of a rock or cliff* n mawere 6 (LHL)

predict *guess* vb -fembera i & t (HHH)

prefer *choose* vb -sarudza t (LLL); -da pana (LH)

pregnant *be with child* vb -va nenhumbu (LHL); -bata pamuviri (HH HLLL); -va napamuviri (LHLLL); *pregnant* adj mai *vana pamuviri (a pregnant woman)*

prejudice *biased opinion formed before one has adequate knowledge* n rusaruro 11 (LLLL) cf -sarura (LLL); *race p.* rusaruraganda 11 (LLLLHH) cf -sarura (LLL)

prepare *make, repair* vb -gadzira t (LLL); *prepare for* vb -gadzirira i (LLLL)

present *gift, offering* n chipo 7 (LH) cf -pa (H)

present *be p.; exist* vb -vapo i; *be absent* vb neg: Haapo. (*He is not here / there.*)

presently *very soon* adv iye zvino 1a (HL HH); gare gare (LH LH)

preserve *keep* vb -chengeta t (LLL)

press *(e.g. a button)* vb -dzvanyidzira i & t (LLLL); *p. out, extract, squeeze* vb -svina i & t (LL); *press to destruction, crush* vb -pwanya t (LL)

presume *expect* vb -karira (LLL)

pretend *imagine* vb -nyepera i (LLL) cf -nyepa (LL)

pretty *be beautiful* adj & vb -naka i (LL) (stative vb); Ane rokwe rakanaka. (*She has a pretty dress.*)

prevent *protect from* vb -dzivirira t (LLLL); -pipira t (HHH)

previous to *before* adv pamberi pa- 16 (LLH); *previously, once* adv -mbo- infix vb

prey *animal or bird killed or hunted as food by other birds or animals.*

price *payment charged for something* n mutengo 3 (LHH) cf -tenga (HH); mubhadharo 3 (LLLL) cf -bhadhara (LLL)

prick *pierce, slaughter* vb -baya i & t (LL)

pride *too high an opinion of oneself* n kudada 15 (LLL); kuzvikudza 15 (LHLH); rudado 11 (LLL) cf -dada (LL)

priest *minister of religion who offers sacrifice to God* n mupristi 1 (LHL) cf Eng.; fata 1a (LL) cf Eng.

Prince of Wales' Feathers' *tree* n mupfuti 3 (LLL); mufuti 3 (LLL)

print *stamp* vb -dhinda t (LL)

print *foot-p.* n tsoka 9 (LL); rutsoka 11 (LLL); *tracks* n matsimba 6 (LLL)

prison *place of punishment for those who break the law* n tirongo 5, matirongo 6 (LHL); jeri 5, majeri 6 (HL) cf Eng.; *prison warder, one who guards prisoners* n mujerigadhi 1 (LHLLL); plur: 2 & 6; *prisoner in jail, convict, person kept in jail* n bhanditi 5, mabhanditi 6 (LHH) cf Eng.; musungwa 1 (LHL) cf -sunga (HH)

prize *reward* n mubayiro 3 (LLLL)

probably *likely to happen* adv zvimwe (LL); dzimwe nguva (LL HH); -nge + noun or noun clause: Mvura inenge ichanaya. (*It will probably rain.*)

probation *be on trial* vb -edzwa i (LL) cf -edza (LL)

proceed from *come from* vb -bva i (L); *proceed, go* vb -enda i & t (LL); -inda i & t K (LL)

procession *line of people, file of people* n mudungwe 3 (LHL)

proclaim *preach* vb -paridza i & t (HHH)

procrastinate *delay, put off* vb -verengera i & t (LLLL)

procure abortion vb -bvisa nhumbu / pamuviri (LL LL/LLLL)

procure *gain, find* vb -wana i & t (LL)

produce *bear fruit* vb -bereka i & t (LLL)

produce *(grain)* n mbesa 9 MZ (HL); mbesanwa 9 (HLH)

profess *expose the truth, say openly* vb -dura i & t (LL); *affirm faith in or allegiance to (religion, God, Christ)* vb -tendera i & t (LLL)

profit *return, advantage* n chimuko 7 (LLL)

profound *be deep, abstruse* vb -dzama i (LL); -dzika i (LL); e.g. rudo rwakadzama (*profound love*)

progress *make p., advance culturally* vb -fambira mberi (HHH LH)

progress *improvement, forward movement* n rubudiriro 11 M (LHHHL) cf -budirira (HHHL)

prohibit *forbid, ban* vb -rambidza t (LLL); -bhana t (HH) cf Eng.

promise *solemnly undertake to do something* vb -tsidza i (LL); -vimbisa i & t (LLL)

promise *firm undertaking to do something* n mhiko 9 (LL) cf -pika (LL); chitsidzo 7 (LLL) cf -tsidza (LL)

prop *support* n chitsigiro 7 (LHHL) cf -tsigira (HHH)

prop up *support* vb -tsiga t (HH); -sendeka t (HHH)

proper *be appropriate* vb -fanira i (HHH) (stative vb); Ndizvo zvakafanira kuitwa navakuru. (*That is what is appropriate for adults to do.*)

properly *correctly, rightly, in the proper way, in the right manner* adv nomazvo (HLH), nomutoo kwawo

property *possesssions (collective)* n pfuma 10 (HL); nhumbi 10 (LH)

prophesy *foretell the future* vb -profita i & t (LLL) cf Eng.; -uka i & t (HH); -fembera i & t (HHH); *prophet, one who foretells the future* n mufemberi 1 (LHHL) cf -fembera (HHH); muprofita 1 (LLHL) cf Eng.

proportionate *be even* vb -ringana i (LLL)

proposal *something that is proposed* n chirongwa 7 (LLH) cf -ronga (LL)

proprietor *owner* n muridzi 1 (LLH); mwene 1 (LH)

prosper *be rich* vb -pfuma i (HH)

prosperous *be well off* vb -garika i (LLL)

prostitute *adulteress, loose woman* n hure 5, mahure 6 (HL) cf Eng. or Afrik.; pfambi 9 (HH); joki 5, majoki 6 (LH)

prostrate *starbur, devil thorn, boot protectors, a thorny seed that pierces the sole of a shoe* n feso 5, mafeso 6 (LL)

protea *sugar bush* n mubonda 3 (LLL); muhonda 3 (LLL) *cf illustration p. 112*

protect from *keep safe from harm* vb -dzivirira t (LLLL)

protrude *jut out* vb -chanjamara i (HHHL)

proud *be vain* vb -dada i (LL) **-zvikudza** (HLH) reflex

proverb *everyday expression full of wisdom or advice* n tsumo 9 MZ (HH); shumo 9 K (HH)

provided that *so long as* conj chero + Partic (LL); *a choice made in the face of some disadvantage; provided that, if* conj: Mvura ikanaya gore rino tichawana kudya kwakąkwana. (*If / provided it rains we shall have enough food this year.*)

provide for *care for, nourish* vb -riritira t (HHHL); -kotsvera t M (HHH)

provoke *make angry, vex* vb -denha i & t (LL)

prowl *go about cautiously looking for a chance to get food, to steal etc. (usu animals)* vb -nyangira i & t (HHH)

prudence *wisdom* n ungwaru 14 (LLH) cf -ngwara (LL)

prudent *be wise* vb -ngwara i (LL) (stative vb); Ana baba vakangwara. (*He has a wise father.*)

prune *trim the edges e.g. fruit tree* vb -pemhena t (LLL)

psalm *a prayerful song of Holy Scripture* n rwiyo 11 (LH); pisarema 5 (HLHL); samu 9 (HL) cf Eng.

pub *bar* n bhawa 5, mabhawa 6 (HL) cf Eng.

pubic region *private parts* n chinena 7 (LLL)

publicly *openly* adv pachena 16 (LLL)

publish *make known to the public, announce* vb -paridza t (HHH)

pudding *dish of sweet food served as part of a meal, usu after the meal* n pudhin'i 9 (HLL) cf Eng.

puddle *mix mortar or mud* vb -kanya t (LL)

puff *heavy breathing after exercise* vb -takwaira i (HHHL); -femereka i (LLLL)

puff adder *sp of fat, poisonous snake; length up to 1m.* n chiva 7 (LL) (gen name for adders) *cf illustration p. 145*

pugnacity *desire to fight* n musindo 3 (LLL)

pull *draw something nearer* vb -zvuva t KoZ (LL); -dhonza t (LL); -kakata t (HHH); -kweva i & t (LL); *pull down, demolish, destroy* vb -paza t (LL); *pull out feathers, pluck* vb -undura i & t (LLL); *pull out plants by the roots* vb -dzura i & t (LL); -dzipura i & t (LLL); -tipura t (LLL); *pull ugly faces, make faces* vb -finyama i (HHH); *pull someone's leg, joke* vb -ita musara i (LL LLL); *pull down branches with a hook* vb -ngova i & t (LL)

pullet *young hen at the stage of first laying* n tseketsa 9 Z (LHL); sheche 9 K (LL)

pump *machine for forcing air or liquid into something* n pombi 9 (LH) cf Eng.; *pump air or liquid* vb -pomba t (HH) cf Eng.

pumpkin *fruit used as a vegetable* n nhanga 5, manhanga 6 (LL); *p. leaves cooked as veg* n muboora 3 (LLLH); *p. pips* n mhodzi 10 (LH)

puncture *of a tyre* n ponji 9 (HL) cf Eng.

punish *administer punishment* vb -ranga i & t (LL); *punishment, pain or discomfort for wrongdoing* n chirango 7 (LLL) cf -ranga (LL)

pupa *insect during the dormant stage, chrysalis, cocoon* n chikukwa 7 (LLL)

pupil *one who learns (usu in school)* n mufundi 1 (LHH) cf -funda (HH); mudzidzi 1 (LHL) cf -dzidza (HH)

pupil of eye *black centre of eye* n mboni 9 (HH)

puppy *young dog* n mbwanana 9 (HHH); kutu 9 (HL); handa 9 MZ (LL)

purchase *buy* vb -tenga i & t (HH)

pure *clean, without evil or sin* adj -tsvene (LH); dzvene 5, tsvene 9

purify *clean* vb -chenesa t (LLL) cf -chena (LL)

purity *holiness* n utsvene 14 (LLH)

purlin *light strip of wood running along length of roof and supporting the covering* n mbariro 9 (LLL)

purple *colour* adj pepuru 9 (HLL) cf Eng.

purr *(of a cat)* vb -n'eura i (HHH)

purpose *intention of doing, what one intends to do* n chido 7 (LH) cf -da (H); vavariro 9 (HHHL) cf -vavarira (HHHL)

purse *container for keeping money on one's person* n chikwama 7 (LHL)

pursue *follow, go after* vb -tevera t (LLL)

purulent *be p.; discharge pus* vb -funuka i (LLL)

pus *yellow liquid discharge from a wound* n urwa 14 (LH)

push *(opposite of pull)* vb -sandidzira i & t (LLLL); -sairira i & t (LLLL); -sundidzira i & t (LLLL); *push over, knock o.* vb -ngundumura t (HHHL)

put *place* vb -isa t (LL); *put away in their right place, arrange* vb -rongedza i & t (LLL); *put against, lean, put upright against* vb -sendeka t (HHH); *put down* vb -isa pasi t (LL LH); *put down from the head, unload* vb -tura i & t (HH); *put down baby from the back* vb -burutsa t MZ (LLL); *put in, put inside, insert* vb -pinza (LL); *put in disorder, dismantle* vb -gurunura t (HHHL); *put in order, arrange* vb -ronga t (LL); *put out, turn out light, extinguish* vb -dzima i & t (HH); *put out of joint, dislocate* vb -minyura t (LLL); *put on clothes, dress* vb -pfeka mbatya (LL LL); *put on guard* vb -chenjedza t (HHH); *put on speed, accelerate, go faster,* vb -mhanyisa i (HHL); *put on weight (humans), get fat* vb -futa i (LL); *(animals)* vb -kora i (LL); *put right, adjust, correct* vb -ruramisa t (LLLL) cf -rurama (LLL); *put to bed* vb -rarisa t (HHH); *put to shame, cause shame* vb -nyadza i & t (HH) cf -nyara (HH); *put up, fix, affix, fasten* vb -rovera t (HHH); *put up (e.g. notice), hang up* vb -turika t (HHH); *put up with, endure* vb -tirira i & t (LLL) — PT & PP put

put off *delay* vb -nonoka i (LLL)

putrid *be rotten, bad* vb -ora i (LL) (stative vb)

puzzle *cause wonder or astonishment* vb -shamisa i & t (HHH); -kangenisa t (HHHL)

pyjamas *loose-fitting jacket and trousers for sleeping in* n mapijama 6 (LLHL) cf Eng.

pyorrhoea *disease of the gums which causes teeth to fall out* n chikutumeno 7 K (LHHLH); chigurameno 7 Z (LHHLH)

python *very large and non-poisonous snake which kills its prey by constriction (4,8 m to 6 m in length)* n shato 9 (HH) *cf illustration p. 145*

parasites

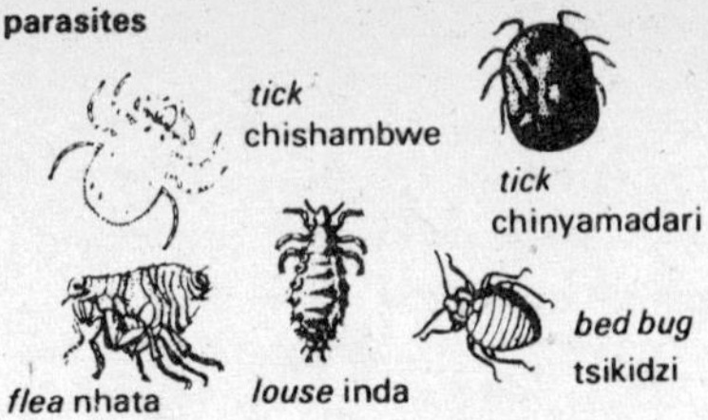

Q

quail chihuta

quail *very small, gregarious, edible, ground-bird* n chihuta 7 (LLL); chipwi 7 M (LH); imwi 9 M (LH); ipwi 9 M (LH) R196

quarrel *grumble or take part in an argument* vb -popota i (HHH); -popotedzana (HHHLL); *quarrel, angry argument or disagreement* n bopoto 5 (HHL) cf -popota

quarter-evil *cattle disease* n chidhiya 7 Z (LHL); chigodora 7 Z (LLLL); chipfura 7 M (LHL)

queen *wife of a king, woman ruler* n hosi 9 (HL); ngosikadzi 9 (HHLL); mambokadzi 1a (LLLL)

quelea *sp of gregarious seed-eating bird* n chimokoto 7 MZ (LLLL); dzemaguru 9 (HLHH) R805

quench *thirst, satisfy t.* vb -bvisa nyota (LL HH)

question *something asked* n mubvunzo 3 MZ (LLL) cf -bvunza (LL)

question *enquire, ask qs.* vb -bvunza i & t (LL); -vhunza i & t KKo (LL); *question, investigate* vb -feya-feya i & t (HHHL)

quick *be q.* vb -kurumidza i (HHHL); -chimbidza i (HHH); Aka**chimbidza** kuuya. (*He came quickly.*)

quickly *without delay* adv nokukurumidza (HLHHHL); nokuchimbidza (HLHHH); -chimbidzo- — infix vb

quiet *be silent* adj & vb -nyarara (HHL) (stative vb); Ndaona vana vaka**nyarara**. (*I found the children silent.*)

quietly *without noise* adv chinyararire 7 (LHHLH)

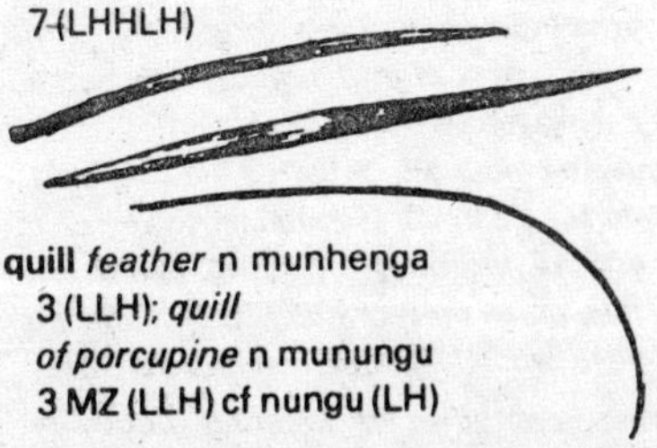

quill *feather* n munhenga 3 (LLH); *quill of porcupine* n munungu 3 MZ (LLH) cf nungu (LH)

quit *go from, leave, depart* vb -bva i (L)

quit *give up, stop doing* vb -regera i & t (LLL)

quiver *tremble* vb -dedera i (LLL); -bvunda i (HL)

R

ratel/ tsere

rabbit *(see* **hare***)* n tsuro 9 (LL)

rabies *disease of dogs producing madness* n chikangiri 7 (LLLL)

race *contest* n mapitse 6 (LLH); mujahwo 3 (LLL); makwikwi 6 (LLH)

race *tribe, variety* n rudzi 11 (LL) *plur:* marudzi 6; udzi 14 Ko (LL)

racial discrimination n rusaruraganda 11 (LLLLHH) cf -sarura (LLL)

radio set n redhiyo 9 (HLL) cf Eng.; wairesi 9 (HLLL) cf Eng.

radio station *broadcasting station* n nhepfenyuro 9 (LLLL)

rag *scrap of material* n mvemve 5, mamvemve 6 (LH); rengenya 5 MZ, marengenya 6 (LLL); dzoto 5, matsoto 6 M (HH)

rage *anger* n hasha 10 (HH) *plur only*

ragged clothes *tatters* n mamvemve 6 (LLH); madhende 6 K (LHH)

rail *railway line* n njanji 9 (LH)

rain *water* n mvura 9 (HH); *early r.* n bumharutsva 5 (LLLH); *drizzle* n mubvumbi 3 (LLH); upfunhambuya 14 (LLLHL); *rain with hail* n chimvuramahwe 7 (LHHHL)

rain vb -naya i & t (LL); -na (L), -niwa (LL) passive form; *r. lightly, drizzle* vb -pfunha i (LL)

rain tree *lance tree* n mupanda 3 (LLL); mupandangoma 3 (LLLLL); muwoworo 3 (LLLL)

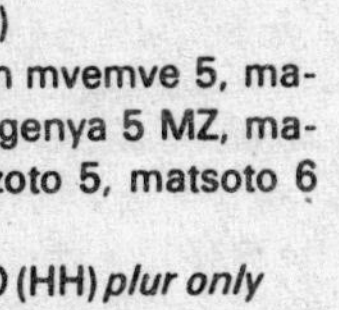

rainbow n murara 3 (LLL); mutswi 3 (LL); muraraungu 3 MZ (LLLHH)

raincoat *outer coat to protect from rain* n chikweshe 7 (LLL); renikoti 9 (HLLL) cf Eng.

rainy season *(Nov. — March)* n zhizha 5 KoZ (LH); zhezha 5 K (LH); maenza 6 MZ (LLH)

raise *breed livestock* vb -pfuya t (HH); -pfuwa t K (HH)

raise *lift up, hoist up* vb -simudza t (HHL); -sumudza t (HHL); *raise dust* vb -pfumbura t (HHH); -tibura t (HHH); *raise money, search for money* vb -tsvaga mari (LL LH)

rake *long-handled tool used for smoothing soil, gathering together dead leaves etc.* n hara 9 (HL) cf Eng.: *harrow;* reki 9 (HL) cf Eng.

rake *make clean with r.* vb -kura t (LL); -kukura t (HHH); -hara t (HH) cf Eng. *cf illustration p. 162*

ram *male sheep* n hondohwe 9 MZ (LHL); gondohwe 5 K, makondohwe 6 (LHL)

ram *force into a hole* vb -tsindira t (HHH)

ran *cf run*

rang *cf ring*

ransack *pillage, plunder* vb -kukura t (HHH)

ransom *pay r.* vb -tsikinura t (LLLL); *ransom, money paid for freeing a prisoner* n tsikinuro 9 MZ (LLLL) cf -tsikinura (LLLL)

rap *at the door, knock* vb -gogodza i & t (HHH)

rape *ravish, violate* vb -bata chibharo t (HH LHH); -manikidza t (HHHL); -bhinya t (LL)

rape *a leaf-vegetable* n repi 5 (HL) cf Eng.; chembere dzagumana (LLL HHLL)

rapid *be quick* vb -kurumidza i (HHHL)

rapids *water-falls* n mangondo 6 (LLL); machiti 6 K (LLL); mapopopo 6 (LLLL)

rapoko grass n mombe 9 (LL)

rascal *dishonest person* n goronyera 5, makoronyera 6 (LLLL)

rat *small animal that gnaws, rodent* n gonzo 5, makonzo 6 (LL); goso 5 Ko, makoso 6 (LL); *giant r.* n mhunzamatura 9 (HHLHL); pinga 1a M (HH)

ratel *honey badger* n chisere 7 K (LLL); chitsere 7 KM (LLL), mbungo 9 Z (LL); mbure 9 Z (LL); tsere 9 MZ (LL) *cf illustration p. 125*

rather than *in preference to* adv: Ndingade mari **pane** zvokudya. (*I would prefer money rather than food.*)

rattle *musical instrument made from a calabash* n hosho 9 (LH)

ravelled *be r. or entangled (of wool and cotton)* vb -katana i (HHH)

raven *white-necked r.* n gunguo 5, makunguo 6 (HHL)

ravish *rape, violate* vb -bata chibharo t (HH LHH); -bhinya t (LL)

raw *uncooked, unripe* adj -mbishi (HH); mbishi 5 & 9 (HH)

rays *of the sun* n maranzi 6 MZ (LLH)

razor blade *sharp, cutting instrument for shaving* n chisvo 7 (LH); reza i (HL) cf Eng

reach *arrive at* vb -svika i & t (LL); *be able to be reached* vb -svikika i & t (LLL) cf -svika (LL)

reach *stretch out for* vb -sveverera i & t (LLLL)

read *follow the meaning of the printed word* vb -rava t K (LL); -verenga i & t (LLL) — PT & PP *read*

ready *be prepared* vb -gadzirira i (LLLL) cf -gadzira (LLL)

real *true, proper* Pronoun in apposition cf p. 196

really *truly* adv chokwadi (HLH); kwazvo (HL); chose K (HH); *really; (footnote)* Ndini chaiye etc. *cf p. 194*

reap *bring in the harvest* vb -kohwa i & t (LL)

rear *bring up, tend small children* vb -rera t (LL); *way of bringing a child up* n murerero 3 (LLHH) cf -rera (LL)

reason *think, consider* vb -funga i (LL)

reason *cause or justification for something* n chikonzero 7 (LHHL) -konzera (HHH)

reasonable *be sensible* vb -va nomusoro (HLHH)

rebel *show resistance to authority* vb -panduka i (LLL); n mupandukiri 1

rebellion *armed rising* n chimurenga 7 (LLLL)

rebound *(as a ball), bounce* vb -dauka i (HHH)

recall *remember* vb -yeuka i & t (LLL)

recede *withdraw, move back* vb -suduruka i (LLLL)

receipt *written statement of something received* n rusiti 11, marusiti 6 (LHL) cf Eng.

receive *take something offered or sent* vb -tambira (HHH); -gashira i & t (LLL)

reckon *think* vb -funga i & t (LL)

recline *lie down, sleep* vb -rara i (HH); -vata i (HH); (stative vbs); Vana **varere**. (*The children are asleep / lying down.*)

recognize *know* vb -ziva t (HH)

recollect *remember* vb -yeuka i & t (LLL); -tondera i & t (HHH)

recollection *reminiscence* n ndangariro 9 (LLLL) cf -rangarira (LLLL)

recommend *speak in favour of (a person), intercede for* vb -reverera t (HHHL)

reconcile *cause persons to become friends after they have quarrelled* vb -wadzanisa t (LLLL) cf -wadzana (LLL)

record *gramophone r.* n rekodhi 9 (HLL) cf Eng.

recover *health, survive* vb -pona i (HH); -naya i (LL).

recover something lost *find* vb -wana t (LL)

recreate *in conversation* vb -tandara i (HHH)

rectify *put right* vb -ruramisa t (LLLL) cf -rurama (LLL)

red *reddisn, brown* adj -tsvuku (LH); dzvuku 5, tsvuku 9; *reddish pink, reddish* adj & vb -tsvukuruka i (LLLL) (stative vb)

red mahogany *tree* n mururu 3 (LLH); muwawa 3 (LLL); *red paper tree* n mukusere 3 (LHLL)

red wings *flowering plant* n bepu 5 (LH)

red-hot *be aglow, be red* vb -tsvuka i (LL)

redeem *set free by payment* vb -nunura t (LLL); *redeemer, one who redeems (Jesus Christ)* n mununuri 1 (LLLL) cf -nunura (LLL)

reduce *take part away* vb -kamura t (HHH)

reed *kind of waterplant which is tall, firm and thin* n tsanga 9 (LL)

reedbuck *rietbok, weight about 65 kg* n bimha 5, mapimha 6 (LL); mhima 9 (LL) *cf illustration p. 89*

reedy place n deve retsanga 5 (LH LHL); dofo 5 (LH)

refine *make better, improve* vb -nakisa t (LLL)

refined *be good-mannered* vb -va netsika i (LHL)

reflect *ponder* vb -rangarira i & t (LLLL); -funga i & t (LL)

refrigerator *apparatus for preserving food at a low temperature* n firiji 9 (HLL) cf Eng.

refuge *place of r.* n diziro 5, matiziro 6 (HHL) cf -tiza (HH)

refuge *take r., fly to safety* vb -potera i (HHH); *refugee* n mupoteri 1

refuse *reject* vb -ramba i & t (LL)

refuse *rubbish, waste-matter* n marara 6 (LLL)

regard *with r. to, about* nezva- (HL)

region *district* n dunhu 5, matunhu 6 (HH); ruwa 5, maruwa 6 (LL)

regret *an omission in the past (e.g. of advice)* vb -kungura i & t (HHH)

registration certificate n chitupa 7 (LLL)

regulation *rule, law* n murau 3 (LLL); mutemo 3 (LHH) cf -tema (HH)

reign *govern, administer* vb -tonga i & t (HH)

rein *strap by which a horse is controlled* n bhandi 5, mabhandi 6 (HL) cf Eng.

reject *refuse* vb -ramba i & t (LL); *throw away* vb -rasa t (HH)

rejoice *be happy* vb -fara i (HH)

relate *tell a story* vb -ita ngano t (LL LL)

relation *relative by blood or by marriage* n hama 9 (HH); *relationship, some degree of being related* n ukama 14 (LHH); *related, belong to the same family* vb -va noukama i

relaxed *be free* vb -sununguka i (HHHL) (stative vb); Ndakasununguka. (*I am relaxed.*)

release *allow to go* vb -regedza t (LLL); -regera t (LLL); *loosen* vb -sunungura t (HHHL) cf -sunga (HH)

reliable *be trustworthy, able to be believed* vb -tendeseka i (LLLL); -vimbika i (LLL); *reliable, sound (moral quality)* adj & vb -tsiga i (HH) (stative vb)

religion *faith, content of belief* n chitendero 7 (LLLL) cf -tendera (LLL)

relish *vegetable or meat (eaten with sadza)* n muriwo 3 MZ (LHH); usavi 14 (LHH)

reluctant *be unwilling through fear* vb -zeza i (LL); *procrastinate* vb -zengurira i (LLLL)

rely on *depend on, put trust in* vb -vimba na- (LL); -temba na- i (HH)

remain *r. behind, be left over* vb -sara i (HH)

remarkable *be astonishing* vb -shamisa i & t (HHH) cf -shama (HH)

remedy *medicine* n mushonga 3 (LLH)

remember *recall* vb -yeuka i & t (LLL); -tondera i & t M (HHH); *fail to r.* vb -kanganwa i & t (HHH); -shaya t (LL)

remind *cause someone to remember* vb -yeuchidza t (LLLL) cf -yeuka (LLL); -fungisa t (LLL) cf -funga (LL); -tondedza t (HHH) cf -tondera (HHH)

reminder *something that reminds or recalls to memory* n chiyeuchidzo 7 (LLLLL) cf -yeuchidza (LLLL)

remit *let off, excuse from payment, forgive* vb -regerera t (LLLL)

remote *place* adv kure kure 17 (LL HH); *remote time past* adv kare kare 12 (LL HH)

remove *take away* vb -bvisa t (LL) cf -bva (I); *remove bark from tree, debark* vb*-svuura t (LLL); *remove honey from hive* vb -mora t (HH); *remove a lid, uncover* vb -kudubura t (HHHL); *remove an object from fire* vb -bura t (LL); *remove a tree-stump and roots* vb -gobora t (LLL); *remove thatch, strip off t.* vb -pfurunura t (HHHL) cf -pfirira (HHH)

rend *tear, rip* vb -bvarura t (HHH)

renew *make new* vb -vandutsa t (LLL); -vandudza t (LLL)

rent *pay r., pay tax* vb -tera i & t (LL); *pay r. for* vb -terera (LLL)

rent *for a house* n rendi 9 (HL) cf Eng.; mutero 3 (LLL) cf -tera (LL)

repaid *cf repay*

repair *mend* vb -gadzira t (LLL)

repay *pay back, retaliate (includes return injury for injury)* vb -tsiva t (LL) — PT & PP *repaid*

repeat *do again* vb -pamhidza i & t (LLL)

repeatedly *time and again* adv nguva nenguva (HH HLL); -ramba + Partic

repent *be sorry* vb -pfidza i (HH)

repentance *sorrow for sin* n rupinduko 11 (LLLL) (*same word used for the Sacrament of Penance*) cf -pinduka (LLL)

repentant *be penitent* vb -pfidza i (HH)

replace *restore to original place* vb -dzorera t (LLL)

replant *r. where previous seeds have not germinated* vb -kaurura t (LLLL)

repleat *be full, have enough to eat* vb -guta i (HH)

reply *give an answer* vb -pindura i & t (LLL); -davira i & t (HHH); *reply, an answer given* n mhinduro 9 (LLL) cf -pindura (LLL)

report *lodge an official complaint to authority* vb -mhan'ara i (LLL)

representative *one who acts for or speaks for someone* n mumiririri 1 (LHHHL) cf -miririra (HHHL); *r. in marriage negotiations* n munyai 1 (LLL)

reproach *reprimand angrily, scold, abuse* vb -tuka i & t (HH)

reptile *cold-blooded animal including snakes, lizards etc.* n *see illustration.*

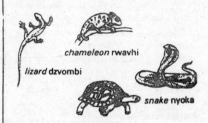

reptiles

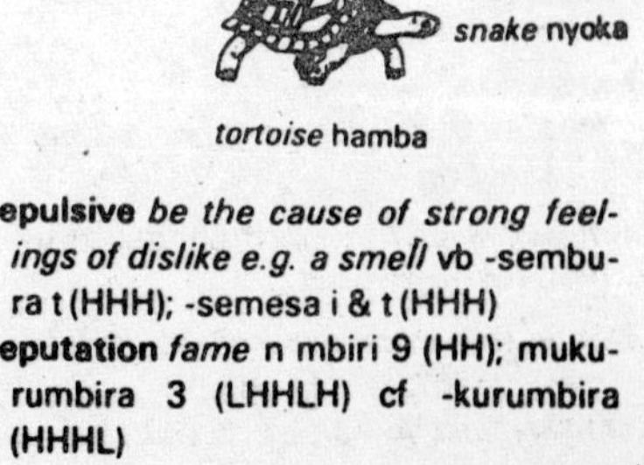

repulsive *be the cause of strong feelings of dislike e.g. a smell* vb -sembura t (HHH); -semesa i & t (HHH)

reputation *fame* n mbiri 9 (HH); mukurumbira 3 (LHHLH) cf -kurumbira (HHHL)

request *earnest r., plea* n chichemo 7 (LHH) cf -chema (HH)

request *ask for* vb -kumbira i & t (HHH)

require *wish for, want* vb -da i & t (H); *required, be needed* vb -dikanwa i (HHH) cf -da (H)

rescue *from harm, save* vb -nunura t (LLL)

resemble *be similar to, be like* vb -fanana na- i (HHH) (stative vb); -todza t KM (HH); *resemble each other* vb -fanana i (HHH); -todzana i KM (HHH) (stative vbs); Vana ava vakafanana. (*These children are alike.*)

reserve *keep back* vb -chengeta i & t (LLL)

reside *live, stay* vb -gara i (LL)

resign *give notice of leaving employment* vb -pa notisi (HLL)

resist *refuse to do what is required* vb -ramba i & t (LL)

resolute *be determined* vb -shinga i & t (HH) (*usu followed by infinitive*): Ashinga kuenda mvura ichinaya. (*He is determined to go while it is still raining.*)

resolve *make up the mind* vb -tsunga mwoyo (HH HL)

resound *echo back sound* vb -ita maun'ira (LL LLLL)

respect *honour, give deference, regard respectfully* vb -kudza t (HH); -remekedza i & t (LLLL); *respect shown, deference* n rukudzo 11 (LHH) cf -kudza (HH); ruremekedzo 11 (LLLLL) cf -remekedza (LLLL)

respiration *breathing* n mafemo 6 (LLL) cf -fema (LL)

respire *breathe* vb -fema i & t (LL)

respond *reply* vb -davira t (HHH)

responsibility *duty, work* n basa 5, mabasa 6 (LL)

rest *be still or quiet* vb -zorora i (HHH); *rest on, lean on* vb -tsamira t (HHH)

rest *the majority remaining* n rudhende 11 (LHH)

resting place *time of rest* n zororo 5, mazororo 6 (HHL)

restore *return, give back* vb -dzorera i & t (LLL)

restrain *prevent, hold back* vb -dzivirira t (LLLL)

resurrection *the rising of the dead* n kumuka muvafi 15 (LLL LLH)

retain *keep, preserve* vb -chengeta t (LLL)

retaliate *revenge, pay back* vb -tsiva i (LL)

retaliation *action taken to pay back* n chitsividzo 7 (LLLL) cf -tsividza (LLL)

retch *vomit* vb -rutsa i & t (HH)

retreat *spiritual r.* n runyararo 11 (LHHL) cf -nyarara (HHL)

retreat *run away, flee* vb -tiza i & t (HH)

return *come back* vb -dzoka i (LL); -petuka i M (LLL); *go b. to point of departure* vb -dzokera i (LLL) cf -dzoka (LL); *give back* vb -dzosera t (LLL); -dzorera t (LLL); -dzokesa t (LLL); dzosa t (LL)

reveal *make to see* vb -onesa t (HHH) cf -ona (HH); *declare openly* vb -isa pachena (LL LLL); *enlighten, teach* vb -dzidzisa i & t (HHL) cf -dzidza HH); *r. by word e.g. secret* vb -dura i & t (LL); -dudza i & t (LL)

revenge *retaliate, repay* vb -tsiva i & t MZ (LL); -tsividza i & t MZ (LLL); *revenge, retaliation* n matsive 6 (LLH) cf -tsiva (LL)

reverence *show honour* vb -remekedza t (LLLL); -kudza t (HH); *reverence, profound respect* n rukudzo 11 (LHH) cf -kudza (HH); -ruremekedzo 11 (LLLLL)

revive *nurse* vb -pepa t (HH)

revolt *be hateful to, be repulsive* vb -semesa i & t (HHH) cf -sema (HH)

revolve *turn around on an axis* vb -tenderera i (HHHL)

revolver *type of pistol* n vhorovhoro 9 (LHLL) cf Eng.

revolution *rebellion* n chimurenga 7 (LLLL)

reward *give prize or gratuity* vb -tusa t (LL)

reward *wage, salary* n mubayiro 3 (LLLL); chituso 7 (LLL) cf -tusa (LL)

rhinoceros *black r., a browsing sp which is the smaller and yet the more vicious of the two rhinoceros sp. A young calf always follows its mother* n nhema 9 (HL); *white r. is a grazing sp somewhat bigger than the black. The white r. was once extinct in Zimbabwe and has now been reintroduced. The calf always goes in front of its mother.* n fura 9 KoZ (LL) *cf p. 65*

Rhodesian ash *tree, wild syringa t.* n mukarati 3 (LHHL); *R. ebony tree* n mushuma 3 (LHL); muchenje 3 (LLL); *R. hibiscus tree, snot apple t. quarters t.* n mutohwe (LHL); *R. holly tree, redwood t., wild oleander* n muminu 3 (LLH); mutswatswa 3 (LLL); *R. ironwood tree* n musaru 3, musharu 3 (LLH); *R. jacaranda tree* n mukuku 3 (LHL); *R. rubber tree* n musikanyimo 3 (LLLLL); mutochwa 3 (LHL); *R. teak* n munhondochuru 3 (LLLLL); mukusi 3 (LHL); *R. wattle, African black-wood t.* n musambanvoka 3 (LLLHH); mupumhamakuva 3 (LHHLHH); *R. wistaria, wild wistaria* n mupangamabwe 3 (LLLLL); mukweshanyama 3 (LHHHL)

rib *any one of the curved bones extending from the backbone round the chest* n mbabvu 9 (LL); rumbabvu 11 (LLL)

rice *type of white grain* n mupunga 3 (LLL); *r. field* n deka 5, mateka 6 (LL); dimbwa 5 Z, matimbwa 6 (LL); doro 5, matoro 6 (LH)

rich *be wealthy* vb -pfuma i MZ (HH)

rich person n mupfumi 1 (LHH) cf -fuma (HH); huzu 9 MZ (HL); *riches, wealth* n upfumi 14 (LHH); pfuma 9 (HL) cf -pfuma (HH)

rid *get r. of, get free of, drive away* vb -tanda t (HH); -dzinga t (HH); *get r. of a thing, throw away* vb -rasa t (HH) — PT & PP *ridded, rid*

ridden *cf ride*

riddle *puzzling question, usu to entertain after supper* n chirahwe 7 Z (LHL); chipari 7 KoM (LHL); chirabwe 7 K (LHL)

ride *get on* vb -tasva t (HH); -kwira t (HH); Zvinonzi navanhu varoyi vanotasva mapere. (*People say that witches ride on hyenas.*) — PT *rode;* PP *ridden*

ridge *line where two sloping surfaces meet* n muhomba 3 (LHL)

ridicule *make fun of* vb -seka i & t (LL); *r. by imitating* vb -edzesera i & t (LLLL)

riem *leather harness, thong, strap* n tambo 9 (LL)

rifle *gun with spiral grooves in the barrel* n pfuti 9 (LL)

right *be morally fit, suitable* vb -kodzera i (LLL)

right *correct* Pronoun in apposition cf p. 196

right *be r. morally, be righteous* adj & vb -rurama i (LLL); -naka i (LL) (stative vbs); Tina baba vakarurama. (*We have an upright father.*); *r. hand* n rudyi 11 (LH); *r. hand side* n kurudyi 17 (LLH); gumbo rokurudyi (*the right hand leg*)

righteousness *justice* n ururami 14 (LLLL) cf -rurama (LLL)

rightly *correctly, properly* adv nomazvo (HLH)

ring *sound* vb -ridza t (LL) — PT *rang, rung;* PP *rung*

ring *for the finger or for the ear* n mhete 9 Z (LH); ringi 9 (HL) cf Eng.

ringworm *infection* n chisasa 7 MZ (LLL)

rinkhals *ring-necked spitting cobra, black beneath with white band across the throat, length 75 cm to 90 cm, found only in E. Districts* n mbeza 9 M (LH)

rinse *remove traces of soap in clean water* vb -dzumburudza t (LLLL); -ngurungudza t M (HHHL)

riot *rebellion* n chimurenga 7 (LLLL)

rip *tear* vb -bvarura t (HHH)

rip open *undo stitching* vb -rudunura t (LLLL)

ripe *ripen, become ripe* vb -ibva i (HH) (stative vb); muchero wakaibva (*ripe fruit*)

ripples *waves* n masaisai 6 (LLLLL)

rise *from bed, wake up* vb -muka i (LL); *r. early* vb -fuma i (HH); *r. from sitting, stand up* vb -simuka i (HHL); *r. of the sun* vb -buda i (HH); *r. against, oppose, turn against* vb -mukira t (LLL) — PT *rose;* PP *risen*

rise *(of dust)* vb -tibuka i (HHH); -mbumuka i (HHH); -pwititika i (HHHL); *(of smoke)* vb -pfumbuka i (HHH)

rise *as dough, bubble, fizz* vb -tutuma i (LLL)

river crossing *ford* n zambuko 5 mazambuko 6 (LLL)

river *small r.* n rukova 11 (LLL); hova 10 *plur* (LL); *large r.* n rwizi 11 (LH); nzizi 10; *r. bank* n hombekombe 9 (LLLL); *rivulet, stream* n kakova 12 (LLL); kakokorodzi 12 (LHHLH)

road *highway* n mugwagwa 3 (LLL); ròdhi 9 (HL) cf Eng.

roam *wander about* vb -famba-famba i (HHHL)

roan antelope *sp of large antelope, weight up to 150 kg* n chengu 9 (LH); ndunguza i Z (LLL) *cf illustration p. 89*

roar *(as a lion)* vb -dzvova i (LL); *(as a fire or river)* vb -tinhira i (LLL)

roast *over open fire* vb -gocha i & t (LL); *roast in pan, fry* vb -kanga t (HH)

rob *steal* vb -ba i & t (H); *take by force, plunder* vb -pamba i (HH)

robber *thief* n mbavha 9 (LH); gororo 5, makororo 6 (LHL)

rock *big stone* n dombo 5, matombo 6 (LH); ibwe 5, mabwe 6 (LL); *flat expanse of granite* n ruware 11 (LLH); *rocks, balancing r.* n matombo akaturikidzana

rock-rabbit *dassie* n mbira 9 (HL) (*to be distinguished from* mbira 9 (LL) = *Shona piano*)

rod *cane* n shamhu 9 (LH)

rode *cf ride*

rodent *kinds of gnawing animals*

roll *r. down* vb -kunguruka i (HHHL); -kungurutsa t (HHHL); *roll down a hillside* vb -koromoka i (HHHL); *roll up sleeves or any part of clothing* vb -kunya t (LL)

roller bird n gatahwa 5, magatahwa 6 (LHL); jenjera 5 M (HHL)

roof *covering of a building providing protection from sun and rain* n denga (remba) 5, matenga 6 (HL)

roof-top *peak of conical roof* n chisuvi 7 (LLL); chiruvi 9 K (LLL)

room *house* n imba 9 (LH); mupanda 3 (LLL)

rooster *male fowl* n jongwe 5, majongwe 6 / machongwe 6 (LH)

root *part of a plant or tree which is under the soil* n mudzi 3 (LL)

root up *pull up by the roots* vb -dzura t (LL); -dzipura t (LLL)

rope *very strong cord* n gambara 5, magambara 6 (LLL); tambo 9 (LL); *r. made from bark-fibre* n bindepinde 5, mabindepinde 6 (HLHL)

rot *go bad, decay* vb -ora i (LL); *rot thoroughly* vb -orera i (LLL)

rotate *turn round* vb -tenderera i (HHHL); -tenderedza t (HHHL)

rotten *be putrid, bad* adj & vb -ora i (LL) (stative vb); Mazai aya aka**ora**. (*These eggs are rotten.*)

round *be spherical* adj & vb -tenderera i (HHHL) (stative vb); Mwedzi wakate**nderera**. (*The moon is spherical.*)

round *wrap r.* vb -moneredza t (HHHL) cf -mona (HH)

round up *gather together (livestock)* vb -kokorodza t (HHHL)

rouse *disturb from sleep* vb -mutsa t (LL) cf -muka (LL)

row *line of objects* n mudungwe 3 (LHL); rundaza 11 (LLH)

row *noise* n ruzha 11 (LH)

row *a boat, paddle* n kwasva i (LL)

rub *r. against, r. to soothe, (e.g. pain) r. to smooth (e.g. sandpaper)* vb -kwiza t (LL); *r. out, erase, remove by erasing* vb -dzima t (HH); *r. ointment, anoint* vb -zora t (LL); *r. eyes* vb -pokotora t (HHHL)

rubber *eraser* n rabha 9 (HL) cf Eng.

rubber hedge *milk bush* n heji yomukaka 9 (HL LHLL); rusungwe 11 (LHL)

rubber tree n mutowa 3 (LHL)

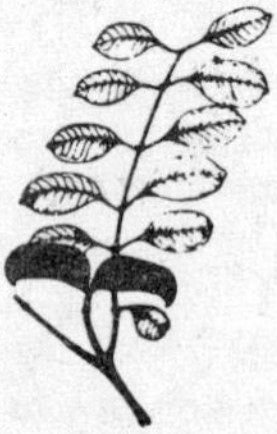

rubbish *waste-material thrown away* n marara 6 (LLL)

rubbish bin *refuse container* n bhini 5,

rodents

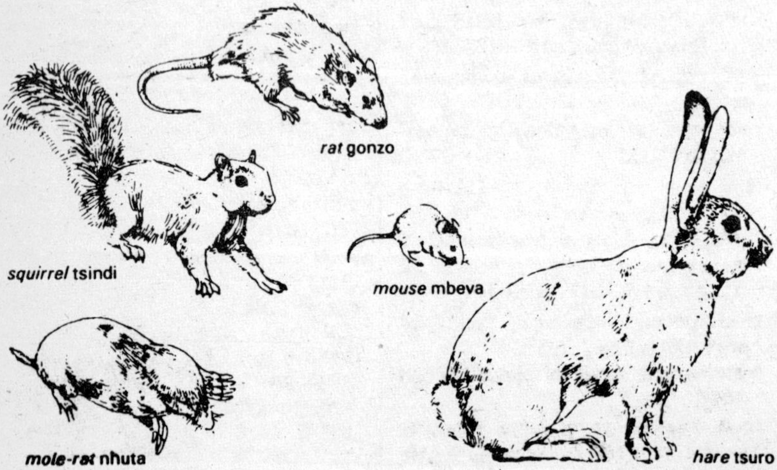

mabhini 6 (HL); dhodhibhokisi 5 (HLHLL) cf Eng.

rude *be bad-mannered* vb -shaya tsika i (LL LL); -shaya unhu i (LL LL)

rug *thick carpet usu small* n jari 5, majari 6 (LH); ragi 5, maragi 6 (HL) cf Eng.

ruin *destroy* vb -paradza t (LLL)

ruin *of a kraal, deserted village* n dongo 5, matongo 6

rule *administer, judge* vb -tonga i & t (HH)

rule *law, ruling* n mutemo 3 (LHH) cf -tema (HH); murau 3 (LLL)

ruler *one who rules* n mutongi 1 (LHH) cf -tonga (HH)

ruler *for drawing* n rura 9 (HL) cf Eng.

rumble *as wagon* vb -gudubuka i (HHHL); *rumble as a bus or thunder* vb -tinhira i (LLL); -dhirima i (LLL); -dhuruma i Z (LLL); -nguruma i (LLL)

rumour *story that requires to be confirmed, statement open to doubt* n guhwa 5, makuhwa 6 (LL); runyerekupe 11 (LLLLL)

run *move at speed* vb -mhanya i (HH); -rumba i M (LL); *run at full speed* vb -rarira pasi (HHH LH) *i.e. run close to the ground; r. fast* vb -mhanyisa i (HHL); *run away, r. from* vb -tiza i & t (HH); *run after, pursue* vb -dzinganisa t (HHHL); -tandanisa t (HHHL) — PT *ran;* PP *run*

run short *be out of stock, have no more* vb -pererwa na- (HHH)

rung *cf ring*

rung *step of ladder* n nera 5 MZ (HL)

rupoko *finger millet, ingredient for good beer* n zviyo 8 (LH)

rush *move with great speed* vb -kurumidza i (HHHL); -mhanya i (HH)

rust *on iron, disease on wheat or mealies* n ngura 9 (LH)

rut *wheel track in the earth* n vhiri rengoro 5, mavhiri engoro 6 (HL HLH)

cane rat tsenzi

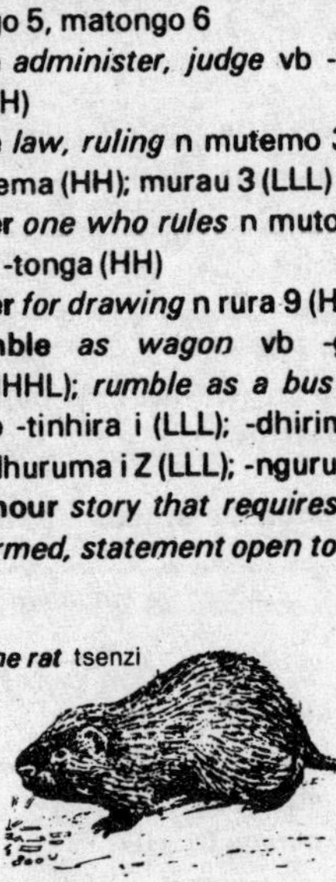

dassie mbira

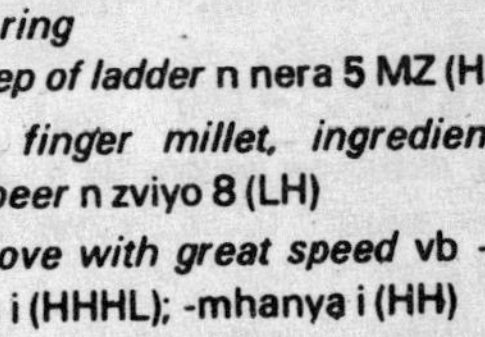

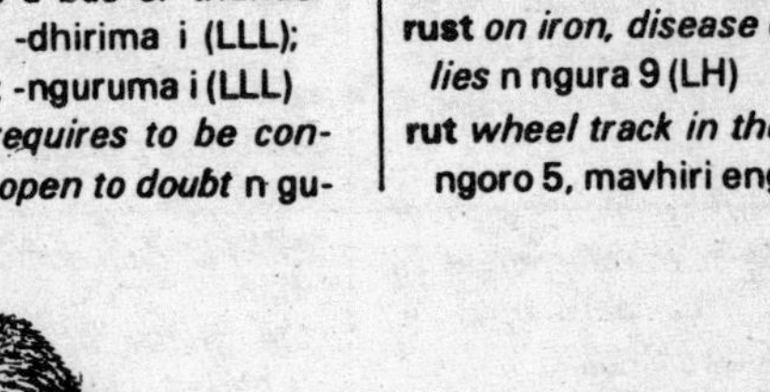

porcupine nungu

S

sable antelope mharapara

sabbath *Jewish day of rest: Saturday; Christian day of rest: Sunday* n sabata 5 & 9 (HLL) cf Eng.

sable antelope *weight up to 225 kg* n mharapara 9 (LLLL); ngwarati 9 MZ (LLL)

sack *large woven container; large, rough bag* n sagi 5, masagi 6 (LH) ; saga 5, masaga 6 (LH); saki 5, masaki 6 (LH) cf Eng.

sacrament *outward religious sign of an inward grace* n sakaramende 5, masakaramende 6 (LLLHL) cf Eng.

sacred *be holy* adj -era i (LL)

sacrifice *make sacrificial offering* vb -pira i & t (HH); -teura i & t (HHH); *sacrifice, sacrificial offering* n mupiro 3 (LHH) cf -pira (HH); muteuro 3 (LHHL) cf -teura (HHH)

sacrum *the last bone of the lower spine* n chididi 7 (LLL)

sad *be depressed* vb -tsamwa i (LL); -suruvara i (HHHL) (stative vbs); chembere yakasuruvara (*a sad old woman*); *sadden, disappoint* vb -tsamwisa i & t (LLL)

saddle *seat for the rider of bicycle or horse* n chisharo 7 (LLL); seduru 9 (HLL) cf Eng.

sadza *5, staple, stiff porridge; stir sadza in the early stages of preparation* vb -kurunga t (HHH); *stir the final stiff porridge* vb -mona t (HH)

safari shirt *khaki bush-s.* n jamba 5, majamba 6 (HL)

safety pin *p. with a guard for the point* n chipeneti 7 (LHLL)

said *be reported* vb -nzi i (L) *passive form of the* vb -ti

said *cf say*

saint *holy person* n musande 1 (LHL) cf Eng.

salary *wage, reward* n mubayiro 3 (LLLL)

sale *offering of goods at low prices for a period* n sero 9 (HL) cf Eng.

sale *put up goods for s., display goods for sale* vb -shambadza t (HHH)

saliva *spittle* n mate 6 (LH)

salt *substance used to flavour food (sodium chloride)* n munyu 3 (LH); sauti 9 (HLL) cf Eng.

salt *apply s.* vb -runga t (LL); *salty, be s., tasting of salt* vb -vava i & t (HH)

salute *greet* vb -kwazisa i & t (HHH); *salutation, greeting* n kwaziso 9 (HHL) cf -kwazisa (HHH)

salute *raising of the hand to the forehead to show respect (in military fashion)* n sarupu 9 (LHL) cf Eng.

salvation *process of saving from sin* n ruponeso 11 (LHHL) cf -ponesa (HHH); kununurwa 15 (LLLL)

same *identical* pronoun functioning as adj cf p. 199

same *be alike* adj & vb -enzana i (LLL); -fanana i (HHH) (stative vbs); Imbwa idzi dzakaenzana. (*These dogs are the same size.*)

samp *mealie-rice, crushed mealies with husks removed* n munyuchu 3 (LHL)

sanctify *make holy* vb -sandisa t (HHH) cf Eng.

sand *tiny grains of worn rock* n jecha 5, majecha 6 (HL)

sand snake *striped s.s.* n maswerwe 9 (LLL); maserwe 9 (LLL); *hissing s.s.* n dzvoti 5, madzvoti 6 (LH)

sandal *open shoe with straps* n shangu 9 (LH)

sandwich *slices of bread with meat, etc. between* n sangweji 5, masangweji 6 (HLL) cf Eng.

sang *cf sing*

sanitary lane *usu a lane running along the back of a property* n sendiraini 9 (HLHLL) cf Eng.

sank *cf sink*

sap *life blood of a tree* n muto 3 (LL)

sari *cotton wrap round the body worn by women* n muganyirwa 3 (LHLH)

sash *worn round the waist* n jindadzi 5, majindadzi 6 (LLL)

sassaby *tsessebe, tesseby* n nondo 9 (LL)

sat *cf sit*

satan *the evil spirit, the devil* n satani 1a (HLL) cf Eng.

satiated *be replete, have satisfied feeling after a good meal* vb -guta i (HH)

satisfaction *for wrong done* n chiripiro 7 (LLLL) cf -ripira

satisfy *satiate* vb -gutsa i & t (HH); *be satisfied* vb -gutswa i (HH); -gutsikana i (HHHL); *s. thirst* vb -pedza nyota (HL HH)

satisfactorily *in a manner that satisfies* adv zvinofadza / zvinogutsa mwoyo

saturated *be soaked* vb -nyn'ata i (LL); -nyata i (LL)

Saturday *sixth day after Sunday* n Chitanhatu 7 Z (LHLH); Mugovera 3 (LLHL)

sauce *liquid added to food to give it extra flavour* n muto 3 (LL)

saucer *curved, round dish in which a cup is placed* n sosa 9 (HL) cf Eng.; mbiya 9 (LH)

sausage *chopped-up meat, etc., put into tube of thin skin* n sochisi 9 (HLL) cf Eng.;

sausage tree B.Bk. 1,47 n mubvee 3 (LHL); mumvee 3 (LHL)

savage man *solitary thug* n gandanga 5, magandanga 6 (LLL); dusvura 5 (LLL); mapakatsine 1a (LHHLH); bhovha 5 (HL)

save *from illness or danger* vb -ponesa i & t (HHH) cf -pona (HH); *keep safe, look after* vb -chengeta t (LLL)

saviour *one who saves* n mununuri (LLLL) cf -nunura (LLL); muponesi 1 (LHHL) cf -ponesa (HHH)

saw *cutting-tool with tooth-edged steel blade* n saha 5, masaha 6 (HL) cf Eng.

saw *cf see*

saw *cut with a saw* vb -cheka nesaha t (HH HLL(— PT *sawed;* PP *sawn, sawed*

say vb -ti i & t (L), *passive form:* -nzi (L), *frequently found in impersonal forms:* Zvanzi, Hanzi *or* Kwanzi (*It is said.*); Zvanzi kudii? (*What was said / What did he say?*); *speak* vb -taura i & t (LLL) — PT & PP *said*

say hello *greet* vb -kwazisa t (HHH)

say goodbye *s. farewell* vb -oneka i (LLL) *(to be distinguished from* -oneka (HHH) *be visible)*

say so *do so* vb -daro i & t (HL)

scab *skin irritation or disease* n gwembe 5 (LH)

scabies *itch, skin-irritation* n mhezi 9 (LH)

scald *burn the skin with very hot liquid* vb -tsva i (H); Ndatsva munwe. (*I have burnt the finger i.e. I am burnt the finger*); -pisa t (HH); *scald, burn* n kutsva 15 (LH); utsva 14 (LH) cf -tsva (H)

scale *instrument for measuring weights* n chikero 7 (LHL) cf Eng.

scandal *harmful gossip or rumour* n makuhwa 6 (LLL)

scar *mark remaining on the surface of skin as the result of injury* n vanga 5, mavanga 6 (LL); mbonje 9 (LL)

scarab beetle *dung b.* n ngoko 9 (LL);

nyamututa 1a (LLHH); *rhinoceros or rhino dung b.* n nyangare 9 (LLL)

scarce *be in short supply* vb -shomeka i (LLL)

scare *terrify, frighten* vb -tyisa i & t (HH); -tyisidzira i & t (HHHL) cf -tya (H)

scatter *disperse* vb -parara i (LLL); *scatter, disperse physically* vb -paradzira t (LLLL) + locative; Paradzira manyowa mumunda. (*Scatter manure on the field.*)

scent *good smell* n kunhuhwira 15 (LLLL); *scent perceived by animals* n hwema 14 KoZ (LL); bwema 14 K (LL)

scent *get the s. of* vb -femedza i & t (HHH); -femba i & t (HH); *follow the s.*

scavengers

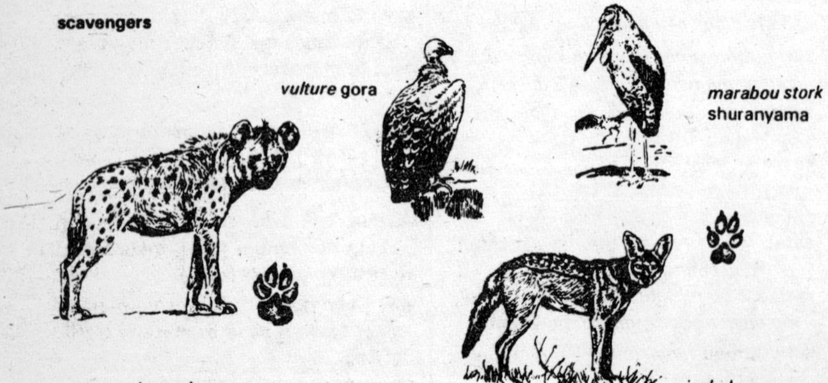

vb -bvumba (ĥwema) i Z (LL); *scented, be sweet-smelling* vb -nhuhwira i (LLL)

scholar *one who learns* n mudzidzi 1 (LHL) cf -dzidza (HH)

school *place of learning* n chikoro 7 (LHL) cf Eng.; *schooling, education* n dzidzo 9 (HL) cf -dzidza (HH); fundo 9 (HH) -funda (HH)

scissors *two-bladed instrument for cutting* n chigero 7 (LLL) cf -gera (LL)

scold *swear at, blame angrily* vb -tuka i & t (HH); -nyomba i & t (HH)

scone *small flattish plain cake* n sikonzi 5 & 9 (LHL) cf Eng.

scoop *ladle liquid, draw water* vb -chera t (HH); *scoop out water* vb -kupa t (HH)

scorch *burn* vb -pisa i & t (HH)

score *record of points* n chibozwa 7 (LLH)

score a goal vb -nwisa t (HH); -gowesa t (HHH)

scorn *despise* vb -zvidza t (LL); -shora t (LL)

scorpion *creature with poisonous sting in the tail* n chinyaride 7 K (LLHL); chinyavada 7 K (LLLL); rize 5, marize 6 (LH); mbambarize 9 (LLLH) *cf illustration p. 80*

scotch cart *two-wheeled cart* n chikochikari 7 (LHLLL) cf Eng.

scour *rub a dirty surface clean* vb -kwesha t (HH)

scourge *flog, thrash* vb -pura t (HH)

scout *keep watch* vb -sora t MZ (HH)

scowl *pull an ugly face* vb -finyama i (HHH)

scrape *skin or surface* vb -para t (HH); -kenga t (HH); *scrape pot interior* vb -kokora t (HHH)

scraping *pot s. when a pot is being cleaned* n goko 5, makoko 6 (HH)

scratch *relieve skin irritation* vb -kwenya i & t (LL); *scratch (as a hen)* vb -para t (LL); -tsvara (LL); *scratch agressively with finger-nails or claws* vb -mara i & t (HH)

scream *high-pitched cry of alarm* n mhere 9 (LL)

scream *cry* vb -ridza mhere (LL LL)

screen *hinder the view* vb -dzikatira t (HHHL)

screw in *fasten or tighten by screwing* vb -monera t (HHH); *unscrew* vb -mononora t (HHHL)

screwdriver *tool used for screwing* n sikurudhiraivha 9 (LLHLLLL) cf Eng.; *cf illustration p. 162*

scripture *Sacred S., Bible* n Bhaibheri 5, maBhaibheri 6 (HLLL) cf Eng.

scrotum *testis* n jende 5 (LL)

scrounge *visit for a meal* vb -kwata i (LL); *scrounger at mealtimes* n mukwati 1 (LLL) cf -kwata (LL)

scrub *close-packed impenetrable brushwood* n jokocho 5 (LLL); bvokocho 5, mabvokocho 6 (LLL)

scrub *rub hard with brush* vb -kwesha t (HH); -korobha t (HHH) cf Eng.

sea *expanse of salty water at the coast* n gungwa 5, makungwa 6 (LL); nyanza 9 MZ (LH)

seal *stick down* vb -nama i & t (LL)

seam *line of stitching* n musono 3 (LLL) cf -sona (LL)

seam *edge of a garment* n mukombero 3 (LLLL) cf -kombera (LLL)

search *look for* vb -tsvaga i & t (LL)

season *a period of the year having a particular climate* n mwaka 3 MZ (LH); *rainy s.* n zhizha 5 (LH); *dry s.* n chirimo 7 (LLL); *winter, cold season* n chando 7 (LL)

seat *chair* n chigaro 7 (LLL) cf -gara (LL)

seated *be s.* vb -gara i (LL); Ndigere. (*I am seated.*)

second a motion *support* vb -tsinhira t (LLL)

second *of a series* adj -chipiri

secretary *one who writes* n munyori 1 (LHH) cf -nyora (HH)

secretary bird *long-legged bird of prey* n hwata 9 MZ (HL); mukwasi 3 (LLL); munditi 3 (LLL) R105 *cf illustration p. 49*

secretly *in a secret manner* adv chiverevere 7 (LLLLL); chinyararire 7 (LHHLH); *in secret* adv muchivande 18 (LLHL)

section *division, part, portion* n chikamu 7 (LHL); chimedu 7 (LHL); *section of people* n chikwata 7 (LLL)

see *use the power of sight* vb -ona i & t (HH); *look at carefully, examine* vb -ongorora i & t (HHHL) — PT *saw;* PP *seen*

seed *element of a plant from which new life can grow* n mbeu 9 (HH); *seed of fruit* n mhodzi 9 (LH); tsongoro 9 (HHL)

seedling *plant in the seed bed* n nhondo 9 (LL)

seed-eater *among our best song-birds* n ngozha 9 (LH); nzviridyamatanda 9 (LHLLHH)

seek *look for, search,* vb -tsvaga i & t (LL); -tsvaka i & t KM (LL) — PT & PP *sought*

seek revenge *avenge* vb -tsiva i & t (LL); -dzorera i & t (LLL)

seem *appear to be* -nge + noun or relative; -nga + noun or relative: Rinenge shizha. (*It seems to be a leaf.*)

seesaw n binyumupinyu 5 (LHHLH)

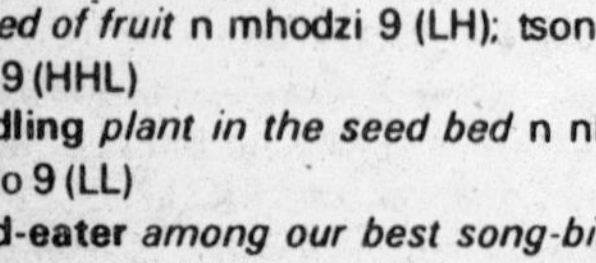

seethe *with anger* vb -viruka nehasha (LLL HLL)

seize *catch, hold* vb -bata i (HH)

seldom *not often, rarely* adv kashoma 12 (LLL)

select *choose* vb -sarudza i & t (LLL)

self adj & n *cf p. 200*

self-government n kuzvitonga 15 (LHLH)

selfish *be self-centred* vb -**zvifunga** i (HLH) cf -funga (LL)

selfishness *too much thinking about one's own needs* n undingoveni 14 (LHLHH)

sell *try to find buyers, exchange goods for money* vb -tengesa i & t (HHH) cf -tenga (HH) — PT & PP *sold; selling price* n mutengo 3 (LHH) cf -tenga (HH)

semen *male seed* n urume 14 (LHH) -cf murume (LHH)

send *cause somebody or something to go* vb -tuma t (HH); *send away, chase away* vb -dzinga t (HH); -tanda t (HH); *send back, return* vb -dzokesa t (LLL); -dzosa (LL); *send for, send someone to obtain* vb -tumira t (HHH) cf -tuma (HH); Ndatumira shuga. (*I have sent for sugar.*) — PT & PP *sent*

sense *good s., common s.* n pfungwa 9 (LH) cf -funga (LL); *have s., be intelligent* vb -chenjera i (HHH) (stative vb); Tino mwana aka**chenjera**. (*We have an intelligent child.*)

sensible *be reasonable* vb -va nomusoro i (HLHH)

sentence *(grammatical)* n chirevo 7 (LHH); mutsetse 3 MZ (LHL)

separate *part mutually* vb -paradzana i (LLLL); *cause mutual parting* vb -siyanisa t (HHHL) cf -siyana (HHH); *s. animals* vb -tsaura t (HHH); *s. milk by machine, churn* vb -gaya t (HH); *s. people fighting, break up a fight* vb -nunura t (LLL); -randutsa t (LLL); *s. by selection* vb -keta t K (LL)

sergeant *rank in army or police force* n sajeni 1a (HLL) cf Eng.

sermon *homily* n mharidzo 9 (HHL) cf -paridza (HHH)

serval cat *yellow cat with black spots/, length 1 m, and long legs* n nzunza 9 (LL); nzudzi 9 M (LL) *cf illustration p. 50*

servant *person working for another* n muranda 1 (LLL); *female s.* n murandakadzi 1 (LLLLL)

serve *(esp serve God)* vb -itira t MZ (LLL); -shumira t K (HHH); *s. out, dish out food* vb -pakura i & t (HHH); *s. as a waiter* vb -sevha i & t (HH) cf Eng.; *s. (in veterinary sense), copulate* vb -kwira t (HH); -tanda t (HH); -dzinga t (HH)

serve *a prison sentence* vb -pika i (LL)

server *in church service* n mubatidzi 1 (LHHL)

set *place, put down* vb -isa t (LL); *set alight* vb -tungidza t (HHH); *set dogs on* vb -svukudzira t (HHHL); *set foot on* vb -tsika t (LL); *set free, release* vb -sunungura t (HHHL) cf -sunga (HH); *set (of the sun)* vb -vira i (HH); -doka i (HH); -nyura i (HH); *set on fire* vb -pisa t (HH); *set up, establish* vb -misa t (HH) cf -mira (HH) — PT & PP *set*

settle *(of sediment), sink to the bottom* vb -gadzana i (LLL)

seven *the number 7* adj -nomwe (LH); nomwe 10 (LH)

sever *cut off* vb -cheka t (HH); -dimura t (HHH); -dambura t (HHH)

several *many* adj -zhinji (HH); zhinji 10 (HH)

sew *stitch* vb -sona i & t (LL) — PT *sewed;* PP *sewn, sewed*

shadow *shade* n mumvuri 3 (LHL)

shaft *of an assegai* n rwiriko 11 (LLL); *plur:* nzwiriko 10 (LLL)

shake *tremble* vb -bvunda i (HL); -dedera i (LLL); -zunguzika i (HHHL)

shake *(liquid) move quickly up & down or from side to side* vb -kuchukudza t (HHHL)

shake *(carpets, trees etc.) s. off* vb -zunza (LL); -bvurudza t (LLL) — PT *shook;* PP *shaken*

shake hands *in greeting* vb -bata chishanu 6 (HH LHL); *in condolence* vb -bata maoko t (HH LHH)

shake the head *in denial, or disagreement* vb -dzungudza t (HHH)

shaky *be s., be not very firm* vb -zhekazheka i (HHHL)

shallot *sp of onion* n sharotsi 9 (HLL) cf Eng.

shame *embarrassment* n nyadzi 10 (HH)

shame *put to s.* vb -nyadza i & t (HHH); -nyadzisa i & t (HHH); cf -nyara (HH); *shamed, be ashamed, be embarrassed* vb -nyara1 (HH)

shape *mould, form s.* vb -umba t (HH)

share *legal s., entitlement* n mugove 3 (LLH) cf -gova (LL)

share *have a share* vb -goverana i (LLLL) cf -gova (LL); *share out* vb -gova t (LL)

sharp *be keen-edged (blade)* vb -pinza i (LL); *be s. -pointed* adj & vb -tesva i (HH) (stative vb); penzura yakatesva (*a sharp-pointed pencil.*)

sharpen *make sharp* vb -rodza t (LL); *sharpening instrument, file, stone* n chirodzo 7 (LLL) cf -rodza (LL); chirodzero 7 (LLLL)

shatter *break, smash into pieces* vb -punza t (HH)

shave *cut hair of the chin with a razor* vb -gusa t (LL); -veura t (HHH); *s. wood, plane* vb -senda t MZ (LL)

shaving-brush albizia *a tree* n muriranyenze 3 (LLLHH)

shawl *large piece of material worn about the shoulders by women or wrapped round a baby* n chari 9 (LH)

shear *cut the wool off sheep* vb -cheka t (HH) — PT *sheared;* PP *shorn, sheared*

sheath *pouch for knife or sword* n hara 5, mahara 6 (LH)

shed blood *from a wound* vb -buritsa ropa (HHH HL); *s. clothes, remove c.* vb -bvisa mbatya (LL LL); *s. tears* vb -buritsa misodzi (HHH LHL) — PT & PP *shed*

sheep n hwai 9 (LL); gwai 5 K, makwai 6 (LL); *lamb, young s.* n hwayana 9 (LLH); *ram, male s.* n hondohwe 9 (LHL)

sheet *bed s.* n shitibhedha 5 (HLLL) cf Eng.; *s. of corrugated iron* n rata 5, marata 6 (HL) *cf p. 35; s. of paper* n pepa 5, mapepa 6 (LL) cf Eng.

shelf *ledge for putting things* n sherufu 9 (HLL) cf Eng.

shell *remove outer covering* vb -menya t (HH)

shell *groundnut s.* n ganda 5, makanda 6 (HH); deko 5, mateko 6 (HH); *egg s.* n gekenya 5, makekenya 6 (HHL)

shelter *made of branches* n musasa (LLL)

shelter *take s., hide from* vb -hwanda i MZ (HH); -vanda i K (HH); *take s. from the rain* vb -dzamba i M (HH); -zamba i K (HH); -vanda mvura K (HL HH)

shepherd *herdsman* n mufudzi 1 (LLL) cf -fudza (LL)

shepherd *herd* vb -fudza t (LL)

shield *piece of armour carried on the arm* n nhoo 9 (HL); shangwi 9 M (LL)

shield *protect from* vb -dzivirira t (LLLL)

shield bug n harurwa 9 (LLH)

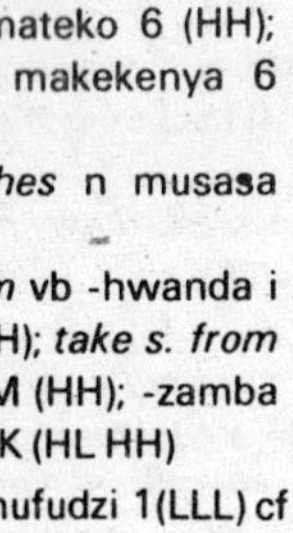

shifting spanner *monkey wrench* n bhobhojani 5, mabhobhojani 6 (LLHL)

shimmer *gleam* vb -nyiminya i (LLL)

shin *bony front of the leg between the knee & the ankle* n mupimbira 3 (LHHL); mupimbiri 3 (LHHL)

shine *give out or reflect light* vb -penya i (LL); -bwinya i (LL) — PT & PP *shone*

ship *large vessel that travels out to sea* n ngarava 9 (LLH)

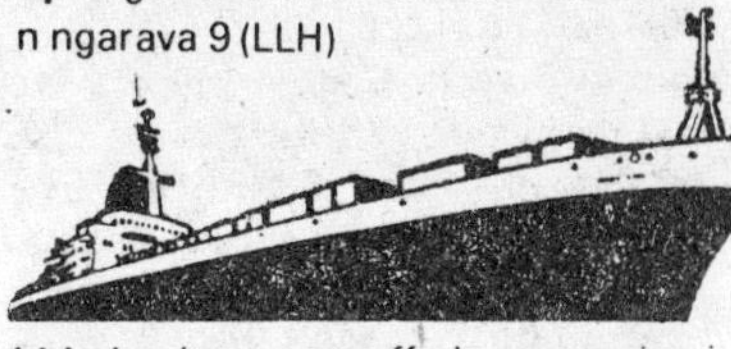

shirk *hesitate, put off* vb -zengurira i (LLLL)

shirt *top garment worn by men* n hembe 9 (HL) cf Afrik.; *khaki bush s., safari s.* n jamba 5, majamba 6 (HL)

shiver *with cold or fear* vb -bvunda i (HL); -dedera i (LLL)

shocked *be electrically s.* vb -batwa negetsi (HH HLL)

shoe *sandal* n shangu 9 (LH); bhutsu 9 (HL) cf Eng.; *shoes, footwear, sandals* n shangu 10 (LH); bhutsu 10 (HL) cf Eng.; *high-heeled s.* n gogo 9 MZ (LH)

shoe lace n tambo yebhutsu 9 (LL HLL)

shone *cf shine*

shook *cf shake*

shoot *with a gun, shoot at* vb -pfura i & t (HH); *s. and miss* vb -potsa i & t (LL) — PT & PP *shot*

shoot *sprout* vb -mera i (LL)

shop *store* n chitoro 7 (LHL) cf Eng.

shop *go buying* vb -shopa i & t (HH) cf Eng.

shop assistant *s. keeper* n mutengesi 1 (LHHL) cf -tengesa (HHH)

shore *bank, water's edge* n hombekombe 5, mahombekombe 6 (LLLL)

shorn *cf shear*

short *measuring little, slight* adj -pfupi (HL); -pfupi 5 & 9; *s., be squat* vb -pfupika i (HHH); -fupika i K (HHH)

short *lack, be s. of something* vb -shaya i & t (LL)

short-cut *make a short-cut* vb -dimburira i (HHHL); dimbidzira t (HHHL)

shortage of n kushomeka kwa- 15 (LLLL)

shorten *make shorter* vb -pfupikisa t (HHHL) cf -pfupika (HHH)

shot *cf shoot*

shot-gun *sporting gun using cartridges containing tiny balls of lead* n chifefe 7 (LLL)

should *ought to* vb -fanira i (HHH)

shoulder *between tip of shoulder and neck* n fudzi 5, mafudzi 6 KM (HL); pfudzi 5 MZ (HL); *shoulder blade* n bendekete 5, mapendekete 6 (HHLH)

shout *say something in a loud voice* vb -zhamba i (HL); -daidzira i (HHHL)

shout *loud call or cry, scream* n mhere (LL)

shout at *abuse in public* vb -shaudha i & t (HHH) cf Eng.; *shout for help* vb -ridza mhere i (LL LL)

shove *push* vb -sandidzira t (LLLL); -sairira t (LLLL)

shovel *spade-like tool used for moving earth* n foshoro 9 (HLL) cf Eng. *cf illustration p. 162*

shovel out *empty with a s.* vb -foshora t (HHH) cf Eng.

show *demonstration* n shoo 9 (HL) cf Eng.

show *demonstrate, indicate* vb -ratidza t (LLL); -rakidza t (LLL); *s. spite, be spiteful* vb -ita pfini (LL HH); *s. off in bad taste* vb -vhaira i (LLL); *show, reveal, expose* vb -onesa t (HHH) cf -ona (HH) — PT *showed;* PP *shown*

shower *of very light rain* n pfunhambuya 9 (LLHL)

shrew *dwarf s. capable of moving by large hops; and insect-eating* n dzwitswitswi 5, madzwitswitswi 6 (HHH) *cf illustration p. 79*

shrike *black-crowned tchagra* n tindiritindiri 9 (LHLHL) R715; *boubou s.* n chinanga 7 (LLL) R709; *fiscal s., butcher bird* n korera 9 (LHH); chikorera 7 (LLHH); chisemaura 7 (LHHHL); nyamatunge 9 (LLHL) R707; *olive bush s.* n chemberebwai-bwai 9 (LLLHLHL) R717; *puff-back s.* n chidhirihora 7 K (LLLHL) R712; *red-backed s.* n bhinya 5 (LL) R708; *white helmet s.; social sp moving in parties of 4—12* n chiteveravadzimba 7 (LLLLLLL); shavishavi 5 K (LLLL) R727 *same word as for butterfly.*

shrink *become smaller* vb -dzoka i (LL); Mastokononzi enhando ano**dzoka** kana agezwa. (*Cheap stockings shrink when washed.*) — PT *shrank, shrunk;* PP *shrunk, shrunken*

shrivel *contract into wrinkles (vegetables and fruits)* vb -svava i (LL); -una i (LL); *curl up, wither* vb -putana i (LLL) (LLL)

shrub *bush* n gwenzi 5, magwenzi 6 (LH)

shudder *shake, shiver, tremble* vb -bvunda i (HL); -dedera i (LLL); -huta i M (HH)

shuffle *playing cards* vb -chokocha t (HHH)

shut *close up* vb -pfiga t (HH); -vhara t (LL) — PT & PP *shut*

shut up *be silent, be quiet* vb -nyarara i (HHL); Vana vaka**nyarara**. (*The children are silent.*)

shy *be s., be bashful* vb -nyara i (HH)

shyness *bashfulness* n nyadzi 10 (HH); manyadzo 6 (LHH)

sick *be ill* vb -rwara i (HH); *be s., vomit* vb -rutsa i & t (HH)

sicken *make ill, affect with disgust or loathing* vb -svota i & t (HH)

sickness *illness, fever giving high temperature* n chirwere 7 (LHH); hosha 9 MZ (LL); *sick person, patient* n murwere 1 (LHH) cf -rwara (HH)

sickle *curved blade with a short handle, used for cutting grass* n jeko 5, majeko 6 (HH)

side *one of two surfaces* n divi 5, mativi 6 (LL); rutivi 11 (LLL); *far side, other side* n mhiri 9 (LL)

sidestep *dodge, evade, elude* vb -nzvenga i & t (HH)

sieve *utensil with wire network to separate finer grains from coarser* n sefa 9 (HL); sevho 9 (HL) cf Eng.

sift *separate by putting through a sieve* vb -sefa t (HH); -sevha t (HH) cf Eng.; *winnow, separate chaff from grains with the help of the wind* vb -pepeta i & t (HHH)

sigh *heave a sigh* vb -tura mafemo befu (HH HLL/LH)

sign *identification mark* n mucherechedzo 3 (LHHHL) cf -cherechedza (HHHL); chiratidzo 7 (LLLL) cf -ratidza (LLL); chioneso 7 (LHHL) cf -onesa (HHH) *informative & indicative s.* n chiziviso 7 (LHHL) cf -zivisa (HHH)

sign *make a mark* vb -cherechedza i (HHHL); *sign a name* vb -saina i (HHH) cf Eng.

sight *power of seeing* n kuona 15 (LHH)

silence *condition of being quiet or silent* n runyararo 11 (LHHL) cf -nyarara (HHL)

silence *make somebody or something silent* vb -nyaradza t (HHH) cf -nyarara (HHL)

silent *be quiet* vb -nyarara i (HHL)

silently *without noise* adv chinyararire (LHHLH)

silliness *stupidity* n upenzi 14 (LHH); ubenzi 14 (LHH)

silly *be stupid* vb -pata i (LL); -penga i (HH)

silver *shining, white precious metal* n sirivha 9 (HLL) cf Eng.; *silver tree, yellow-wood t.* n **mukonono** 3 (LLLL); mususu 3 (LHL) B.Bk. 1,38

similar *be alike* vb -todzana i (stative vb) (HHH); -fanana i (stative vb) (HHH); Hembe idzi **dzakafanana**. (*These shirts are identical.*)

simple *be easy* vb -reruka (HHH) (stative vb); Basa iri **rakareruka**. (*This is simple work.*)

simple *s.-minded, stupid* adj & vb -remara i (stative vb) (HHH) mukomana **akaremara** (*stupid boy*)

simpleton *simple person* n rema 5, marema 6 (HH); fuza 5, mafuza 6 (LL)

simply *in a simple manner* adv -ngo- infix vb: **Ndangomuti enda**. (*I simply told him to go.*)

simultaneously *at the same time* adv panguva imwe chete

sin *act that breaks God's laws, immoral act* n chitema 7 (LLH); chitadzo 7 (LHH) cf -tadza (HH); rutadzo 11 (LHH) cf -tadza; chivi 7 (LH)

sin *do wrong, commit s.* vb -tadza i (HH); *sin against, offend* vb -tadzira t (HHH)

since *for the reason that* conj sezvo (LH); PC zva- (L); **Zvawaneta enda undorara**. (*Since you are tired go to bed.*)

since *from the time that* adv kubvira (LLL) — (*often followed by the Participial*)

sinew *strong cord joining a muscle to a bone* n gakava 5, makakava 6 (HHL); runda 5, marunda 6 (LH)

sing *make continuous musical sounds with the voice* vb -imba i & t (HH); *lead the singing* vb -shaura i & t Z (HHH) — PT *sang;* PP *sung; singer, one who sings* n muimbi 1 (LHH) cf -imba (HH)

sink *go down below the surface of a liquid* vb -nyura i (HH) — PT *sank;* PP *sunk, sunken*

sinner *one who breaks God's laws (usu seriously)* n mutadzi 1 cf -tadza (HH);

munyangadzi 1 (LHHL) -nyangadza (HHH)

sip *drink a very small quantity at each mouthful* vb -dzvuta i & t (LL)

sir *respectful form of address to a man* n changamire 1a (LLLL)

sisal *plant producing fibre* n konje 9 (LL)

sister *(of a boy)* n hanzvadzi 9 (HHL); hazvanzi 9 K (HHL); *sister of father-in-law (of man)* n tete 1a (LH); younger s. (of a girl) n munin'ina 1 (LHHL); *elder s. (of a girl)* n mukoma 1 (LHL)

sister-in-law (*of man*) muramu 1 (LHH); mwaramu 1 M (LHH); *older than wife* n maiguru 1a (HLHH); *younger than wife* n mainini 1a (HLHL); *sister-in-law (of a woman)* n vatete 2a (HLH); vamwene 2a (HLH)

sit *live, stay* vb -gara i & t (LL); *s. on eggs, incubate* vb -rarira i & t MZ (HHH); -vatira i & t K (HHH); -hamira Ko (HHH); *sit on haunches, crouch* vb -chochomara i Z (HHHL), -chonjomara i (HLHL) — PT & PP *sat*

sitting *cross-legged s.* n chisero 7 (LLL); chibondokoto 7 (LLLLL)

situation *employment, work* n basa 5, mabasa 6 (LL)

six *the number 6* adj -tanhatu (HLH); nhanhatu 10 (HLH)

sixth *(of a series)* adj -chitanhatu (LHLH) mwedzi wechitanhatu (*sixth month*)

sixty *the number 60* n makumi matanhatu 6 (LHH LHLH)

size *degree of largeness or smallness* n saizi 9 (HLL) cf Eng.; ukuru 14 (LHH)

size *of man or animal* n mumhu 3 (LH); mhiri 9 M (LH)

sjambok *weapon for inflicting punishment (usu made from hippo hide)* n chamboko 7 (LHL) cf Afrik.

skaapsteker *striped s., sp of snake* n maserwe 9 (LLL)

skeleton *bony framework of an animal body* n mapfupa 6 (*lit. bones*) (LHH) rangwanda 5, marangwanda 6 (HHH)

sketch *picture* n chifananidzo 7 (LHHHL) cf -fananidza (HHHL)

skid *slide* vb -tsvedza i (LL)

skilful man *with his hands* n mhizha 9 (LH); tsanzu 9 (LH)

skilful man *able, clever, champion* n nyanzvi 9 (LH); shasha 9 (LL)

skim *the surface of a liquid* vb -yerura t MZ (LLL)

skin *hide* n ganda 5, makanda 6 (HH); *s. of animal, hide* n dehwe 5, matehwe 6 (LL)

skin *remove skin* vb -vhiya i & t (LL); -vhuya i & t M (LL)

skink *sp of short-legged, striped lizard* n dzvinyu 5 (LH); dzvombi 5 (LH)

skip *jump* vb -svetuka i & t (HHH)

skirt *female outer garment that hangs from waist* n siketi 9 (LHL) cf Eng.

skull *bony framework of the head* n dehenyn'a 5, madehenyn'a 6 (HLH); rutemhei M (LHLH); dehenya 5 KM (HLH)

sky *ceiling, roof* n denga 5, matenga 6 (HL)

slab *of loose flat rock* n fendefa 5, mafendefa 6 (HHL)

slake *dampen* vb -nyatisa t (LLL)

slake thirst *satisfy t.* vb -pedza nyota (HL HH)

slam door *close with a bang* vb -kwatidza gonhi (HHL HL); -rovera gonhi ([illegible]HL HL)

slander *malign, back-bite, tell rumours* vb -ita makuhwa (LL LLL)

slap *quick blow with the open hand* n mbama 9 (HL)

slap *beat with the palm of the hand* vb -rova nembama t (HH HLL); -pamhadza t (HHH); -mbamura t (HHH)

slasher *flat-iron instrument for cutting grass* n bhemba 5, mabhemba 6 (HL)

slaughter *slay, kill* vb -uraya i & t (HHH); -baya t (LL)

slave *person taken into captivity and becomes the property of another* n nhapwa 9 (HL) cf -tapa (HH); *slavery, condition of being a slave* n utapwa 14 (LHL) cf -tapa (HH)

sledge *vehicle without wheels that slides along the ground* n chirei 7 (LHL) cf Eng.

sleep *be in a condition which provides unconsciousness and rest* vb -kotsira i (LLL); -rara i (HH); -vata i (HH) — PT & PP *slept*

sleep *sleepiness* n hope 10 (HH); *sleepy, be drowsy* vb -va nehope (HLL); *nod with sleep* vb -dzimwaira (HHHL)

slice *thin, flat piece cut off something* n chimedu 7 (LHL) cf -medura; *s. of pumpkin* n mbai 9 MZ (LL); mbadzi 9 K (LL)

slice *cut into slices* vb -medura t (HHH)

slid *cf slide*

slide *slippery place* n mutserendende 3 (LLLLL)

slide *as children at play* vb -ita mutserendende (LLLLL) — PT *slid;* PP *slid, slidden*

downward slope materu

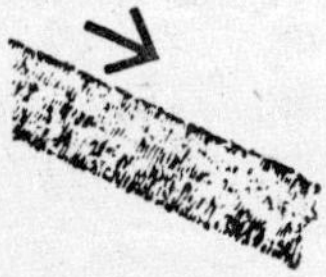

upward slope mukwidza

slightly *very little* adv zvishomanana (LLLHH)

sling *baby s.* n mbereko 9 (LLL) cf -bereka (LLL) *cf p. 11*

slip *from hands* vb -svotoka i (LLL); *slip with feet, be slippery, slide* vb -tsvedza i (LL); -tedza i (LL)

slip *error, mistake* n chikanganiso 7 (LHHHL) cf -kanganisa (HHHL); mhosho 9 K (HL)

slop about *spill over the edge* vb -gabhagabha i MZ (HL HL); -kabakaba i (HL HL)

slope *upward s.* n mukwidza 3 (LHL); makata 6 Z (LLL); *downward s.* n materu 6 (LHL) *cf illustrations*

sloth *laziness, idleness* n nungo 10 (LL); usimbe 14 (LLL)

slough *cast off skin (snakes)* vb -vhunura i (HHH); *slough, discarded skin* n vhunurwa 5 (HLH)

slow *be s., delay* vb -nonoka i (LLL); *slowly* adv zvishoma nezvishoma (LLL LHLL)

slowness *of action* n chinono 7 (LLH) cf -nonoka (LLL)

slow-worm *blind w.; small harmless reptile between snakes and lizards* n tsukukuviri 9 (HHHLH)

slug *shell-less snail* n hozhwa 9 (HL) *same word as for snail cf p. 80*

slyness *guile to deceive* n muzvambarara 3 (LLLLL)

smack *punish with flat hand* vb -kwachamura t (HHHL)

small *diminutive* adj -diki (HL); diki 5 & 9; -doko KM (HL); doko 5 & 9; -duku (HL); duku 5 & 9

small *be s.* vb -dupika i (HHH); -dukupa i (HHH); **smaller** adj -duku pana: Wachi yako *iduku pane* yangu. (*Your watch is smaller than mine.*); **smallest** adj Wachi yako **iduku pane dzose** dzandakaona. (*Your watch is the smallest I have seen.*); *make small, reduce the size of* vb -dukupisa t (HHHL)

small mahogany *tree* n chikwaku 7 (LLL); *s. wild gardenia t.* n chidambi 7 (LHL)

smallpox *severe, contagious disease* n chibhokisi 7 (LHLL) cf Eng.

smart *be clever* vb -svinuka i (LLL) (stative vb); Varume vaka**svinuka** vanopfuma. (*Sharp-witted men get rich.*); -chenjera i (HHH) (stative vb); MaJapani rudzi rwaka**chenjera**. (*The Japanese are a clever people.*)

smash *shatter, s. against* vb -punza t (HH); *s. into, bump into* vb -dhuma t (LL); *s. in, bash in, disfigure* vb -fonyedza t (HHH)

smear with *anoint with* vb -zora t (LL); *s. the floor* vb -dzura t (HH); *s. the wall, plaster* vb -nama t (LL)

smell *scent, odour (perceived by animals)* n hwema 14 (LL); bwema 14 K (LL)

smell *unpleasantly* vb -nhuhwa i (LL); *bad s., rotten s.* n kunhuhwa 15 (LLL); *s. pleasantly* vb -nhuhwira i (LLL); *good s., sweet s.,* n kunhuhwira 15 (LLLL) — PT & PP *smelt, smelled; smell an odour, take a s.* vb -nhuhwidza t (LLL); -nhuwidza t MZ (LLL); *begin to corrupt* vb -ita mweya (LL LH)

smile *express amusement or happiness by the face* vb -nyemwerera i (LLLL); -sekerera i & t (LLLL)

smith *craftsman* n mhizha 9 (LH); mupfuri 1 (LHH) cf -pfura

smoke *grey vapour from something burning* n utsi 14 (LH)

smoke *(of a fire), produce s.* vb -pfungaira i (HHHL); *smoke (tobacco), take snuff* vb -svuta i & t (LL); -puta i & t (LL); *be smoky* vb -na utsi: Mumba muno utsi. (*The house is smoky (inside).*)

smooth *be free of roughness* vb -tsetseka i (LLL); *smooth by scraping* vb -kwenenzvera t (HHHL)

smother *prevent from breathing* vb -pfumbira t (LLL)

smudge *besmirch* vb -nyangadza t (HHH); -svipisa t (LLL)

smuggle in *introduce contrary to instructions* vb -verevedza t (LLLL)

snail *small, soft creature with a shell on its back* n hozhwe 9 (HL); hozhwa 9 (HL) *cf illustration p. 80; same word for slug*

snake *legless, crawling reptile; sometimes poisonous* n nyoka 9 (HH)

snakes

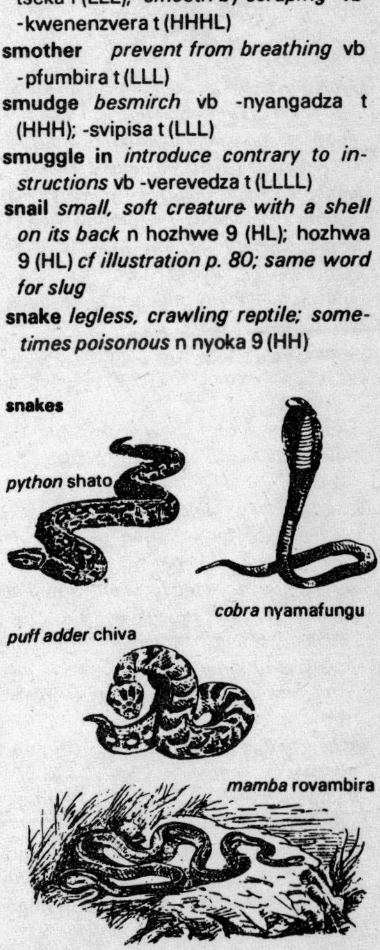

snake bean *tree* B.Bk. 1,12 mucherechese 3 (LLLHL); mukosha 3 (LLL); mucherekese 3(LLLHL)

snake bird *sp of water bird with slender neck and long, pointed beak; darter* n shambira 5 (LLL)

snake weasel *snake polecat* n chidembo 7 (LLL) *cf illustration p. 182*

snap *break suddenly under strain* vb -papfuka i (HHH); -dimbuka (HHH)

snare *catch in a trap* vb -teya t (HH); *whip s.* n dhibhu 5, madhibhu 6 (HL)

snarl *growl menacingly (like a dog)* vb hon'a i (LL); -n'ara i (LL)

snatch *take away suddenly and roughly* vb -bvuta i & t (LL)

sneak away *go away quietly and secretly* vb -svova i & t (LL); -verevedza i & t (LLLL)

sneer *contemn, show contempt despise* vb -svora i & t (LL); -zvidza i & t (LL)

sneeze *make a s., make an outburst of air caused by irritation in the nose* vb *-hotsira i (HHH)*

sniff *when attracted by scent, smell attentively (like a dog)* vb -funidza t (HHH); -femba t (HH); *s. when the nose is running, draw up mucus into the nose* vb -kwiridzira dzihwa (HHHL LH)

snip *a hedge with shears* vb -chetura t (HHH)

snipe *painted s.* n nhapata 9 (LLL) *general name for water fowl*

snore *noisy breathing in sleep* n ngononо 10 (LLL); *snore, breathe roughly and noisily while sleeping* vb -ita ngononо

snot-apple *tree, Rhodesian tree hibiscus, quarters* n mutohwe 3 (LHL) B.Bk. 1,33

snout *flat nose of a pig* n svusvudza 9 (LLL)

snowberry n muchagauwe 3 (LLLHH) B.Bk. 1,24

snuff *tobacco* n fodya 9 (HL); *s. box* n nhekwe 9 (LL); chibako 7 (LHL); nyere 9 (LL); *take s., inhale s.* vb -femba t (HH); -puta t (LL); -svuta t (LL)

snug *be comfortably warm* vb -dziyirwa i (HHH) cf -dziya (HL)

so *that is the reason why, hence, therefore* conj saka + Partic or indicative

so long as *provided that* conj chero (LL) + Partic: Ndicharamba ndichisevenza, **chero** ndichiwana mari. (*I shall continue working, so long as I get money.*)

so-and-so *what's-his-name* n nhingi 1a (LH); nhingirikiri 1a (LHHHH)

soak *immerse in liquid* vb -nyika t (HH)

soap *substance used for washing* n sipo 9 (LL) cf Afrik.; murota 3 Z (LLL)

soapstone *soft, local stone used for carving* n munyakwe 3 MZ (LHL); munyaka 3 KM (LHL)

sob *draw in the breath sharply in sorrow* vb -pfikura i (HHH)

society *organisation of men or women* n chita 7 (LH), nzanga 9 (LL)

sock *short stocking* n sokisi 5, masokisi 6 (HLL) cf Eng.; *socks* n masokisi 6 (LHLL) cf Eng

soft *not firm or hard* adj -nyoro (HH); nyoro 5 & 9

soft *be s.* vb -nyorova i (HHH); *be s. to touch as ripe fruit, be ever-ripe* vb -tebvenyuka i (LLLL); -tubvunyuka i (LLLL)

soften *make soft* vb -nyorovesa t (HHHL); *soften solid* vb -pfavisa t (LLL); *cause solid to melt* vb -nyungudisa t (LLLL)

softly *gently* adv zvinyoronyoro (LHHLH); *soggy, be s.* vb -nyata M (LL); nyn'ata i MZ (LL)

soil *earth* n ivhu 5 KoMZ (LH); vhu 5 K (H); mavhu 6; *red s.* n mhukutu 9 (LLL); jiho 5 KM, majiho 6 (LL)

soil *make dirty* vb -svipisa t (LLL)

soil-erosion n gukuravhu 5 Z (HHLH); guve 5 MZ (LL)

sold *cf sell*

soldier *member of the army* n soja 5, masoja 6 (HL) cf Eng.

soldier termite *kind of white ant* n juru 5, majuru 6 (LH); *cf illustration p. 159*

soloist *in collective singing, leader* n mushauri 1 (LHHL) cf -shaura (HHH)

solution *rubber s., liquid rubber adhesive* n shurushuru 9 (LHLL) cf Eng.

some -mwe *cf p. 186 someone* n mumwe 1 (LL); *something* n chimwe 7 (LL); *sometimes* adv dzimwe nguva (LL HH); mamwe mazuva (LL LHH); mimwe misi (LL LH); *somewhere* adv kumwe (LL)

some -ti *in rel mood* — Akarwara kwamazuva akati. (*He was ill for some days.*)

somersault *action of turning head over heels* n mhidigari 9 (HHLH)

son n mwanakomana 1 (LHLLL); *first born s.* n nevanji 1a (HLH); *s. of sister of girl's mother* n hanzvadzi 9 (HHL); *s. of brother of girl's mother* n sekuru 1a (LHL); *s. of sister of boy's mother* n mukoma 1 (LHL)/ munin'ina 1 (LHHL); *s. of brother of boy's mother* n sekuru 1a (LHL); *s. of brother of girl's father* n hanzvadzi 9 (HHL); *s. of brother of boy's father* n mukoma 1 (LHL) / munin'ina 1 (LHHL); *s. of sister of boy's father* n muzukuru 1 (LHHL); *sons and daughters of girl's father's sister* n vana 2 (LH); *son-in-law, husband of daughter* n mukuwasha 1 (LHHL); mukwambo 1 (LHL)

song *psalm* n rwiyo 11 (LH) *plur:* nziyo 10 (LH)

soon *before long, in a short time* adv zvino zvino (HL HL); gare gare (LH LH); *as soon as -ngo- infix vb:* Pata**ngo**pinda mumba mvura yatanga kunaya.) *The rain came as soon as we entered the house.*); Kurumidza kuuya. (*Come soon.*)

soot *pitch, black deposit from smoke* n chin'ai 7 (LLL)

soothe *comfort* vb -nyaradza t (HHH) cf -nyarara (HHL); *s. by rubbing* vb -kwiza t (LL)

sorcerer *sorceress, witch* n muroyi 1 (LLL) cf -roya (LL)

sore *wound* n ronda 5, maronda 6 (LL)

sore *be painful* vb -rwadza i & t (HH)

sorghum *kaffir corn, sp of millet* n pfunde 5, mapfunde 6 (HH); bvunde 5, mapfunde 6 (HH); *sweet s., the sweet, edible cane* n ipwa 9 (LH); pwa 9 K (H)

sorrel *garden s., donkey weed, oxalis* n gungwe 5 (LL) B.Bk. 1,65

sorrowful *be sad* vb -suwa i & t (HH); *sorry, be s., regret* vb -suwa i (HH); Ndino urombo. (*I am sorry.*); inter pepa K (HL)

sort *species, race* n rudzi 11 (LL); marudzi 6; mhando 9 MZ (LL)

soul *spirit* n mweya 3 (LH)

soul *of deceased pagan, ancestor* n mudzimu 3 (LHH); *soul of deceased foreigner* n shave 5, mashave 6 (LL)

sound *noise that is heard* n kutinhira 15 (LLLL); kurira 15 (LLL)

sound *give forth a s.* vb -ridza t (LL); -rira i (LL)

soup *gravy* n muto 3 (LL); svupu 9 (HL) cf Eng.

sour *be bitter, turn s.* vb -vava i (HH)

sour milk *curdled m.* n mukaka wakakora 3 (LLL LHHL)

sour plum *tree* n mutsvanzva 3 (LHL); mutengeni 3 (LHHL)

south *direction to the right when facing the sunrise* n maodzanyemba (LLLLL) (*less common:* chamhembe 7 (LHH))

sow *plant seed* vb -dyara t (HH); -dzvara t K (HH); *s. by broadcasting* vb -kusha t K (HH); -mwaya t Ż (LL); -kusa t M (HH) — PT *sowed;* PP *sown, sowed*

space *place* n nzvimbo 9 (LL)

space out *widen intervening spaces* vb -taranza t (HHH)

spade *tool for digging* n foshoro 9 (HLL) cf Eng. illustration p. 162

spanner *tool for gripping and turning nuts* n chipanera 7 (LHLL) cf Eng.; *monkey wrench, shifting s.* n bhobhojani 5 (LLHL) *cf illustration p. 162*

sparkle *glitter, flash with light* vb -vaima i (LLL); -n'ąima i (LLL)

sparrow-hawk *very small sp of hawk* n rukodzi 11 (LHL); ruvangu 11 (LLH) *cf illustration p. 49*

spat *cf spit*

speak *use the voice to share or exchange views* vb -taura i & t (LLL); *speak out, s. clearly, s. loudly* vb -taurisa i (LLLL) cf -taura (LLL); *s. out, own up* vb -dura i & t (LL) — PT *spoke;* PP *spoken*

speaker *one who speaks* n mutauri 1 (LLLL) cf -taura (LLL)

spear *weapon thrown by hand* n pfumo 5, mapfumo 6 (HH)

spear grass n tsine 9 (LH)

specialist *expert* n nyanzvi 9 (LH); mazvikokota 1a (LHLLL)

species *kind, type, tribe* n rudzi 11 (LL), plur: ndudzi 10

spectacles *pair of glasses for the eyes* n magirazi 6 (LLHL) cf Eng.

spectator *one who watches (usu a game)* n muyevi 1 (LLL) cf -yeva (LL)

speech *talk given in public* n nhauro 9 (LLL) cf -taura (LLL); *manner of speaking* n mutauriro 3 (LLHHH) cf -taura (LLL)

spell *name or write the letters of a word in their proper order* vb -pereta t (HHH); -peretera t (HHHL); -perengera t (HHHL); -sopera t (HHH) — PT & PP *spelt, spelled*

spend *the day* vb -swera i (LL); *spend the night, sleep* vb -vata i (HH); -rara i (HH)

spend *money wastefully* vb -paradza mari (LLL LH) — PT & PP *spent*

spendthrift *improvident, wasteful person without suggesting poverty* n rombe 5, marombe 6 (LL)

spent *cf spend*

spew *vomit, retch* vb -rutsa i & t (HH)

spherical *be round like a ball* vb -urungana i (HHHL) (stative vb); Ano kumeso **kwakaurungana**. (*She has a round face.*)

spider *creature with eight legs which spins a web* n dandemutande 5, matandemutande 6 (LLLLL); buwe 5, mabuwe 6 (LL); *spin a web* vb -tanda t (LL) *cf illustration p. 80*

spider flower *common weed whose leaves are edible* n nyevhe 9 (LH)

spider's web *also single thread of a spider's web* n dandadzi 5, madandadzi 6 (LLL) *cf illustration p. 175*

spill out *flow over the side of a container* vb -deuka i (HHH); -deura t (HHH); *s. by accident* vb -deuka i (HHH) — PT & PP *spilt, spilled*

spin *make string or rope* vb -kosa t (HH); *s. round an axis e.g. wheel* vb

-tenderera i (HHHL); -zeya i (HH); *cause to s. round* vb -tenderedza t (HHHL); -zeya t (HH) — PT *spun, span;* PP *spun*

spinach *wild s., poor man's s.* n mowa 5 (LL)

spindle pod n mujakari 3 (LHHH)

spine *backbone* n muzongoza 3 (LHLH); zongoza 5 (HLH)

spinster *woman who has not married* n tsikombi 9 (HLH)

spirit *soul* n mweya 3 (LH); *aggrieved s.* n ngozi 9 (LL); *ancestral s., s. of a senior relative* n mudzimu 3 (LHH); *ceremony to unite ancestral s. with s. world* n kurova guva 15 (LHL HH); *foreign possessing s.* n shavi 5, mashavi 6 (LL); *ghost, spook* n chipoko 7 (LHL) cf Eng. & Afrik.; *God, Supreme Spirit, Creator* n Mwari 1a (LH); Dzivaguru 1a (LLHH); Chidzachapo 1a (LLLH); Wamatenga 1a (HLHL); Musiki 1a (LLL); Musikavanhu 1 (LLLLL); Nyadenga 1a (LHL); Mubvandiripo 1a (LLHLH); Samasimba 1a (HHLH); *tutelary, guardian s. of a tribe* n mhondoro 9 (LLL); *person who possesses a t. s., tutelary s. medium* n svikiro 5, masvikiro 6 (LLL); *water s.* n nzuzu 9 (LH)

spirit-level *builder's or bricklayer's instrument* n puranga manzi 9 (LHL HL)

spirt *spurt, gush out in a jet or stream* vb -tsatika i (HHH)

spit *s. out* vb -svipa i & t (HH); -pfira i & t (HH) — PT & PP *spat*

spite *desire to cause somebody pain or damage* n pfini 9 (HH)

spiteful *be s., show spite* vb -ita pfini (LL HH)

spitefulness *quality of desiring or causing pain or damage* n chinya 7 (LL)

spittle *saliva* n mate 6 (LH)

splash *cause liquid to fly about in drops* vb -pfachura t (HHH)

splinter *sharp-pointed fragment usu of wood* n banzu 5 (LH); rubanzu 11 Z (LLH)

split *be cracked* adj & vb -tsemuka i (LLL); Ndine ndiro yakatsemuka. (*I have a cracked plate.*); *split, break lengthwise* vb -tsemura t (LLL); -banzura t (LLL) — PT & PP *split*

spoil *pamper, over-indulge* vb -tunhira t Z (LLL); -jaidza t (HHH); mwana akatunhirwa (*spoiled child*)

spoil *sully, blemish* vb -nyangadza i & t (HHH) — PT & PP *spoilt, spoiled*

spoke *bar or wire connecting the hub of a wheel with the rim* n chipokisi 7 (LHLL); sipokisi 9 (LHLL) cf Eng.

spoke, spoken *cf speak*

sponge *veg matter from the sea used by man for washing* n chiponji 7 (LHL); chipanji 7 (LHL); chishambo 7 KoZ (LLL)

sponge *scrounge food* vb -kwata i (LL)

spoon *utensil for preparing or eating food* n chipunu 7 (LHL) cf Eng.

spoon *wooden s.* n mugwaku 3 (LHL); rugwaku 11 (LLH); *ladle (calabash)* n mukombe 3 (LHL)

spoor *tracks, footprints* n matsimba 6 (LLL); gwara 5, makwara 6 (LH)

spot *place* n nzvimbo 9 (LL)

spot *see, observe* vb -ona i & t (HH)

spot *in colouration* n vara 5, mavara 6 (HH)

spout *pipe through which liquid pours* n muromo 3 (LLL)

sprain *wrench (ankle, wrist etc.) violently; twist a limb* vb -minyura t (LLL); -svodogora t (HHHL)

sprang *cf spring*

sprawl *lie outstretched* vb -zvambarara i (HHHL); -tambarara i MZ (HHHL); -rashuka i K (HHH)

spray *scatter drops of liquid, throw liquid in the form of a spray, sprinkle an object with s.* vb -mwaya t (LL); -fafaidza (HHHL)

spread *distribute* vb -paradzira t (LLLL); *s. bread* vb -zora t (LL); *s. out like branches* vb -pasa i (LL); *s. out like a runner plant* vb -tambarara i (HHHL); *s. out as in bed-making* vb -waridza t K (LLL); -warira t MZ (LLL); *s. in sun to dry* vb -yanika t (HHH) — PT & PP *spread*

spring *of water, place where water rises from the ground* n chisipiti 7 (LHHH)

spring *jump, leap* vb -svetuka i & t (HHH) — PT *sprang;* PP *sprung*

springhare *springhaas, sp of rodent* n nhire 9 (LH); gwizo 5 KM (LL); gwete 5 KoM (HH)

sprinkle *send a shower of water or liquid onto a surface* vb -mwaya t (LL); -sasa t KM (LL); -sasaidza t Z (LLLL); -mwamwaidza t Z (LLLL)

sprout *from the ground* vb -mera i (LL); *s. from the stem* vb -tunga i (HH)

sprung *cf spring*

spun, span *cf spin*

spurwing goose n hanzi 9 (LH) cf Afrik.

spy *watch secretly* vb -sora i & t MZ (HH); *spy, enemy observer* n musori 1 MZ (LHH) cf -sora (HH); musvori 1 K (LHH)

squander *waste anything* vb -paradza t (LLL)

square *figure with four equal sides* n sikweya 9 (LHL) cf Eng.

squarely *evenly (in a way which is even)* adv zvakaenzana (LHHLL) rel

squash *crush* vb -pwanya t (LL)

squash *Shona vegetable* n budzi 5, mapudzi 6 (LH)

squat *crouch on haunches* vb -chochomara i (HHHL); -tonona i KM (LLL)

squeak *make a shrill cry or sound (humans or animals)* vb -swinya i (HH)

squeaker *sp of fish* n korokoro 9 (LLLL)

squeal *(of a pig), utter a shrill cry* vb -zhwinya i (HL)

squeeze *wring out liquid content* vb -svina t (LL)

squint *look with half-closed eyes because of glare* vb -remara maziso i (HHH LHH); *be cross-eyed* vb -tswinya ziso i (LL HH)

squirm *wriggle* vb -zvongonyoka i (HHHL)

squirrel *small rodent that climbs trees* n tsindi 9 (HH); shindi 9 K (HH). *There are 3 species found in Rhodesia: bush s., sun s. and red s. The last 2 are found in the Eastern Districts; cf illustration p. 132*

squirt *spurt in a stream, liquid coming out forcefully* vb -tsatika i (HHH)

stab *pierce* vb -baya t (LL)

stable *building in which horses are kept* n danga ramabhiza 5 (LH LHLH); chitevere 7 (LHLL) cf Eng.

stack *pile one thing on top of another* vb -turikidza t (HHHL)

staff *rod, walking stick* n mudonzvo 3 (LHL) cf -donzva (HH)

stagger *walk unsteadily, swaying from side to side* vb -dzadzarika i (LLLL)

stain *soil, dirty* vb -svipisa t (LLL); *s. permanently* vb -tindivadza i & t (LLLL)

stale bread n chingwa chagara 7 (LL LHL) *i.e. which has stayed a long time*

stalk *dry s.* n shanga 5 (LL)

stalk *(wild game), creep up unobserved* vb -nyangira t (HHH)

stammer *stutter, nervous disorder of talking* vb -ndandama i (LLL)

stamp *(postage), piece of printed paper stuck on envelopes* n chitambi 7

(LHL) cf Eng.; *stamp (rubber or metal), article for making a stamp mark* n chidhindo 7 (LLL) cf -dhinda (LL)

stamp *with mortar and pestle to crush grain* vb -tswa i & t MZ (H)

stand *keep an upright position* vb -mira i (HH); -ima i M (HH); *stand aside, give way to, move out of the way* vb -peuka i Z (HHH); -tsauka i (HHH); *stand in a line, line up* vb -ita rundaza i (LL LLH); *stand on tip-toe* vb -dadama i (LLL); -susumhira i Z (HHHL); *stand in one's light, over-shadow* vb -dzikatira (HHHL); *stand up* vb -simuka i (HHL); *stand upright, s. up straight* vb -twasuka i (LLL) — PT & PP *stood*

stank *cf stink*

star *one of the heavenly bodies that shine at night* n nyenyedzi 9 MZ (HLH); nyeredzi 9 KM (HLH)

starbur *upright s., a S. American weed* n chibayamahure 7 (LLLLHL); chidhongi 7 (LLH)

stare at *look fixedly at, gaze with fixed attention* vb -dzvokora t (LLL)

starling *sp of bird, Cape glossy s.* n hwidzikwidzi 9 (LHLL); husvu R737 (LH); *long tailed s.* n hwirikwiri 9 (LHLL) R742; *red-winged s.* n ngwitsvo 5 Z, mangwitsvo 6 (HL); sviho 5 (HL); *violet-backed s.* n nyerure 9 K (LLL) R745

start *begin, commence* vb -tanga i (HH); -vamba i (LL); *start motor car* vb -mutsa motokari (LL)

startle *alarm, give a fright to* vb -vhundutsa t (LLL); *s. game from a cover* vb -mutsa t (LLL); *be startled, alarmed* vb -vhunduka i (LLL)

starve *be famished, be very hungry* vb -ziya i (HL); -fa nenzara i (H LHL)

statement *at court* n sitatimende 9 (LHLLL) cf Eng.; *statement of account* n akaunzi 9 (LHLL) cf Eng.

station *halting place of trains or buses* n chiteshi 7 (LHL) cf Eng.

statue *solid likeness carved or moulded from stone, wood, etc.* n mufananidzo 3 (LHHHL) cf -fananidza (HHHL)

stature *build of body* n chimiro 7 (LHH)

stay *s. at, dwell at* vb -gara i (LL); *s. behind* vb -sara i (HH); *s. up all night* vb -pupudza i (HHH)

steady *be self-possessed* adj & vb -dzikama i (LLL) (stative vb); Munhu akadzikama haataurisi. (*A self-possessed person does not talk excessively.*); *secure, make something stand firmly* vb -tsigisa t (HHH)

steal *take another's property without permission* vb -ba i & t (H) — PT *stole*; PP *stolen*

steal off *steal away, quietly disappear,* vb -svova i MZ (LL); -verera i (LLL)

steam *(same word as smoke)* n utsi 14 (LH)

steep *in liquid, soak, submerge* vb -nyika t (HH)

stembuck *steenbok, very small antelope, weight about 14 kg* n mhene 9 (LH) cf illustration p. 89

stemfruit n musaswa 3 (LLL); muhorongwa 3 (LLLH) B.Bk. 1,42

step *distance taken by each foot when walking* n nhanho 9 Z (LL); nhano 9 M (LL); *s. of ladder* n danhiko 5 (LLL); *s. of staircase* n sitepisi 5 (LHLL) cf Eng.

sterile man *m. who cannot beget children* n ngomwa 9 (LH)

sterile cow *c. that cannot bear young* n mhanje 9 (HL)

stick *dry piece of firewood* n rukuni 11 (LHH); *any stick or short piece of branch* n chimuti (LLH); *stirring stick for cooking* n mugoti 3 (LHL); *walking s.* n mudonzvo 3 (LHL) cf -donzva (HH); mubhadha 3 (LLL); *stick insect* n hwizarukuni 9 Z (HLLHH); mhashurukuni 9 K (LLLHH)

stick *apply glue, stick together* vb -namatidza t (LLLL); *stick, adhere to* vb -namatira i (LLLL); *stick in mud, sink down* vb -nyura i (HH); *stick out, put out* vb -buritsa t (HHH) — PT & PP *stuck*

sticky *be s.* vb -tsvetera i (LLL)

stiff *be hard* adj & vb -oma i (HH) (stative vb); Huni idzi dzakaoma. (*This is hard wood.*); *stiffen, make stiff, make hard* vb -omesa t (HHH) cf oma (HH)

stifle *suffocate* vb -vhumira t MZ (HHH); -pwitira t K (LLL); -fungaidza t (HHHL)

still *even up to the present time or the moment mentioned.* Use Progressive Implication: Ndichiri kurwara. (*I am still sick.*)

sting *of a bee* n rumborera 11 (LLLL)

sting *as a bee* vb -ndurira KoZ (LLL); -ruma i & t (HH) — PT & PP *stung*

stinginess *great unwillingness to spend money, meanness* n rutsuta 11 MZ (LLL); ruomera 11 Z (LHHL)

stingy *be mean, stint* vb -nyima i & t (HH)

stink *smell badly* vb -nhuwa i (LL); -nhuhwa i (LL); *s. very badly* vb -kanda gwema / hwema / mweya i (LL LL) — PT *stank, stunk;* PP *stunk*

stink *bad smell, bad odour* n kunhuwa 15 (LLL); gwema 5 (LL)

stint *be stingy, mean* vb -nyima i & t (HH)

stir *(a pot), make contents move round and round* vb -kurunga i & t (HHH); -kodzonga i & t (HHH); stir the fire, *stoke* vb -kuchidzira moto (LLLL LH)

stirring-stick n mugoti 3 (LHL)

stitch *sewing s.* n sitichi 9 (LHL) cf Eng.

stitch *sew* vb -sona i & t (LL)

stocking *tight-fitting covering for the foot and leg* n stokononzi 5, mastokononzi 6 (HLLL) cf Eng.

stoep *verandah* n vharanda 5, mavharanda 6 (LHL) cf Portuguese

stoical *be brave at enduring pain; show no sign of pain* vb -shiva i (LL)

stole *cf steal*

stomach *belly* n dumbu 5, matumbu 6 (LL) *first stomach (of ruminants); food container in the body* n guru 5, makuru 6 (LH) (*to be distinguished from* guru 5 (LL) *a burrow, and* guru 5 (HH) *a polygamus union*); *stomach-ache, diarrhoea* n manyoka 6 (LHH)

stone *very hard natural mineral matter* n ibwe 5, mabwe 6 (LL); dombo 5, matombo 6 (LH); *flat, loose s.* n fendefa 5, mafendefa 6 (HHL)

stonechat *small grassland bird which feeds on insects* n sheranjera 1a M (LLLL); mujesi 3 (LHL); mhindirira 9 (LLLL) R576

stood *cf stand*

stool *small portable seat* n chigaro 7 (LLL) cf -gara (LL); chituru 7 (LHL) cf Eng.

stool *human excrement* n tsvina 9 (LL) (*euphemism:* dirt); *liquid s.* n rupanzo 11 (LHH) cf -panza (HH)

stoop *bow down, bend over* vb -kotama i (LLL)

stop *bus s.* n sitopi 9 (LHL) cf Eng.; chiteshi 7 (LHL) cf Eng.

stop *cease moving, stand, halt* vb -mira t (HH); *cause to s., bring to a s.* vb -misa t (HH) cf -mira (HH)

stop doing *give up* vb -regera i & t (LLL); *leave off, cease, desist from* vb -rega (LL) + Infinitive: Rega kuenda! (*Don't go!*); *put an end to* vb -pedza t (HH); *stop a hole, s. up, block the entrance* vb -vhara t (LL); -dzivira t (LLL); -pfiga t (HH)

stopper *cork or plug for closing an opening* n chidziwo 7 (LLL); mudzivo 3 M (LLL)

store *shop* n chitoro 7 (LHL) cf Eng.

stork *large, long-legged bird which usu feeds on locusts, insects, lizards etc.* n dambiramurove 5 K, madambiramurove 6 (HHHHLH); shuramurove 5 KoMZ, mashuramurove 6 (LLLLH) **General names**; *marabou stork, carrion-eating bird having naked head and neck and repulsive appearance* n svorenyama 9 (LLLL) R73; *white bellied stork, a non-breeding visitor from N. Africa; appears in flocks Oct — March, hence also called rain-stork* n svore 5 (LL); shohwori 5 K, mashohwori 6 (HLH); jororwi 5 Z (HLH); hororwi 9 (HLH); mun'ori 3 M (LHL); mushore (LLL) R78

story *fable* n ngano 9 (LL); nyaya 9 (LH); rungano 11 (LLL); ngano 10 (LL)

stout *fat, thick-set* adj -kobvu (LH); gobvu 5, hobvu 9

stout *be fat (humans)* vb -futa i (LL) (stative vb)

stoutness *fatness, tendency to fat* n ukobvu 14 (LLH)

stove *apparatus for cooking* n chitofu 7 (LHL) cf Eng.

straggle *be untidily drawn out* vb -tsauka i (HHH)

straight *be without curve or bend* adj & vb -twasuka (LLL) (stative vb); Mapango aka**twasuka** ndiwo anodiwa. (*Straight poles are the ones required.*); *be s., morally upright* vb -rurama i (LLL)

straighten *make straight* vb -twasanura t MZ (LLLL); -ruramisa t MZ (LLLL); -swatudza t MZ (LLL)

strain *filter* vb -mimina t (LLL); *s., stretch, pull fence-wire* vb -kakata t (HHH)

strainer *vessel for straining liquid* n chisvino 7 (LLL) cf -svina (LL); chimimino 7 (LLLL) cf -mimina (LLL)

strange *be odd, cause astonishment* vb -shamisa i (HHH) cf -shama (HH)

stranger *visitor who is not known* n mweni 1 (LL); muenzi 1 Z (LLH)

strangle *kill by squeezing the throat and stopping the breathing* vb -dzipa i & t (HH)

strap *band, usu of leather, for fastening things* n bhandi 5, mabhandi 6 (HL) cf Eng.

stream *small river* n rukova 11 (LL); *plur:* hova 10 (LL)

stream *run in a thin s.* vb -chururuka i (HHHL)

street *main road* n mugwagwa 3 (LLL)

strength *power* n simba 5, masimba 6 (LH)

strengthen *make firm or strong* vb -simbisa t (LLL) cf -simba (LL)

stretch *extend (elastic)* vb -dhadhamura t (LLLL); -tatamura t (LLLL); -dhadhamuka i (LLLL); *s. hide* vb -kaka t (LL); *stretch out hand* vb -tambanudza ruoko (HHHL LHH); *stretch out for, reach for* vb -sveverera t (LLLL);

stretch one's limbs vb -zamura i (HHH); *stretch legs, straighten l.* vb -tambarara i (HHHL)

stride *take step* vb -kanda nhanho i (LL LL); n nhanho 9 Z (LL); nhano 9 M (LL) — PT *strode;* PP *stridden, strid*

strike *beat, hit* vb -rova i & t (HH); passive: -rohwa: -nera i & t M (LL); *s. a match* vb -kwenya t (LL) — PT *struck;* PP *struck, stricken*

string *fine cord for tying things* n mukosi 3 (LHL)

string *beads together* vb -tunga chuma (HH LH) — PT & PP *strung*

strip off bark vb -svuura t (LLL); *s. off thatch, remove t.* vb -pfurunura t (HHHL)

strive after *endeavour, try* vb -vavarira t (HHHL) — PT *strove;* PP *striven*

stroke *an animal* vb -puruzira t (LLLL)

strong *be healthy* adj & vb -simba i (LL); -gwinya (HH) (stative vbs); Munhu uyu aka**simba**. (*This person is healthy.*)

strong *be powerful* adj & vb -simba i (LL); mukomana ane simba (*a powerful boy*)

strongly *in a strong manner, powerfully* adv zvine simba (LH LH) rel

strut *walk proudly* vb -kanyaira i (HHHL)

stuck *cf stick*

student *one who learns* n mudzidzi 1 (LHL) cf -dzidza (HH); mufundi 1 (LHH) cf -funda (HH)

study *obtain knowledge by learning or discovering* vb -dzidza i & t (HH); -funda i & t (HH)

stuff inside *fill up* vb -paka t (HH)

stumble *strike the foot against something and nearly fall* vb -dzadzarika i (LLLL); *s. and fall, trip* vb -pingirishwa i (HHHL)

stump *of a tree* n chigutsa 7 (LLH); gutsa 5, magutsa 6 (LH)

stump *remove s. from the ground* vb -gobora t (LLL)

stung *cf sting*

stunk *cf stink*

stupid *be foolish* vb -pusa i (LL); -remara i (HHH); -zingaira i (HHHL)

stupid person *fool* n rema 5, marema 6 (HH); fuza 5, mafuza 6 (LL); *stupidity, foolishness* n urema 14 (LHH); ufuza 14 (LLL)

stutter *stammer owing to nervous disorder of speech* vb -kakama i (LLL); -ndandama i (LLL)

stutterer *person who stutters* n chimata 7 M (LLL)

sty *pig s., enclosure for pigs* n danga renguruve 5 (LH LHLL)

style *manner of doing anything* n sitaira 9 (LHLL) cf Eng.

subdue *overcome* vb -kurira i & t (HHH)

submerge *soak, steep in liquid* vb -nyika t (HH)

submit *agree* vb -bvuma i & t (LL)

subside *go down in level* vb -serera i (LLL)

subtract *take away* vb -bvisa t (LL); -tapudza t (HHH)

succeed *follow* vb -tevera t (LLL)

succeed *in work* vb -budirira i (HHHL)

successor *follower* n muteveri 1 (LLLL) mutevedzeri 1 (LLLLL) cf -tevera (LLL)

such *which is like that* adj zvakadaro (LHLH); *s. as, for example, for instance* adv sokuti (LHL)

suck *(sweets), slowly dissolve in the mouth* vb -svisvina t (HHH); *s. from a wound using the mouth* vb -sveta t (LL); *feed, suck from the breast* vb -yamwa i (HH); -mwa i K (H); *suckle, breastfeed* vb -yamwisa t (HHH) cf -yamwa (HH); -mwisa t K (HH)cf -mwa (H)

suffer *go through a process of suffering* vb -tambudzika i (LLLL); *be long-*

suffering, patient in suffering vb -tirira i (LLL)

sufficient *be enough* adj & vb -kwana i (HH) (stative vb); Tine mvura yaka**kwana**. (*We have sufficient water.*)

sugar *sweet substance obtained from various plants e.g. sugar cane* n tsvigiri 9 (HLH); shuga 9 (LL) cf Eng.; *sugar-cane, tall plant with sweet juice* n nzimbe 9 (HL); pwarungu 9 (HHH)

sugar bush *protea* n mubonda 3 (LLL)

suicide *commit s., self murder* vb **-zvi**sungirira i (HLLLH) reflex

suit *set of outer clothing of the same material* n sutu 9 (HL); svutu 9 (HL) cf Eng.

suitable *be worthy, proper* vb -kodzera i (LLL) (stative vb); Vabereki vaka**kodzera** kuremekedzwa. (*Parents are worthy of respect.*)

suit-case *travelling case for carrying clothes* n sutukesi 9 (HLLL) cf Eng.

sulk *be in a bad temper and show unwillingness to talk* vb -ita chiramwa (LL LLH)

sully *blemish, spoil* vb -nyangadza i & t (HHH); -svibisa t (LLL)

summer *hot season (Nov. — March)* n zhizha 5, mazhizha 6 (LH)

summersault *action of turning head-over-heels* n mhidigari 9 Z (HHLH)

summit *on top* n pamusoro 16 (LLHH)

summon *call, beckon* vb -daidza t (HHH); -shevedza t (HHH)

sun *heavenly body which lights up and warms the earth* n zuva 5, mazuva 6 (HH); *sunbeam, beam, ray of light* n ranzi 5, maranzi 6 (LH); museve wezuva 3 (LLL HLL); *sunshine* n mushana 3 (LLH)

sunbird *sp of bird that lives on nectar from flowers* n tsodzi 9 (LH); kadzvororo 12 (LLLL); kadzonyn'a 12 (LHL); tsodzo 9 (HH); todzvo 9 (HL)

Sunday *day of rest* n Svondo 9 (LL); Sondo 9 (LL); cf Afrik.

sung *cf sing*

sunglasses *dark glasses which protect the eyes from bright light* n magogorosi 6 (LHLLL) cf Eng.

sunhemp *rotation crop bearing black seeds* n hundubwe 9 (HHL); jerenjere 5 (LLLL)

sunrise *at s., when the sun rises* adv zuva robuda (HH HHL); *sunset, at s., when the sun sets* adv zuva rodoka (HH HHL)

sunk, *sunken cf sink*

superb *excellent, very good, splendid, pre-eminent, expert* adj mandorokwati (LLLHL); Vatambi venhabvu **vamandorokwati**. (*They are excellent football players.*)

supervise *without actually doing the work, give orders* vb -pikita t (LLL)

supper *eat s., eat the evening meal* -rarira t (HHH); *supper, evening meal* n chirariro 7 (LHHL) cf -rarira (HHH)

supply *give* vb -pa i & t (H)

support *a motion, second* vb -tsinhira t (LLL)

support *prop up* vb -tsigira t (HHH)

suppose *think, assume* vb -funga i (LL)

supposed to *ought to, should* vb -fanira i (HHH)

sure *be certain* vb -va nechokwadi i (HLLH); Ndine chokwadi. (*I am certain.*); Une shuwa here? (*Are you sure?*)

surely *truly* adv chokwadi (HLH); zviro kwazvo (LL HL)

surpass *do or be better than* vb -pfuura t (HHH); -kunda t K (HH); -pinda t (LL)

surprise *astonish* vb -shamisa i & t (HHH) cf -shama; *catch in the act* vb -dimbura t Z (LLL); *take by s.* vb -futa i (HH)

surrender *give up, stop fighting* vb -tera i (LL); -sarenda i (LLL)

surround *shut in on all sides, be all round* vb -komberedza t (HHHL); -komba t (HH)

survive *continue to live* vb -pona i (HH); -rarama i (LLL)

suspect *have an idea that* vb -fungira i & t (LLL); -fungidzira i & t (LLLL)

suspicion *feeling of a person who suspects* n fungidziro 9 Z (LLLL); fungwa 9 K (LH)

suspicious *be s., having suspicion* vb -nyumwa i (LL)

swagger *walk proudly* vb -kanyaira i (HHHL)

swallow *cause something to go down the throat* vb -medza i & t MZ (LL); -minya i & t K (LL)

swallow *small, fast-flying bird* n nyenganyenga 9 (HLHL); mherepere 9 M (LLLL) *general terms*

swam *cf swim*

swarm of bees *large colony or family of b.* n bumha renyuchi 5 (HL HLL); mukuze 3 (LHL)

sway *to and fro, move unsteadily from one side to the other* vb -tepuka i (HHH)

swear at *scold* vb -tuka i & t (HH)

swear to *s. on oath, promise* vb -pika i (LL) — PT *swore;* PP *sworn*

sweat *give out s.* vb -tikitira i (HHHL); *sweat, perspiration* n dikita 5 (LLH) cf -tikitira (HHHL); ziya 5 K (LH)

sweep *brush away or clean with a broom* vb -tsvaira i & t (HHH); -psvaira M (HHH) — PT & PP *swept*

sweet *flavoured sugar, chocolate, etc.* n siwiti 9 (LHL); chiwitsi 7 (LHL) cf Eng.

sweet *be s., taste like sugar* vb -tapira i (HHH)

sweet potato *plur: potatoes; plant with tubers eaten as a vegetable* n mbambaira 9 (LLLL); *cf illustration p. 170*

sweet thorn tree n munenje 3 (LHL)

sweetheart *loved one* n mudiwa 1 (LHL) cf -diwa (HH)

sweet pea *wild s.p.* n karumanyemba 12 (LHHHL) B.Bk. 1,63

swell *become greater in size* vb -zvimba i (HH) — PT *swelled;* PP *swollen, swelled*

swelling *glandular s. in the groin or armpit* n mwambabvu 3 (LHH)

swelling *swollen place on the body* n bundu 5, mapundu 6 (HH)

swept *cf sweep*

swill *with water, last rinse before drying* vb -sukurudza t (LLLL)

swim *move through the water by bodily movement* vb -tuhwina i (LLL); -tiva i (LL); -shambira i (LLL); *s. under water* vb -ita chamunyurududu i (LL HLHHLH) — PT *swam;* PP *swum*

swimming pool *any p. suitable for swimming* n dhigidho 5 KM, madhigidho 6 (LLL); duhwino 5 Z (LLL)

swing *seat held by ropes for swinging on* n mudzuwerere 3 MZ (LHLLL)

switch out *s. off, extinguish* vb -dzima t (HH)

switch *electrical device for controlling current* n swichi 9 (HL) cf Eng.

swollen *cf swell*

sword *weapon like a long knife* n bakatwa 5, mapakatwa 6 (HLH)

sympathy *pity* n tsitsi 10 (LH); *sympathetic, having or showing feelings of pity* adj chiremba ane tsitsi (*a sympathetic doctor.*)

syphilis *a venereal disease* n njovhera 9 (LHL)

syrup *thick, sweet liquid* n manyuchi 6 (LHH)

T

tsessebe nhondo

table *piece of furniture with flat top and usu 4 legs* n tafura (HLL) cf Afrik.; dara 5, matara 6 (HH); teburu 9 (HLL) cf Eng.

tacky *be extremely sticky* vb -rembuka i (HHH)

tadpole *young of a frog before full development* n zunguzurwa 5 Z, ma-

zunguzurwa 6 (LLLH); buruuru 5, maburuuru 6 (LLLL); burunga 5 M (LLL)

tail *movable part of the lower end of the spine of an animal* n muswe 3 MZ (LH); mwise K (LH); *tail of bird or fish* n besu 5, mapesu 6 (HL)

tailor *maker of suits* n musoni 1 (LLL); cf -sona (LL); tera 1a (HL) cf Eng.

take *carry away and remove* vb -tora t (HH); *accept, receive* vb -tambira i & t (HHH); *take away, move away* vb -bvisa t (LL); *take away, move away* vb -torera t (HHH); *take away, remove, subtract* vb -bvisa t (LL); -bhisa t (LL); -tapudza t (HHH); *take down (e.g. from a shelf)* vb -turura t (HHH); *take down from the head* vb -tura t (HH); *take from the fire* vb -bura t (LL); *take by force* vb -pamba t (HH); *take a handful of* vb -dzamura t (LLL); *take by surprise, t. unawares* vb -futa i & t (HH); *take leave, say goodbye* vb -oneka i & t (LLL); *take an oath, promise* vb -pika (LL); *take off (clothes), undress* vb -kumura t (HHH); -kurura t (HHH); -bvisa t (LL) *take offence for little reason* vb -gumbukira t (LLLL); *take out* vb -buritsa t (HHH); *take out a thorn* vb -tumbura munzwa (LLL LH); *take out of the eye* vb -fura t (HH); *take a pinch of* vb -tswinya t (LL); *take quickly from the fire, snatch* vb -chachura t (LLL); *take a round about way* vb -monerera i (HHHL); *take shelter from the rain* vb -hwanda mvura (HL HH); *take to pieces, take apart* vb -gurunura t (HHHL); *take unawares, t. by surprise* vb futa i & t (HH); *take up, lift up* vb -simudza t (HHL) — PT *took;* PP *taken*

tale *story* n nyaya 9 (LH); rungano 11 (LLL); ngano 9/10 (LL)

talk *speak* vb -taura i & t (LLL); *talk in sleep, have a night-mare* vb -vhumuka i (HHH); *talk nonsense, speak foolishly* vb -bvotomoka i (HHHL); -taura nhando (LLL LH); *talk much, t. too much, speak loudly* vb -taurisa i (LLLL); -zavaza i (LLL)

tall *high* adj -refu (LH); refu 5, ndefu 9

talon *claw* n nzara 9 (LH); runzara 11 (LLH); *same word for finger nail*

tame an ox *break-in* vb -pingudza t (LLL); *tame a wild animal* vb -pfuya t (HH)

tampan *house tick* n humba 9 (LL)

tangarine *naartjie* n nachisi 5 & 9, manachisi 6 (HLL) cf Afrik.

tangle *be in a t., be tangled* vb -katana i (HHH); -monana i (HHH) (stative vbs); Shinda iyi yakamonana. (*This wool is tangled.*)

tank *large container used for liquid* n tangi 5 & 9, matangi 6 (HL) cf Eng.

tantalise *raise hopes that are to be disappointed* vb -nyemudza t (LLL)

tap *device to stop the flow — usu of liquid* n pombi 9 (LH); tepi 9 (HL) cf Eng.

tap *adminster quick light blow* vb -dodódza i & t (HHH)

tar *black substance obtained from coal, used mainly in the construction of roads* n tara 9 (HL) cf Eng.

task *work* n basa 5, mabasa 6 (LL)

tassel *male element of maize plant which grows at the top* n muchekechera 3 (LLLLH); ngarara 9 (LLL)

taste *eat/drink a sample* vb -ravira i & t (LLL); -raira i & t (LLL); *taste bitter, t. sour* vb -vava i (HH); *t. good* vb -naka i (LL); *t. sweet* vb -tapira i (HHH)

tatoo mark *tribal identification mark* n nyora 9 (HL)

tatters *ragged clothes* n mamvemve 6 (LLH); marengenya 6 (LLLL); madzoto 6 (LHH); marengenyn'a 6 (LLLL)

taught *cf teach*

tax *sum of money paid by citizens to the government for public services (education, health, roads, etc.)* n mutero 3 (LLL)

tax *pay t., pay rent* vb -tera i (LL)

tea *drink made by adding boiling water to dried tea leaves* n tii 9 (HL) cf Eng.; *t. leaves (used or unused)* n masamba 6 (LLL); *tea pot, container for making tea* n tiipoti 9 (HLLL) cf Eng.

teach *give or pass on knowledge* vb -dzidzisa i & t (HHL)cf -dzidza (HH); fundisa i & t (HHH) cf -funda (HH) — PT & PP *taught*

teacher *person who teaches* n mudzidzisi 1 (LHHL) cf -dzidzisa (HHL); ticha 1a (HL) cf Eng.; *lady t.* n misitiresi 1a (HLLLL) cf Eng.

team *persons playing game together and forming one side* n timu 9 (HL) cf Eng.

tear *t. in shreds (clothing)* vb -bvarura t (HHH); -bvaruka i (HHH); *tear the skin, scratch the s.* vb -mara t (HH); *tear surface of skin, graze* vb -svuura t (LLL); *tear off, unstick* vb -kwatura t (LLL); *tear meat, usually cooked, into two* vb -dunzura t KoZ (HHH) — PT *tore;* PP *torn*

tear *t. drop* n musodzi 3 (LHL)

teaspooon *common, small spoon used for stirring tea* n tiispunu 9 (HLHL) cf Eng.

teat *nipple* n munyatso 3 (LLL)

tedious *be tiring* vb -netesa i (LLL)

teenage boy *young man* n jaya 5, majaya 6 (LH); *teenage girl, young woman* n mhandara 9 (LLL)

teethe *cut teeth* vb -mera mazino i (LL LHH)

telegram *message sent by radio or wire* n tenigramu 9 (HLLL) cf Eng.

telephone *instrument for talking to somebody at a distance* n runhare 11 (LHL); foni 9 (HL) cf Eng.

telephone *use the t. for a conversation* vb -chaya foni (LL HL)

tell *narrate, speak* vb -taura i & t (LLL)

tell *inform* vb -udza t (HH); -taurira t (LLLL); *tell lies, t. tales, lie* vb -nyepa i (LL); -reva nhema (HH LH); *t. on another* vb -reva mumwe (HH HL); *tell the truth, speak out* vb -dura t (LL) — PT & PP *told*

temper *severe anger* n hasha 10 (HH)

temperature *degree of heat or cold* n tembiricha 9 (HLLL) cf Eng.

temple of head *side of face between the eye and the ear* n chao 7 (LL)

tempt *attempt* vb -edza t MZ (LL); -idza t K (LL); *try to persuade somebody to do wrong* vb -furira (HHH); -runzira t (HHH); *ensnare, trap* vb -teya t (HH); *coax* vb -nyengetedza t (HHHL); *temptation, something that tempts* n chiedzo 7 (LLL); cf -edza (LL)

ten *the number 10* adj gumi 5, makumi 6 (HH); *to indicate 10 objects* **gumi** *is used as a noun in apposition;* Ndipewo mazai gumi. (*Please give me 10 eggs.*)

tender *soft* adj -nyoro (HH); nyoro 5, nyoro 9

tendon *tough cord that joins muscle to bone* n runda 5, marunda 6 (LH)

tennis shoes n tenesi 9 (HLL) cf Eng.; *t. ball* n tenesi 9 (HLL) cf Eng.

tent *movable shelter made of canvas* n tende 9 (LL) cf Eng.

term *school t.* n temu 9 (HL) cf Eng.

terminate *come to an end* vb -guma i (HH); -pera i (HH)

termite *'white ant'* n ishwa 9 (LH); *queen t.* n zimai reshwa 21 (LHL HL);

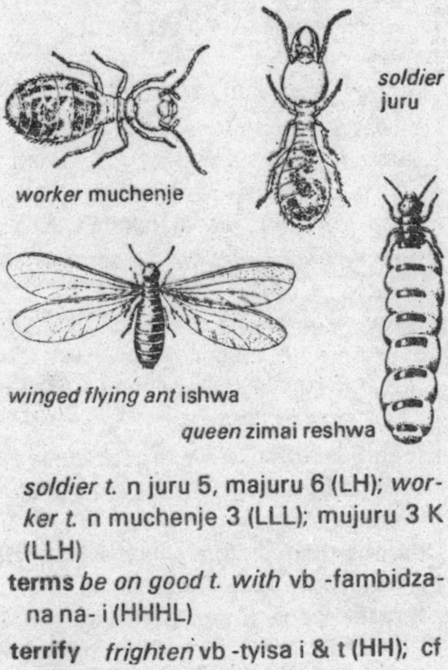

soldier t. n juru 5, majuru 6 (LH); *worker t.* n muchenje 3 (LLL); mujuru 3 K (LLH)

terms *be on good t. with* vb -fambidzana na- i (HHHL)

terrify *frighten* vb -tyisa i & t (HH); cf -tya (H)

territory *land, region* n nyika 9 (LL); dunhu 5, matunhu 6 (HH)

tessebe *the fastest of our antelopes (also tsessebe or sassaby)* n nhondo 9 (LL) *cf illustration p. 157*

test *try* vb -edza i & t (LL)

test *examination* n bvunzo 9 MZ (LL) cf -bvunza (LL); zamanisheni 5, mazamanisheni 6 (LLHLL) cf Eng.

testicle *male organ* n jende 5, machende 6 (LL); svada 5, masvada 6 (LL); gandi 5 (LH)

testify *give evidence* vb -fakaza i (LLL); -pupura t (HHH); *give testimony, witness* vb -fakaza i (LLL); -pupurira t (HHHL); -pa umboo i (LLH)

testimony *evidence, usu in a court of law* n umboo 14 MZ (LLH); uchapupu 14 (LLHH); ufakazi 14 (LLLL)

than conj kupinda (LLL); kukunda (LHH); kupfuura (LHHH); pana (LH); John anoziva kupinda Mary. (*John knows better than Mary.*); Paul mukuru pana John. (*Paul is bigger than John.*)

thank *express gratitude* vb -tenda i & t (LL); Mazviita. /Ndatenda. (*Thank you.*)

that *in order that* conj kuti (LL) + subjunctive; *that is the reason why* conj saka (LL); ndosaka (HLL) + Partic or Indic; *that is so* conj ndizvozvo (HLH); *that is to say* conj ndokuti (HLL)

that *dem cf p. 205*

thatch *cover a roof with grass* vb -pfirira t (HHH); -pfurira t (HHH)

therefore *for that reason* conj naizvozvo (LHLH); nokudaro (HLHL); saka (LL)

thereupon *and then* conj & adv ndokubva (HLL) + Rec Past Partic

thick *thickset, stout* adj -kobvu (LH); gobvu 5, hobvu 9

thicket *mass of trees, bushes, etc. growing together* n bvokocho 5, mabvokocho 6 (LLL)

thief *person who steals* n mbavha 9 (LH); gororo 5, makororo 6 (LHL)

thieve *steal* vb -ba i & t (H)

thigh *leg above the knee* n chidya 7 (LL)

thin *opposite of fat* adj -tete (LL); dete 5, nhete 9

thin *be emaciated* adj & vb -tetepa (LLL); -onda (HH) (stative vbs); Akaonda kwazvo. (*He is very thin.*) *make* *t.* vb -ondesa i & t (HHH); -onza i & t (HH)

thing *material object, usu lifeless* n chinhu 7 (LL); chiro 7 (LL)

think *suppose, t. of, t. about, t. over, consider* vb -funga i & t (LL); -ti i & t (L) — PT & PP *thought*

third *(of a series)* adj & pron -chitatu (HLH)

thirst *great desire for liquid* n nyota 9 (HH); *be thirsty, have thirst* vb -va nenyota

this dem *cf p. 205*

this evening adv mauro 6 (LLH); manheru ano 6 (LLH HL); *this morning* adv mangwanani ano 6 (LHLH HL)

thong *narrow leather strip or strap* n tambo 9 (LL)

thorax *part of an insect body between the neck and the waist* n dundundu 5 (HHH)

thorn *sharp-pointed growth on a plant* n munzwa 3 MZ (LH); muhwa 3 K (LH)

though *although* conj nyangwe (LL); kunyange (LLL); kunyangova (LLLH) + Partic

thought *in the mind* n pfungwa 9 KoMZ (LH); *memory of the past, reminiscence, preoccupying thought* n ndangariro 9 (LLLL)

thought *cf think*

thousand *1 000* n chiuru 7 (LLL); churu 7 (LL)

thrash *flog* vb -pura t (HH); -zvinda t (LL); *thrash to death, murder, flog* vb -ponda i & t (LL)

thread *wool, cotton* n shinda 9 (LL); chinda 9 K (LL)

thread beads *sew beads onto a thread* vb -tunga chuma (HH LH); *thread cotton (into a needle)* vb -tungira shinda patsono (HHH HL)

thread *of a nut* n nyembo 9 Z (HH)

threaten *menace, frighten* vb -tyisidzira t (HHHL); *threat, gesture to frighten or to hurt* n kutyisidzira 15 (LHHHL)

thresh corn *beat the grain from the dry, outer covering* vb -pura t (HH); *threshing floor* n ruware 11 (LLH); buriro 5, mapuriro 6 (HHL) cf -pura (LLH); *t. stick* n mupuro 3 (LHH); mhuro 9 (HH)

threshold *stone or plank under a doorway* n chiguvare 7 (LLLL)

threw cf *throw*

thrice *three times* adv katatu 12 (LLH)

throat *front part of neck* n huro 9 (LL)

throb *(of the heart-beat)* vb -pfura i (HH); *t. of the head* vb -tema i (HH); *t. of a wound or pain* vb -banda i (LL)

throttle *obstruct the air passage* vb -dzipa i & t (HH)

throw *fling, cast* vb -kanda i & t (LL); -potsera i & t (LLL); *throw away, discard* vb -rasa t (HH); -rasha t K (HH) — PT *threw;* PP *thrown*

thumb *short, thick finger* n chigunwe 7 MZ (LLL); gunwe 5 K (LL); *t. nail* n chara 7 (LH)

thunbergia n mufurambudzi 3 (LLLHH); mukuvamvura 3 (LHLHH) B.Bk. 1,89

thrush *(general name)* n zvichirori 5 (HHLH)

thrust *prod with a pointed weapon* vb -dyunga t (HH)

thunder *make a loud noise of t.* vb -dhirima i (LLL); -tinhira i (LLL)

thunder *rumble of t.* n kudhirima 15 (LLLL); mupande 3 K (LLH); *clap of t.* n bhanan'ana 5, mabhanan'ana 6 (LLLL)

Thursday *fourth day after Sunday* n China 7 (LL)

tick *(found on cattle, dogs etc.)* n chikwekwe 7 (LLL); chishambwe 7 (LLL); *blue t.* chinyamadari 7 (LLLLH); *bond-legged itick* n dari 5 (LH) *cf illustration p. 124*

tick bird *cattle egret* n fudzamombe 5, mafudzamombe 6 (LLLL); dzoramombe 5, madzoramombe 6 (LLLL)

tickle *rub or touch sensitive parts of the skin e.g. under the arms* vb -sekenyedza t (LLLL); -tekenyedza t (LLLL)

tidy *put in order* vb -rongedza t (LLL)

tie *fasten with string* vb -sunga t (HH); *t. a knot* vb -pfunda t (HH); *t. together, join by tying* vb -sunganidza t (HHHL)

tie *neck t.* n tai 9 (HL) cf Eng. *cf illustration p. 106*

tiger fish *sp of fierce Zambezi fish* n cheni 9 (HL); mucheni 3 (LHL); muvanga 3 K (LHH) *cf illustration p. 174*

tight *be firm* vb -simba i (LL) (stative vb); Sunga zvaka**simba**. (*Tie it tightly.*) *ly.*)

tighten *make tight* vb -kaka t (LL); *t. a nut* vb -mona t (HH)

till *until* adv kusvikira (LLL) + Partic

till soil *plough* vb -rima i & t (LL)

tilt *lean over* vb -rereka i & t (HHH)

time *measure of the passing of events* n nguva 9 (HH); nhambo 9 K (LL); *short t.* n chinguva 7 (LHH); *very short t.* n chinguvana 7 (LHHH)

timid *be afraid, fear* vb -tya i & t (H)

tin-opener *bottle-opener* n chivhuro 7 (LLL) cf -vhura (LL)

tiny *dimunitive* adj 1) -diki (HL); 2) *usu classes 12 & 13: kadiki (LHL)*

tip-toe *walk quietly on the toes* vb -susumhira i (HHHL); -dadama i (LLL)

tire *make weary* vb -netesa t (LLL); *tired, be fatigued, weary* vb neta i (LL); *tiring, be tedious* vb -netesa i (LLL)

toad-stool *sp of mushroom* n fodya yegudo 9 (HL LHL)

tobacco *snuff* n fodya 9 (HL) cf Portuguese = folha; *t. barn* n dhirihora 5, madhirihora 6 (LLHL)

today *this day* adv nhasi 1a (HL)

toe *one of the front members of the foot* n chigunwe 7 Z (LLL); chigumwe 7 K (LLL); *same term used for birds' toes*

together *in one company* adv pamwe chete (LH LH)

told *cf tell*

tomato *(plur: tomatoes), fruit eaten as a veg* n buno 5, mapuno 6 (LL); domasi 5, madomasi 6 (LHL) cf Eng. *cf illustration p. 170*

tomorrow *day following today* adv mangwana 6 (LHH); *day after t.* adv kuseramangwana 15 (LLLLHH)

tongue *movable organ in the mouth* n rurimi 11 (LHH); *language* n rurimi 11 (LHH); plur: ndimi 10 (HH); mutauro 3 (LLLL) cf -taura (LLL)

tonight *at sometime after darkness* adv usiku huno (LHL HL); *this evening* adv manheru ano (LLH HL)

took *cf take*

tools *weapons, implements* n zvombo 8 (LL)

tooth *outgrowth from the jaws used for eating* n zino 5, mazino 6 (HH); *back t., molar t.* n zeyo 5, mazeyo 6 (LL); *incisor, front t.* n zino repamhanza 6

top *on top* adv pamusoro 16 (LLHH)

torch *portable light* n mwenje 3 (LL); tochi 9 (HL) cf Eng.

tore *cf tear*

torment *inflict great suffering* vb -tambudza t (LLL)

torn *cf tear*

torn *be rent* vb -bvaruka i (HHH) (stative vb); **Ane bhurukwa rakabvaruka.** (*He has torn trousers.*)

tortoise *slow-moving reptile growing a portable shell* n hamba 9 (HH); kamba 9 Z (HH) *cf illustration p. 128*

toss *throw* vb -kanda t (LL)

totem *usu an animal chosen as the symbol of a clan* n mutupo 3 (LHH)

touch *hold* vb -bata t (HH); *touch lightly, graze, brush past* vb -nzvenzvera t (HHH)

tough meat *sinewy m.* n runda 5, marunda 6 (LH)

tough *to chew, work etc.* vb -tana i (HH)

towel *napkin used for drying* n tauro 5, matauro 6 (HLL) cf Eng.

town *commercial and residential centre* n taundi 5, mataundi 6 (HLL) cf Eng.; dhorobha 5, madhorobha 6 (LHL) cf Afrik.

township *residential suburb* n taundishipi 9 (HLLLL) cf Eng.; rukisheni (LHLL) cf Eng.

trace *piece evidence together, track* vb -ronda i & t (LL); -rondedzera i (LLLL)

trachea *wind-pipe in the throat* n gurokuro 5, makurokuro 6 (LLLL)

track *follow spoor or tracks* vb -ronda i (LL)

track *foot-marks on the ground* n dzimba 5, matsimba 6 (LL)

tractor *farm vehicle for hauling* n tirakita 9 (LHLL) cf Eng.

some tools

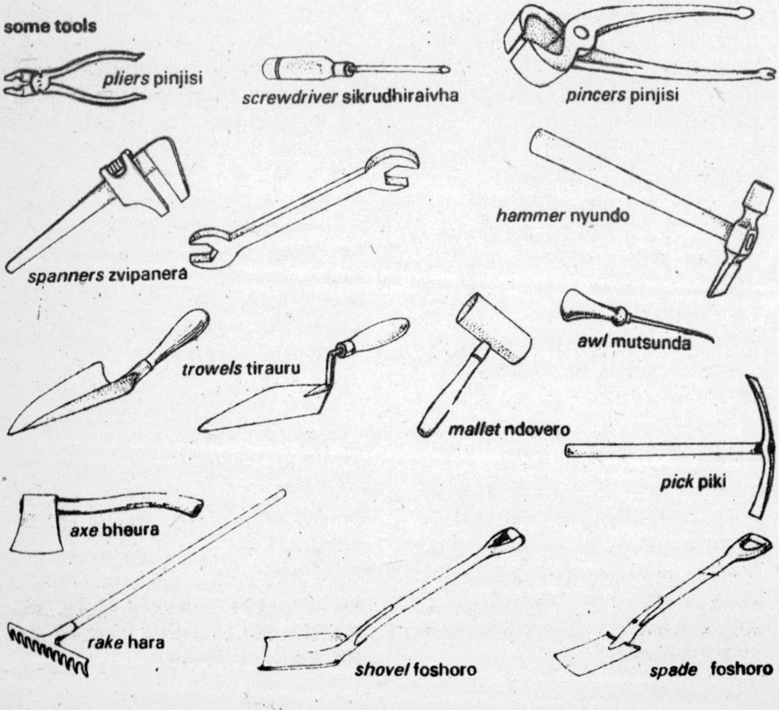

trade *hawk, sell* vb -shambadza i & t (HHH); *trader, person who buys and sells* n mutengesi 1 (LHHL) cf -tengesa (HHH); mushambadzi 1 (LHHL) cf -shambadza (HHH)

trail *drag along the ground* vb -zvuzvurudza t (HHHL)

train *railway t.* n chitima 7 (LHL) cf Eng.; tireni 9 (LHL) cf Eng.

train animals *break-in* vb -pingudza t (LLL)

traitor *political t.* n chombe 1a (HL); mutengesi 1 (LHHL)

trample *run over* vb -tsika t (LL); *t. mud, mix mortar, puddle* vb -kanya t (LL)

transfer *from one place to another* vb -tuta t (HH); *move village* vb -tama i (HH)

transgress *break a regulation, law, etc.* vb -tadza i (HH); -darika mutemo i (HHH LHH); *transgression, sin* n rutadzo 11 (LHH) cf -tadza (HH)

tanslate *from one language to another* vb -turikira i (HHHL); *translator, person who translates* n muturikiri 1 (LHHHL)

transparent *be t., able to be seen through* vb -njenjemera i (LLLL); -onekera i (HHHL)

transplant *remove from one place to grow in another* vb -sima t (HH)

transport *carry* vb -takura t (LLL)

trap *set a t., snare* vb -teya t (HH)

trap *spring t. for mice* n chikirimbani 7 (LLHLL); *whip snare* n dhibhu 5 (HL); *cage t.* n chizarira 7 (LLHL); *falling-stone t.* n riva 5, mariva 6 (HL); *falling-log t.* n mukuni 3 (LHH); mudhanda 3 (LHL)

travel *walk* vb -famba i (HH); *traveller, person who travels* n mufambi 1 (LHH) cf -famba (HH); *traveller's joy, woody climbing plant* n chifemedza 7 (LHHL) B.Bk. 1,60

travel *journey* n rwendo 11 (LL), nzendo 10 (LL)

tray *flat framework for carrying* n tureya 9 (LHL) cf Eng.

tread *t. on, put the foot down on* vb -tsika t (LL) — PT *trod;* PP *trodden. trod*

treasure *riches* n pfuma 9 (HL) cf -pfuma (HH)

treasurer *person who is given the task of looking after money* n sahomwe 1a (HLL); mubati wehomwe 1 (LHH HLL)

treat *give medicine* vb -rapa i & t (LL)

treat cruelly *mistreat* vb -va noutsinye i (LHLL)

treat with contempt *despise* vb -shora i & t (LL); *treat well, look after* vb -bata zvakanaka t (HH LHHL)

tree *large plant providing wood* n muti 3 (LH) *also used for medicine; tree stump* n chigutsa 7 (LLH)

tree snake *cf boomslang*

trek ox *ox used for hauling* n dhonza 5, madhonza 6 (LL); gwaimani 5, magwaimani 6 (LHLL)

tremble *shiver* vb -dedera i (LLL); -bvunda i (HL)

trench *ditch, gully* n goronga 5, makoronga 6 (LHL)

trial *temptation* n chiedzo 7 (LLL) cf -edza (LL)

tribe *nation, race* n rudzi 11 (LL); marudzi 6

tribulation *great grief* n rushambwa 11 (LLH); dambudziko 5, matambudziko 6 (LLLL) cf -tambudzika (LLLL)

trim *(e.g. a hedge), take away or cut uneven parts* vb -chechenedza t (HHHL)

trip *stumble, catch the foot and lose balance* vb -pingirishwa i (HHHL); **Apingirishwa akapunzika.** (*He tripped and fell.*); *trip up, cause to lose balance* vb -gumbura t (LLL); -pingirisha t (HHHL)

trod, *trodden cf tread*

trolley *small wagon that moves on rails* n ngorovhani 9 (LHLL)

trot *go at a pace between a walk and a run* vb -nzunzuta i (HHH)

trouble *cause inconvenience* vb -netsa i & t (LL); -tambudza i & t (LLL); *be troubled, upset* vb -netseka i (LLL)

trousers *outer garment for the legs* n bhurukwa 5, mabhurukwa 6 (LHL); bhurukwe 5, mabhurukwe 6 (LHL); *short t.* n chikabudura 7 (LLLLL); kabudura 12 (LLLL); *long t.* n mudhabha 3 (LLL); mudhebhe 3 (LLL); tirauzi 5, matirauzi 6 (LHLL) cf Eng.

trowel *bricklayer's instrument for spreading mortar on bricks; very small gardening instrument* n troforo 9 (HLL); trauru 9 (HLL) cf Eng. *illustration p. 162*

truck *railway t.* n tiroko 5, matiroko 6 (LHL) cf Eng.

true *real* chaiye etc. (LHL) *cf p. 196*

truly *truthfully, in truth* adv chokwadi (HLH); zvechokwadi (HLLH)

truncheon *short, thick club* n nduni 9 (LL)

trunk *of elephant* n musinga 3 (LLL); musingo 3 (LLL); mhuno yenzou 9 (LL LHL)

trust *rely on* vb -vimba na- (LL); -nyinda na- M (LL)

trust *confidence* n chivimbo 7 (LL) cf -vimba (LL)

trustworthy *be reliable* vb -vimbika i (LLL); -tendeka i (LLL)

truth *quality or state of being true* n chokwadi 7 (HLH); idi 5 MZ (LH)

try *test* vb -edza t (LL); -idza t K (LL)

tsessebe *the fastest of our antelopes* n nondo 9 (LL); nhondo 9 (LL); *cf p. 157*

tsetse fly *fly that carries and causes sleeping sickness* n mhesvi 9 Z (HL)

tube *pipe esp of rubber* n chubhu 9 (HL) cf Eng.

tuberculosis *T.B.* n chikosoro chorurindi 7 MZ (LHHL LHLH); rutakatira 11 (LLLLL); tibhii 9 (HHL) cf Eng.

tuck in *fold or push in* vb -funyira mukati (LLL LLH)

Tuesday *second day after Sunday* n Chipiri 7 (LLH)

tuft *of hair on the head* n zhumu 5, mazhumu 6 (LH) *as on the head of a duiker*

tug *pull sharply and vigorously* vb -gwina t (LL)

tumble off *fall off, t. down* vb -koromoka i (HHHL); -kurumuka i (HHHL)

tumble weed *flowers appear from a large bulb August—September* B.Bk. 1,52 n munzepete 3 (LHLL)

tumour *boil, abscess* n mota 5, mamota 6 (LL)

tumult *commotion, noise* n ruzha 11 (LH)

tune *song* n rwiyo 11 (LH); plur: nziyo 10 (LH)

turaco n *cf lourie*

turbid *be muddy* vb -bvunduka i MZ (LLL)

turkey *large poultry bird* n garikuni 5, makarikuni 6 (LLHH); toki 9 (LH) cf Eng., *cf illustration p. 119*

turn *against, rise up against* vb -mukira t (LLL); *t. back, t. round* vb -tendeuka i (HHHL); *t. back, return* vb -dzokera i (LLL); *do in turn* vb -ravana i & t (LLL); *t. inside out* vb -pindura t (LLL); -sandura t (LLL); *t. upside down, invert, t. over* vb -pindura t (LLL); -sunamisa t (HHHL); *look back* vb -cheuka i (HHH); *t. off, branch off* vb -tsauka i (HHH); *t.*

tsetse fly mhesvi

over vb -pinduka i (LLL); -sanduka i (LLL); *t. over a page* vb -bhedhenura t (LLLL); -penengura t (HHHL); *t. over in a vehicle* vb -bheuka i (LLL); *t. round, face a different direction* vb -tendeuka i (HHHL); *t. round* vb -tendeudza t (HHHL); -tenderedza t (HHHL); *spin round (by human agent)* vb -sika t (LL); *t. one's back on someone, t. away* vb -furatira t (HHHL)

turnip *sp of root veg* n tenipi 9 (HLL) cf Eng. *cf illustration p. 170*

turpentine *tree, Rhodesian ironwood t., balsam t.* n musaru 3 (LLH)

tusk *tooth structure of an elephant* n nyanga yenzou 9 (LH LHL)

twice *two times* adv kaviri 12 (LLH); ruviri 11 K (LLH)

twig *dry t.* n tsotso 9 (HH)

twig snake *vine snake, back-fanged poisonous s.* n kangamiti 9 (HHLH); kangemiti 9 (HHLH)

twilight *faint half-light, a.m.* n mavambakwedza 6 (LLLLL); *p.m.* n rukunzvikunzvi 11 (LHHLH)

twine *thin string* n mukosi 3 (LHL)

twine *wrap round, coil round* vb -moneredza t (HHHL); *t. threads together to make string* vb -kosa t (HH)

twinkle *shine with an unsteady light* vb -bwinya i (LL); -vaima i (LLL); -taima i (LLL)

twins *two children born at the same time of the same mother* n mavíri 6 (LLH); mapatya 6 (LLL)

twist *wind or turn one around another* vb -mona t (HH); *twisted, be bent* vb -kombama i (HHH)

two *the number 2* adj -viri (LH); mbiri 10 (LH)

type *print with a typewriter* vb -taipa i & t (HHH) cf Eng.

typewriter *typing machine* n tapureta 9 (HLLL)

tyre *rubber covering around the rim of a wheel* n tai 5, matai 6 (HL); taya 5, mataya 6 (HL) cf Eng.

twig snake kangamiti

mombe mbiri

miti miviri

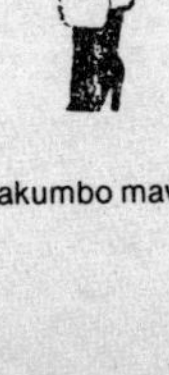

makumbo maviri

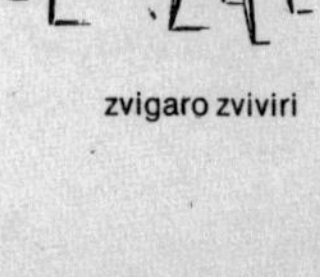

zvigaro zviviri

U

udder *of a cow, part of a cow that produces milk* n zamu 5, mazamu 6 (HH)

ugly *be bad to look at* vb -ipa i (HH); (stative vb); Akaipa pameso. (*She has an ugly face.*)

ultimately *finally* conj pokupedzisira (HLHLHL); *eventually* conj **-zo-** infix vb. **Akatsvaga** mhou kwose kwose akazoiwana padyo norukova. (*He searched everywhere for the cow and eventually found it by the river.*)

ululate *make shrill sound of rejoicing, esp made by women* vb -pururudza i (HHHL)

umbilical cord n rukuvhute 11 (LHHL)

umbrella *portable metal folding-frame covered by cloth to provide shelter from the rain* n amburera 5 (LLHL); sumburera 5 (LLHL) cf Eng. (*Protects from rain or sun.*)

umbrella thorn *tree* n muunga 3 (LLL)

unable *be incapable of* vb -tadza i (HH); Ndatadza kuuya. Ndakoniwa kuuya. Ndakundikana kuuya. Handina kubudirira kuuya. Handina kukwanisa kuuya. (*I was unable to come.*)

unbind *untie* vb -sunungura t (HHHL) cf -sunga (HH)

unbutton *undo the buttons* vb -koponora t (HHHL) cf -kopera (HHH)

unchaste *be impure* vb -va nounzenza i (HLHH)

uncle *paternal u.* n babamukuru 1 (LHLHH); babamudiki /munini 1a (LHLHL / LHL) *depending upon the seniority compared with my father; maternal u.* n sekuru 1a (LHL) *same term for grandfather*

uncoil *unwind, untwist* vb -mononora t (HHHL); -mononoka i (HHHL)

uncooperative *be unhelpful* vb -sada kubatsira i (LH LHHH)

uncork *remove cork or stopper* vb -dziura t (LLL)

uncouple *unfasten* vb -kochonora t (LLLL)

uncover *take away covering* vb -fugura t (HHH); *take off the lid* vb -pfudugura t (HHHL); -kudubura t (HHHL)

under *underneath* adv pazasi 16 (LLH); zasi 17 (LH); pasi 16 (LH)

underbelly *of a four-legged animal* n muhamba 18 (LHH)

underground *beneath the ground* n pasi 16 (LH)

underpart *base, support* n garo 5, magaro 6 (LL) cf -gara (LL)

understand *hear, perceive* vb -nzwa i & t (H) — PT & PP *understood; understanding, good comprehension* n nzwisiso 9 (HHL) cf -nzwa (H)

understood *be clear of meaning* vb -nzwika i (HH)

undo stitching *unpick sewing* vb -rudunura t (LLLL); *undo a nut, unsrew* vb -kumura t KM (HHH); *undo, untie* vb -sunungura t (HHHL)—PT *undid;* PP *undone*

undone *come u. (stitching)* vb -rudunuka i (LLLL); (*a knot*) vb -sungunuka i (HHHL)

undoubtedly *beyond dispute* adv zvisina nharo (LHH HL) rel

undress *remove clothes* vb -bvisa hembe / mbatya t (LL HL / LL); -kumura t (HHH)

unearth *remove earth covering* vb -fukunura t (LLLL)

unfasten *undo, untie* vb -sunungura t (HHHL) cf -sunga (HH)

unfinished *leave undone* vb -tindika t (LLL); Akatindika basa. (*He left the work unfinished.*)

unfold *open out* vb -petenura t (LLLL); -bhedhenura t (LLLL)

unfolded *be left u.* vb -petenuka i (LLLL)

unhappy *be sad* vb -suwa i (HH)

unharness oxen *outspan* vb -kurura i (HHH); -kumura t (HHH)

unhook *uncouple* vb -kochonora t (LLLL)

uniform *style of common dress e.g. worn by members of police and army* n nyufomu 9 (HLL); yunifomu 9 (HLLL) cf Eng.

unimportant *of no importance* adj -nhando (LH); Kutaura kwake ndokwe**nhando**. (*His conversation is of no importance.*)

unimportant *insignificant* adj -sina maturo (. . . *which has no importance*) Anotaura zvisina maturo. (*He talks matters of no importance / rubbish.*)

union *state of being in harmony* n ruwadzano 11 (LLLL) cf -wadzana (LLL)

unite *bring together* vb -batanidza t (HHHL) cf -batana (HHH); -sanganisa t (LLLL) cf -sangana (LLL)

unite *be one in union of mind, be united* vb -batana pamwe i (HHH HH); *be in unison, harmony* vb -wadzana i (LLL)

university *place of higher learning* n yunivhesiti 9 (LLHLL) cf Eng.

unkempt *be untidy (the hair)* adj -nyandanuka i (LLLL) (stative vb)

unlawfully *in a way which is contrary to law* vb -zvisiri pamurau (LHL LLLL); zvisiri pamutemo (LHL LLHH)

unless *if not, except when* conj kusatoti (LLLL) + Partic

unlike *be different* vb -siyana t (HHH) (stative vb)

unload *a vehicle* vb -buritsa zvinhu mumotokari

unlock *unfasten the mechanism of a door by turning a key* vb -kiinura t (HHHL) cf -kiya (HH)

unloose *untie, undo* vb -sunungura t (HHHL) cf -sunga (HH); -pfetenura t (LLLL)

unlucky *be unfortunate* vb -va nerombo rakaipa i; -va nomunyama i; munhu ano **munyama** (*an unfortunate person*)

unmarried man *bachelor* n pfunda 9 (LL); *confirmed b.* n tsvimborume 9 (HLHL)

unobliging *be unhelpful, ungenerous* vb -kondoroka i Z (LLLL)

unpick *sewing, undo stitching* vb -rudunura t (LLLL)

unpleasant *be nasty* vb -ipa (HH) (stative vb); Munhu uyu aka**ipa**. (*He is an unpleasant person.*)

unprogressive *be backward* vb -sarira shure i (HHH HL)

unpunctual *be late* vb -nonoka i (LLL)

unravel *disentangle, unwind* vb -pfudzunura t (HLHL); -mononora t (HHHL) cf -mona (HH)

unripe *(vegetable or fruit)* adj -mbishi (HH), mbishi 5 & 9

unscrew *remove a screw* vb -mononora t (HHHL); *disengage a metal joint, undo* vb -kumura t (HHH)

unselfish *be the opp. of self-seeking* vb -sazvida (LHL)

unspeakable *cannot be described* adj upfumi husinga**tauriki** (*unspeakable wealth*)

unsuccessful *be without success, fail* vb -kundikana (HHHL) usu + infin Ndakundikana kuuya. (*I failed to come.*)

untidiness *disarrangement, disorderliness* n uyanga 14 MZ (LHH)

untie *undo* vb -sunungura t (HHHL) cf -sunga (HH)

untie *a knot* vb -pfutunura t (LLLL)

until *up to a later time* conj kudzimara (LHHH); kusvikira (LLLL); dzimara (HHH); dakara (HHH) + Partic

untruth *falsehood* n nhema 9 (LH); manyepo 6 (LLL) cf -nyepa (LL)

unwilling *be reluctant* vb -ramba i & t (LL)

unwind *uncoil, untwist* vb -mononora t (HHHL) cf -mona (HH); -mononoka i (HHHL)

unwrap *remove outer covering (e.g. parcel)* vb -pfutunura t (LLLL)

up *be time up, finished* vb -pera i (HH); Nguva **yapera**. (*Time is up.*)

upon *on top* adv pamusoro pa- 16 (LLHH)

upright *be morally u.* vb -rurama i (LLL) (stative vb); Ane murume **akarurama**. (*She has an upright husband.*); *be erect* vb -twasanuka i (LLLL) (stative vb); Bango iri **rakatwasanuka**. (*This pole is upright.*)

uprightness *of character, righteousness* n ururami 14 (LLLL) cf -rurama (LLL)

uproar *outburst of noise* n mheremhere 9 (LLLL)

uproot *pull up veg matter by hand with roots still attached* vb -tipura t (LLL); -dzura t (LL); *u. stumps, remove stumps from the ground* vb -gobora t (LLL)

upset *be offended* vb -gumbuka i (LLL); *hurt the feelings of* vb -gumbura t (LLL) — PT & PP *upset*

upset *(liquid), knock a container of liquid over* vb -deura t (HHH); (*solids*) -punza t (HH); -ngundumura t (HHHL)

upset tummy *stomach ache* n manyoka 6 (LHH); Ana manyoka. (*He has an upset tummy.*)

upside down *turn u.d.* vb -sunamidza t (HHHL) cf -sunama (HHH)

upside down *with the upper part under* adv -sunama i (HHH) (stative vb)

upwards *above* adv kumusoro 17 (LLHH); kuuzuru 17 (LLHL)

urge *encourage* vb -kurudzira t (HHHL)

urinate *pass water* vb -rasa m̃vura i (HL HH); -ita dope i (LL LL); -tunda i & t (LL); -ita weti (LL HL) cf Eng.

urine *waste liquid of the body from the bladder* n mutundo 3 (LLL); dope 5 (LL); weti 9 (HL) cf Eng.

use *utilise, make use of* vb -sevenzesa t (HHHL) cf -sevenza (HHH); -shandisa t (HHH) cf -shanda (HH)

used to *be accustomed to* vb -jaira i & t (HHH); **Ndajaira** kutaipa. (*I am familiar with typing.*); -zivira i & t (HHH); -rovedzera i & t KM (HHHL); *be in the habit of* Past habitual tense: Ndaive nehuku. (*I used to have chickens.*); Ndaishanda kuHarare. (*I used to work at Salisbury.*)

useful *be of profit or advantage* vb -va nebasa i (LHL); *be useless (inanimate things)* vb motokari isina basa (*useless motor car*)

usually *often, many times* adv kazhinji 12 (LHH); -wanzo- infix vb

utensil *household u. (e.g. pots & pans)* n mudziyo 3 (LHH)

uterus *womb* n mimba 9 (HH); nhumbu 9 (LL)

utilize *use, make use of* vb -shandisa t (HHH) cf -shanda (HH); -sevenzesa t (HHHL) cf -sevenza (HHH)

V

valley nhika

vaccinate *protect against disease by developing a resistance (usu to small pox)* vb -baya nhomba (LL LH)

vaccination *innoculation against small pox* n nhomba 9 (LH)

vagina *female organ* n sikarudzi 5, masikarudzi 6 (LLLL); mheche 9 (HH); beche 5 (HH)

vain *be conceited, proud, having too high an opinion of one's beauty or ability* vb -dada i (LL)

valley *territory placed between hills* n dinha 5, matinha 6 (LH); nhika 9 (LH)

valuable *be precious* vb -kosha i (LL); -komba i (LL)

valve *of pneumatic tyre* n vharufu 9 (HLL) cf Eng.

vanish *disappear* vb -tsakatika i (LLLL); -nyangarika i (LLLL)

vanity *high opinion of one's looks* n mandionekwe 6 (LHHHH)

vanquish *conquer, overcome* vb -kurira t (HHH)

vapour *air charged with steam or mist* n mweya 3 (LH)

vaseline *a petroleum product like ointment* n vhasirina 5 (LLHL) cf Eng.

vast *huge, great* adj -kuru (HH), guru 5, huru 9, -kurukuru (HHLH); guruguru 5, huruhuru 9 *reduplicated adj*

veal *meat of a calf* n nyama yemhuru 9 (LL HLH)

vegetable *plant or its products* n muriwo 3 (LHH); vhejitebhuru 5 (HLHLL) cf Eng.; dried v. n mufushwa 3 (LHL); mutsotso 3 M (LHH); musone 3 M (LLH); *dry v.* vb -fusha t (HH)

vehicle *motor v.* n motokari 9 (HLLL) cf Eng.

vein *artery, small passage for delivery or return of blood* n tsinga 9 (HH); rutsinga 11 (LHH) *same word for muscle; jugular v.* n uzhwa (LH)

veld *open savannah with scattered trees* n sango 5, masango 6 (HH)

vengeance *take v., pay back* vb -tsiva i & t (LL)

venom *organic poison (usu snake v.)* n uturu 14 (LHH)

verandah *part of a house, open on at least one side* n berevere 5, maperevere 6 (HHHH); vharanda 5, mavharanda 6 (LHL) cf Portuguese

verb *(grammatical), doing word, word that describes an action* n chiito 7 (LLL) cf -ita (LL)

verse *of scripture, passage* n ndima 9 (LH); *v. of poetry* n vhesi 9 (HL)

vertigo *dizziness from heights* n dzungu 5 (HL)

vervet monkey n tsoko 9 (LH); shoko 9 K (LH); soko 9 (LH); *mutupo of the vaShawasha people*

very *v. much* adv kwazvo (HL); *v. much, exceedingly* adv zvakaipa (LHLL) *slang*

very few *little* adv -shomashoma (LLHH)

some vegetables

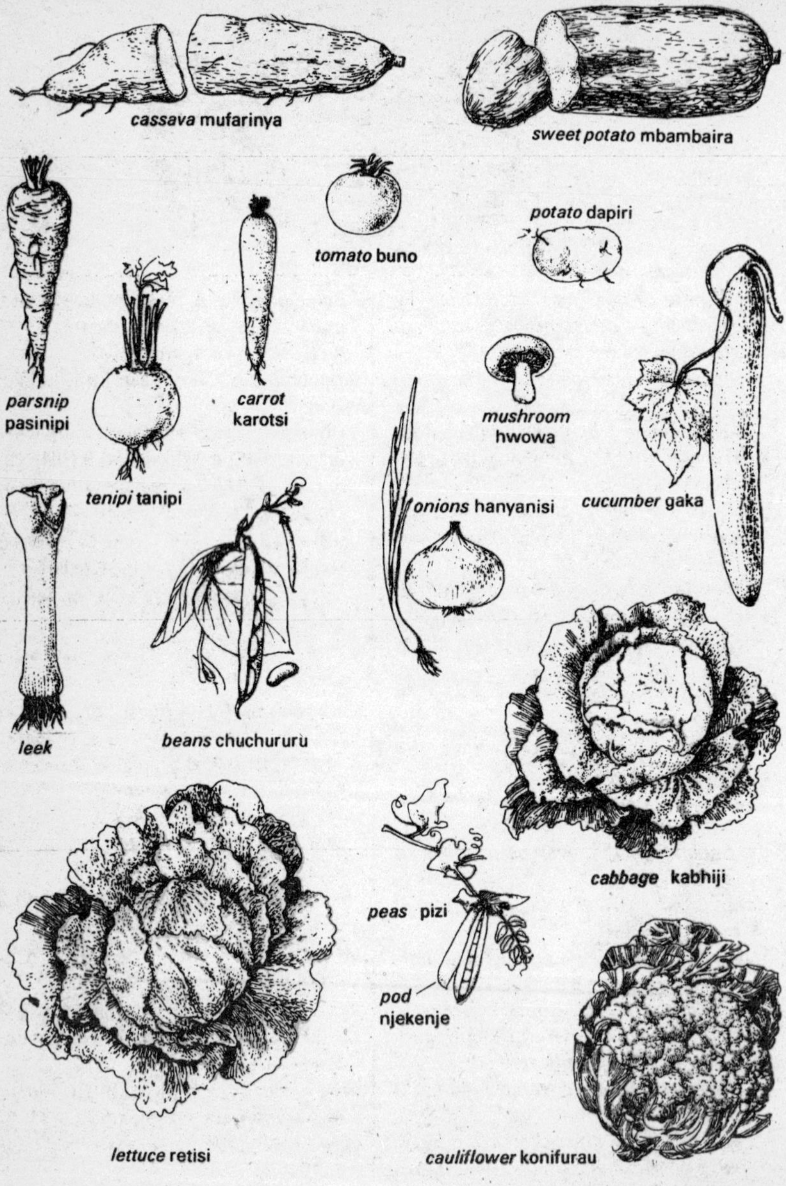

cassava mufarinya
sweet potato mbambaira
potato dapiri
tomato buno
parsnip pasinipi
carrot karotsi
mushroom hwowa
tenipi tanipi
onions hanyanisi
cucumber gaka
leek
beans chuchururu
cabbage kabhiji
peas pizi
pod njekenje
lettuce retisi
cauliflower konifurau

very soon *presently* adv iye zvino 1a (HL HH); gare gare (LH LH)

vessel *for drinking, usu for beer* n gaba 5, magaba 6 (LH)

vest *top undergarment* n vhesi 5, mavhesi 6 (HL) cf Eng.

vex *tire, annoy, weary* vb -netsa i & t (LL); *v. with noise* vb -nyaudza i & t (HHH); *make angry* vb -shatirisa i & t (HHHL)

vice *instrument for gripping, fastened to a work-bench* n rumano 11 MZ

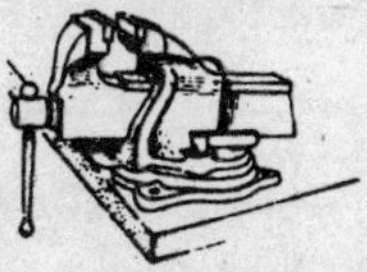

(HHL); chimano 7 (LHH); vhaisi 9 (HLL) cf Eng.

vice *bad conduct of a particular kind: stealing, lying, drinking etc (see virtue)* n tsika yakaipa 9 (LL LHLL)

victor *winner* n mukundi 1 (LHH) cf -kunda (HH)

vie *with one another* vb -pishana i (HHH)

view *look at* vb -tarisa t (LLL)

vigour *power, strength* n simba 5, masimba 6 (LH)

village *home* n musha 3 (LH); *abandoned v. site* n dongo 5, matongo 6 (LL)

vine *climbing plant that bears grapes* n muwaini 3 (LHLL) cf Eng.; muvhaini 3 (LHLL) cf Eng.

vine snake *twig snake* n kangemiti 9 (HHLH)

violate *the law, break the l.* vb -darika mutemo i (HHH LHH); -darika murau i (HHH HLL)

violence *great force* n simba 5, masimba 6 (LH)

violet tree n mufufu 3 (LHL) B.Bk. 1,23

virgin *pure, untouched girl* n mhandara izere 9 (LLL LHH); muvirigo i (LHLL) cf Latin

virgin agricultural land *land not yet cultivated* n gombo 5, makombo 6

virtue *good conduct (see vice)* n tsika yakanaka 9 (LL LHHL)

viscera *intestines, bowels* n ura 14 (LL); matumbu 6 (LLL)

visible *be seen* vb -oneka i (HHH) (*to be distinguished from:* -oneka (LLL) *to say goodbye*)

visit *go to see* vb -tara i & t (HH); -shanya i (HH); -shanyira t (HHH)

visitor *person or stranger who visits* n mweni 1 (LL); muenzi 1 (LLH)

vitex *wild plum tree* n mutsvubvu 3 (LHL) B.Bk. 1,45

vlei *open land, often damp* n bani 5, mapani 6 (HL); deve 5, mateve 6 (LL); *damp fertile soil* n deka 5, mateka 6 (LL); doro 5, matoro 6 (LH); *water-logged v.; bog* n dofo 5, madofo 6 (LH); jahwi 5, majahwi 6 (LH)

vlei lily n durura 5 (LLL) B.Bk. 1, 53

vlei rat otomys n dapi 5, matapi 6 (LH)

voice *sound made when speaking* n izwi 5, mazwi 6 (LH); inzwi 5 K (LH)

vomit *retch, bring up contents of the stomach* vb -rutsa i & t (HH); *vomit, spew, contents of the stomach which spill out* n marutsi 6 (LHL)

vote *express an opinion for or against* vb -vhota i (HH) cf Eng.

vow *solemnly promise* vb -pika i (LL); -tsidza i (LL)

vow *solemn promise* n mhiko 9 (LL) cf -pika (LL); chitsidziro 7 (LLLL) cf -tsidzira (LLL)

voyage *journey* n rwendo 11 (LL), nzendo 10 cf -enda

vulture *bird which eats dead animals and carrion* n gora 5, magora 6 (HL); wanga 5, mawanga 6 (HL); ngwanga 5 K, mangwanga 6 (LL)

vundu *sp of very large cat-fish resembling barbel weighing up to 45 kg* n mvumba 9 (LL) *cf illustration p. 174*

W

wart hog
njiri

wild pig humba

wag *the tail* vb -pinimidza muswe (HHHL LH)

wage *payment made or received for work done* n mubayiro 3 (LLLL)

wager *bet* vb -bheja i & t (LL) cf Eng.

wagon *vehicle with four wheels* n ngoro 9 (LH); *w. with two wheels* n chikochikari 7 (LHLLL) cf Eng.

wagtail *sp of bird which gets its name from its habits of running short distances, stopping after each short run and wagging its tail* n kadzvidya 12 Z (LLH); kanzvidya 12 K (LLH); ndondoza 9 (HHL)

waist *part of the body above the hips* n chiuno 7 (LHH)

waistcoat *top sleeveless garment with buttons down the front* n nhuruvagi 9 (HHLH); mhasikiti 9 (HLLL) cf Eng.

wait *delay acting, w. a moment* vb -mira i (HH); *wait for, await* vb -mirira t (HHH) cf -mira (HH)

wait *on someone, serve at table* vb -perekera t (HHHL); *waiter, person who serves food and waits at table* n weta 1a (HL) cf Eng.

wait-a-bit thorn tree *wag'nbietjieboom* n muchecheni 3 (LHHL)

wake *get up, arise* vb -muka i (LL); *waken, cause to wake up* vb -mutsa t (LL) — PT *woke, waked;* PP *waked, waken, woke*

wake up *recover consciousness* vb -pepuka i (LLL)

walk *travel* vb -famba i (HH); *w. fast, briskly* vb -fambisa i (HHL); *w. about, take a stroll* vb -famba-famba i (HHHL); *w. across, cross to the other side* vb -darika t (HHH); -bira t (HH); *w. away, turn one's back on* vb -furatira t (HHHL); *w. lame, limp* vb -gumina i (LLL); -kamhina i (LLL); *w. backwards* vb -dududza i (HHH); *w. proudly* vb -kanyaira i (HHHL); -nangaira i Z (HHHL); *w. quietly, not wishing to attract attention* vb -nyahwaira i (HHHL); *w. round* vb -poterera i & t (HHHL); *w. with the aid of a stick or staff* vb -donzva i (HH)

walking stick *stick used to aid walking* n mudonzvo 3 (LHL) cf -donzva (HH); mubhadha 3 (LLL)

wall *outer and inner* n madziro 6 (LLL); *outer w.* n chengo 7 (LL); *w. of stone* n rusvingo 11 (LLL)

wallet *purse* n chikwama 7 (LHL)

wander *about, walk about* vb -famba-famba i (HHHL) cf -famba (HH)

want *wish for* vb -da i & t (H); *w. strongly, desire very much* vb -disa t (HH) cf -da (H)

want *be unable to find, lack* vb -shaya i & t (LL)

war *battle* n hondo 9 (HH)

warbler *cisticola, very small sp of bird which inhabits long grass* n kasiisii 12 (LHLHL); chitsiitsii 7 (LHLHL); dhimba 5 (LH); dhiidhii 5 (HLHL); chidhiidhii 7 (LHLHL)

ward *in a hospital* n wadhi 9 (HL) cf Eng.

ward *off blow, parry* vb -vhika i & t (LL); -dziva i & t (LL); -tava i K (LL)

warm *be w.* vb -dziya i (HL); *take warmth from* vb -dziya t (HL); *w. up* vb -dziyisa t (HHH); -sasika t (HHH); *warm hands* vb -dziyisa t (HHH); -sasika maoko t (HHH LHH); *w. oneself by the fire* vb -dziya moto (HL LH); *w. oneself in the sun, sun-bathe* vb -zambira zuva i (HHL HH); -shanira i K (HHH)

warn *caution, forewarn* vb -yambira t (LLL); -vambira t KM (LLL)

warrior *warlike fighter* n murwi 1 (LL) cf -rwa (L)

wart *small growth on the skin* n mhopo 9 (HL)

warthog *large pig-like animal that possesses two large side-growths on the face* n njiri 9 (LL) *cf p. 172*

was, *were cf be*

wash *clothes* vb -geza t (LL); *w. the body, bathe* vb -geza i & t (LL); -shamba i & t (LL); *w. utensils and teeth* vb -suka t (LL)

washer *flat ring pierced with a hole, used for assembling machinery* n washa 9 (HL) cf Eng.

washing line *l. on which washing is dried* n mutariko 3 (LHHL), mutariro 3 (LHHL)

wash-basin n dhishi 5, madhishi 6 (HL) cf Eng.

wasp *flying insect with painful sting* n igo 5 (LL); go 5 K (L); *mason w.* n mbuzambuza 9 (HLHL); mbuzvambuzva 9 K (HLHL)

waste *use without good purpose* vb -paradza t (LLL); -ruza t (LL) cf Eng.; *w. time* vb -pedza nguva t (HL HH)

waste away *be thin* vb -onda i (HH)

waste matter *rubbish* n tsvina 9 (LL); marara 6 (LLL)

watch *small instrument for telling the time* n wachi 9 (HL) cf Eng.

watch *set w. over* vb -garirira t (LLLL); -rindira t (LLL); *w. over, look after, keep from danger* vb -tarisa t (LLL); *be careful of* vb -chenjerera i & t (HLHL); *watch secretly, spy* vb -sora i & t MZ (HH)

water *product of rain* n mvura 9 (HH)

water *irrigate* vb -diridza t (LLL); *w. at the mouth, salivate* vb -rwerwa mate Z i (LL LH)

water-berry tree *waterboom* n mukute 3 (LHL) B.Bk. 1,36

water-bottle *liquid container* n chigubhu 7 (LHL)

waterbuck *large antelope, weight up to 180 kg* n dhumukwa 5 MZ, madhumukwa 6 (LHL); dhumuka 5 K, madhumuka 6 (LHL) cf *illustration p. 88*

waterfall *fall of water from one level to another* n bopoma 5, mapopoma 6 (LLL); ngondo 5, mangondo 6 (LL)

water-fowl *(general term)* n hukurwizi 9 (HHLH); gukurwizi 5 (HHLH)

water beetle n nyungururwi 9 (LLLH)

water lily n hapa 5, mahapa 6 (LH)

water-melon *very juicy sp of melon* n

-nwiwa 5, manwiwa 6 (HL); vise 5, mavise 6 (HL)

water scorpion n zimai redziva 21 (LHL LHL)

water snake *green* n nyarufuro 9 M (LLLL); mbunzvi 9 K (LH); nyokamuriwo 9 (HHLHH)

water-pot *pot used for carrying w.* n chirongo 7 (LLH)

water-spring *well, fountain* n tsime 5, matsime 6 (HL)

wattle *bagworm* n tumbare 9 (LLL); kondo 9 (HH)

wattle *false black w.* n muzeze 3 (LLL) B.Bk. 1,14

wave *raise hand in greeting* vb -simudzira ruoko t (HHHL LHH)

wave *of water, ridge of water between two hollows* n saisai 5, masaisai (LLLL); sandairira 5, masandairira 6 K (LLLLL)

wax *substance made by bees and by man for making candles* n namo 9 (LL) cf -nama (LL); *discharge from ear, ear wax* n mafunzu 6 (LHH)

waxbill *blue w., sp of seed-eating bird* n kadhiidhii 12 (LHLHL); kasiisii 12 (LHLHL); chisiisii 7 (LHLHL); katsiitsii 12 (LHLHL); *yellow-backed w.* n njikenjike 9 (HLHL); *Jameson's ruddy w.* n tondondo 9 (HHH); tondoro 9 (HHH)

way *path* n nzira 9 (LL); zhira 9 K (LL); gwanzi 5 M (HH)

weak *be feeble, sickly* adj & vb -rukutika i (LLLL) (stative vb); Ano mwana akarukutika. (*She has a sickly child.*)

weakness *moral or physical w., state of being weak* n utera 14 (LLH); undonda 14 (LLL)

wealth *(including w. of cattle)* n upfumi 14 (LHH); pfuma 9 (HL); ufumi 14 K (LHH) cf -pfuma (HH)

wealthy *be rich* adj & vb -fuma i (HH) (stative vb); Ano murume akapfuma. (*She has a wealthy husband.*); *wealthy person, rich person* n mupfumi 1 (LHH) cf -pfuma (HH)

wean *accustom a young baby or animal to food different from mother's milk* vb -rumura i & t (HHH)

weapons *implements, tools* n zvombo 8 (LL)

wear *put on clothes* vb -pfeka i & t (LL) — PT *wore;* PP *worn*

wear out *become old through wear* vb -sakara i (LLL); -sakadza t (LLL)

weariness *tiredness, fatigue* n kuneta 15 (LLL)

weary *be tired* vb -neta i (LL); *w. by tedious talk, bore* -finha i & t (HH); *make tired* vb -netesa i & t (LLL)

weasel *sp of small, flesh-eating animal cf snake weasel* n chidembo 7 (LLL) *cf illustration p. 182*

weather *the condition out-of-doors* n (*use a vb to describe the condition with the subject cc of class 17 (kunze)*) Nhasi kuri kutonhora. (*It is cold today.*)

water creatures

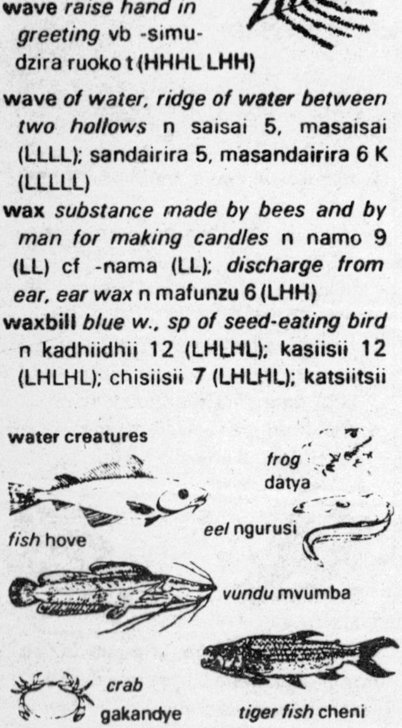

weave *knit* vb -ruka i & t (LL) — PT *wove;* PP *woven, wove*

weaver *sp of bird which weaves its nest from grass or other fibre* n jesa 5, majesa 6 (HL) **general term;** *masked w.* n nzvidya 9 (LH); dombwa 5, matombwa 6 (LH)

web *spider's w.* n dandemutande 5,

wedge chibanzuro

matandemutande 6 (LLLLL); dandadzi 5, matandadzi 6 (LLL)

wedding feast *w. ceremony* n mucha-to 3 (LLL) cf -chata (LL)

wedge *for splitting wood* n chibanzuro 7 (LLLL) cf -banzura (LLL)

Wednesday *third day after Sunday* n Chitatu 7 (LLH)

weed *wild plant growing where it is not wanted* n sora 5, masora 6 (LL); *black-jack* n mhuu 9 (HL); mhuyuyu 9 (HHH)

weed by hand vb -dzura t (LL); -tipura t (LLL); *w. with a hoe* vb -sakura i & t (LLL)

week *a period of seven days* n svondo 5 & 9 (LL); sondo 5 & 9 (LL); vhiki 5 & 9 (HL) cf Eng.; *this w.* n svondo rino 5 (LL HL); *next w.* n svondo rinouya 5 (LL LHHH); *last w.* n svondo rakapera 5 (LL LHLL)

weep *cry* vb -chema i & t (HH) — PT & PP *wept*

weevil *insect which eats and damages grain* n chipfukuto 7 (LLLL) cf -pfukuta (LLL); chikumo 7 (LLL)

weigh *measure on a weighing machine* vb -era t (LL); -pima t KM (LL); -ira t K (LL)

weight *heaviness of a thing when weighed* n uremu 14 KM (LLH); kure-ma 15 (LLL); uremi 14 (LLL); uremo 14 Z (LLL)

welcome *a guest, receive g.* vb -gashi-ra t MZ (LLL); -tambira t MZ (HHH)

weld together *join surfaces of metal usu by heat* vb -namatidza t (LLLL) cf -nama (LL); -weredha t (HHH) cf Eng.

well *be in good health* vb -simba i (LL); -va wadi M (HL)

well *very w.* adv zvakanaka (HHHL) (Lit: *It is well.*)

well dressed *w. groomed* vb -shambi-dzika i (LLLL)

well off *be wealthy* vb -pfuma i (HH)

well-being *life in peace and plenty* n kugarika 15 (LLLL)

well-built *of good build* adj chimiro chakanaka 7 (LHH LHHL); mutambi ane chimiro chakanaka 7 (*a well-built player*)

well-known *be widely known* vb -zivi-kanwa i (HHHL); *well-known, famous* adj mabhuku ane mbiri (*famous books*)

well-mannered *be well-behaved* vb -va netsika dzakanaka i (LHL LHHL); *well-mannered* adj jaya rine tsika (*a well-mannered young man*)

well *of water* n tsime 5, matsime 6 (HL)

went *cf go*

wept *cf weep*

west *where the sun sets* n madokero 6 (LHHL); mavirira 6 (LHHL)

wet *be raining* vb -naya i (LL); *be w. through, be soaked* adj & vb -tota i (LL); -nyata i (LL); -nyn'ata i (LL)

what's-his-name n nhingi 1a (LH); *what's-its-name* n -nhingi *adding noun concord*

what? *interrogative suffix* -i? Wazviitirei? (*What did you do it for? / Why did you do it?*) Chii? (*What is it?*)

what Rel Moods: Ini **chinondishamisa** ndechokuti . . . (*What astonishes me is . . .*) **Zva**ndinoreva ndezvizvi . . . (*What I mean is this . . .*)

whatever *every* chipi nechipi (HL LHL) *cf p. 187*

what-you-call-it (*when the exact vb cannot be remembered*) vb -nhingirika (LLLL)

wheat *grain from which flour is made, sp of grass* n koroni 9 (LLL)

wheel *circular frame turning on an axle* n vhiri 5, mavhiri 6 (HL) cf Eng.

wheelbarrow *garden vehicle with one wheel and two handles* n bhara 5, mabhara 6 (HL) cf Eng.

when (*referring to a time in the future*) conj kana (LL); kunge (LL) + Rec Past Partic; (*referring to a time in the past*) conj zva- PC class 8 (*Indirect Rel. construction*); *and then when, when finally* conj kuzoti (LLL) + Rec Past Partic; *when?* adv rini? 1a (HL)

whenever *at every time when* (in past narrative) adv -ti Past Continuous Tense — Amai vaiti vakabuda panze mwana ochema. (*Whenever the mother went outside the child cried.*) For time in the future use kana + Partic — **Kana** uchida kufambisa motokari, isa peturu. (*If you want to use the motor car put in some petrol.*)

whereas *but* conj asi (LH)

wherever *at every place where* adv kupi nokupi (HL LHL) *cf p. 187*

whether *if* conj kana (LL) + Partic

whey *liquid part of sour milk* n mutuvi 3 (LHH)

which interrogative adj -pi *cf p. 187* Wabvepi? / Wabva **kupiko**? (*Which place have you come from? / Where have you come from?*)

which usu Rel Mood / *by which:* Ndiyo nzira yandauya *nayo*. (*This is the path by which I came.*); *with which:* Ndipewo kii yokupinda *nayo*. (*Give me the key with which to enter.*); Locatives: *at which* Indirect Rel: Ndipo **paanose**venza. (*That is the place (at which) where he works.*); *from which:* Ndiko **kwandiri** kubva. (*That is the place from which I am coming.*) *in which:* Ndimo **mandinochengetera** mari. (*That is the place (in which) where I keep money.*); *to which:* Ndiko **kwa**anoenda. (*That is the place to which he goes.*)

which is *Impersonal Copulative cf p. 184*

while *when* adv -ti Indic Mood + Partic: Ndakati ndichienda kutaundi ndakamiswa nomupurisa. (*While proceeding to town I was stopped by a policeman.*)

while away *the time with, pass the time pleasantly in company* vb -varaidza t (HHHL)

whip *length of cord; strip of leather, fastened to a handle* n chiwepu 7 (LHL) cf Afrik.: tyava 9 (LL)

whip *beat with a whip* vb -rova i & t (HH); *w. severely, thrash, flog* vb -zvinda i & t (LL); -pura i & t (HH)

whip snare *(general term)* n dhibhura 5 (HHL)

whirlwind *swift circling movement of air* n chamupupuri 7 (HLHLH); chinyamupupuri 7 (LL HHH)

whisper *almost silent conversation* n zevezeve 5 (LLLL)

whisper *to speak quietly, almost silently* vb -ita zevezeve i (LL LLLL)

whistle *with lips* vb -ridza murudzi

/muridzo (LL LHL / LHL); *w. with finger* vb -ridza mheterwa (LL LHL); *whistle, clear sound made by forcing air through a small opening* n murudzi 3 (LHL); mheterwa (LHL); muridzo 3 (LHL)

whistle *instrument for making a sharp noise* n pito 9 (HL); nyere 9 (LL); pembe 9 (HL)

white *the colour of pure milk* adj -chena (LL); jena 5, chena 9

white *be free of dirt, clean* vb -chena i (LL) (stative vb); Ndine hembe yakachena. (*I have a clean shirt.*); *whitish, be w.* adj & vb -chenuruka (LLLL)

white ant *(large, edible) termite* n juru 5, majuru 6 (LH); *w. a: (small, not edible)* n muchenje 3 (LLL)

white eye *yellow w. sp of small, yellow gregarious bird* n chimaranga 7 (LLLL) PG 25

white man *European* n muRungu 1 (LLL)

white mahogany tree n muchichiri 3 (LLLH); *w. syringa tree* n mubvumira 3 (LLLL)

who? interrog pron 1a ani? (LH) — *plur:* vanaani? (LHLH)

whoever *any person who* pron upi noupi (HL LHL) etc. *cf p. 187*

whole adj & n quantitative -se (H) *cf p. 188* muviri wose / wese (*the whole body*)

whom *use Indirect Rel Mood; for whom, from whom:* Indirect Rel + Applied form; Ndiye munhu waakabira mari. (*She is the one from whom he stole the money.)*

whooping cough *infectious disease causing a severe cough* n chikosoro chorutakatira 7 (LHHL LHLLLL)

why? *for what reason?* adv Sei + Partic — Sei achidaro? (*Why does he do that?*); nemhaka yei? pamusana pei?

whydah *widow bird; long-tailed, seed-eating, parasitic bird* n tsvikidza 9 (HHL) PG 26; tsekedzamutsetse 9 (LHLLHL); tsekedzamakaya 9 (LHLLHL) R846; *cf widow bird*

wicked *be morally bad* vb -ipa i (HH) (stative vb)

wide *measuring much from side to side* adj -pamhi (LH), bamhi 5, mhamhi 9; *be broad* vb -pamhamha i (LLL)

widow *woman who has lost her husband through death* n chirikadzi 9 (LLHL)

widow bird *whydah* n muswewadepa 3 (LHHLL); muswewadepura 3 (LHHLLL); tswetswe 9 (LL) *general terms for a seed-eater with a long*

tail; pin-tailed w. b. n tsvikidza 9 (HHL); tsvikidzamakwaya 9 (LHLLHL); tsekedzamakaya 9 K; tsekedzamutsetse 9 (LHLLHL); mutsetse 3 M (LHL); nyabundu 9 (LLL) R846

width *distance across* n upamhi 14 (LLH) cf -pamhamha (LLL)

wife *married woman* n mukadzi 1 (LHH); mudzimai 1 (LLHH)

wild *be mad* vb -penga i (HH); *growing in the wild* adj e.g. *wild fruit* michero yesango; *w. cat* n nhiriri 9 (LLL); bonga 5, maponga 6 M (LL); *w. custard apple tree* n muroro 3 (LHL); *w. dog, Cape hunting dog* n mhumi 9 (LH); *w. Dutchman's pipe* n chividze 7 (LHL); *w. pig* n humba 9 (LL) (*also totem*); *w. fig tree* n mukuyu 3 (LHL); muonde 3 (LLH); *w. gardenia tree* n mutarara 3 (LLLL); *w. gentian flowering plant* n tswarinzwa 9 (LHL) B.Bk. 1,73; *w. loquat tree* n muzhanje 3 (LLL); mushuku 3 (LLL); *w. lupin* n jero 5 (LL); *w. medlar tree* n mutufu 3 (LLL); *w. oleander tree, red wood t.* n muwona 3 (LHL); *w. orange tree, klapper apple t.* n mutamba 3 (LLH); *w. grape tree* n mudzambiringa 3 (LLHLL); *wild pear tree* n mutongotowa 3 (LHHLH); *w. plum tree* n mutsubvu 3 (LHL); *w. sweet pea* n karumanyemba 12 (LHHHL); *w. syringa tree* n mukarati 3 (LHHL); *w. violet tree* n mufufu 3 (LHL); *w. willow tree (grows along banks of rivers)* n mupuma 3 (LHL); mutete 3 (LLL); musambangwena 3 (LLLLL)

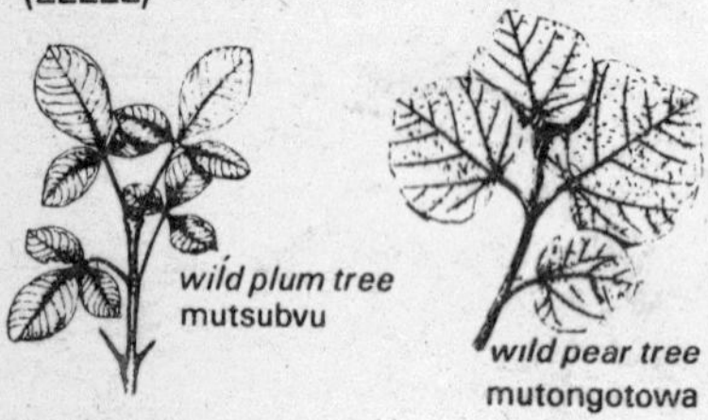

wild plum tree mutsubvu

wild pear tree mutongotowa

wildebeest *blue; gnu* n kongoni 9 (LLL); mvumba 9 (LL) *cf illustration p. 88*

will *shall (Fut tense)* vb Ndichada. (*I shall want.*)

will *mental power which directs a man's thoughts and actions* n kuda 15 (LH); Tichaonana **nokuda** kwaMwari. (*We shall meet again according to the will of God, i.e. if God wishes.*)

will *wish, desire, purpose* n chido 7 (LH) cf -da (H); Ane **chido** chokuramba ari mupenyu. (*He has a will to continue living.*)

wilt *wither, lose freshness* vb -svava i (LL); -una i (LL)

win *find* vb -wana t (LL); -hwina t (LL) cf Eng.; *w. a fight* vb -kurira t (HHH) — PT & PP *won*

wind *strong current of air* n mhepo 9 (HH); *whirlwind, strong circular motion of air occurring on hot days* n chamupupuri 7 (HLHLH)

wind round *twist (string, wire etc.)* vb -mona t (HH); *w. as a path or road* vb mona i (HH) — PT & PP *winded, wound*

winding *be winding, twist and turn (as a road)* adj & vb -monyoroka i (HHHL) (stative vb); mugwagwa wakamonyoroka (*a winding road*)

wind-pipe *trachea* n gurokuro 5, makurokuro 6 (LLLL)

window *frame admitting light into room* n fafitera 5, mafafitera 6 (HLLL); windo 5, mawindo 6 (HL) cf Eng.

windy *be gusty* adj: Kunze kune mhepo. (*It is windy out-of-doors.*)

wing *flying limb of a bird* n bapiro 5, mapapiro 6 (LLL)

wink *open and shut an eye quickly* vb -tsonya i MZ (HH); -chonya i (HH)

winnow *separate grain from dry outer coverings with the help of the wind* vb -urutsa i & t MZ (LLL); -rudza t K (LL); -pepeta t (HHH)

winter *cold season* n chando 7 (LL)

winter thorn *white thorn, apple-ring acacia* n mutsangu 3 (LHL)

wipe *dry, dust, w. off, w. clean* vb -pukuta t (LLL); *w. off with foot, erase* vb -pfukudza t (HHH)

wire *long, thin, drawn-out metal, sometimes insulated for conducting electricity* n waya 9 (HL) cf Eng.; *telegram* n terigramu 9 (HLLL) cf Eng.

wireless *radio* n wairesi 9 (HLLL); wairosi 9 (HLLL) cf Eng.

wisdom *intelligence, cleverness* n ungwaru 14 (LLH); *practical w.* n uchenjeri 14 (LHHL) cf -chenjera (HHH)

wise *be clever* adj & vb -ngwara i (LL); -chenjera i (HHH) (stative vbs); Ndine mwana aka**chenjera**. (*I have a clever child.*) *wise person* n Munhu ano **ungwaru**. (*He is a wise person.*)
wish *want, desire* vb -da i & t (H); *w., desire, purpose* n chido 7 (LH) cf -da (H)
wisteria *tree w.* n mupaka 3 (LHH) B.Bk. 1,18

witch *person who uses magic for evil purposes* n muroyi 1 (LLL) cf -roya (LL)
witchcraft *attempt to exert power over another by casting a spell* n uroyi 14 (LLL) cf -roya (LL)
witch-doctor *diviner, person who claims to explain underlying causes in the affairs of men* n n'anga 9 (LL)
witchweed n bise 5, mabise 6 (HL) cf -pisa (HH)
with *by* prep na + a = na: **navanhu** (LHL) (*with people*); na + *u* = no: **nomunhu** (LHL) (*with a person*); na + i = ne: **nebanga** (HLL) (*with a knife*) *For tonal behaviour* cf and
withdraw *retrace steps* vb -bva i (L); *remove* vb -bvisa t (LL) cf -bva (L) — PT *withdrew;* PP *withdrawn*
wither *droop, dry up* vb -svava i (LL) (stative vb); Maruva aya **akasvava**. (*These flowers are withered.*)
within *inside* adv mukati 18 (LLH)
without *outside* adv panze 16 (LH); kunze 17 (LH)
witness *give evidence* vb -pupura i & t (HHH)
witness *person who gives evidence* n mufakazi 1 (LLLL); chapupu 7 (LHH); mboo 9 (LH); mupupuri (LHHL) cf -pupura (HHH)
witness *evidence given* n uchapupu 14 (LLHH) cf -pupura (HHH); umboo 14 M (LLH)
woe *sorrow, tribulation* n dambudziko 5, matambudziko 6 (LLLL) cf -tambudzika (LLLL)
woman *human adult female* n mukadzi 1 (LHH); munhukadzi 1 (LLLL); mudzimai 1 (LLHH); *w. who has born a child* n mvana 9 (LH); *old w.* n chembere 9 (LLL); *womanly way of acting or speaking* n chikadzi 7 (LHH) cf mukadzi

womb *uterus* n nhumbu 9 (LL); mimba 9 (HH)
won *cf win*
wonder pipi 5, mapipi 6 (HH); *miracle* n chishamiso 7 (LHHL)
wonder *feel wonder at* vb -shama i (HH)
wonderful *be astonishing* vb -shamisa i (HHH) cf -shama (HH)
woo *make love* vb -nyenga i & t (HH); -pfimba i & t (HH)
wood *firewood* n huni 9 (HH); *bundle of f., faggot* n svinga 5, masvinga 6 (HH); *log of wood* n danda 5, matanda 6 (HH)
woodpecker *sp of bird which nests in holes pecked out of the trunks or branches of dead trees* n hohodza 9 (HHL); chingogogo 7 (LHHH); chigogodza 7 (LHHL) *general terms*

wood-borer *insect which bores wood* n chikumo 7 (LLL)

wool *fur, animal hair* n mvere 9 (LL); *cotton w.* n donje 5, matonje 6 (LL); *wool, cotton, thread* n shinda 9 (LL); *sheep's w.* n wuru 9 (HL) cf Eng.

word *something said* n izwi 5, mazwi 6 (LH); inzwi 5 K, manzwi 6 (LH); *message* n shoko 5, mashoko 6 (LL)

wore *cf wear*

work *employment, duty* n basa 5, mabasa 6 (LL); *job of w.* n mushando 3 (LHH) cf -shanda (HH)

work *apply oneself to perform a task* vb -sevenza i & t (HHH); -shanda i & t (HH); -bata basa (HH HL) — PT & PP *worked*

workman *employee* n musevenzi 1 (LHHL) cf -sevenza (HHH); mushandi (HHH) cf -shanda (HH)

world *pysical creation on earth* n pasi 16 (LH); nyika 9 (LL)

worm *grub, maggot* n honye 9 (LL); gonye 5, makonye 6 (LL) *cf illustration p. 70*

worn *used and shabby* adj -tsaru (HL); dzaru 5, tsaru 9

worn *cf wear*

worn out *be finished* vb -pera i (HH); -sakara i (LLL)

worry *be distressed* vb -tambudzika i (LLLL); *upset, disturb* vb -tambudza i & t (LLL); -netsa i & t (LL)

worship *pray* vb -namata i & t (LLL)

worthless *cheap, poor quality* adj Noun + PC + mutowenyemba (LLLHL); bhurukwa romutowenyemba (*a cheap pair of trousers*)

worthy *be suitable, becoming* adj & vb -kodzera i (LLL) (stative vb); Tine musevenzi **akakodzera**. (*We have a worthy employee.*)

wound *hurt* vb -kuvadza i & t (HHH)

wound *injury done to the body involving damage to the skin* n ronda 5, maronda 6 (LL)

woven, *wove cf weave*

wrap *in paper, w. up* vb -putira t (LLL)

wrath *anger, rage* n hasha 10 (HH)

wrestling *physical struggle without striking blows* n tsimba 9 MZ (LH); *wrestle, grapple* vb -ita tsimba i MZ (LL LH)

wriggle *twist and turn the body (as a snake), writhe in pain* vb -zvonyongoka i (HHHL); -zvongonyoka i (HHHL)

wring *clothes, remove excess liquid* vb -svina t (LL)

wring *the neck (fowl), kill* vb -shonyonga t (HHH); -monya t (HH); -monyora t (HHH) — PT & PP *wrung*

wrinkle *line in the skin of the forehead* n nanda 5 MZ, mananda 6 (LL)

wrinkled *be crumpled up* vb -unyana i (LLL); -finyama i (LLL)

wrist *joint between hand and arm* n chiningoningo 7 (LHLHL)

write *put words into writing* vb -nyora i & t (HH); *w. badly* vb -taratadza t (HHHL) — PT *wrote;* PP *written; writer, person who writes* n munyori 1 (LHH) cf -nyora (HH)

writing *manner or style of w.* n raitin'i 9 (HLLL) cf Eng.

writing instrument *(any kind)* n chinyoreso 7 (LHHL) cf -nyora (HH); runyoro 1 (LHH) cf -nyora (HH)

written *cf write*

wrong *do w.* vb -tadza i MZ (HH); -kanganisa i (HHHL); *w. someone, offend* vb -tadzira t (HHH) cf -tadza (HH)

wrong *the incorrect* adj -ri *in the neg cf p. 195; what's w.* Zvaita sei? (*What has happened?*)

wrong way round *be up-side down* vb -sunama i (HHH)

X

X-ray *instrument for photographing the internal structure of the body* n ekisireyi 9 (HLLLL) cf Eng.

Y

yoke joko

yard *open space around a dwelling* n chivanze 7 (LHL)

yard *playground; large, open, clear space* n nhandare 9 (LLL); *yard, one pace as a measure of distance* n yadhi 9 (HL) cf Eng.

yawn *sign of weariness accompanied by opening the mouth* vb -shama nyai Z (HH HH); -zhamura i (HHH); -shama n'ai K (HH HH)

year *a cycle of four seasons (spring, summer, autumn, winter)* n gore 5, makore 6 (LH); *last y.* n gore rakapera 5 (LH LHLL); makei 1a (LHL); *this y.* n gore rino 5 (LH HL); naka 1a (HL); *next y.* n gore rinouya 5 (LH LHHH); makei 1a (LHL); *month* n mwedzi 3 (LH); *week* n svondo 5 & 9 (LL); *day* n zuva 5, mazuva 6 (HH); musi 3 (LH)

yearly *year by year* adv gore negore (LH HLH)

yearn *long for, wish for* vb -suwa i & t (HH); -panga i & t (LL)

yearning *strong desire* n chisuwo 9 MZ (LLL) cf -suwa (HH)

yeast *substance used in the making of bread to make it rise* n mbiriso 9 (LLL) cf -virisa (LLL)

yell *make a loud shout* vb -zhamba i (HL)

yellow heads *flowering plant* n chitupatupa 7 (LHLHL) B.Bk. 1,71

yellow star flower *common flower of the highveld just before the rains* n hodzori 9 (HHL); nhindiri 9 (LLL) B. Bk. 1,54

yellow wood tree n mushava 3 (LHH); muvara 3 (LLL)

yellowfish *large-scaled y.* n kuyu 9 (L

yes *word of agreement* adv -hor (HL); ee (LL); ehunde M (LHL); ehoc (LHL); hengu K (HL)

yesterday *day before today* n nezuro 1a (HHL); zuro 1a (LL); *day before y.* n marimwezuro 1a Z (LLLLL); zwana 1a M (HH)

yet *up to the present time* adv -ti + Rec Past Partic — Wati waona Bopoma reVictoria here? (*Have you seen the Victoria Falls yet?*); *not yet* conj *Stative form of vb* -gara + infin; -gere: Ndigere kuchata. (*I am not yet married.*); Neg form of vb -ti + Rec Past Partic — Handisati ndachata. (*I am not yet married.*)

yield *bear (of plants)* vb -bereka i & t (LLL); *submit, surrender* vb -tera i (LL)

yodel *a song sung in the manner of changing frequently from the ordinary voice to a higher pitch and back again* n chigure 7 (LHL); vb -ita chigure (LL LHL)

yoke *bar of wood placed across the necks of oxen when pulling* n joki 5, majoki 6 (HL) Afrik.; *Y.-pin* n chikei 7 (LHL) cf Afrik. *cf illustration above*

yolk of egg *yellow part of e.* n mhondo 9 (HH)

young *small living thing* adj -duku (HL); duku 5 & 9 (*also* -diki *and* -doko); *y. bird, fledgeling, nestling* n nyn'ana 5, manyn'ana 6 (LH); nyana 5, manyana 6 KM (LH); *y. buck, fawn* n tsvana 9 (HL); *y. child; baby* n mucheche (LLL); *y. dog, puppy* n mbwanana 9 (HLH); handa 9 M (LL); imbwanana 9 (LHLH); *y. donkey* n dhongana 5 (LHH); *y. fowl, chicken* n hukwana 9 (HHH); *y. goat, kid* n mbudzana 9 (HLH) *y. horse, foal* n mwana webhiza 1 (LH HLH); *y. man, unmarried m.* n jaya 5, majaya 6 (LH); *y. ox, calf* n mhuru 9 (LH); *y. pig, piglet* n ngurwana 9 (HLH); *y. unmarried woman* n mhandara 9 (LLL)

yoke joko

Z

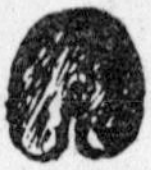

zebra mbizi

Zambian *of Z. origin* adj e.g. hembe yechiZambia (*a Zambian shirt*)

zeal *enthusiasm* n ruchamiro 11 MZ (LLLL) cf -chama (LL)

zealous *be earnest* vb -shinga i (HH); -chama (LL); *z. person* n mushingi 1 (LHH) cf -shinga (HH)

zebra *striped, horse-like animal* n mbizi 9 (LH) *mutupo:* tembo (HH); dhuve (HL)

Zimbabwe creeper *climbing shrub with pink flowers* n gwebwa 5 (LL) B.Bk. 1,84

zorilla *striped polecat, African skunk* chidembo 7 (LLL)

snake-weasel chidembo

zorilla chidembo

Inflection Tables

Copulatives, Demonstratives, Pronouns

AG G. Fortune, **An Analytical Grammar of Shona** (Longman, 1955) out of print

E G. Fortune, **Elements of Shona** (Longman, 1968)

J S.K. Jackson, **Shona Lessons** (Morgenster, 1967)

O'N J. O'Neil S.J., **A Shona Grammar** (Longman, 1948) out of print

L Derek Fivaz & Jeanette Ratzlaff, **Shona Language Lessons** (Word of Life Publications in association with the Rhodesia Literature Bureau, 1969)

SC D. Dale S.J., **Shona Companion** (Mambo Press, 1974)

IMPERSONAL COPULATIVES	+	ABSOLUTE PRONOUNS	
	Ndini	shamwari yako.	It is I who am your friend.
	Ndiwe	wakanganisa.	It is you who has done wrong.
1	**Ndiye**	mwana wako.	It is he who is your child.
	Ndisu	tasvika.	It is we who have arrived.
	Ndimi	mune zano rakanaka.	It is you who have a good plan.
2	**Ndivo**	vasikana vaibika.	It is the girls who were cooking.

1a	**Ndiye**	Mwari ndiye wakandisika.
2a	**Ndivo**	Ambuya ndivo vaitidzidzisa.
3	**Ndiwo**	Ndiwo musha wedu.
4	**Ndiyo**	Mitemo ndiyo yatinochengeta.
5	**Ndiro**	Gudo ndiro rinodya chibahwe.
6	**Ndiwo**	Magejo ndiwo anorimisa munda.
7	**Ndicho**	ChiRungu ndicho chinotaurwa.
8	**Ndizvo**	Ndizvo zvakanaka izvi zvawaita.
9	**Ndiyo**	Imbwa ndiyo yakaba nyama.
10	**Ndidzo**	Mombe dzedu ndidzo dzinokuma.
11	**Ndirwo**	Rudo ndirwo runosunga ukama.
12	**Ndiko**	Kashumba ndiko kanonetsa mhuru.
13	**Nditwo**	Tusikana nditwo tunotamba.
14	**Ndihwo**	Uchi ndihwo hunotapira.
15	**Ndiko**	Kunamata ndiko kutaura naMwari.
16	**Ndipo**	Pamusoro ndipo panopfirirwa.
17	**Ndiko**	Ndiko kwandinogara.
18	**Ndimo**	Mumusha ndimo mune nhamo.

The normal form in the negative is:
Handisirini, Hausiriwe, Haasiriye,
Handisini, Hausiwe, Haasiye, etc. (Cf. p. 195)

(Cf. AG §837; L 89)

In the negative:
Handichokwadi here? **Sandichokwadi here? M. (Is it not true?)**
Handizvoba! Sandizvoba! M. (It is not so!)
Handiniba! Sandiniba! M. (It is not I.)

(AG §849)

What? What kind?		**ENUMERATIVES**	
a child of what kind, what sex?	mwanai?	mwana **mui?**	1
which people were they taken by?	naani?	zvatorwa navanaani?	2
what sort of tree?	mutii?	*muti **mui?**	3
what is inside?	(copulative)	chiri mukati **chii?**	7
what kind of bread?	chingwai?		
what sort of things do we want?	zvinhui?	tinoda **zvii?**	8
what little goat?	kambudzii?	kambudzi **kai?**	12
what kind of meal, flour?	upfui?	upfu **ui?**	14
at what house?	pambai?	pamba **pai?**	16
into which house?	mumbai?	mumba **mui?**	18

Tinoda dhora pai? Pagore.
(We want a dollar how often? Once a year.)
Vanobva kui? Kubasa.
(Where have they come from? From work.)
Vaenda kui? Kumaodzanyemba.
(Where abouts did they go? To the south.)

For what purpose?

medicine for what purpose?	mushonga **wei?**	3
gardens for what purpose?	minda **yei?**	4
what is the knife meant for?	ibanga **rei?**	5
pills for what purpose?	mapiritsi **ei?**	6
for what reason?	nemhosva **yei?**	9
flour for what purpose?	upfu **hwei?**	14
for what reason?	pamusana **pei?**	16

(Cf. AG §273, 330; E 96; J 144, 146; L 45)

The interrogative -i? may be suffixed to verbs with the effect of changing the final vowel -a to -e (i.e. the suffix can be regarded as -i-i? with latent vowel -i-).

Munodei? (**What** do you want?)
Izwi iri rinorevei? (**What** does this word mean?)

When suffixed to the applied form of the verb the meaning can be rendered as **What for**? **Why**? **For what reason**?

Vanonwirei doro vari pabasa? (Why do they drink beer while on duty? i.e. They drink beer for what, they being at work?)

Uri kuchengeterei mari? (What are you keeping the money for?)
Unotaurirei naye? (Why do you speak to her?)

ENUMERATIVES	**Other**
1 **mumwe** murume	another man
2 **vamwe** varwi	other warriors
1a **mumwe** baba mudiki	another junior paternal uncle
2a **vamwe** vadzimambo	other kings
3 **mumwe** mushonga	another medicine
4 **mimwe** mikombe	other ladles
5 **rimwe** zuva	another day
6 **mamwe** matambudziko	other troubles
7 **chimwe** chinhu	another thing
8 **zvimwe** zvokudya *	other food
9 **imwe** nguva	another time
10 **dzimwe** mbudzi	other goats
11 **rumwe** rupenyu	another life
12 **kamwe** karume	another little man
13 **tumwe** twana tudiki	other little children
14 **umwe** upfumi	other riches
15 **kumwe** kushanda	other work
16 **pamwe** panzvimbo	in another place
17 **kumwe** kurutivi	on the other side
18 **mumwe** mudhorobha	in another town

(Cf. AG §273, 328; E 95; O'N 86, 91; L 45)

Note: Another usage of the enumerative puts the qualifier **after** the noun it qualifies, with the stem **-MWE** of high tone. The meaning thus becomes: **one** or **the same.**
E.g. Ndawana zai **rimwe** chete. (I found only one egg.)

* In class 8 the qualifier often functions alone as an adverbial meaning **perhaps.** E.g. Zimwe ndichauya. (Perhaps I shall come.)

Locative ideas, when using this enumerative and a noun are expressed with verb **-na.**

E.g. Mazwi edu mazhinji akabva **kune** mimwe mitauro.
(Many of our words have come from other languages.)

Handifungi kuti ndizvo zvinoitwa **kune** zvimwe zvikoro.
(I don't think that such things are done at other schools.)

Which one? **ENUMERATIVES**

Which woman?	Mukadzi **upi?**	1
Which servants?	Varanda **vapi?**	2
Which tree am I to cut?	Ndotema muti **upi?**	3
Which vegetables have we eaten?	Tadya miriwo **ipi?**	4
On which day does he come?	Anouya nezuva **ripi?**	5
What books have you found?	Wawana mabhuku **api?**	6
Which chair do you want?	Unoda chigaro **chipi?**	7
What gifts was he given?	Akapiwa zvipo **zvipi?**	8
Which church do you go to?	Munoenda kuchechi **ipi?**	9
Which needles do we want?	Tinoda tsono **dzipi?**	10
What kind of tobacco?	Fodya yorudzi **rupi?**	11
Which little boy?	Kakomana **kapi?**	12
Which little birds?	Tushiri **tupi?**	13
Which grass do you mean?	Munoreva uswa **hupi?**	14
What kind of cooking?	Kubika **kupi?**	15
Where shall I put it?	Ndochiisa **papi?**	16
Where is the village?	Musha uri **kupi?**	17
In which house is the sick man?	Murwere ari mumba **mupi?**	18

(Cf. AG §329, 273; E 96; J 143; O'N 55; L 61)

The interrogative suffix **-ko?** is often suffixed to this enumerative.
E.g. Muri kureva upi**ko?** (Who are you talking about?)
When repeated after a noun, the enumerative pronoun may be translated into English as: **any at all, every, whatever.** (Cf. AG §274, 330; J 129, O'N 57) Consider the following examples:—

Muti **upi noupi** unobereka mashizha.
(Every kind of tree bears leaves.)
Shiri **dzipi nedzipi** dzine minhenga.
(Birds of every kind have feathers.)

To render **anyone at all,** ani naani is used.
Ani naani angapinde zvake. (Anyone can go in.)

QUANTITATIVES — **The whole, All**

1	**wose**	the whole person	munhu wose
2	**vose**	all servants	varanda vose
1a	**wose**	the whole Christ	Kristo wose
2a	**vose**	all the ladies	vanamai vose
3	**wose**	the whole heart	mwoyo wose
4	**yose**	all commandments	mitemo yose
5	**rose**	the whole day	zuva rose
6	**ose**	all the years	makore ose
7	**chose**	the whole chin	chirebvu chose
8	**zvose**	all things, everything	zvinhu zvose
9	**yose**	all riches, wealth	pfuma yose
10	**dzose**	all races, tribes	ndudzi dzose
11	**rwose**	the whole story	rungano rwose
12	**kose**	even the slightest (adv)	nakashoma kose
13	**twose**	all the little girls	tusikana twose
14	**hwose**	the whole night	usiku hwose
15	**kwose**	the whole mind	kufunga kwose
16	**pose**	the whole world	pasi pose
17	**kwose**	at the entire village	kumusha kwose
18	**mose**	the whole interior	mukati mose

(Cf. AG §331f; E 80; J 117, 129)

Note: Another qualifier using exactly the same concords is **-GA** meaning **alone**. Like **-SE** it may qualify a noun, or absolute pronoun, or may be used by **itself**.

E.g. With nouns:	chimwe choga (One thing alone)
With absol. pronouns:	Ini ndoga (I alone)
By itself:	Ndinoshanda ndoga (I work alone)

ndoga	I alone	**toga**	we alone
woga	you alone	**moga**	you alone
oga	he/she alone	**vose**	they alone

A Manyika form of quantitative concord substitutes e for o:—

E.g. Ini ndega	**Vanhu vese**	**Ndapedza zvese**
(I alone)	**(All people)**	**(I have finished everything.)**

Good, Real, True	Quantitative concord + -MENE	
I myself	ini ndómené	
you yourself	iwe wómené	
he himself	iye wómené	1
	ómené	1
we ourselves	isu tómené	
you yourselves	imi mómené	
they themselves	ivo vómené	2
the king himself	mambo ómené	1a
grandmother herself (hon. plur.)	ambuya vómené	2a
on the very day	nomusi wómené	3
good fruit	michero yómené	4
the blind man himself	bofu rómené	5
the police themselves	mapurisa ómené	6
a real store	chitoro chímené	7
truly, really	zvómené *	8
the widow herself	chirikadzi yómené	9
the old men themselves	harahwa dzómené	10
real love, true love	rudo rwómené	11
the little boy himself	kakomana kómené	12
the little children themselves	twana twómené	13
real poverty	urombo hwómené	14
real suffering	kutambudzika kwómené	15
right outside	panze pómené	16
right at my home	kumusha kwangu kwómené	17
right inside	mukati mómené	18

(Cf. AG §331f, J 127)

* In this example the qualifier functions as an adverbial.

Note: This qualifier is typically Karanga. (Cf. AG §334)
Where -MENE qualifies a person, the better rendering, according to context, is the reflexive -self; where it qualifies anything else, real, good or fine is often the more appropriate English translation.

MPERSONAL COPULATIVES

1	**Mumwe mudyari, mumwe mukohwi.**	**One is a sower, another is the harvester.**
2	Ava **vapenyu**, avo **varwere**.	These (here) are well, those over there are the sick.
1a	**Ndíani?**	Who is it?
	Ndíbaba.	It is father.
2a	**Ndavádzimai** (pl. of number).	They are the women.
	Ndávanání? / Ndívanaani?	Who are they?
	Ndavásekuru (honorific).	It is uncle.
3	**Mú**nda wakanaka.	It is a good field.
4	**Mí**chero yakaibva.	They are ripe fruits.
5	Mambo **í**dombo rangu.	The Lord is my rock.
6	Aya **mábwe.**	These (here) are rocks.
7	**Chí**rwere.	It is an illness.
8	**Zví**nhu zvakakosha.	They are valuable things.
9	**Í**mhuka.	It is a wild animal.
10	**Í**mombe.	They are cattle.
11	**Rú**vara.	It is a colour.
12	**Kásikana.**	It is a little girl.
13	**Túshomanana.**	It is very little.
14	**Ú**nhu hwakanaka.	It is good manners.
15	Doro **kúdya.**	Beer is food.
16	**Pási** patinovata.	It is on the ground that we sleep.
17	Denga **kúmusha** kwedu.	Heaven is our home.
18	**Múkati** maagere.	It is the inside where he is.

(Cf. AG §831, 835; E 69f; J 92f; O'N 102)

The formation of Impersonal Copulatives fits into three categories:—

1) **Where the copulative formative Ndi-(1a) or Nda-(2a) is prefixed to the noun.**
2) **Where the noun prefix, if one exists, is raised to a high tone. E.g. Classes 1-4.**
3) **Where, in the absence of a noun prefix, a copulative formative i- of high tone is prefixed to the noun. I.e. Classes 5, 9 and 10.**

NDA- with Enumeratives **IMPERSONAL COPULATIVES**

Which is the shepherd?	**Mufudzi ndoúpi?**	1
Which are the owners?	**Varidzi ndavápi?**	2
Which is the Master?	**Tenzi ndoúpi?**	1a
Which is the paternal aunt? (hon. plural)	**Vatete ndavápi?**	2a
Which is the commandment?	**Mutemo ndoúpi?**	3
Which are the villages?	**Misha ndeípi?**	4
Which is the proper word?	**Izwi chairo nderípi?**	5
Which are the flowers?	**Maruva ndaápi?**	6
Which one is the lighter?	**Chinoreruka ndechípi?**	7
Which are the bricks?	**Zvitina ndezvípi?**	8
Which is the thief?	**Mbavha ndeípi?**	9
Which are the clothes?	**Nhumbi ndedzípi?**	10
Which is the reserve?	**Ruzevha ndorúpi?**	11
Which is the little sheep?	**Kahwai ndakápi?**	12
Which are the little birds?	**Tushiri ndotúpi?**	13
Which is righteousness?	**Ururami ndoúpi?**	14
Which is the food?	**Kudya ndokúpi?**	15
Which is the side?	**Parutivi ndapápi?**	16
Where is it you are going?	**Kwamuri kuenda ndokúpi?**	17
Which is the inside?	**Mukati ndomúpi?**	18

(Cf. AG §842)

Many other copulatives are formed from Qualificative Pronouns. For a number of examples cf. AG §840f.

Rules of elision

Nda- before a prefix of the vowel a- remains Nda-

Nda- before a prefix of the vowel i- becomes Nde-

Nda- before a prefix of the vowel u- becomes Ndo-

LOCATIVE DEMONST. COPULATIVES **(HA + Near Demonst.)**

The locative demonstrative copulatives are used when introducing or presenting a person or object that is physically present. For Example:

1	**Hoyu** musikana.	Here is the girl.
2	**Hava** vashandi.	Here are the workers.
1a	**Hoyu** tenzi wangu.	Here is my master.
2a	**Hava** vasekuru.	Here is grandfather (honorif. pl.).
3	**Hoyu** moto.	Here is the fire.
4	**Heyi** michero.	Here is the fruit.
5	**Heri** jira.	Here is the cloth.
6	**Haya** maruva.	Here are the flowers.
7	**Hechi** chigaro.	Here is the chair.
8	**Hezvi** zviwitsi.	Here are the sweets.
9	**Heyi** nguwani.	Here is the hat.
10	**Hedzi** mbatya.	Here are the clothes.
11	**Horwu** rukweza.	Here is the rapoko
12	**Haka** kambwa.	Here is the puppy.
13	**Hotwu** tuhove.	Here are the little fish.
14	**Hohwu** upfu.	Here is the flour.
15	**Hoku** kuita.	Here is the way to do (it).
16	**Hapa** pokurara.	Here is the place to sleep.
17	**Hoku** kumba kwako.	Here is your home.
18	**Homu** mumba.	Here is the house interior.

The Near **Precised** Demonstrative Copulative is similarly formed from the **Precised** Near Demonstrative:
Houno (here **he** is); havano; houno, heino, etc.
E.g. **Houno** mumwe muenzaniso. (Here is another example.)
(Cf. AG §860; E 179; J 100f; O'N 163)

Rules of elision

Ha- before a demonstrative of the vowel **a-** remains **Ha-**
Ha- before a demonstrative of the vowel **i-** becomes **He-**
Ha- before a demonstrative of the vowel **u-** becomes **Ho-**

Hoyo mukomana.	There is the boy.	**hoyo**	**1**
Havo varume.	There are the men.	**havo**	**2**
Hoyo mambo.	There is the lord.	**hoyo**	**1a**
Havo madzishe.	There are the chiefs.	**havo**	**2a**
Hoyo munda.	There is the garden.	**hoyo**	**3**
Heyo mipichisi.	There are the peach trees.	**heyo**	**4**
Hero gomo.	There is the hill.	**hero**	**5**
Hayo mapurisa.	There are the police.	**hayo**	**6**
Hecho chibahwe.	There is the maize.	**hecho**	**7**
Hezvo zvidhinha.	There are the bricks.	**hezvo**	**8**
Heyo mhuru.	There is the calf.	**heyo**	**9**
Hedzo tsotsi.	There are the hooligans.	**hedzo**	**10**
Horwo rwiyo.	There is the psalm (song).	**horwo**	**11**
Hako katsono.	There is the little needle.	**hako**	**12**
Hotwo tushiri.	There are the little birds.	**hotwo**	**13**
Hohwo hwahwa.	There is the beer.	**hohwo**	**14**
Hoko kunwa.	There is the drink.	**hoko**	**15**
Hapo pakati.	There is the centre.	**hapo**	**16**
Hoko kumusha.	There is the village	**hoko**	**17**
Homo mukati.	There is the inside.	**homo**	**18**

(Cf. AG §860; E 179; J 100f)

RIGHT **(When the object referred to is physically present)**

1	**Ndiyeyu*** mukomana chaiye.**	It is the right boy.
2	**Ndivava** varume chaivo.	They are the right men.
1a	**Ndiyeyu** ticha chaiye.	He is the right teacher.
2a	**Ndivava** vanamai chaivo.	They are the right mothers.
3	**Ndiwoyu** muchero chaiwo.	It is the right fruit.
4	**Ndiyoyi** minda chaiyo.	They are the right fields.
5	**Ndirori** bhuku chairo.	It is the. right book.
6	**Ndiwawa** mapadza chaiwo.	They are the right badzas (hoes).
7	**Ndichochi** chigaro chaicho.	It is the right chair.
8	**Ndizvozvo** zvidhina chaizvo.	They are the right bricks.
9	**Ndiyoyi** huku chaiyo.	It is the right chicken.
10	**Ndidzodzi** mbudzi chaidzo.	They are the right goats.
11	**Ndirworwu** rudzi chairwo.	It is the right kind (sort).
12	**Ndikaka** kakomana chaiko.	It is the right little boy.
13	**Nditwotwu** tusikana chaitwo.	They are the right little girls.
14	**Ndihwohwu** hwahwa chaihwo.	It is the right beer.
15	**Ndikoku** kudya chaiko.	It is the right food.
16	**Ndipapa** pamusoro chaipo.	It is the right top.
17	**Ndikoku** kunhu chaiko.	It is the right direction.
18	**Ndimomu** mukati chaimo.	It is the right inside.

*** In these examples the copulative form of the emphatic near demonstrative (Cf. p. 183) is used.**

**** Another use of the pronoun (chaiye) takes on the meaning of the English adverb really. For example:**

Ndini **chaiye.**	It is really me.
Ndiwe **chaiye.**	It is really you.
Ndiye **chaiye.**	It is really him.
Ndisu **chaivo.**	It is really us.
Ndimi **chaivo.**	It is really you.
Ndivo **chaivo.**	It is really them.
Ndiyo **chaiyo** mari yangu.	It really is my money
Ndidzo **chaidzo** mombe dzedu.	They really are our cattle.

It is the wrong girl.	Musikana **haasiri** iye *.	1
They are the wrong men.	Varume **havasiri** ivo.	2
He is the wrong doctor.	Dhokotera **haasiri** iye.	1a
They are the wrong mothers.	Vadzimai **havasiri** ivo.	2a
It is the wrong fruit.	Muchero **hausiri** iwo.	3
They are the wrong fields.	Minda **haisiri** iyo.	4
It is the wrong book.	Bhuku **harisiri** iro.	5
They are the wrong eggs.	Mazai **haasiri** iwo.	6
It is the wrong chair.	Chigaro **hachisiri** icho.	7
They are the wrong bricks.	Zvitinha **hazvisiri** izvo.	8
It is the wrong chicken.	Huku **haisiri** iyo.	9
They are the wrong keys.	Kiyi **hadzisiri** idzo.	10
It is the wrong kind.	Rudzi **harusiri** irwo.	11
It is the wrong little boy.	Kakomana **hakasiri** iko.	12
They are the wrong little girls.	Tusikana **hatusiri** itwo.	13
It is the wrong honey.	Uchi **hahusiri** ihwo.	14
It is the wrong food.	Kudya **hakusiri** iko.	15
It is the wrong top.	Pamusoro **hapasiri** ipo (handipo).	16
It is the wrong direction.	Kunhu **hakusiri** iko (handiko).	17
It is the wrong interior.	Mukati **hamusiri** imo (handimo).	18

Where the **relative mood** is used in the negative, the form becomes:

Cl. 5 bhuku **risiriro:** the wrong book (the book which is not it)
Watora gwara risiriro. (risiri iro)
Watora nzira isiriyo. (isiri iyo)
Both mean: (You have taken the wrong path/You have missed the point)

(Cf. AG §733; E 112)

Note: Sometimes contraction occurs:-
Watora gwara risiro. (risiri iro) You have missed the point.
Watora nzira isiyo. (isiri iyo) You have missed the point.

PRONOUN IN APPOSITION — **Genuine, Good, Proper, Real, True**

(Cha- + Absolute Pronoun)

1	**chaiye**	true man	munhu chaiye
2	**chaivo**	real men	vanhu chaivo
1a	**chaiye**	true God	Mwari chaiye
2a	**chaivo**	real ancestors	vadzitateguru chaivo
3	**chaiwo**	a genuine heart	mwoyo chaiwo
4	**chaiyo**	proper trees	miti chaiyo
5	**chairo**	real work	basa chairo
6	**chaiwo**	real fools	mapenzi chaiwo
7	**chaicho**	real bread	chingwa chaicho
8	**chaizvo** *	real gifts	zvipo chaizvo
9	**chaiyo**	true relative	hama chaiyo
10	**chaidzo**	true friends	shamwari chaidzo
11	**chairwo**	true love	rudo chairwo
12	**chaiko**	a real little house	kamba chaiko
13	**chaitwo**	proper little shoes	tushangu chaitwo
14	**chaihwo**	genuine friendship	ushamwari chaihwo
15	**chaiko**	a genuine illness	kurwara chaiko
16	**chaipo** **	right in the middle	pakati chaipo
17	**chaiko**	the real home	kumusha chaiko
18	**chaimo**	right in Salisbury in Salisbury proper	muHarare chaimo

* This pronoun is extensively used in Cl. 8, as an adverb meaning **very much.**

Examples:
Ziso rinorwadza **chaizvo.**
(The eye hurts **very much.**)
Ndinofara **chaizvo.**
(I am **very** happy.)
Zvinoshatirisa **chaizvo.**
(It is **very** annoying.)

(Cf. AG §285, J 127, O'N 161)

** Compare the following Cl. 16 pronouns:

Panze **chaipo**
(Right outside)

Pamusoro **chaipo**
(Right at the top)

Genuine, Good, Real, Proper, True

PRONOUN FUNCTIONING AS ADJECTIVE

(Kwa- + Absolute Pronoun)

a good husband	murume **kwaye**	1
good parents	vabereki **kwavo**	2
the good chief	ishe **kwaye**	1a
a good grandmother (honorific pl.)	ambúya **kwavo**	2a
proper way	mutoo **kwawo**	3
fruits deserving the name	michero **kwayo**	4
right word	izwi **kwaro**	5
good eggs	mazai **kwawo**	6
proper food	chokudya **kwacho**	7
special millet	zviyo **kwazvo**	8
car in running order	motokari **kwayo**	9
really good manners	tsika **kwadzo**	10
real happiness	rufaro **kwarwo**	11
a proper little house	kamba **kwako**	12
good model cars	tumotokari **kwatwo**	13
true relationship	ukama **kwahwo**	14
good singing	kuimba **kwako**	15
real home	pamusha **kwapo**	16
at really good grazing	kumafuro **kwako**	17
a good interior (of a house)	mumba **kwamo**	18

(Cf. AG §285; J 128; O'N 128)

This pronoun is extensively used (in Cl. 8) as an adverb meaning very much.

Examples: **Gumbo rinorwadza kwazvo.**
(The leg is very painful.)
Ndine nyota kwazvo.
(I have a great thirst.)
Ndakatambudzwa kwazvo.
(I was troubled very much.)

ABSOLUTE PRONOUN + POSSESSIVE PRONOUN of Class 7

	ini pachangu	I myself, I personally
	iwe pachako	you yourself
1	**iye** pachake	he himself
	isu pachedu	we ourselves
	imi pachenyu	you yourselves
2	**ivo** pachavo	they themselves
3	**iwo** muti pachawo	the tree itself
4	**iyo** minwe pachayo	the fingers themselves
5	**iro** rokwe pacharo	the dress itself
6	**iwo** majuzi pachawo	the jerseys themselves
7	**icho** chando pachacho	the winter itself
8	**izvo** zviyo pachazvo	the millet itself
9	**iyo** hama pachayo	the relative himself
10	**idzo** mhosva pachadzo	the crimes themselves
11	**irwo** rufu pacharwo	death itself
12	**iko** kakomana pachako	the little boy itself
13	**itwo** tunhu pachatwo	the little things themselves
14	**ihwo** hwahwa pachahwo	beer itself
15	**iko** kudya pachako	food itself
16	**ipo** pakati pachapo	in the centre itself
17	**iko** kunze pachako	the outside itself
18	**imo** mukati pachamo	the inside itself

(Absolute Pronouns: AG §250f; E 18, 111, 180f; J 39; O'N 20f; L 42)
To stress ownership, we say in English:—
Imari yangu pachangu. (It is my own money.)

In Shona we can stress ownership in the following way:
Aka kambwa ndekangu pachangu. (It is my own little dog.)
Iropa rake pachake. (It is his own blood.)
Unofanira kuenda woga iwe pachako. (You must go on your own.)
Ngaakutaurire iye pachake. (Let him tell you himself.)

The adverbial **na-** can be joined to the Absolute Pronoun with change of vowel through elision in the 1st and 2nd person.
In the 3rd person there is no elision. For example:-

neni	with/by me	**nesu**	with/by us
newe	with/by you	**nemi**	with/by you
naye	with him/her	**navo**	with/by them

Ndakarumwa nayo (imbwa) nezuro. (I was bitten by it yesterday.)

(Possessive pronoun + **-kare-** + far demonstrative cf p 205)

the same boy	mukomana wakareyo	1
the same people	vanhu vakarevo	2
the same king	mambo wakareyo	1a
the same paternal aunt (hon.)	vatete vakarevo	2a
the same day	musi wakarewo	3
the same trees	miti yakareyo	4
the same year	gore rakarero	5
the same words	mazwi akarewo	6
the same time	chinhambwe chakarecho	7
in like manner, likewise	(ndakaita) zvakarezvo *	8
the same road	nzira yakareyo	9
the same cattle	mombe dzakaredzo	10
the same colour	ruvara rwakarerwo	11
the same little child	kamwana kakareko	12
the same chickens	tutiyo twakaretwo	13
the same night	usiku hwakarehwo	14
the same food	kudya kwakareko	15
at the same time, immediately **	pakarepo	16
at the same place **	kwakareko	17
in the same house **	mumba makaremo	18

* In this example the pronoun functions as an adverb.

** The locatives of this pronoun often function as adverbs. But notice the following examples in which the pronoun agrees with the noun it qualifies:

16 Panguva yakareyo. (At the same time.)
17 Akabva kumusha wakarewo. (He came from the same village.)
18 Vari mumba yakareyo. (They are in the same house.)

(Cf. O'N 94; L 109)

ABSOLUTE PRONOUNS **Reduplicated Emphatic Forms**

			Alternative
	inini *	I myself, my very self	**iyeni** *
	iwewe *	You yourself, your very self	**iyewe** *
1	**iyeye** *	He himself, that very one	
	isusu *	We ourselves, our very selves	**iyesu** *
	imimi *	You yourselves, your very selves	**iyemi** *
2	**ivavo** *	They themselves, those very ones	
3	**iwoyo**	It itself. Muti iwoyo wakarohwa nemheni. (The tree itself was struck by lightning.)	
4	**iyoyo**	Michero iyoyo yakaora.	
5	**iroro**	Ruva iroro idzvuku.	
6	**iwayo**	Mazino iwayo akachena.	
7	**ichocho**	Chirei ichocho chakatyoka.	
8	**izvozvo**	Zvingwa izvozvo zvakaora.	
9	**iyoyo**	Nguva iyoyo yakasvika.	
10	**idzodzo**	Huku idzodzo dzakatengeswa.	
11	**irworwo**	Rumbo irworwo runofadza.	
12	**ikako**	Kasikana ikako kakauya.	
13	**itwotwo**	Tumbuyu itwotwo tunoruma.	
14	**ihwohwo**	Usiku ihwohwo hwakasviba.	
15	**ikoko**	Kuimba ikoko kwaifadza.	
16	**ipapo**	Ndakakurira panzvimbo ipapo.	
17	**ikoko**	Kumusha ikoko kwakafa munhu.	
18	**imomo**	Mupani imomo ndomaiswa mazai.	

(Cf. AG §252; E 175, 182; O'N 59, 73)

* The reduplicated absolute pronouns can take on the meaning: 'Who me? Do you mean me?'
E.g. Unogara kupi? **Inini?** (or **Iyeni?**)
The form: **Inini** ndinofunga . . . can be rendered: I **personally** think . . .

EMPHATIC DEMONSTRATIVES

Near demonstratives (This very ... This here ...)		Far demonstratives (That very ...)	
iyeyu	mukomana iyeyu	**iyeyo**	**1**
ivava	varume ivava	**ivavo**	**2**
iwoyu	munda iwoyu	**iwoyo**	**3**
iyoyi	misha iyoyi	**iyoyo**	**4**
irori	banga irori	**iroro**	**5**
iwaya	mapadza iwaya	**iwayo**	**6**
ichochi	chingwa ichochi	**ichocho**	**7**
izvozvi	zvimedu izvozvi	**izvozvo**	**8**
iyoyi	hwai iyoyi	**iyoyo**	**9**
idzodzi	nzira idzodzi	**idzodzo**	**10**
irworwu	rudzi irworwu	**irworwo**	**11**
ikaka	kamwana ikaka	**ikako**	**12**
itwotwu	tupwere itwotwu	**itwotwo**	**13**
ihwohwu	ukuru ihwohwu	**ihwohwo**	**14**
ikoku	kurima ikoku	**ikoko**	**15**
ipapa	At this very place	**ipapo**	**16**
ikoku	To this very place	**ikoko**	**17**
imomu	In this very place	**imomo**	**18**

(Cf. AG §318; E 182; J 71f; O'N 59)

These locative demonstratives are often used adverbially:

PLACE

Ipapo paiva netsime. (At that place there was a well.)
Ipapo painge paino uswa uzhinji. (There was much grass in the place.)

TIME

Ipapo mheni yakabva yapenya. (At that point lightning flashed.)
Ipapo akashaya kuti oita sei.
(At that point he had no idea what to do.)
(Other **reduplicated demonstratives** are dealt with by Fortune.
(AG §316f; E 175)

PRECISED NEAR DEMONSTRATIVE This / These (here)

This demonstrative **refers** to **things which are physically present** (e.g. **this** eye) or **temporally relevant** (e.g. this week) to the speaker.

Copulative Form			**Non-copulative form**
1	**únó**	this boy	mukomana **úno**
2	**vánó**	these men	varume **váno**
1a	**únó**	today	**nhasi úno**
2a	**vánó**	these fathers	vadzibaba váno
3	**únó**	this month	mwedzi úno
4	**ínó**	these trees	miti íno
5	**rínó**	this year	gore ríno
6	**ánó**	these days	mazuva áno
7	**chínó**	this maize	chibahwe chíno
8	**zvínó**	these chairs	zvigaro zvíno
9	**ínó**	this time	nguva íno
10	**dzínó**	these countries	nyika dzíno
11	**rwúnó**	this arm	ruoko rwuno
12	**kánó**	this little book	kabhuku káno
13	**twúnó**	these little boys	tukomana twúno
14	**hwúnó**	this night (i.e. last night)	usiku hwúno
15	**kúnó**	this illness	kurwara kúno
16	**pánó**	here on earth	pasi páno
17	**kúnó**	here in Rhodesia	kuRhodesia kúno
18	**múnó**	here in Salisbury	muHarare múno

16 Uya ugare **pano** apa. (Come and sit here.)
17 Uya **kuno** uku. (Come in this direction.)
18 Mumusha **muno** umu muno ruzha. (There is much noise in this village.)

(Cf. AG §314; E 65; J 70; L 61)

Note: There are two cases in which this pronoun bears variant tonal behaviour: in the copulative form, e.g. **Ndoúnó** (It is this one); and in the form where the noun it qualifies is understood, e.g. Ndoupi mukomana waunoda? Ndinoda **únó.** (I want this one).

This demonstrative may refer to things not necessarily physically present.

this girl	musikana **uyu**	**1**
these workers	vashandi **ava**	**2**
this chief	ishe **uyu**	**1a**
these lords	vadzimambo **ava**	**2a**
this share	mugove **uyu**	**3**
these feathers	minhenga **iyi**	**4**
this idea, opinion, advice	zano **iri**	**5**
these words	mazwi **aya**	**6**
this nail	chipikiri **ichi**	**7**
right now, this moment	iye zvino **izvi**	**8**
this country	nyika **iyi**	**9**
these cattle	mombe **idzi**	**10**
this tribe, race, nation	rudzi **urwu**	**11**
this little child	kamwana **aka**	**12**
these little vegetables	tumuriwo **utwu**	**13**
this wisdom	ungwaru **uhwu**	**14**
this praying	kunamata **uku**	**15**
this lower part	pazasi **apa**	**16**
in this place	kunzvimbo **uku**	**17**
in this school	muchikoro **umu**	**18**

(Cf. AG §312; E 66; J 70)

The **Far Demonstrative** form of this pronoun is simply formed by altering the final vowel to **-o** in each case.
E.g., **uyu**, avo, uyo, iyo, etc. (that one **over there**)
Uyo ndiye munhu. (**That** is the person.)

When this Demonstrative is introduced by the Impersonal Copulative **nda-** (it is), elision may take place.
E.g. Mwana wangu **ndo**uyu; vana vake **nda**ava.
(My child is this one; her children are these.)
Basa rangu **nde**iri. (This is my work.)

PRECISED FAR DEMONSTRATIVE PRONOUN (Selectors)

The one referred to or talked about (not physically present)

This demonstrative (selector) is used when its context is clear to the understanding of the speakers.

E.g. Murume **uya** akasvika. (That man (I told you about) arrived.)
Vanhu **vaya** vakandibatsira. (Those people (I met) helped me.)

that father

	Copulative Form	Non-copulative Form	
1	**úyá**	murimi úya	that farmer
2	**váyá**	vaKristo váya	those Christians
1a	**úyá**	baba úya	that father
2a	**váyá**	vadzitateguru váya	those grandfathers
3	**úyá**	mupfudze úya	that manure
4	**íyá**	mitemo íya	those commandments
5	**ríyá**	gomo ríya	that hill, mountain
6	**áyá**	maruva áya	those flowers
7	**chíyá**	chingwa chíya	that bread
8	**zvíyá**	zvifundo zvíya	those lessons
9	**íyá**	nzira íya	that path
10	**dzíyá**	chembere dzíya	those old women
11	**rwúyá**	rukova rwúya	that river
12	**káyá**	kahwai káya	that little sheep
13	**twúyá**	tuvhudzi twúya	those little hairs
14	**hwúyá**	uipi hwúya	that evil
15	**kúyá**	kutambudzika kúya	that tribulation
16	**páyá**	pashure páya	at that part behind
17	**kúyá**	kuruboshe kúya	at that left side
18	**múyá**	mudondo múya	in that forest

The final vowel of the pronoun is always as above in Karanga and Manyika; but the final vowel in Zezuru is always -e.
(Cf. AG §321: Demonstratives of the 2nd precised position; E 65; O'N 60; J 73: Relative demonstrative pronoun; L 61)

TABLE OF DEMONSTRATIVES

Near demonst. (Cf. p. 253)	Far demonst.	Demonst. concords	Precised near demonst. selectors	Precised far demonst. selectors	
uyu	uyo	u-	uno	uya	1
ava	avo	va-	vano	vaya	2
uyu	uyo	u-	uno	uya	3
iyi	iyo	i-	ino	iya	4
iri	iro	ri-	rino	riya	5
aya	ayo	a-	ano	aya	6
ichi	icho	chi-	chino	chiya	7
izvi	izvo	zvi-	zvino	zviya	8
iyi	iyo	i-	ino	iya	9
idzi	idzo	dzi-	dzino	dziya	10
urwu	urwo	rwu-	rwuno	rwuya	11
aka	ako	ka-	kano	kaya	12
utwu	utwo	twu-	twuno	twuya	13
uhwu	uhwo	hwu-	hwuno	hwuya	14
uku	uko	ku-	kuno	kuya	15
apa	apo	pa-	pano	paya	16
uku	uko	ku-	kuno	kuya	17
umu	umo	mu-	muno	muya	18

(Cf. AG §310f; E 65; J 70f; O'N 59; L 52)

Near demonstratives (this/these) refer to things not necessarily physically present.

Far demonstratives (that/those) refer to things at some distance from the speaker.

Precised near demonst. (this/these) refer to things physically present or temporally relevant to the speaker.

Precised far demonst. (that/those) refer to things referred to or talked about, which are not physically present.

CONCORDS OF THE VERB

		Subject Concord	Past Subj. Cc.	Exclusive Subj. Cc.	Object Concord
1st P. sing.	I	ndi-	nda-	ndo-	-ndi-
2nd P. sing.	you	u-	wa-	wo-	-ku-
3rd P. sing.	he/she	a- (1)	a-	o-	-mu-
1st P. plur.	we	ti-	ta-	to-	-ti-
2nd P. plur.	you	mu-	ma-	mo-	-ku-
3rd P. plur.	they	va- (2)	va-	vo-	-va-
Class **1a**		a-	a-	o-	-mu-
2a		va-	va-	vo-	-va-
3		u-	wa-	wo-	-u-
4		i-	ya-	yo-	-i-
5		ri-	ra-	ro-	-ri-
6		a-	a-	o-	-a-
7		chi-	cha-	cho-	-chi-
8		zvi-	zva-	zvo-	-zvi-
9		i-	ya-	yo-	-i-
10		dzi-	dza-	dzo-	-dzi-
11		ru-	rwa-	rwo-	-ru-
12		ka-	ka-	ko-	-ka-
13		tu-	twa-	two-	-tu-
14		hu-	hwa-	hwo-	-hu-
15		ku-	kwa-	kwo-	-ku-
16		pa-	pa-	po-	-pa-
17		ku-	kwa-	kwo-	-ku-
18		mu-	ma-	mo-	-mu-
References:		L 35	L 56	L 122	L 92

ABSOLUTE PRONOUNS AND QUALIFICATIVE CONCORDS

	Absolute Pronouns	QC	AC	EC	PC	Poss. stems	
1st P. sing.	ini	ndo-				-ngu	
2nd P. sing.	iwe	wo-				-ko	
3rd P. sing.	iye	o-	mu-	mu-	wa-	-ke	(1)
1st P. plur.	isu	to-				-idu	
2nd P. plur.	imi	mo-				-inyu	
3rd P. plur.	ivo	vo-	va-	va-	va-	-vo	(2)
Class 1a	iye	o-	mu-	mu-	wa-	-ke	1a
2a	ivo	vo-	va-	va-	va-	-vo	2a
3	iwo	wo-	mu-	mu-	wa-	-wo	3
4	iyo	yo-	mi-	mi-	ya-	-yo	4
5	iro	ro-	(ri-)	ri-	ra-	-ro	5
6	iwo	o-	ma-	ma-	a-	-wo	6
7	icho	cho-	chi-	chi-	cha-	-cho	7
8	izvo	zvo-	zvi-	zvi-	zva-	-zvo	8
9	iyo	yo-		i-	ya-	-yo	9
10	idzo	dzo-		dzi-	dza-	-dzo	10
11	irwo	rwo-	ru-	ru-	rwa-	-rwo	11
12	iko	ko-	ka-	ka-	ka-	-ko	12
13	itwo	two-	tu-	tu-	twa-	-two	13
14	ihwo	hwo-	u-	u-	hwa-	-hwo	14
15	iko	kwo-	ku-	ku-	kwa-	-ko	15
16	ipo	po-	pa-	pa-	pa-	-po	16
17	iko	kwo-	ku-	ku-	kwa-	-ko	17
18	imo	mo-	mu-	mu-	ma-	-mo	18

QC Quantitative Concord — EC Enumerative Concord
AC Adjectival Concord — PC Possessive Concord

(Possessive pronouns: Cf. AG §338f; E 70f; 66f; O'N 48f; L 67)

INDICATIVE PARADIGM Compound predicate: **NGA / NGE**

The verb -NGE here is indicative. It has a participial complement.

NDINENGE	FUTURE	(Cf. SC p. 84)
Ndinenge ndiri kudya. (I shall be + I eating, I shall be eating.) Ndinenge ndiina mazai. (I shall have eggs.)	SC p. 285	Ndinenge ndisiri kudya. (I shall be + I not eating, I shall not be eating.) Ndinenge ndisina mazai. (I shall not have eggs.)
Ndinenge ndichidya. (I shall be eating.) Ndinenge ndadya. (I shall have eaten.) Ndinenge ndichadya. (I shall be yet to eat.)	SC p. 282	* Ndinenge ndisingadyi. (I shall not be eating.) Ndinenge ndisina kudya. (I shall not have eaten.) * Ndinenge ndisingadyi. (I shall not be yet to eat.)

NDANGA	PAST (today)	(Cf. SC p. 82)
Ndanga ndiri kudya. (I was eating.) Ndanga ndiina mazai. (I had some eggs.)	SC p. 280	Ndanga ndisiri kudya. (I was not eating.) Ndanga ndisina mazai. (I had no eggs.)
Ndanga ndichidya. (I was eating.) Ndanga ndadya. (I had eaten.) Ndanga ndichadya. (I was yet to eat.)	SC p. 278	* Ndanga ndisingadyi. (I was not eating.) Ndanga ndisina kudya. (I had not eaten.) * Ndanga ndisingadyi. (I was not yet to eat.)

still PROGRESSIVE **no longer**

FUTURE

still	**no longer**
Ndinenge ndichiri kudya. **(I shall still be eating.)** **Ndinenge ndichina mazai.** **(I shall still have eggs.)**	Ndinenge ndisisiri kudya. (I shall no longer be eating.) Ndinenge ndisisina mazai. (I shall no longer have eggs.)

PAST

still	**no longer**
Ndanga ndichiri kudya. (I was still eating.) Ndanga ndichina mazai. (I still had eggs.)	Ndanga ndisisiri kudya. (I was no longer eating.) Ndanga ndisisina mazai. (I no longer had eggs.)

Note: The same participial complements may be compounded with the remote past tense **ndakanga** and the past continuous tense **ndainge** in the same way as the future form ndinenge (or **ndichange** or **ndinonga** M.) and the recent past form **ndanga**.

INDICATIVE PARADIGM

	PRESENT	
Present Habitual	ndinoenda	handiendi
(May include Future)	(I go)	(I do not go)
Present Continuous	ndiri kuenda	handisi kuenda
(Now or later)	(I am going)	(I am not going)
	Stative	
Past in form:	ndava kuenda	handisati ndava kuenda
Present in meaning:	(I am now going)	(I am not yet going)
Commencing a state:-	ndakwana	handina kukwana
	(I am full, replete)	(I am not full, replete)
	ndakanaka	handina kunaka
	(I am beautiful)	(I am not beautiful)
	PAST	
Recent Past (today)	ndaenda	handina kuenda
Remote Past	ndakaenda	handina kuenda
(yesterday)	(I went)	(I did not go)
Continuous Past	ndaienda	ndaisaenda
	(I used to go)	(I used not to go)
	Compound Forms	Cf. opposite
Recent Past	ndanga ndichienda	* ndanga ndisingaendi
Remote Past	ndakanga ndichienda	* ndakanga ndisingaendi
	(I was going)	(I was not going)
Pluperfect	ndanga ndaenda	ndanga ndisina kuenda
	ndakanga ndaenda	ndakanga ndisina kuenda
	(I had gone)	(I had not gone)
Past Future	ndanga ndichaenda	* ndanga ndisingaendi
	ndakanga ndichaenda	* ndakanga ndisingaendi
	(I was yet to go)	(I was not going yet)
	FUTURE	
Simple Future	ndichaenda	handichaendi
	(I will go)	(I will not go)
	Compound Forms	Cf. opposite
Future Continuous	ndinenge ndichienda	ndinenge ndisingaendi
	(I shall be going)	(I shall not be going)
Future Perfect	ndinenge ndaenda	ndinenge ndisina kuenda
	(I will have gone)	(I will not have gone)

*** There is no strictly future Negative Participial. The Present Participial serves in its place.**

PARTICIPIAL PARADIGM

The Participial Mood in Shona is always dependent grammatically upon a main verb. Notice that there is no strictly Future Negative Participial. References are to **Shona Companion**.

PRESENT p.72f

Example: Kana ndichienda, ndichamuona.
(If I go, I shall see him/her.)

ndichienda	p.292	**ndisingaendi** *	p.293

PAST p.73f

Example: Kana ndaenda, uchamuona.
(When I have gone, you will see him/her.)

ndaenda	p.294	**ndisina kuenda**	p.295
ndakanaka	(stative)	**ndisina kunaka**	p.297f
pp.82, 284, 296f			

FUTURE

Example: Handizivi kana achaenda.
(I don't know if he will go.)

ndichaenda	p.308	**ndisingaendi** *	p.308

Verb **-RI**	ndiri	pp.118, 302	ndisiri	pp.119, 303
Pres. Continuous	ndiri kuenda	p.276	ndisiri kuenda	p.81
Verb **-NA**	ndina / ndiina	p.112	ndisina	p.113
Past Compound verb			ndisina kuenda	p.113

(still) PROGRESSIVE IMPLICATION (no longer)

Verb **-RI**	ndichiri	p.120	ndisisiri	pp.121, 307
Pres. Continuous	ndichiri kurwara	p.286	ndisisiri kurwara	p.121
Verb **-NA**	ndichina	p.114	ndisisina	pp.115, 307
Stative Verbs	ndichakarara		ndisisina kurara	
Non-stative verbs	ndichiri kuuya	p.306	ndisisauyi	p.307

EXCLUSIVE IMPLICATION

ndoenda	p.304	ndisati ndoenda	p.305

RELATIVE PARADIGM

SC

DIRECT RELATIVE

	PRESENT		p.310f
Habitual	ndinoenda	ndisingaendi *	
	PAST		p.313f
Recent P.	ndaenda	ndisina kuenda	
Remote P.	ndakaenda	ndisina kuenda	
Habitual	ndaienda	ndaisaenda	
	FUTURE		p.314f
	ndichaenda	ndisingaendi *	Cf p.109
Verb -RI	ndiri	ndisiri	p.318f
Pres. Continuous	ndiri kuenda	ndisiri kuenda	p.318f
Verb -NA	ndina	ndisina	p.318f
Potential Mood	ndingaende	ndisingaendi	p.324

INDIRECT RELATIVE

p. 310f

Note: The Concord in bold print may be replaced by the Concord of any Class. The tone behaviour following it is that of the Participial Mood.

	PRESENT		
Habitual	zvandinoedza	zvandisingaedzi	p.310f
Continuous	zvandiri *kuedza	zvandisiri kuedza	
	PAST		
Recent Past	zvandaedza	zvandisina kuedza	p.312f
Remote Past	zvandakaedza	zvandisina kuedza	p.312f
Habitual Past	zvandaiedza	zvandaisaedza	p.314f
	FUTURE		
	zvandichaedza	zvandisingaedzi	p.314f
Verb -RI	zvandiri *	zvandisiri	p.320f
Verb -NA	zvandiina	zvandisina	p.320f
Potential Mood	zvandingaende		p. 324